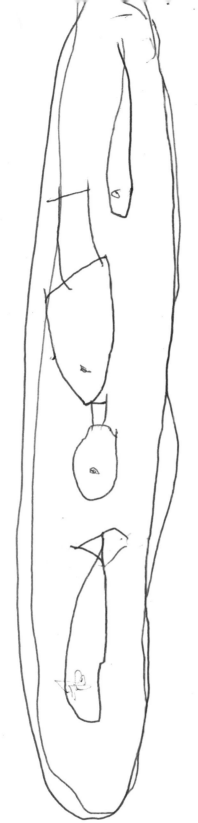

Commercial Insurance

Commercial Insurance

Arthur L. Flitner, CPCU, ARM, AIC
Assistant Vice President
American Institute for CPCU/Insurance Institute of America

Jerome Trupin, CPCU, CLU, ChFC
Partner
Trupin Insurance Services

First Edition

American Institute for Chartered Property Casualty Underwriters/
Insurance Institute of America
720 Providence Road, Malvern, Pennsylvania 19355

First Edition • Seventh Printing • July 2006

Library of Congress Control Number: 2002110394

ISBN 978-0-89463-114-6

Foreword

The American Institute for Chartered Property Casualty Underwriters and the Insurance Institute of America (the Institutes) are independent, not-for-profit organizations committed to expanding the knowledge of professionals in risk management, insurance, financial services, and related fields through education and research.

In accordance with our belief that professionalism is grounded in education, experience, and ethical behavior, the Institutes provide a wide range of educational programs designed to meet the needs of individuals working in property-casualty insurance and risk management. The American Institute offers the Chartered Property Casualty Underwriter (CPCU®) professional designation. You select a specialization in the CPCU program with either a commercial or a personal risk management and insurance focus, depending on your professional needs. In addition to this specialization, the CPCU program gives you a broad understanding of the property-casualty insurance industry.

The Insurance Institute of America (IIA) offers designations and certificate programs in a wide range of disciplines, including the following:

- Claims
- Commercial underwriting
- Fidelity and surety bonding
- General insurance
- Insurance accounting and finance
- Insurance information technology
- Insurance production and agency management
- Insurance regulation and compliance
- Management
- Marine insurance
- Personal insurance
- Premium auditing
- Quality insurance services
- Reinsurance
- Risk management
- Surplus lines

No matter which Institute program you choose, you will gain practical knowledge and skills that will help you to grow personally and professionally.

The American Institute for CPCU was founded in 1942 through a collaborative effort between industry professionals and academics, led by the faculty members at The Wharton School of the University of Pennsylvania. In 1953, the American Institute for CPCU merged with the IIA, which was founded in 1909 and which remains the oldest continuously functioning national organization offering educational programs for the property-casualty insurance business. The Institutes continuously strive to maximize the value of your education and qualifications in the expanding insurance market. In 2005, the Institutes extended their global reach by forming the CPCU Institute of Greater China (CPCUIGC). In addition, many CPCU and IIA courses now qualify for credits towards certain associate's, bachelor's, and master's degrees at several prestigious colleges and universities, and all CPCU and IIA courses carry college credit recommendations from the American Council on Education (ACE).

The Insurance Research Council (IRC), founded in 1977, helps the Institutes fulfill the research aspect of their mission. The IRC is a division of the Institutes and is supported by industry members. The IRC is a not-for-profit research organization that examines public policy issues of interest to property-casualty insurers, insurance customers, and the general public. IRC research reports are distributed widely to insurance-related organizations, public policy authorities, and the media.

Our textbooks are an essential component of the education we provide. Each book is specifically designed both to provide you with the practical knowledge and skills you need to enhance your job performance and career and also to deliver that knowledge in a clear manner. The content is developed by the Institutes in collaboration with insurance and risk management professionals and members of the academic community. We welcome comments from our students and course leaders because your feedback helps us to continuously improve the quality of our study materials. Through our combined efforts, we will truly be *succeeding together*.

Peter L. Miller
President and CEO
American Institute for CPCU
Insurance Institute of America

Preface

This book was originally published in 1987 as the text for the Commercial Insurance course (INS 23) in the Institutes' Program in General Insurance. The current edition of the text is now assigned in the CPCU and ARe programs, as well as the INS program.

Although commercial insurance policies have undergone considerable change since *Commercial Insurance* was first published, the purpose of the text remains the same: to provide the reader with a broad understanding of the property and liability loss exposures faced by most organizations and the corresponding types of insurance for covering those loss exposures.

Many individuals in a variety of jobs within the insurance business have reviewed one or more chapters of the text to verify that the material is correct, complete, and at an appropriate educational level. We are grateful to the following reviewers, as well as any that we might have inadvertently omitted: Patricia M. Arnold, CPCU, ALCM; Howard E. Candage, CPCU, AMIM, AAI; Barbara P. Cobb, CPCU, CPIW; Richard Cohen, CPCU, ARM, CIC; Christina Cronin, CPCU; Lisa Eimbinder, CPCU; Lowery D. Finley III, CPCU, AAI, PFP; Rosemarie Friend, CPCU; Gary Grasmann; Stephen Horn II, CPCU, ARM, AAI; Nanette R. Jennings, CPCU; Larry L. Klein, CPCU, AIM, AAI; Melissa McBratney, CPCU, GCA; Loretta Newman, CPCU; Louis E. Nunez, CPCU, AU, ARM; Kevin M. Quinley, CPCU, ARM, AIC; Maurice Southwell, CPCU, CLU, ChFC; and Mary Lou Speckheuer, CPCU, AMIM, CPIW.

For more information about the Institutes' programs, please call our Customer Service Department at (800) 644-2101, e-mail us at cserv@cpcuiia.org, or visit our Web site at www.aicpcu.org.

Arthur L. Flitner
Jerome Trupin

Contributing Authors

The Institutes and the authors acknowledge, with deep appreciation, the work of the following contributing authors:

Robert J. Gibbons, PhD, CPCU, CLU
Executive Director and President
International Insurance Foundation

Stephen Horn II, CPCU, ARM, AAI
Stephen Horn Insurance Services

Anita W. Johnson, CPCU, CLU, ChFC
Director of Examinations
AICPCU/IIA

Bernard L. Webb, CPCU, FCAS, MAAA
Professor Emeritus of Actuarial Science and Insurance
Georgia State University

W. Jeffrey Woodward, CPCU, CIC
Senior Research Analyst
International Risk Management Institute, Inc.

Contents

1   Overview of Commercial
     Insurance   1.1
     Insurance as a Risk Management
     Technique   1.3
     Lines of Business   1.5
     Commercial Insurance Policies   1.9
     Summary   1.15

2   Commercial Property
     Insurance, Part I   2.1
     Policies Providing Commercial
     Property Coverage   2.3
     Overview of the Commercial
     Property Coverage Part   2.5
     Building and Personal Property
     Coverage Form   2.8
     Insuring Fluctuating Values   2.28
     Blanket Insurance   2.30
     Summary   2.32

3   Commercial Property
     Insurance, Part II   3.1
     Causes-of-Loss Forms   3.3
     Other Commercial Property
     Coverage Forms   3.15
     Endorsements   3.21
     Commercial Property Conditions   3.25
     Rating Commercial Property
     Coverage   3.29
     Summary   3.34

4   Business Income Insurance   4.1
     Business Income Loss Exposure   4.4
     Business Income Coverage Forms   4.7

     Other Forms and Endorsements   4.21
     Rating Business Income Coverage   4.24
     Summary   4.24

5   Commercial Crime Insurance   5.1
     ISO Commercial Crime Program   5.4
     Financial Institution Bonds   5.28
     Summary   5.28

6   Equipment Breakdown
     Insurance   6.1
     Insuring Agreements   6.4
     Exclusions   6.11
     Limits of Insurance   6.13
     Conditions   6.14
     Summary   6.18

7   Inland and Ocean Marine
     Insurance   7.1
     Development of Inland Marine
     Insurance   7.3
     Inland Marine Exposures   7.4
     Inland Marine Insurance   7.9
     Ocean Marine Exposures   7.18
     Ocean Marine Insurance   7.19
     Summary   7.25

8   Commercial General Liability
     Insurance, Part I   8.1
     Liability Loss Exposures   8.3
     Overview of Commercial General
     Liability Insurance   8.9

Coverage A—Bodily Injury and
Property Damage Liability   8.10

Coverage B—Personal and
Advertising Injury Liability   8.25

Supplementary Payments   8.28

Coverage C—Medical Payments   8.29

Summary   8.30

9 Commercial General Liability
Insurance, Part II   9.1

Who Is an Insured?   9.3

Limits of Insurance   9.6

CGL Conditions   9.9

Claims-Made CGL Coverage Form   9.14

CGL Endorsements   9.17

Rating CGL Coverage   9.19

Miscellaneous Liability
Coverage Forms   9.22

Summary   9.24

10 Commercial Automobile
Insurance   10.1

Automobile Loss Exposures   10.3

Business Auto Coverage Form   10.6

Garage Coverage Form   10.29

Motor Carrier Coverage Form   10.34

Rating Commercial Auto
Insurance   10.36

Summary   10.39

11 Businessowners Policies and
Farm Insurance   11.1

Businessowners Policies   11.3

Farm Insurance   11.17

Summary   11.22

12 Workers Compensation and
Employers Liability Insurance   12.1

Workers Compensation Statutes   12.3

The Workers Compensation and
Employers Liability Policy   12.15

Rating Workers Compensation
Insurance   12.26

Summary   12.30

13 Miscellaneous Coverages   13.1

Excess and Umbrella Liability
Insurance   13.3

Professional Liability Insurance   13.12

Aircraft Insurance   13.24

Environmental Insurance   13.27

Coverage for Foreign Operations   13.29

Surety Bonds   13.30

Summary   13.36

Index   1

Chapter 1

Direct Your Learning

OUTLINE

Insurance as a
Risk Management
Technique

Lines of Business

Commercial Insurance
Policies

Summary

Overview of Commercial Insurance

After learning the content of this chapter, you should be able to:

■ Describe property loss exposures and liability loss exposures, and analyze them in a given case.

■ Describe the risk management process.

- Identify the six steps involved.

- Identify four noninsurance risk management techniques.

■ Briefly describe each of the lines of business discussed in this assignment.

■ Analyze the components of the ISO commercial package policy.

■ Describe each of the provisions found in the Common Policy Conditions of the commercial package policy.

■ Describe the major features of the Terrorism Risk Insurance Act of 2002, including covered acts, covered insurers, and the obligations and funding methods of private insurers and the federal government.

Develop Your Perspective

What are the main topics covered in the chapter?

This chapter examines commercial insurance within the larger context of risk management. Several common types (or "lines") of commercial insurance are described, as are the components of a commercial package policy.

Review a Commercial Package Policy (CPP) used by your company or one of the insurers you represent. Compare it with the CPP presented in Exhibit 1-2 (p. 1.11).

- Which forms are included in the policy?
- Which forms are not?

Why is it important to learn about these topics?

By recognizing a commercial loss exposure and the type of commercial policy that would cover the exposure, you will begin to understand how insurance works as a method of managing risks.

Consider the range of coverages available in commercial package policies.

- Why might an insurer be generally unwilling to include some lines of coverage—such as aircraft or ocean marine insurance—in a commercial package policy?

How can you use what you will learn?

Examine a particular customer's property and operations.

- What risk management techniques, in addition to insurance, might be appropriate for this customer?
- Of the various coverages surveyed in this assignment, are there any that your customer definitely would *not* need?

Chapter 1
Overview of Commercial Insurance

Just as individuals and families buy homeowners insurance and personal auto insurance, businesses and other organizations buy insurance to protect themselves against the adverse financial effects of property and liability losses. Insurance covering for-profit businesses and nonprofit organizations—such as educational, religious, or governmental entities—is called **commercial insurance**, in contrast with the personal insurance that individuals and families buy to cover their generally nonbusiness insurance needs.

The distinction between personal insurance and commercial insurance is fundamental to property and liability insurers. Some insurers provide only commercial insurance, and some provide only personal insurance. Many insurers provide both types of insurance, but typically they do so through separate personal and commercial divisions. In general, the property and liability insurance needs of businesses and other organizations are more complex than those of individuals and families. Accordingly, commercial insurance involves a far greater number of policy forms and endorsements than those used to provide personal insurance.

This chapter provides an overview of commercial insurance by examining the following topics:

- Insurance as a risk management technique
- Commercial lines of business
- Commercial insurance policies

Subsequent chapters of the text will focus on the various commercial insurance coverages introduced in this chapter.

> **Commercial insurance**
> Insurance that covers for-profit businesses or nonprofit organizations against the adverse financial effects of property and liability losses.

INSURANCE AS A RISK MANAGEMENT TECHNIQUE

Insurance enables a person or an organization (called "the policyholder" or "the insured") to transfer the financial consequences of a loss to an insurer. The insurer, in turn, pays the policyholder for covered losses and distributes the costs of losses among all policyholders. Insurance is just one technique that organizations use as part of an overall process known as risk management. **Risk management** is the process of identifying, analyzing, and managing loss exposures in such a way that an organization can meet its objectives.

> **Risk management**
> The process of identifying and analyzing loss exposures, evaluating the feasibility of risk management techniques to address the loss exposures, selecting and implementing the best techniques, and monitoring results.

Loss exposure
Any condition or situation that presents a possibility of loss, whether or not loss actually occurs.

A **loss exposure** is a possibility of loss. In other words, if an organization could suffer a particular loss, it is exposed to that type of loss. For example, buildings in the Midwest are exposed to tornado damage and thus are said to have a tornado loss exposure. Violent tornadoes do not occur in most West Coast states; therefore, buildings in those states do not have a tornado loss exposure.

The loss exposures to which commercial insurance responds include both property loss exposures and liability loss exposures.

Property loss exposure
The possibility that a person or an organization will sustain a financial loss as the result of the damaging, destruction, taking, or loss of use of property in which that person or organization has a financial interest.

- A **property loss exposure** is the possibility that a person or an organization will sustain a financial loss as the result of the damaging, destruction, taking, or loss of use of property in which that person or organization has a financial interest. The possibility of tornado damage, noted above, is an example of a property loss exposure.

- A **liability loss exposure** is the possibility that a person or an organization will sustain a financial loss as the result of a claim being made against that person or organization by someone seeking monetary damages or some other legal remedy. An example of a liability loss exposure is the possibility that a restaurant will be sued by one of its customers who has slipped and fallen because of a water spill on the restaurant's floor.

Liability loss exposure
The possibility that a person or an organization will sustain a financial loss as the result of a claim being made against that person or organization by someone seeking monetary damages or some other legal remedy.

Property and liability loss exposures can be identified and treated through the risk management process. The risk management process consists of the following steps:

1. Identifying loss exposures
2. Analyzing loss exposures
3. Evaluating the various techniques for treating the loss exposures
4. Selecting the most effective technique or techniques
5. Implementing the selected techniques
6. Monitoring the program and making needed corrections or adjustments

Although this text is concerned primarily with insurance, insurance is only one of several risk management techniques, and it is almost always used in combination with other techniques. These noninsurance techniques include the following:

Avoidance
A risk management technique by which an organization avoids a loss exposure by choosing not to own a particular item of property or not to engage in a particular activity.

- **Avoidance**. Avoidance occurs when an organization avoids an identified loss exposure by choosing not to own a particular item of property or not to engage in a particular activity. For example, by not manufacturing a new product, a manufacturer can avoid the potential liability for injuries resulting from the new product.

Loss control
A risk management technique that prevents losses from occurring or reduces the size of losses that do occur.

- **Loss control**. Loss control includes any measure to prevent losses from occurring (such as storing gasoline in sealed, approved containers) or to reduce the size of losses that do occur (such as installing an automatic sprinkler system in a building).

- **Retention**. An organization that pays all or part of its own losses is said to retain or "self-insure" its losses. For example, a business might choose to self-insure certain exposures or to purchase large deductibles on its insurance policies. When an organization has the financial ability to absorb some or all of its own losses, retention may be less costly *in the long run* than buying insurance to cover the same losses.

- **Noninsurance transfer**. Noninsurance transfer occurs when an organization (such as a building owner) obtains the promise of a second, *noninsurance* organization (such as a remodeling contractor) to pay for certain losses that would otherwise fall on the first organization. Also known as hold harmless agreements or indemnity agreements, noninsurance transfers are commonly included in a wide variety of contracts, such as leases, construction contracts, and purchase agreements.

Retention
A risk management technique by which an organization pays all or part of its own losses due to its loss exposures.

Noninsurance transfer
A risk management technique by which an organization obtains the promise of a second organization (other than an insurer) to pay for certain losses that would otherwise be the financial responsibility of the first organization.

LINES OF BUSINESS

Commercial insurance can be divided according to particular lines of business. A **line of business**, or simply a line, is an identifiable type of insurance. The divisions used to identify lines of business depend on the purpose for which the lines are being identified. For example, the lines of business listed in the "annual statement" form that insurers use to report financial data to state insurance regulators differ in some ways from the lines of business commonly referred to by insurance companies and practitioners in their everyday operations. The divisions used in this text, listed in Exhibit 1-1 and summarized in the sections that follow, conform generally to those used by insurers in their everyday operations.

Line of business
A general classification of insurance, such as commercial property, commercial general liability, commercial crime, or commercial auto.

EXHIBIT 1-1

Lines of Commercial Insurance

- Commercial property insurance
- Business income insurance
- Crime insurance
- Equipment breakdown (boiler and machinery) insurance
- Inland and ocean marine insurance
- Commercial general liability insurance
- Commercial automobile insurance
- Businessowners insurance

- Farm insurance
- Workers compensation and employers liability insurance
- Excess and umbrella liability insurance
- Professional liability insurance
- Aircraft insurance
- Environmental insurance
- Surety bonds

Commercial Property Insurance

As a general term, commercial property insurance refers to any type of commercial insurance that covers loss to property. In this general sense, several of the lines of business listed above are commercial property insurance (as opposed to commercial liability insurance). In a narrower sense, the term "commercial property insurance" is used to describe insurance covering commercial buildings and their contents against loss caused by fire, windstorm, and other perils. Commercial property insurance (in its narrower meaning) provides little, if any, coverage for property while in transit or otherwise away from the insured location and omits most crime-related perils as well as mechanical or electrical breakdown or steam boiler explosion. Most references to commercial property insurance in this textbook pertain to the narrower concept of the commercial property line of business rather than to the broader concept of all insurance covering property loss exposures.

Business Income Insurance

When property is physically damaged, the owner suffers a financial loss equal to the reduction in the property's value. Damage to property can also result in lost income and increased expenses. Though sometimes called an "indirect" loss, the loss of income or the increased expenses needed to continue operations can have a devastating financial effect. Business income insurance provides organizations a way to protect against this possibility. Although generally included within the commercial property line, business income insurance is so different from insurance against physical loss to buildings and contents that it is treated separately in this text.

Crime Insurance

Commercial crime insurance covers property and perils that are not covered by most commercial property policies. For example, money and securities are generally excluded types of property, and employee dishonesty is almost always an excluded cause of loss in commercial property policies. Various commercial crime coverages are available to insure (1) money and securities against a wide range of perils (not limited to crime perils) and (2) property other than money and securities against various crime perils, such as employee dishonesty, burglary, robbery, theft, and extortion.

Equipment Breakdown Insurance

Equipment breakdown insurance (also known as boiler and machinery insurance) is another type of insurance that fills a gap in commercial property policies. Mechanical breakdown, electrical injury (other than lightning), and steam boiler explosion are causes of loss that are typically excluded from commercial property policies. Boiler and machinery insurance can be used to cover damage to property resulting from these perils, as well as resulting business income losses. If, for example, a store lost business income because its air conditioning system suffered a mechanical breakdown during the hottest week of the summer, a properly arranged equipment breakdown policy would cover both the physical damage and the resulting loss of business income.

Inland and Ocean Marine Insurance

In most of the world except the United States, marine insurance principally means insurance on vessels and their cargoes. In the United States, marine insurance is divided into ocean marine and inland marine insurance. Ocean marine insurance conforms to the international meaning of marine insurance, whereas inland marine insurance includes a wide variety of risks that in the United States were first insured by marine underwriters. These risks include property in domestic transit, mobile equipment, buildings in the course of construction, property essential to transportation or communication (such as bridges, tunnels, and radio and television towers), and many other classes of property that typically involve an element of transportation.

Commercial General Liability Insurance

Every business, even one that has little or no property exposed to loss, faces the threat of claims and lawsuits for damages arising from its acts or omissions in conducting its operations. The basic protection for this exposure is commercial general liability insurance. Commercial general liability insurance covers the loss exposures arising from an organization's premises and operations, its products, or its work. It also covers various other offenses that may give rise to claims or suits, such as libel, slander, false arrest, and invasion of privacy.

Most Covers
The Claims.

Commercial Automobile Insurance

Commercial property insurance does not cover physical damage to automobiles. Moreover, commercial general liability insurance excludes liability arising out of the ownership, maintenance, or use of automobiles in most circumstances. Both automobile physical damage insurance and automobile liability insurance are available under a commercial automobile insurance policy or in the commercial auto coverage part of a package policy. Various coverages can be added to an auto policy by endorsement, such as auto medical payments coverage and uninsured/underinsured motorists coverage. Commercial auto insurance also encompasses specialized forms for trucking firms and auto dealers.

Businessowners Insurance

The businessowners policy combines, in a simplified manner, most of the property and liability coverages, other than auto and workers compensation, needed by small and medium-sized businesses such as stores, offices, and

Prop & lib

apartment buildings. Smaller organizations can thus avoid the more complex structure of a policy containing many separate forms providing the various coverages described above. Several optional coverages that are printed in the businessowners policy form can be activated by the insured's payment of an additional premium, and a limited number of other optional coverages can be added to the policy by endorsement.

Farm Insurance

Because many farmers and ranchers live and work on their own land, they need a combination of personal insurance and commercial insurance. Farm insurance provides this blend of coverages. The personal insurance aspect is similar to a homeowners policy, covering the farmer's home and household property. The commercial insurance aspect is similar to commercial property and inland marine coverage, covering property used in farming operations, including livestock, mobile equipment and machinery, and farm structures such as barns and outbuildings. Farm insurance also covers liability arising out of either personal or farming activities. When farm insurance is written for an agribusiness organization, the personal coverages are omitted from the policy.

Workers Compensation and Employers Liability Insurance

Workers compensation laws, which apply throughout the United States, obligate employers to pay specified medical, disability, rehabilitation, and death benefits for their employees' job-related injuries and diseases. The obligation to pay these benefits exists regardless of whether the employer was in any way at fault. In theory, employees are precluded from suing their employers for injuries or diseases covered by the applicable workers compensation law. However, in some cases employees are permitted to sue their employers for work-related accidents. Workers compensation and employers liability insurance provides two coverages: (1) coverage for benefits the insured employer is obligated to pay under workers compensation laws and (2) coverage for employee injury claims made against the insured employer that are not covered by workers compensation laws.

Excess and Umbrella Liability Insurance

Most commercial insureds want higher coverage limits than they can obtain in their primary liability coverages, such as commercial general liability and commercial auto liability. Insureds can obtain the additional coverage limits through excess liability policies. A common type of excess liability policy is the umbrella liability policy, which not only provides excess limits above primary policy limits but also "drops down" to cover some claims that are not covered by the insured's primary policies.

Professional Liability Insurance

Traditionally, the term "professional liability insurance" has referred to policies covering professionals such as doctors, lawyers, and engineers against liability arising out of their rendering, or failing to render, professional services. Today, the term is used to describe policies written to protect a much broader spectrum of occupations than the "learned professions" listed above, and it is also used to describe similar liability coverages such as directors and officers liability insurance, fiduciary liability insurance, and employment practices liability insurance.

Aircraft Insurance

Commercial general liability insurance excludes liability for aircraft, and commercial property insurance excludes physical damage to aircraft owned or used by the insured. Insureds that own or operate aircraft can obtain aircraft insurance policies that provide aircraft liability coverage, aircraft physical damage coverage, and other aircraft coverages.

Environmental Insurance

Injury, damage, or cleanup costs resulting from the release of pollutants are largely excluded under most commercial insurance policies. Organizations that wish to insure their pollution loss exposures can obtain various types of environmental insurance.

Surety Bonds

A surety bond is an agreement by one party (the surety) to answer for the failure of another (the principal) to perform as the principal has promised. Most surety bonds are provided by insurance companies, and surety bonding is regulated in the same manner as insurance. Contract surety bonds are widely used to guarantee that a contractor will complete a building project according to specifications, that the contractor will pay certain bills for labor and materials, and that the contractor's work will be free from defects for a specified period. Commercial surety bonds are used to provide a wide range of other guarantees in any number of situations.

COMMERCIAL INSURANCE POLICIES

This text will focus primarily on the policy forms developed by Insurance Services Office (ISO), an advisory organization serving insurers throughout the United States. Some insurers use similar policy forms developed by the American Association of Insurance Services (AAIS), an advisory organization similar to ISO. For some lines of business, neither ISO nor AAIS offers a standard form. Thus, any insurer wishing to underwrite one of those lines must develop its own policy forms. Even when a standard policy form exists, many insurers develop their own forms, usually to broaden the coverage in an attempt to gain a competitive advantage over other insurers.

A commercial insurance policy can be either a monoline policy or a package policy. A **monoline policy** includes only one line of business. A **package policy** includes two or more lines of business. In practice, most organizations have a package policy that provides most or all of their needed coverages. In addition to their package policies, many organizations also have one or more mono-line policies from other insurers providing coverages that the package insurer either does not write or is unwilling to provide to the insured. For example, an architect's office might have an insurance program that consists of the following policies:

1. A package policy covering the following lines:
    *   Commercial property
    *   Commercial crime
    *   Commercial inland marine
    *   Commercial general liability
    *   Commercial automobile

2. A monoline workers compensation and employers liability policy
3. A monoline architects professional liability policy

Monoline policy
Policy that covers only one line of business.

Package policy
Policy that covers two or more lines of business.

ISO Commercial Package Policy Program

Under the rules and forms developed by ISO and used by many insurance companies, a **commercial package policy (CPP)** includes the following components:

1. Common policy declarations
2. Common policy conditions
3. Two or more coverage parts

A policy that contains items 1 and 2 above but only *one* coverage part is a monoline policy. These three components are described in more detail below and are illustrated in Exhibit 1-2.

Commercial package policy (CPP)
Policy that covers two or more lines of business by combining ISO's commercial lines coverage parts.

Common Policy Declarations

The **common policy declarations** (often called the common "dec" page) are printed on one or more pages and are usually located at the front of the policy. They show the following information:

*   Policy number
*   Names of the insurance company and the producer
*   Name, address, and business description of the named insured
*   Effective date and expiration date of the policy
*   Premium for each coverage part included in the policy
*   Total premium

Common policy declarations
A required CPP component that provides basic information about the insurer, the policyholder, and the insurance provided.

EXHIBIT 1-2

Components of the ISO Commercial Package Policy (CPP)

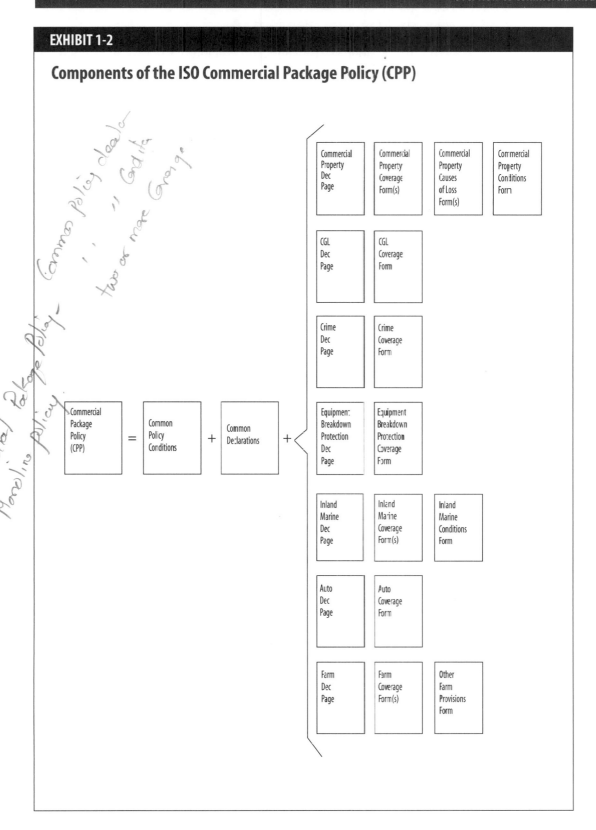

The common policy declarations page may also include a general statement, known as the "in consideration" clause. In this clause, the insurance company agrees with the named insured to provide the insurance as stated in the policy in return for the payment of premium and subject to all the terms of the policy.

Common Policy Conditions

Common Policy Conditions
A required CPP component that contains six conditions applicable to all coverage parts unless a coverage part states otherwise.

The **Common Policy Conditions** are a separate form that is attached to the policy. The form contains six conditions that apply to all coverage parts in the policy unless a particular coverage part states otherwise. This approach avoids the need to repeat the Common Policy Conditions in each coverage part. The six conditions in the form are titled as follows:

- Cancellation
- Changes
- Examination of your books and records
- Inspections and surveys
- Premiums
- Transfer of your rights and duties under this policy

Cancellation

The insured may cancel the policy at any time by mailing or delivering written notice of cancellation to the insurance company. If two or more insureds are listed in the declarations, only the one listed first (called the first named insured) can request cancellation.

The insurance company can cancel the policy by mailing or delivering written notice of cancellation to the first named insured. In order to provide reasonable time for the insured to obtain other insurance, the insurance company is required to give advance notice of cancellation. Notice of cancellation must be mailed or delivered to the insured (1) at least ten days before the date of cancellation if the cancellation is for nonpayment of premium or (2) at least thirty days before the date of cancellation for any other reason.

If the notice of cancellation is mailed, the insurance company is not required to prove that the insured actually received the notice. It is required to prove only that the notice was mailed to the first named insured at the mailing address shown on the policy.

If the cancellation results in a return premium, the refund will be sent to the first named insured. In effect, the first named insured is designated as the agent who can act on behalf of all other insureds for all transactions related to cancellation of the policy.

In almost every state, the cancellation provision is superseded by state law and an endorsement is added to the policy. That endorsement modifies the cancellation provisions to conform with the applicable law. The state laws

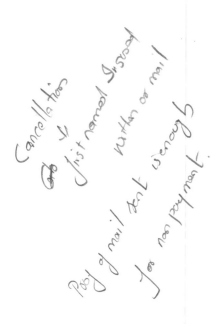

commonly address permissible reasons for cancellation and the advance notification period.

Changes

The Common Policy Conditions include a clause concerning changes in the policy. This clause states that the policy constitutes the entire contract between the parties. The policy can be changed only by a written endorsement issued by the insurance company. Such changes may be made, with the insurance company's consent, upon the request of the first named insured. Only the first named insured has the authority to request policy changes, and the insurance company is authorized to make changes upon the request of the first named insured without specific permission of any other insured.

Examination of Books and Records

The insurance company reserves the right to examine and audit the insured's books and records related to the policy at any time during the policy period and for up to three years after the termination of the policy. This provision is included because many commercial insurance policies are issued with estimated premiums. The final premium is determined after the policy expires, based on reported values of the insured property, the amount of the insured's sales or payrolls, or some other variable premium base.

The insured is required to report the final figures to the insurance company, and the insurance company may accept the insured's reports without verification. However, this provision permits the insurance company to make an on-site verification as it deems necessary. The insurer's rights under this provision may also be exercised during the loss adjustment process.

Inspections and Surveys

The insurance company has the right, but not the obligation, to inspect the insured's premises and operations at any reasonable time during the policy period. The inspections may be made by the insurer's own personnel or by another organization acting on behalf of the insurer. Such inspections are important in determining the insurability of the insured's property and operations, in setting proper insurance rates, and in making loss control recommendations.

The insurance company *may* inform the insured of the results of such inspections and *may* recommend changes. However, it does not have a duty to do either.

The inspections and surveys provision makes it clear that the insurer (1) does not make safety inspections, (2) does not guarantee that conditions are safe or healthful, and (3) does not guarantee that the insured is in compliance with safety or health regulations. These disclaimer clauses have been included in the policy in an effort to protect the insurance company against suits (1) by persons who allege that they were injured as a result of the insurer's failure to detect a hazardous condition or (2) by the insured alleging that the insurer failed to detect a violation of laws or regulations, with a resulting fine or other penalty against the insured. Several such suits against insurers have occurred in recent years.

Premiums

The first named insured is responsible for paying the premium under the policy. Also, as previously mentioned, the insurer must pay any return premium under the policy to the first named insured.

[handwritten margin note: first named Insured]

Transfer of Rights and Duties Under the Policy

The insured cannot transfer any rights or duties under the policy to any other person or organization without the written consent of the insurance company. For example, if the insured sells the property covered by the policy, the coverage cannot be transferred to the new owner of the property without the written consent of the insurer. Such a transfer of coverage is generally referred to as an *assignment* of the policy, but that terminology is not used in the Common Policy Conditions.

[handwritten margin note: transfer policy to another person not possible without consent of the Insurer]

The transfer of rights and duties condition also provides specifically for the automatic transfer of coverage upon the death of an individual named insured. Upon death, the insured's rights and duties under the policy are automatically transferred to the insured's legal representatives, or, if the insured's legal representatives have not yet been appointed, to any person having proper temporary custody of the insured property.

Coverage Parts

> **Coverage part**
> A CPP component in a line of insurance (such as commercial property or commercial general liability) that comprises the coverage part's declarations page, one or more coverage forms, applicable endorsements, and in some cases a general provisions form.

A **coverage part** consists of the following components illustrated in Exhibit 1-2:

- A declarations page that pertains only to that coverage part
- One or more coverage forms, which contain insuring agreements, exclusions, and other policy provisions
- Applicable endorsements, which modify the terms of the coverage form(s) to fit the needs of the particular insured

Some coverage parts include a conditions form containing general provisions that could apply to any of the coverage forms included in the coverage part. Other coverage parts use coverage forms that include all the applicable general provisions and therefore do not need a conditions form.

The coverage parts that may be used in an ISO commercial package policy correspond generally to the lines of business discussed earlier in this chapter and include the following:

- Commercial property (including business income)
- Commercial crime
- Equipment breakdown (boiler and machinery)

- Commercial inland marine
- Commercial general liability
- Commercial auto
- Farm

These coverage parts and their components will be discussed in subsequent chapters of this text. Some insurers add other, non-ISO coverage parts to their commercial package policies.

Package Modification Factors

An important element of the commercial package policy (CPP) program is the package discount the insured may receive. The premium for a CPP is determined using the same rules that would apply if each coverage part were being issued as a monoline policy. If both property and liability coverages are provided in the CPP, the application of **package modification factors** often provides a premium discount for the insured. This discount is justified by the greater efficiency of issuing a single package policy instead of several monoline policies for an insured.

The package discount is determined by applying the appropriate package modification factors to the premiums for the various coverage parts included in the policy. The package modification factors reflect the type of business (apartment, office, mercantile, and so forth), the particular coverage part being rated, and other eligibility requirements. A package modification factor of 0.75, for example, means that the premium for that coverage part will be three-fourths of the premium that would apply if the coverage part were issued in a monoline policy. The factors vary from state to state and from insurer to insurer.

Package modification factor
A factor (such as 0.75) that is multiplied by the regular policy premium of any CPP that includes both property and liability coverages, resulting in a premium discount.

Example of Package Modification Factor	
Total policy premium (if coverage parts were written as monoline policies)	$25,220
Package modification factor	× .75
Final package policy premium	$18,915

SUMMARY

The subject of this text is commercial insurance, which is property and liability insurance for businesses and other organizations such as schools and churches. Commercial insurance is one of several techniques used in risk management, which is the process of identifying, analyzing, and managing loss exposures so that an organization can meet its objectives. Other risk management techniques, often used in combination with insurance, include avoidance, loss control, retention, and noninsurance transfer.

Commercial insurance is divided into several lines of business, or distinct coverages. The material in this text is organized along essentially the same divisions as shown in Exhibit 1-1.

Commercial insurance is often provided in a package policy, which is a policy that covers two or more lines of business. In some cases, a policyholder may need to obtain additional coverages under monoline policies. A monoline policy is a policy that provides only one line of coverage, such as a workers compensation and employers liability policy.

Under the commercial package policy (CPP) program of Insurance Services Office (ISO), a package policy consists of common policy declarations, Common Policy Conditions, and two or more coverage parts.

- The common policy declarations page contains essential information about the policyholder and the coverages being provided.
- The Common Policy Conditions form contains six basic conditions that apply to all coverage parts included in the policy.
- Each coverage part consists of a declarations page for that coverage part, one or more coverage forms, and, for some coverage parts, a separate conditions form.

The various coverage parts that can be included in a CPP—especially the coverage forms that spell out the insuring provisions of each coverage part—are the main subjects of several chapters in this text. Some insurers add additional, non-ISO coverage parts to their package policies.

The premium for a CPP is often lower than if the same coverages in the CPP were issued in separate monoline policies. This premium reduction results because some coverage parts in a CPP qualify for a discount based on the various advantages to an insurer of issuing a package policy rather than a monoline policy or policies. The discount is determined by multiplying the monoline premium by a package modification factor (such as 0.75). Package modification factors vary by state and by insurer.

Chapter 2

Direct Your Learning

Commercial Property Insurance, Part I

After learning the content of this chapter, you should be able to:

■ Given a case about a commercial property loss, explain whether coverage applies and determine the amount, if any, the insurer will pay for the loss, applying both coinsurance and deductible.

- Determine which types of property are and are not covered under the Building and Personal Property Coverage Form (BPP).

- Describe each of the additional coverages and coverage extensions included in the BPP.

- Describe each of the conditions appearing in the loss conditions or additional conditions section of the BPP.

- Explain how each of the optional coverages printed in the BPP modifies the basic coverage of the BPP.

■ Describe the purpose of each the following endorsements:

- Functional Building Valuation Endorsement

- Functional Personal Property Valuation Endorsement

■ Explain how the Value Reporting Form and the Peak Season Limit of Insurance Endorsement provide solutions to the problem of fluctuating values.

■ Compare specific insurance and blanket insurance.

OUTLINE

Policies Providing Commercial Property Coverage

Overview of the Commercial Property Coverage Part

Building and Personal Property Coverage Form

Insuring Fluctuating Values

Blanket Insurance

Summary

Develop Your Perspective

What are the main topics covered in the chapter?

This chapter surveys the documents that make up the commercial property coverage part of a commercial package policy. The most important document of that coverage part, the Building and Personal Property Coverage Form (BPP), is described, and several coverage options for tailoring the BPP to meet a customer's individual needs are identified.

Examine a commercial property coverage form used by your company or a company you represent.

- Is this a coverage form other than the BPP?

- Consider the reasons why this particular form was chosen.

Why is it important to learn about these topics?

Almost every commercial insured is covered under the BPP or a similar form. Knowing which coverages are provided by the BPP and which are not will enable you to help your customers select appropriate insurance to cover their commercial loss exposures.

Obtain a copy of an application for commercial property insurance from your underwriting division.

- Examine the applicant's property loss exposures.

- Identify the commercial property forms and endorsements that you would recommend for this applicant.

How can you use what you will learn?

Review a claim file for a loss covered under the BPP or a similar coverage form.

- If you were the claim adjuster handling this loss, what policy provisions would you need to review before deciding whether the loss would be covered and (if covered) how much would be payable?

Chapter 2
Commercial Property Insurance, Part I

Whether it is the office furniture, fixtures, equipment, records, and supplies of a small insurance agency, the stock and fixtures of a main-street merchant, the complex machinery of an automated computer chip manufacturer, or the office and apartment buildings owned by a large real estate developer, all commercial enterprises use at least some tangible property. For almost all of them, property insurance is a necessity. This chapter is called "*Commercial* Property Insurance," following industry usage. However, despite that title, the various policies and forms to be discussed are also used to insure nonprofit and governmental organizations.

Even those enterprises that feel they could absorb any loss or damage to their property without carrying insurance are often required to carry property insurance when they want to obtain financing. Financial institutions that lend money based on a security interest in property want to be sure that the buyer will be able to repay the loan if the property is destroyed. Therefore, insurance coverage naming the lender as a loss payee is an almost universal requirement for mortgages and many other types of loans. It is hard to envision the construction and financing of our country's homes, offices, shopping malls, and factories without property insurance.

POLICIES PROVIDING COMMERCIAL PROPERTY COVERAGE

Commercial property insurance can be provided under any of the following:

- A businessowners policy (BOP)
- A commercial property coverage part
- A policy designed for "highly protected risks" (HPRs)
- Inland marine coverages, including output policies

Commercial property insurance
Insurance that covers loss to commercial property; more narrowly, a line of insurance that covers buildings and business personal property against loss caused by a wide range of perils.

A businessowners policy (BOP) is a combination of property, liability, and other coverages that, in many ways, resembles the homeowners policies used for personal insurance. BOP policies are intended for smaller, less-complex businesses. Underwriting and rating are simplified and often highly automated. Most small businesses are insured under BOPs.

A commercial property coverage part offers a broader range of optional coverages to meet the needs of larger or more diverse firms. These firms are sometimes referred to as the "middle-market," meaning that they are larger than the typical small business but smaller than national or international accounts. However, there is no restriction on the size of firms that can be covered under the commercial property coverage part. It can be issued as part of a package policy or as a monoline policy.

HPR policies are designed to be issued only to organizations with superior loss protection characteristics, for example, fire-resistant, sprinklered buildings. HPR forms are typically the basis of property coverage for the largest enterprises. The coverage is broader and the terms and conditions more liberal than most commercial property coverage parts.

Firms of any size can use inland marine forms. Specialized policies such as data processing or contractors equipment floaters can be used to cover particular types of property. The output policy, which has its roots in inland marine, can cover almost all of a firm's property exposures. Inland marine policies are particularly suitable for property in transit.

These groupings are not absolute. On the one hand, a large business may choose a BOP because it offers the coverages it wants at an attractive price. On the other hand, firms large or small may purchase the commercial property coverage part because it better fits their needs. HPR policies are written for some middle-market businesses but seldom for truly small businesses because of the expense of meeting and maintaining HPR status. Inland marine policies, as noted above, are used by firms of all sizes.

The balance of this chapter and the next two chapters will focus on the commercial property coverage part. Later chapters will discuss BOPs, HPR policies, and inland marine insurance. It will be easier to understand the advantages and disadvantages of the other forms once you have mastered the details of the commercial property coverage part.

This text focuses on the commercial property coverage part of Insurance Services Office (ISO). Many insurers, including the largest writers of commercial property insurance, use their own forms, but they usually base their forms on the ISO form and often use some ISO wording. The commercial property forms of the American Association of Insurance Services (AAIS), used by some insurers, are also similar to the ISO forms. An understanding of the ISO forms should enable you to evaluate other commercial property forms.

Types of Property

Property can be classified in various ways. Here are four important classifications for insurance purposes:

Real property: Land and whatever is growing or erected on or affixed to the land. Sometimes referred to as "immovable property." Few insurance policies use the term "real property" in describing covered property; most policies cover specified types of real property, such as buildings and structures.

Personal property: All property other than real property. Sometimes referred to as "movable property." Insurance policies often use the phrase "personal property" in describing covered property, for example "business personal property." Insurance practitioners commonly refer to personal property usually situated in a building as "contents."

Tangible property: All property that can be touched and that has physical existence. It can be either real or personal property. Most property insurance policies cover only tangible property.

Intangible property: Property that cannot be touched because it has no physical existence. Examples of intangible property are patents, copyrights, and trademarks. Most property insurance policies do not cover intangible property.

OVERVIEW OF THE COMMERCIAL PROPERTY COVERAGE PART

A **commercial property coverage part** consists of the following documents:

1. Commercial property declarations
2. One or more commercial property coverage forms
3. One or more causes-of-loss forms
4. Commercial Property Conditions
5. Any applicable endorsements

Commercial property coverage part
A CPP coverage component that provides a broad range of coverages to "middle-market" or larger firms to insure buildings and business personal property.

Commercial Property Declarations

A **commercial property declarations** page contains the following information pertaining specifically to property insurance:

1. A description of the property insured
2. The kinds and amounts of coverage provided and the covered causes of loss (basic, broad, or special)
3. A list of mortgagees, if any
4. The deductible amount
5. A list of the property coverage forms and endorsements attached to the policy
6. The applicable coinsurance percentage(s)
7. Any optional coverages

Commercial property declarations page
A required commercial property coverage part component that provides basic information about the policyholder and the insurance provided.

Supplemental declarations can be added, as needed, on a separate sheet of paper. For example, if an insured such as a fast-food franchise had too many locations to show on the declarations page, a supplemental schedule could be added to show all locations. Exhibit 2-1 shows a specimen declarations page for a commercial property coverage part.

EXHIBIT 2-1

Commercial Property Declarations Page

COMMERCIAL PROPERTY
CP DS 00 10 00

COMMERCIAL PROPERTY COVERAGE PART
DECLARATIONS PAGE

POLICY NO. SP 001   **EFFECTIVE DATE** 10 / 1 / 2002   [X] **"X" If Supplemental**
Declarations Is Attached

NAMED INSURED

ABC Corporation

DESCRIPTION OF PREMISES

Prem. No.	Bldg. No.	Location, Construction And Occupancy
001	001	2000 Industrial Highway, Workingtown, PA 19000 Joisted Masonry Storm Door Manufacturing

COVERAGES PROVIDED   Insurance At The Described Premises Applies Only For Coverages For Which A Limit Of Insurance Is Shown

Prem. No.	Bldg. No.	Coverage	Limit Of Insurance	Covered Causes Of Loss	Coinsurance*	Rates
001	001	Building	2,000,000	Special	80%	(See Sched.)
		Your Bus. Personal Prop.	1,120,000	Broad	80%	
		Personal Prop. of Others	50,000	Broad	80%	
		Bus. Income & Extra Expense	680,000	Broad	80%	

*If Extra Expense Coverage, Limits On Loss Payment

OPTIONAL COVERAGES   Applicable Only When Entries Are Made In The Schedule Below

Prem. No.	Bldg. No.	Agreed Value			Replacement Cost (X)		
		Expiration Date	Cov.	Amount	Building	Pers. Prop.	Including "Stock"
001	001	10/1/2003	Building	$2,000,000	X		

Inflation Guard (%)		*Monthly Limit Of Indemnity (Fraction)	Maximum Period Of Indemnity (X)	*Extended Period Of Indemnity (Days)
Bldg.	Pers. Prop.			
3%	3%			

*Applies to Business Income Only

MORTGAGEHOLDERS

Prem. No.	Bldg. No.	Mortgageholder Name And Mailing Address
001	001	Workingtown Savings and Loan Assn. 400 Main Street Workingtown, PA 19000

DEDUCTIBLE

$1000. **Exceptions:**

FORMS APPLICABLE

To All Coverages: CP 00 10, CP 00 30, CP 00 90, CP 10 30

CP DS 00 10 00   Copyright, Insurance Services Office, Inc., 1999   Page 1 of 1 □

Commercial Property Coverage Forms

The ISO commercial package policy program includes several different commercial property coverage forms. Each **commercial property coverage form** contains an insuring agreement, describes the property covered and not covered, sets forth the additional coverages and coverage extensions, and includes provisions and definitions that apply only to that coverage form. Commercial property coverage forms do not list the causes of loss for which the described property is covered. That function is performed by the causes-of- loss forms, discussed later.

This chapter describes the Building and Personal Property Coverage Form, which can be used for most organizations. More specialized coverage forms for insuring buildings under construction, condominium association buildings, and the property of condominium commercial unit owners will be discussed in Chapter 3. Coverage forms for insuring the loss of business income (an exposure to be discussed later) will be examined in Chapter 4. Depending on the nature of the insured's loss exposures, more than one commercial property coverage form may be included in a commercial property coverage part.

Commercial property coverage form
A commercial property coverage part component that can be any of several commercial property forms containing an insuring agreement and related provisions.

Causes-of-Loss Forms

The **causes-of-loss forms** specify the perils covered by a commercial property coverage part. The three forms available—termed "basic," "broad," and "special"—allow the insured to select from a range of covered perils.

A commercial property coverage part may contain more than one causes-of-loss form. One causes-of-loss form (such as the special form) may apply to buildings, and another causes-of-loss form (such as the broad form) may apply to personal property. The commercial property declarations indicate which form applies to each type of property at each location.

The causes-of-loss forms will be examined in more detail in Chapter 3.

Causes-of-loss form
A required component of the commercial property coverage part that specifies perils covered; choices include basic, broad, or special form.

Commercial Property Conditions

The **Commercial Property Conditions**, which are printed as a separate form, apply to all coverage forms included in a commercial property coverage part, unless a coverage form contains a condition to the contrary. Like the Common Policy Conditions, the Commercial Property Conditions eliminate the need to repeat these conditions in each coverage form. The Commercial Property Conditions will be described in more detail in Chapter 3.

Commercial Property Conditions
A required component of the commercial property coverage part that contains conditions applicable to all commercial property coverage forms unless a coverage form contains a contradictory condition.

Endorsements

Many endorsements are available to tailor commercial property coverage to meet the specialized needs of particular insureds. Some of these endorsements are noted in the sections that follow.

BUILDING AND PERSONAL PROPERTY COVERAGE FORM

Building and Personal Property Coverage Form (BPP)
A commercial property coverage form that can be used to cover buildings, "your business personal property," and personal property of others.

The **Building and Personal Property Coverage Form (BPP)** is the most commonly used commercial property coverage form. It includes the nine sections listed below and is designed to provide coverage for physical damage to buildings and personal property used for business purposes.

Nine Sections of BPP Coverage Form

- Covered property
- Property not covered
- Additional coverages
- Coverage extensions
- Limits of insurance

- Deductible
- Loss conditions
- Additional conditions
- Optional coverages

Covered Property

The property that can be covered by the BPP consists of the following categories:

1. Buildings
2. Business personal property of the insured
3. Personal property of others in the custody of the insured

Coverage can be provided on any combination of these categories. The insured's selection of coverages is indicated on the commercial property declarations page by entering a limit of insurance for each chosen category of covered property.

An example of the entries on a declarations page is shown in Exhibit 2-1. If there is no entry for one of the categories of covered property (for example, "Building"), then no coverage applies to that category even if the insured owns property fitting that category.

Covered property is insured against direct loss or damage at the described premises caused by a covered cause of loss. Covered causes of loss are determined in the separate causes-of-loss forms.

Building (as defined in the BPP)
The building described in the policy; the building's completed additions; fixtures, including outdoor fixtures; permanently installed machinery and equipment; personal property owned by the insured and used to maintain or service the building or its premises.

Building

The policy covers buildings or structures listed and described in the declarations. The BPP's definition of **building** also includes the following property:

1. Completed additions to covered buildings
2. Fixtures including outdoor fixtures

3. Permanently installed machinery and equipment
4. Personal property owned by the insured and used to maintain or service the building or its premises (for example, fire extinguishing equipment, outdoor furniture, floor coverings, and equipment for refrigeration, ventilation, cooking, dishwashing, or laundering)

In addition, if they are not otherwise insured, the building description covers additions, alterations, or repairs in progress, including materials, equipment, and supplies used in connection with such work. However, such materials, equipment, and supplies are covered only if they are located within 100 feet of the premises. "Premises" includes the grounds on which the building is situated.

Fixtures are items attached to a building or to the land. Outdoor fixtures would include items outside the building but attached to the land, such as light poles and flagpoles. The term "fixtures" is broad enough to include fences and outdoor signs, but these items are specifically excluded from coverage for reasons discussed below under "Property Not Covered."

Business Personal Property of the Insured

"**Your business personal property**" covers personal property owned by the insured and used in the insured's business in or on the described building or in the open (or in a vehicle) within 100 feet of the premises. It includes furniture and fixtures, machinery and equipment, stock, and other similar personal property except those items excluded under the property not covered section. The form defines *stock* as "merchandise held in storage or for sale, raw materials and in-process or finished goods, including supplies used in their packing or shipping." Business personal property of the insured also includes labor, materials, or services furnished by the insured on personal property of others.

> **Your business personal property** (as defined in the BPP) Personal property owned by the named insured and, in some cases, personal property owned by others (such as leased property and improvements and betterments).

The insured's interest in improvements and betterments is also insured as business personal property, even though improvements and betterments are actually a part of the building. **Improvements and betterments** are alterations or additions made to the building at the expense of an insured who does not own the building and who cannot legally remove them. For example, a restaurant that rents space in a commercial building might install expensive wall and ceiling treatments that could not be removed when the lease is terminated. It is not uncommon for some commercial tenants to spend $1 million or more upgrading their premises. The tenant's interest in these improvements and betterments would be insured as part of its business personal property. It is important to consider these expenditures when setting the amount of insurance that an insured should carry.

> **Improvements and betterments** Alterations or additions made to the building at the expense of a tenant who does not own the building and who cannot legally remove them.

The business personal property item also includes leased personal property for which the named insured has a contractual responsibility to procure coverage. An example of such property is phone or computer equipment leased by the insured under an agreement requiring the insured to purchase insurance on the leased equipment.

Personal Property of Others

This coverage is designed to protect the insured against loss or damage to the **personal property of others** while such property is in the custody of the insured. It is intended for businesses (generally referred to as "bailees") that have customers' property in their custody, such as dry cleaners, lawn mower repair shops and furniture upholstery shops. The BPP covers such property only while it is (1) in the insured's care, custody, or control and (2) in or on the building described in the declarations or within 100 feet of the described premises.

Even if the insured does not buy coverage for personal property of others (as indicated by an amount of insurance being shown for that category on the declarations page), the BPP still provides a coverage extension for personal property of others, which is limited to $2,500 at each insured location. This coverage extension is discussed later in this chapter.

Property Not Covered

All three classes of covered property may be modified by this section of the form. The covered property section and the property not covered section must be read together in order to determine whether a specific kind of property is insured.

There are several reasons for excluding some kinds of property from coverage. First, it may not be legal to insure some kinds of property, such as illegal narcotics being held for sale. Second, some property, such as foundations of buildings, may not be subject to loss by the perils insured against. Finally, some kinds of property are excluded because they can be insured more advantageously under other forms. Automobiles and aircraft are examples of such property. The commercial property forms do not provide satisfactory insurance for automobiles because the coverage would apply only while the insured property (the automobile) was on the described premises or within 100 feet of the described premises, whereas the most serious loss exposures for automobiles are off premises. The BPP coverage form lists several classes of property or kinds of property loss that are not covered, as shown in Exhibit 2-2.

Insurance is available for almost all of the items listed in the property not covered section. Only contraband or property in the course of illegal transportation or trade is totally uninsurable. ISO manual rules permit removing the exclusion of many of the other items, and limited coverage is provided for some items in the BPP coverage extensions discussed below. Many items can be insured either by an endorsement adding them to the BPP or, as mentioned, in another policy more specifically designed for insuring such property. Policies that cover property excluded by the BPP will be discussed in later chapters of this text.

Property otherwise insured is not totally excluded (see item k in Exhibit 2-2). The BPP will still cover such property, but only in excess of the other insurance. For example, assume that a computer system valued at $150,000 is

---

Personal property of others
A category of property that the BPP can cover and that includes personal property of others (such as the named insured's customers) while the property is in the named insured's custody.

EXHIBIT 2-2

Property Not Covered Under BPP

Covered Property does not include:

a. Accounts, bills, currency, deeds, food stamps or other evidences of debt, money, notes or securities. Lottery tickets held for sale are not securities;

b. Animals, unless owned by others and boarded by you, only as "stock" while inside of buildings;

c. Automobiles held for sale;

d. Bridges, roadways, walks, patios or other paved surfaces;

e. Contraband, or property in the course of illegal transportation or trade;

f. The cost of excavations, grading, backfilling or filling;

g. Foundations of buildings, structures, machinery or boilers if their foundations are below:

    (1) The lowest basement floor; or

    (2) The surface of the ground, if there is no basement;

h. Land (including land on which the property is located), water, growing crops or lawns;

i. Personal property while airborne or waterborne;

j. Bulkheads, pilings, piers, wharves or docks;

k. Property that is covered under another coverage form of this or any other policy in which it is more specifically described, except for the excess of the amount due (whether you can collect on it or not) from that other insurance;

l. Retaining walls that are not part of a building;

m. Underground pipes, flues or drains;

n. The cost to research, replace or restore the information on valuable papers and records, including those which exist on electronic or magnetic media, except as provided in the Coverage Extensions;

o. Vehicles or self-propelled machines (including aircraft or watercraft) that:

    (1) Are licensed for use on public roads; or

    (2) Are operated principally away from the described premises.

This paragraph does not apply to:

    (a) Vehicles or self-propelled machines or autos you manufacture, process or warehouse;

    (b) Vehicles or self-propelled machines, other than autos, you hold for sale; or

    (c) Rowboats or canoes out of water at the described premises;

    (d) Trailers, but only to the extent provided for in the Coverage Extension for Non-Owned Detached Trailers.

p. The following property while outside of buildings:

    (1) Grain, hay, straw or other crops;

    (2) Fences, radio or television antennas (including satellite dishes) and their lead-in wiring, masts or towers, signs (other than signs attached to buildings), trees, shrubs or plants (other than "stock" of trees, shrubs or plants), all except as provided in the Coverage Extensions.

insured under the general category of business personal property in a BPP issued by Building Fire Insurance Company and is also insured for $100,000 under a separate data processing policy issued by Computer Casualty and Surety. Assume further that the computer system is totally destroyed by fire, a cause of loss insured under both policies. Since the policy of Computer Casualty more specifically describes the computer system, it must pay its limit ($100,000) before Building Fire pays anything. Building Fire Insurance Company would then pay the difference between the limit of Computer Casualty and the amount of loss otherwise payable under the Building Fire Insurance Company policy.

Some coverage is provided for vehicles or self-propelled machines (see item o. in Exhibit 2-2). The BPP *does* cover the following:

1. Vehicles or self-propelled machines or autos that are manufactured, processed, or warehoused by the insured

2. Vehicles or self-propelled machines, other than autos, that are held for sale by the insured

3. Rowboats or canoes that are out of the water at the described premises

4. Trailers, as provided in the coverage extension discussed later in this chapter.

Moreover, the exclusion applies only to vehicles or self-propelled machines that are licensed for use on public roads or are operated principally away from the described premises. Consequently, unlicensed vehicles and vehicles operated principally on the described premises are covered. For example, a truck used only to move steel beams in the storage yard of an iron and steel wholesaler would be covered.

Additional Coverages and Coverage Extensions

The BPP provides several supplemental coverages in addition to the basic coverages for buildings, the insured's business personal property, and the property of others described above. These supplemental coverages are set forth under two subheadings: (1) additional coverages and (2) coverage extensions.

Additional Coverages

The five additional coverages are titled as shown in the box below.

Additional Coverages

1. Debris removal
2. Preservation of property
3. Fire department service charge
4. Pollutant cleanup and removal
5. Increased cost of construction

Debris Removal

Following a major loss, large amounts of debris may remain on the premises, and the cost of removing the debris may be substantial. The debris removal additional coverage addresses that cost. The coverage pays for the removal of debris of covered property only. It would not, for example, pay for the removal of the debris of the insured's licensed automobiles, since they are not covered property.

The debris removal provision in the additional coverages section applies only to the cost of removing debris of covered property resulting from a covered cause of loss during the policy period. The removal expenses will be paid only if they are reported in writing within 180 days of the loss. Under the debris removal provision, the most that will be paid for such debris removal is 25 percent of the sum of the direct loss payment plus the deductible amount. However, this amount may not be sufficient in some cases. Therefore, an additional $10,000 limit per location is provided if (1) the direct loss plus debris removal expense exceeds the limits of insurance or (2) the debris removal expense exceeds the 25 percent limitation of direct losses. The $10,000 additional limit can be increased by endorsement.

The cost to clean up pollution caused by an insured peril is covered. For example, if "building" is shown as covered property, the cost to clean up debris from a fire that causes the release of toxic chemicals onto the floor of the insured's building would be covered. However, the debris removal provision does not apply to costs for cleanup or removal of pollutants from land or water. Limited coverage for these costs is available under the provisions of another additional coverage, which is discussed later in this section.

Preservation of Property

It is sometimes necessary to move the covered property to another location to protect it. The preservation of property additional coverage extends the policy to protect the covered property while it is being moved and for up to thirty days at the new location. This coverage is broader than the normal coverage under the policy. It protects against "any direct physical loss or damage" and is not limited to either the covered causes of loss or locations stipulated in the coverage form. The protection provided under this clause is subject to the limits of insurance stated in the declarations. Thus, no protection is provided by this clause if the limits of insurance are exhausted by payment for the physical loss.

Fire Department Service Charge

In some areas, the fire department may make a charge for its services in controlling or extinguishing a fire. The fire department service charge additional coverage pays such charges up to $1,000 if the charges are assumed by contract prior to loss or are required by local ordinance. This coverage limit is payable in addition to the limit of insurance shown in the declarations and is not subject to any deductible.

Examples of Debris Removal Losses

Each of the examples that follow involves a BPP with a limit of $100,000 on the insured's building and a $1,000 deductible.

Example 1—Debris removal is less than 25% of the sum of loss payment plus deductible.

Amount of loss: $10,000 damage to building, $2,000 debris removal

Insured collects:

$10,000	for building damage
2,000	for debris removal
$12,000	
− 1,000	deductible
$11,000	

Example 2—Debris removal is greater than 25% of the sum of loss payment plus deductible.

Amount of loss: $36,000 damage to building, $22,000 debris removal

Insured collects:

$36,000	for building damage
− 1,000	deductible
$35,000	amount insurer pays for direct physical loss
+19,000	for debris removal*
$54,000	

*The insured collects only $19,000 for the debris removal because the coverage for debris removal is limited to 25% of the sum of the insurer's payment for physical loss plus the deductible ($9,000, calculated as .25 × [$35,000 + $1,000 deductible]) plus the $10,000 additional limit of insurance for debris removal.

Example 3—Building loss exceeds the amount of insurance.

Loss: $105,000 damage to building, $20,000 debris removal

Insured collects:

$100,000	for building damage (limit of insurance)
10,000	for debris removal (additional limit of insurance)
$110,000	

In Example 3, the insurer's payment is not reduced by the deductible. The deductible is subtracted from the amount of the loss (not from the limit), and the remainder exceeds the limit of insurance.

Pollutant Cleanup and Removal

The pollutant cleanup and removal additional coverage provides limited coverage for the cleanup and removal of pollutants from land or water at the described premises. The BPP defines "pollutant" as follows:

> any solid, liquid, gaseous or thermal irritant or contaminant, including smoke, vapor, soot, fumes, acids, alkalis, chemicals and waste. Waste includes materials to be recycled, reconditioned or reclaimed.

This additional coverage pays the insured's expenses to extract pollutants from land or water at the described premises if the release, discharge, dispersal, seepage, migration, or escape of the pollutants is the result of a covered cause of loss that occurs during the policy period. These expenses must be reported in writing within 180 days after the loss. An aggregate limit of $10,000 per location applies to all such expenses that occur during each separate twelve-month period.

Increased Cost of Construction

As Chapter 3 will discuss in more detail, an ordinance or law exclusion in the causes-of-loss forms excludes the increased cost to comply with ordinances or laws regulating the repair, rebuilding, or replacement of covered buildings. The increased cost of construction additional coverage provides a small amount of insurance to cover this exposure. The amount of insurance is equal to 5 percent of the amount of insurance or $10,000, whichever is less. It is paid in addition to the policy limit. This additional coverage applies only if the replacement cost option, to be discussed later in this chapter, has been selected.

No coverage applies to (1) loss to any undamaged portion of the building that an ordinance or law does not permit to remain in use or (2) the cost to demolish the undamaged portion of the structure and remove its debris. Coverage for these excluded items, as well as higher limits for the increased cost to repair or reconstruct, can be provided by the Ordinance or Law Coverage Endorsement, discussed in Chapter 3.

Coverage Extensions

The protection provided by the coverage extensions section of the BPP coverage form applies only if at least 80 percent coinsurance or a value reporting period symbol is shown in the declarations. (Coinsurance requirements and value reporting period symbols are described later in this chapter.) The amounts that may be paid under the coverage extensions are additional amounts of insurance and are not subject to the limits of insurance stated in the declarations.

The BPP coverage extensions are titled as shown in the box below.

> ## BPP Coverage Extensions
>
> 1. Newly acquired or constructed property
> 2. Personal effects and property of others
> 3. Valuable papers and records—cost of research
> 4. Property off-premises
> 5. Outdoor property
> 6. Non-owned detached trailers

Newly Acquired or Constructed Property

If the policy covers a building, the newly acquired or constructed property extension provides automatic coverage for a new building being constructed *at the premises described in the declarations.* Automatic coverage is also provided for newly acquired buildings at other locations provided (1) the newly acquired building will be used for a purpose similar to the use of the building described in the declarations or (2) the newly acquired building will be used as a warehouse. The maximum coverage is $250,000 at each building.

If the policy covers business personal property, the extension also provides automatic coverage for the following:

- Business personal property at any newly acquired location other than fairs, trade shows, or exhibitions
- Business personal property located at newly constructed or acquired buildings at the location described in the declarations
- Newly acquired business personal property at the described premises

The limit for this coverage is $100,000 at each building. The extension does not apply to personal property of others temporarily in the named insured's possession (1) in the course of installing or performing work on the property or (2) in the course of the insured's manufacturing or wholesaling activities.

The coverage for buildings and business personal property provided by this extension is temporary. It terminates automatically at the earliest of the following dates:

1. On the expiration date of the policy
2. Thirty days after the acquisition of the new location or the start of construction of the new building
3. On the date the insured notifies the insurer of the new location or new building

Premium for the coverage is calculated from the date of acquisition or start of construction, regardless of when the insurer is notified.

Personal Effects and Property of Others

The personal effects and property of others extension provides a limited amount of coverage for personal effects (such as a personal radio in an office) owned by an individual insured or a partner, a member, an officer, a manager, or an employee of the insured while on the premises described in the declarations. Personal effects are not covered for loss by theft.

The extension also covers property of others in the care, custody, or control of the insured. However, the limit on all property covered by this extension (personal effects *and* property of others) is $2,500 at each described location. If the value of property of others is greater, insurance can be purchased on such property by showing a limit of insurance for personal property of others coverage, as described earlier; or by purchasing inland marine bailee coverage, as discussed in Chapter 7.

Valuable Papers and Records—Cost of Research

The valuation provision of the BPP coverage form limits any payment for loss of valuable papers and records to the sum of (1) the cost of blank materials for reproducing the records and (2) the cost of labor to transcribe or copy the records. If the damage is so severe that the records cannot be copied or transcribed, the use of this valuation formula could result in a gap in coverage. It would not pay for the cost of research to reconstruct the information on the damaged or destroyed records.

The valuable papers and records—cost of research extension provides limited protection for the cost of research and reconstruction of the information contained on destroyed records, including those that exist on electronic or magnetic media. The limit for this extension is $2,500 at each described location unless a higher limit is shown in the declarations.

Property Off-Premises

The property off-premises extension provides up to $10,000 coverage for covered property while it is away from the described premises. In addition to property temporarily at locations that the insured does not own, lease, or operate, the extension also covers (1) property in storage at a location leased after the inception of the current policy and (2) property at any fair, trade show, or exhibition.

This extension does not apply to property in or on a vehicle or in the custody of the insured's salespersons unless the property in custody is at a fair, trade show, or exhibition.

Outdoor Property

The outdoor property extension covers loss to outdoor fences, radio and television antennas including satellite dishes, signs not attached to buildings, and trees, shrubs, and plants. Unlike the other coverage extensions, the coverage for outdoor property has its own list of covered causes of loss. It covers only loss by fire, lightning, explosion, riot or civil commotion, and aircraft. Some of the more likely causes of loss to outdoor property—windstorm, vehicles, and vandalism—are not covered. The limit of coverage is $1,000, including debris removal expense, but not more than $250 may be applied to any one tree, shrub, or plant. These limits apply regardless of the types or number of items lost or damaged in one occurrence. Coverage for more perils can be provided on outdoor property by adding a description and limit to the policy declarations as a separate item or by covering the property under an inland marine form.

Non-Owned Detached Trailers

Insureds frequently lease trailers to expand office space or to provide additional storage or work areas at their own premises. The leases usually require that the lessee provide insurance for the trailer while it is leased. The non-owned detached trailers extension permits the insured to extend the business personal property coverage to apply to such trailers. The trailer must be used in the insured's business and be in the insured's care, custody, or control at the described premises. Moreover, the insured must have a contractual responsibility to pay for loss or damage to the trailer.

The coverage does not apply while the trailer is attached to any motor vehicle or motorized conveyance, whether or not it is in motion. Nor does it apply during hitching or unhitching operations or when a trailer becomes accidentally unhitched from a motor vehicle or conveyance.

The limit of liability for this extension is $5,000 unless a higher limit is shown in the declarations, and the coverage is excess over any other insurance covering the trailer. Increased limits can be provided on such trailers by adding a description and limit to the policy declarations or by covering the property under an inland marine form.

Limits of Insurance

The limits of insurance section states that the most the insurer is obligated to pay for loss in any one occurrence is the applicable limit of insurance shown in the declarations. In some loss situations, however, the amount of loss payment may be restricted. In others, payment of amounts in addition to the limit of insurance may be made. Payment for loss to outdoor signs attached to buildings is limited to $1,000 per sign in any one occurrence. Losses are paid in addition to the limit of insurance under all of the coverage extensions and under the additional coverages for fire department service charges, pollutant cleanup and removal, and increased cost of construction. Exhibit 2-3 lists the maximum amounts payable under the additional coverages and coverage extensions and indicates whether the payment is in addition to the policy limit.

Under the provisions of other clauses in the form, the insurer may pay less than the applicable limit of insurance. These clauses are discussed in subsequent sections.

Deductible

The insurer is not obligated to pay anything to the insured unless the loss exceeds the deductible; the limit of insurance then applies to the loss in excess

EXHIBIT 2-3

Maximum Limits for BPP Additional Coverages and Coverage Extensions

	Maximum Payment	In Addition to Policy Limit?
Additional Coverages		
Debris Removal	25% of sum of loss payable and deductible, plus up to $10,000	No, except for the additional $10,000
Preservation of Property	Applicable policy limit	No
Fire Department Service Charge	$1,000	Yes
Pollutant Cleanup and Removal	$10,000 per policy year	Yes
Increased Cost of Construction	$10,000 or 5% of the building limit, whichever is less	Yes
Coverage Extensions		
Newly Acquired or Constructed Property		
• Buildings	$250,000 at each building	Yes
• Personal Property	$100,000 at each building	Yes
Personal Effects and Property of Others	$2,500 at each location	Yes
Valuable Papers and Records—Cost of Research	$2,500 at each location (can be increased)	Yes
Property Off Premises	$10,000	Yes
Outdoor Property	$1,000 per occurrence but only $250 per tree, shrub, or plant	Yes
Non-Owned Detached Trailers	$5,000 (can be increased)	Yes

of the deductible. In less formal language, the deductible comes off the loss, not off the limit of insurance. For example, payment under a policy with a $100,000 limit on a building and a $1,000 deductible in each of the following losses would be as follows:

- $500 loss: no payment (loss is less than deductible)
- $100,000 loss: $99,000 payment ($100,000 – $1,000 deductible)
- $110,000 loss: $100,000 payment ($110,000 – $1,000 deductible exceeds limit of insurance)

The deductible applies per occurrence, not separately to each category of covered property (building, business personal property of the insured, or personal property of others). If the occurrence involves loss to more than one category of covered property and a separate limit of insurance applies to each category, loss to any category that is less than the deductible is disregarded. The full deductible will be deducted from the loss for one category that exceeds the deductible; if no category sustains a loss greater than the deductible, no payment is made.

If coinsurance or agreed value optional coverage penalties apply, the amount of the loss is first reduced by any penalty under those provisions before applying the deductible. The coinsurance condition and the agreed value option are discussed later in this chapter.

The standard deductible is $500, but it may be reduced to $250 for an additional premium or increased to a higher amount, which reduces the premium. A $1,000 deductible is common for middle-market insureds. The savings for higher deductibles are seldom attractive to insureds, but underwriters like higher deductibles because they save the insurer the expense of handling small claims.

Loss Conditions

The loss conditions section of the BPP coverage form stipulates the duties of the insured and the insurer after a loss has occurred, explains methods for establishing the value of damaged property, and provides procedures for adjusting claims. These loss conditions apply in addition to the Common Policy Conditions and the Commercial Property Conditions.

Abandonment

Abandonment condition
A condition that prohibits the insured from abandoning damaged property to the insurer.

Under the **abandonment condition**, the insured cannot abandon damaged property to the insurer. Although the insurer reserves the right to take all or any part of the damaged property after payment of loss, the decision to take it is at the option of the insurer. The insured cannot require the insurer to take any of the property.

Appraisal

Appraisal condition
A process that the insurer and the insured must follow for resolving disputes about the insured property's value or amount of loss.

The **appraisal condition** sets forth a method for resolving disputes regarding the *value* of the insured property or the amount of loss. It does not apply to disputes regarding policy coverage or lack of coverage.

If the insured and the insurer cannot agree on the value of the property or the amount of loss, either party may demand an appraisal. The demand for appraisal must be written. Each party appoints a competent and impartial appraiser, and the two appraisers appoint an umpire. If the appraisers cannot agree on an umpire, either of them may request the appointment of an umpire by a judge of a court having jurisdiction over the case. Each appraiser then prepares a statement of the property value and the amount of loss. If the appraisers do not agree, they submit to the umpire the items on which they disagree. A decision agreed to by any two of the three will be binding on all parties.

The insured and the insurer each pay their own appraiser. They share equally the fee for the umpire and the other expenses of the appraisal. Submission to appraisal does not preclude the insurer from denying coverage for the claim.

Duties in the Event of Loss or Damage

The BPP imposes several duties on the insured when a loss occurs. If the insured fails to perform any of these duties, the insurer may not have to pay for the loss. The insured must do the following:

- Notify the police if the loss appears to have resulted from a violation of law, such as arson or theft.
- Give the insurer prompt notice of the loss, including a description of the property damaged.
- Provide information as to how, when, and where the loss occurred.
- Take all reasonable steps to protect the property from further loss, prepare an inventory and, if feasible, set the damaged property aside and in the best possible order for examination. The insured is required to keep a record of expenses incurred in protecting the property, which will be considered when the claim is settled.
- At the insurer's request, furnish the insurer with inventories of the damaged and undamaged property and permit the insurer to inspect the property and records and take samples of the property for testing and analysis.
- Submit to examination under oath regarding any matter related to the loss.
- Cooperate with the insurer in the adjustment of the loss.
- Send a signed, sworn proof of loss to the insurer within sixty days after the insurer requests one. A **proof of loss** is a statement of the facts surrounding the loss. It includes information as to the time, place, and cause of loss; the value of the property before and after loss; any other insurance applicable to the loss; any mortgages or other liens against the property; the interest of the insured in the property; and other pertinent information. The insurer is required to supply the insured with the necessary form for submitting the proof of loss.

Proof of loss
A statement of facts about a loss for which the insured is making a claim.

Loss Payment

If loss or damage is covered, the insurer has four loss payment options:

1. Pay the amount of loss or damage
2. Pay the cost of repairing or replacing the damaged property
3. Take over all or any part of the property and pay its agreed or appraised value
4. Repair, rebuild, or replace the damaged property with other property of like kind and quality

The last option is seldom exercised because the insurer might then become a guarantor of the repaired or replaced property. If the repaired or replaced property proves to be unsatisfactory, the insurer might be required to make it satisfactory even if the cost of doing so exceeds the applicable limit of insurance.

The loss payment clause also states that regardless of the value of the loss, the insurer will pay no more than the insured's financial interest in the covered property. In addition, if the damaged property belongs to someone other than the insured, the insurer may adjust the loss with the owner. If the insurer elects to defend the insured against suits made by property owners, the insurer must pay the defense costs.

The insurer is required to notify the insured of its intent either to pay the claim or to deny payment within thirty days after receipt of a satisfactory proof of loss. Denial of payment might, for example, be due to lack of coverage under the policy or failure of the insured to comply with one or more of the policy conditions. Actual payment is due within thirty days after the parties have agreed on the amount of loss or an appraisal has been completed.

Recovered Property

If either the insurer or the insured recovers property for which the insurer has paid a loss, the party that makes the recovery is obligated to promptly notify the other party. The insured has the option of taking the recovered property and refunding the loss payment to the insurer. The insurer would then pay the cost of recovering the property and the cost, if any, of repairing it. If the insured elects not to take the recovered property, the insurer may dispose of the property as it sees fit.

Vacancy

If the building where a loss occurs has been vacant for more than sixty consecutive days before the loss occurred, the insurer will not pay if the loss is caused by (1) vandalism, (2) sprinkler leakage unless the sprinkler was protected against freezing, (3) breakage of building glass, (4) water damage, (5) theft, or (6) attempted theft. If any other covered peril causes the loss, loss payment will be reduced by 15 percent.

The vacancy conditions apply differently for a tenant than for a building owner or general lessee. A general lessee is an entity that leases the entire building and subleases portions of the building to others.

In the case of a tenant, a vacant "building" means the unit or suite rented or leased to the tenant. A building is vacant when it does not contain enough business personal property to conduct customary operations. Thus, a tenant's coverage could be reduced or eliminated even though the remainder of the building is fully occupied.

If the policy covers a building owner or general lessee, "building" means the entire building, and it is considered vacant unless at least 31 percent of its total square footage is (1) rented to a lessee or sub-lessee and used by that party to conduct its customary operations or (2) used by the building owner to conduct its customary operations. Buildings under construction or renovation are not considered to be vacant.

Valuation

The valuation clause sets forth rules for establishing the value of insured property. Subject to the exceptions summarized in Exhibit 2-4, the insured property is valued at its **actual cash value (ACV)**. The form does not include a definition of actual cash value, but ACV is usually considered to be the cost to replace the property with new property of like kind and quality less depreciation. Depreciation includes any reduction in value because of wear and tear or obsolescence of the property. Thus, depending on the property's age, the quality of maintenance, and other factors, the actual cash value of a particular piece of property can range from being equal to its replacement cost to being much less than its replacement cost. Exhibit 2-4 summarizes the BPP's valuation provisions.

Actual cash value (ACV)
Cost to replace property with new property of like kind and quality minus depreciation.

EXHIBIT 2-4

BPP Valuation Provisions

Property Type	Valuation Basis
Property other than that specifically listed	Actual cash value
Building damage of $2,500 or less	Replacement cost except for awnings, floor coverings, appliances, and outdoor equipment or furniture
Stock sold but not delivered	Selling price less discounts and unincurred costs
Glass	Replacement cost for safety glazing if required by law
Improvements and betterments:	
(a) replaced by other than the insured	Not covered
(b) replaced by insured	Actual cash value
(c) not replaced	Percentage of cost based on remaining life of lease
Valuable papers and records	Cost of blank media plus cost of transaction or copying ($2,500 research cost as coverage extension)

The valuation provisions can be modified by any of several available endorsements. The replacement cost optional coverage and functional valuation endorsements will be discussed later in this chapter. Other specialized endorsements that can be used to modify the loss valuation provisions are beyond the scope of this text.

Additional Conditions

The BPP provides two additional policy conditions to supplement those found in the Common Policy Conditions and the Commercial Property Conditions. These deal with coinsurance and the interests of a mortgageholder (mortgagee).

Coinsurance

Coinsurance clause
Clause that requires the insured to carry insurance equal to at least a specified percentage of the insured property's value.

The **coinsurance clause** requires the insured to carry insurance equal to at least a specified percentage of the actual cash value of the property insured. The percentage is shown in the declarations. If the amount of insurance carried is equal to or greater than the required percentage, the insurer will pay covered losses in full (subject to any applicable deductible) up to the limit of insurance. If the amount of insurance carried is less than the required percentage, loss payments will be reduced proportionately.

If the amount of insurance carried does not meet the coinsurance requirement, the amount the insurer will pay (subject always to the limit of insurance) is calculated by the following formula:

$$\text{Loss payment} = \left(\frac{\text{Amount of insurance carried}}{\text{Amount of insurance required}} \times \text{Loss} \right) - \text{Deductible}.$$

The amount of insurance required is the actual cash value of the property *immediately before the loss occurred* multiplied by the coinsurance percentage. The deductible is subtracted *after* the coinsurance penalty has been calculated. The example in Exhibit 2-5 will help to clarify the calculation.

EXHIBIT 2-5

Coinsurance Example

Actual cash value of covered building at time of loss	$200,000
Limit of insurance	$140,000
Coinsurance percentage	80%
Amount of loss	$40,000
Deductible	$500

Amount of insurance required = .80 × $200,000 = $160,000.

$$\text{Loss Payment} = \left(\frac{\$140,000}{\$160,000} \times \$40,000 \right) - \$500$$

$$= \left(\frac{7}{8} \times \$40,000 \right) - \$500$$

$$= \$35,000 - \$500 = \$34,500.$$

If the amount of insurance carried had been $160,000 or more, the insurer would have paid $39,500, the amount of loss less the deductible.

Some property policies, unlike the BPP, call for subtraction of the deductible *before* the coinsurance penalty is calculated, which results in a slightly higher recovery for the insured. In the coinsurance example above, if the deductible had been applied before calculating the coinsurance penalty, the amount payable would have been $34,562.50 instead of $34,500.

Mortgageholder

If a mortgageholder is shown in the declarations, the insurer is obligated to include the mortgageholder in any payment for loss to the mortgaged property. In practice, the loss payment check or draft is usually made payable jointly to the insured and all mortgageholders so that they can agree on the division of the payment. In most cases, the loss payment is used to repair or rebuild the mortgaged property, and the mortgages continue in force as before.

Any act or default of the insured does not impair the rights of the mortgageholder, providing the mortgageholder pays any premium due that the insured has not paid, submits a proof of loss if requested, and has notified the insurer of any change in ownership, occupancy, or substantial increase in risk of which the mortgageholder is aware. Consequently, the insurer is sometimes obligated to make a loss payment to the mortgageholder even though it has denied coverage, for example, to an insured who has committed arson. In such cases the insurer, at its option, can (1) take over the rights of the mortgageholder to the extent of such payment and collect the amount of payment from the insured or (2) pay off the outstanding balance of the mortgage and take over all of the rights of the mortgageholder.

If the insurer cancels the policy because the insured failed to pay the premium or if the insurer does not renew the policy for any reason, it must notify the mortgageholder ten days before the termination of coverage. If the insurer cancels the policy for any reason other than nonpayment of premium, it must give thirty days' advance notice to the mortgageholder. If the insurer fails to give the required notice to the mortgageholder, the policy remains in force for the protection of the mortgageholder even though it may not provide any protection for the insured.

Optional Coverages

The optional coverages section of the BPP contains provisions for four optional modifications of the BPP: (1) agreed value, (2) inflation guard, (3) replacement cost, and (4) extension of replacement cost to personal property of others. The optional coverages apply only when an appropriate notation is made on the declarations page. The optional coverages for agreed value, inflation guard, and replacement cost may be used for buildings only, personal property only, or both buildings and personal property.

Agreed Value

Agreed value optional coverage
Coverage that suspends the coinsurance clause if the insured carries the amount of insurance that the insurer and insured agree to be the property's full value.

To activate the **agreed value optional coverage**, an amount is entered under the agreed value heading in the declarations for each category of property (building, personal property, or both) to which the option applies. This option enables the insured to remove the uncertainty as to whether the amount of insurance carried complies with the coinsurance clause. With the option in force, the insurer and the insured have agreed in advance that the amount stated in the declarations—the agreed value—is adequate for coinsurance purposes.

The BPP coinsurance provision does not apply to property insured under the agreed value option. However, it is replaced by a provision that, while not called coinsurance, is the practical equivalent of 100 percent coinsurance based on the agreed value. The agreed value option provides that if the limit of insurance equals or exceeds the agreed value stated in the declarations, losses will be paid in full up to the limit of insurance. If the limit of insurance is less than the agreed value, the amount of loss payment is calculated by the following formula:

$$\text{Loss payment} = \left(\frac{\text{Limit of insurance}}{\text{Agreed value}} \times \text{Loss} \right) - \text{Deductible}.$$

Coverage under this option extends until the agreed value expiration date shown on the declarations or the expiration date of the policy, whichever occurs first. If the coverage option is not renewed, the coinsurance condition is reinstated.

Inflation Guard

Inflation guard optional coverage
Coverage for the effects of inflation that automatically increases the limit of insurance by the percentage of annual increase shown in the declarations.

The **inflation guard optional coverage** provides a means for automatically increasing the limit of insurance. The limit of insurance automatically increases by the percentage of annual increase indicated in the declarations. This percentage is applied on a pro rata basis, from the date the limit of insurance became effective to the date of the loss, before the loss payment is computed. The percentage of annual increase is shown separately for buildings and personal property.

Replacement Cost

Replacement cost optional coverage
Coverage for losses to most types of property on a replacement cost basis (with no deduction for depreciation or obsolescence) instead of on an actual cash value basis.

The **replacement cost optional coverage** replaces actual cash value with replacement cost in the valuation section of the form. That is, the insurer is obligated to pay the cost to replace the damaged or destroyed property with new property of like kind and quality without any deduction for depreciation or obsolescence.

The insurer is not obligated to pay replacement cost until the property has been repaired or replaced, and then only if such repair or replacement is completed in a reasonable time. If repair or replacement is not completed in a reasonable time, the loss payment will be based on the actual cash value at the time of loss.

The insured may make a claim on the basis of actual cash value, with the difference between actual cash value and replacement cost to be paid upon completion of repair or reconstruction. The insurer must be notified within 180 days after the occurrence of loss that a claim will be made for replacement cost.

If the replacement cost option is activated, the coinsurance provision continues to apply but with one important difference. The amount of insurance required by the coinsurance provision is found by multiplying *replacement cost* by the coinsurance percentage if the claim is made on a replacement cost basis. If the insured makes a claim on an ACV basis, coinsurance is also calculated on an ACV basis.

If the replacement cost option is selected, tenants' improvements and betterments are also valued at replacement cost if the tenant actually repairs or replaces them, at its own cost, as soon as reasonably possible after the loss.

The replacement cost option does not apply to (1) property of others, (2) contents of a residence, (3) manuscripts, or (4) works of art, antiques, or rare articles. It also does not apply to stock unless indicated in the declarations.

Extension of Replacement Cost to Personal Property of Others

Rather than purchase needed equipment, insureds frequently lease photocopiers, computers, phone systems, and other equipment. These leases or agreements may make the insured responsible for the replacement cost of these items in the event they are damaged by a covered loss. To cover this exposure, insureds who have selected the replacement cost option may also elect to have the personal property of others valued at replacement cost. The amount of the loss will be calculated according to the written agreement between the insured and the owner of the property, but it will not exceed the replacement cost of the property or the applicable limit of liability.

Functional Building and Personal Property Valuation Endorsements

Old or obsolete buildings and personal property can present difficult insurance problems. For example, assume that a four-story building constructed of brick and heavy mill timbers was once used for textile manufacturing but is now occupied as a warehouse with only the lowest floor in use; the upper floors are boarded up and unoccupied. To rebuild the building as originally constructed would be very expensive, far more than the building's market value. A one-story building of lighter construction would be much less expensive to construct and could serve the same function. Even actual cash value, if calculated as replacement cost less depreciation, may be more than the market value of the building.[1]

Insureds are unwilling to purchase amounts of insurance in excess of the market value of their buildings. Insurers, fearing moral and morale hazards, also do not want to write the insurance for such amounts. To cope with this problem, two endorsements are available: (1) functional building valuation and (2) functional personal property valuation (other than stock).

Functional replacement cost
The cost of replacing damaged property with similar property that performs the same function but might not be identical to the damaged property.

These endorsements provide for loss settlement on the basis of functional replacement cost. **Functional replacement cost** is the cost of replacing the damaged property with similar property that will perform the same function but may not be identical to the damaged property. For example, if the interior walls of an older building were constructed of three-coat plaster on wire lath, the walls could be replaced using sheetrock. The sheetrock walls would be functionally equivalent to the previous walls but would cost far less than an exact replacement. The amount of insurance required for functional replacement may be less than that needed for replacement cost or actual cash value coverage. The functional replacement cost value is agreed upon in advance by the insured and the insurer. If the property is not replaced, recovery is limited to the smallest of the following:

- The limit of insurance
- The market value of the building or personal property
- The functional replacement cost

Coinsurance does not apply to property insured under this endorsement.

INSURING FLUCTUATING VALUES

Many business organizations experience wide fluctuations (increases and decreases) in personal property values, especially the value of stocks of goods held for sale. The BPP does not provide a totally satisfactory method to cover fluctuating values. If the insured organization carries high enough limits to cover the maximum value, it is overinsured for much of the year and pays too much in premiums. If it carries less than the maximum value, it is underinsured during its peak inventory period.

The Value Reporting Form and the Peak Season Limit of Insurance Endorsement provide possible solutions to the problem of fluctuating values. They are used in conjunction with the BPP or the Condominium Commercial Unit Owners Coverage Form.

Value Reporting Form

Value reporting form
Form that covers the fluctuating values of business personal property by providing insurance for the insured's maximum expected values and requiring the insured to periodically report property values to the insurer.

Under the **Value Reporting Form,** the insured is required to report the value of the insured business personal property to the insurer periodically during the policy period. The frequency of reporting is indicated by a symbol entered in the declarations. For example, MR, the most common choice, calls for reporting values on hand on the last day of the month, with the report due within thirty days after the end of the month. Daily, weekly, quarterly, and annual periods can also be selected as a basis for reports by entering other codes in the declarations.

As long as the insured reports values accurately and on time, the insurer will pay the full amount of any loss that occurs (subject to the policy limit and deductible), even if the values on hand at the time of the loss are greater than those last reported to the insurer. To illustrate, assume that Tri-State Supply, a wholesaler, insures its business personal property under a Value Reporting Form subject to a limit of $1 million for its single warehouse location. Tri-State's last monthly report of values was made on time and accurately showed the full value of business personal property—$800,000—as of the date of the report. Three weeks later, a fire destroyed the warehouse and its contents. Even though the value of covered personal property had increased to $900,000 since the last report, the loss was covered in full (minus the deductible).

Penalties for Improper Reporting

To encourage accurate and timely reports, the value reporting form provides penalties for failure to comply with the reporting requirements set forth in the form. Separate rules apply when (1) no report is made, (2) one or more reports are past due after the initial report, and (3) reports are inaccurate.

Determining Premium

The insured pays an advance premium at the inception of the policy. The advance premium is based on 75 percent of the limit of insurance. The final premium is determined after the policy anniversary, based on the reported values. The premium is based on the values reported, even if the values reported exceed the policy limit. However, the insurer is not obligated to pay more than the policy limit in the event of loss, even if the reported values are higher. Thus, care should be taken to set the limit high enough to cover any possible increase in value.

Peak Season Limit of Insurance Endorsement

The **Peak Season Limit of Insurance Endorsement** provides differing amounts of insurance for certain time periods during the policy term. For example, a toy store may have a policy providing $100,000 coverage on personal property with a peak season endorsement increasing coverage to $200,000 during the period from October 1 to December 31, when it expects to have higher inventory values. This would have exactly the same effect as endorsing the policy on October 1 to increase the coverage and endorsing it again on December 31 to reduce the coverage. The peak season endorsement eliminates the bother of these extra transactions and the possibility that they might be overlooked.

Peak Season Limit of Insurance Endorsement
Endorsement that covers the fluctuating values of business personal property by providing differing amounts of insurance for certain time periods during the policy period.

The peak season endorsement is usually attached when the policy is issued (although it may be added mid-term), and a pro rata premium is charged for the period during which the limit is increased.

The peak season endorsement is suited to smaller businesses that have regular fluctuations in inventory. Although the value reporting form might be more effective at matching coverage to exposures, many smaller firms do not have accounting systems of sufficient sophistication to generate the required reports accurately and on time. Furthermore, many insurers would decline to issue a Value Reporting Form for a smaller insured because the premium may not be large enough to warrant the added expense of processing the reports and calculating the final premium.

BLANKET INSURANCE

The basic method of insuring buildings and personal property is to schedule a specific amount of insurance in the declarations for each building and a specific amount of insurance for personal property at each location. This approach is called **specific insurance**. An example of how specific insurance might be indicated in the declarations of a commercial property policy is as follows:

Specific insurance
Insurance that covers each building for a specific limit of insurance and personal property at each building for a specific limit of insurance.

- $1,000,000 on the building at 123 Main St., Des Moines, IA
- $800,000 on your business personal property at 123 Main St., Des Moines, IA

The alternative to specific insurance is blanket insurance. **Blanket insurance** is insurance that covers either of the following with *one* limit of insurance:

Blanket insurance
Insurance that covers either of the following with one limit of insurance: (1) two or more types of property (such as buildings and business personal property) or (2) one or more types of property at more than one location.

1. Two or more types of property
2. One or more types of property at more than one location

No special endorsement is required to effect blanket insurance. The word "blanket" is simply added to the statement of coverage in the declarations. If the property described above was insured on a blanket basis, the statement of coverage in the declarations might read as follows:

- $1,800,000 blanket on the building and your business personal property at 123 Main St., Des Moines, IA

Property at different locations can also be covered on a blanket basis. In that case, coverage can apply to one or more types of property at more than one location, for example:

- $5,000,000 blanket on buildings and business personal property at:
    760 Walnut St., Cincinnati, OH
    987 Third St., Cincinnati, OH
    12 Elm St., Fort Thomas, KY

    —or—

- $7,500,000 blanket on buildings at:
    78 Broadway, Malvern, PA
    971 Tenth St., Philadelphia, PA
    88 Highland Rd., Pottstown, PA

Coinsurance Requirement for Blanket Insurance

Blanket insurance may involve an additional cost. The minimum coinsurance clause is 90 percent, but the rates are the same as for 80 percent coinsurance. The insured with blanket insurance must insure to 90 percent of value to avoid a coinsurance penalty but does not receive the 5 percent discount that applies to specific insurance with a 90 percent coinsurance clause. Thus, to meet coinsurance requirements, the insured with blanket insurance must buy more insurance than otherwise would be required.

Advantages of Blanket Insurance

Why would an insured want to spend the additional premium to obtain blanket insurance? To understand the reasons, consider the example of Contemporary Furniture, Inc. (CFI), which owns and operates furniture stores at two locations. Assume that the value of CFI's business personal property in each store is $1,000,000 at the inception of the policy. To comply with the 80 percent coinsurance clause, CFI might purchase specific insurance with a limit of $800,000 on its business personal property at each location. In that event, if the loss exceeds $800,000, CFI will be uninsured for the portion in excess of $800,000. If CFI purchased a blanket policy with a limit of $1,800,000 (90 percent of $2,000,000), CFI would be fully insured for the loss at any one location up to $1,800,000 as long as the total amount of insurance satisfied the coinsurance clause.

Or, suppose that at the time of the loss the value of CFI's property at one store has increased to $1,200,000 and the value of the property at the other store has decreased to $800,000. If the amount of insurance has not been adjusted, a total loss at the first store would leave CFI with a $400,000 uninsured loss if CFI had specific insurance even though the total amount of insurance was adequate. With blanket insurance, CFI's $1,200,000 loss would have been paid in full. CFI's large uninsured loss (without blanket insurance) might be reduced by the newly acquired or constructed property coverage extension. That extension would provide coverage for up to $100,000 on property that CFI had acquired within the thirty-day period before the loss.

Additional debris removal coverage is another advantage of blanket insurance. Even if CFI purchased insurance equal to 100 percent of its insurable value on a specific basis ($1,000,000 at each location), a total loss at either location would leave only the $10,000 additional coverage for debris removal. Debris removal for a large business could exceed $100,000. If only one location was involved in the loss, blanket insurance could cover the loss, including debris removal, in full.

Furthermore, CFI may not be exactly sure of the insurable value at each location. With specific insurance, CFI would either have to purchase a higher amount of insurance to provide a cushion against error in estimating insurable values or risk an uninsured loss. With blanket insurance, assuming the two locations are not likely to be damaged by the same occurrence (such as a hurricane that devastates a wide area), the minimum amount of insurance needed to comply with coinsurance would be sufficient to protect CFI's property fully.

Underwriters are often reluctant to offer blanket coverage because ascertaining that the insured is carrying insurance to value can be difficult.

Combining the Agreed Value Option With Blanket Insurance

Most risk managers, consultants, and other experienced insurance practitioners regard the combination of the agreed value option with blanket insurance as the preferred method to provide property insurance. The agreed value clause avoids any coinsurance penalty, and if separate locations are involved that are not subject to the same loss, the danger of underinsurance is greatly reduced.

SUMMARY

Many of the basic property coverages an organization needs are commonly provided under a commercial property coverage part. A commercial property coverage part consists of (1) commercial property declarations, (2) one or more commercial property coverage forms, (3) one or more causes-of-loss forms, (4) Commercial Property Conditions, and (5) any applicable endorsements.

The most commonly used commercial property coverage form is the Building and Personal Property Coverage Form (BPP). The BPP can be used to insure (1) buildings, (2) business personal property of the named insured, and (3) personal property of others in the named insured's care, custody, or control. With only minor exceptions, property is covered only while located on or within 100 feet of the insured premises. The property not covered section lists the various types of property that are not covered by the BPP. However, most types of property not covered can be insured by adding optional coverage endorsements to the BPP.

The BPP provides several additional coverages and coverage extensions to supplement its basic coverage for buildings and personal property. The additional coverages apply to (1) debris removal, (2) preservation of property, (3) fire department service charges, (4) pollutant cleanup and removal, and (5) increased cost of construction. The coverage extensions provide limited coverage for (1) newly acquired or constructed property, (2) personal effects and property of others, (3) the cost to reconstruct information on destroyed records, (4) property while off the insured premises, (5) certain types of outdoor property, and (6) non-owned detached trailers.

The BPP contains various conditions that address such matters as the insured's duties after loss, the insurer's loss payment options, valuation of covered property, mortgageholders' rights and duties, and coinsurance requirements.

The BPP also contains four optional coverages. The agreed value option suspends the coinsurance requirement. The inflation guard option automatically increases the limits of insurance in accordance with a percentage shown in the declarations. The replacement cost option modifies the BPP valuation condition to apply to most property on a replacement cost basis instead of an actual cash value basis. When the replacement cost option is selected, the extension of replacement cost valuation to personal property of others is also available.

The BPP can be supplemented by either of two forms to address the problem of fluctuating (increasing and decreasing) personal property values: the Value Reporting Form and the Peak Season Limit of Insurance Endorsement.

The Value Reporting Form requires the insured to report the value of covered property periodically (usually monthly) during the policy period. Premiums are then based on the values reported. As long as the insured makes timely and accurate reports, the insurer will pay the full amount of any loss that occurs (subject to the policy limit and deductible), even if the values on hand at the time of the loss are greater than those last reported to the insurer.

The Peak Season Limit of Insurance Endorsement provides differing amounts of insurance for certain time periods during the policy term. Although the Value Reporting Form can do a better job of matching coverage (and premiums) to exposures, the peak season endorsement is often preferred by smaller businesses that do not want to make the reports required by the Value Reporting Form.

The basic approach to insuring buildings and personal property is called specific insurance, whereby a limit is shown for each covered building and for personal property at each building. An alternative to specific insurance is blanket insurance, whereby two or more types of property at one location or one or more types of property at multiple locations are covered under a single limit of insurance.

Blanket insurance is subject to a 90 percent coinsurance requirement instead of the usual 80 percent coinsurance requirement. However, blanket insurance can provide better coverage than specific insurance because the full blanket limit can be applied to any one loss. The blanket approach is often combined with the agreed value option.

CHAPTER NOTE

1. In many states, problems with calculating the actual cash value for older, obsolete buildings and equipment have led the courts to adopt the "broad evidence rule." The broad evidence rule states that all indicators of value, such as replacement cost, market value, assessed value, and many others, must be considered in setting actual cash value.

Chapter 3

Direct Your Learning

Commercial Property Insurance, Part II

After learning the content of this chapter, you should be able to:

■ Given a case about a commercial property loss, explain whether coverage applies.

- Determine which perils are covered and which perils are excluded or limited by the basic, broad, and special causes-of-loss forms.

- Explain how each of the following coverage forms differs from the BPP in order to provide insurance that is appropriate for the exposures each is specifically designed to insure.

  - Builders Risk Coverage Form

  - Condominium Association Coverage Form

  - Condominium Commercial Unit-Owners Coverage Form

■ Describe the purpose of each of the following ISO endorsements:

- Ordinance or Law Coverage

- Manufacturers' Consequential Loss Assumption

- Brands and Labels

- Flood Coverage

- Earthquake and Volcanic Eruption Coverage

■ Describe the provisions of the Commercial Property Conditions.

■ Explain how commercial property coverage is rated.

OUTLINE

Causes-of-Loss Forms

Other Commercial Property Coverage Forms

Endorsements

Commercial Property Conditions

Rating Commercial Property Coverage

Summary

Develop Your Perspective

What are the main topics covered in the chapter?

This chapter continues the survey of commercial property insurance by describing the causes-of-loss forms, specialized coverage forms for buildings under construction and for condominium associations and unit owners, common endorsements, the Commercial Property Conditions Form, and rating.

Consider the factors that normally affect the price of commercial property insurance.

- What events might cause a sudden increase in property insurance rates?

Why is it important to learn about these topics?

Effective handling of commercial property insurance requires a solid understanding of the perils that can be insured against, the ways to configure coverage to meet individual needs, and the conditions that govern many aspects of commercial property coverage. Knowing the process of rating will help you understand how commercial property premiums are affected by various factors.

Compare the basic, broad, and special causes-of-loss forms.

- How does the broad form improve on the basic?
- How does the special form improve on the broad?
- What perils that are not covered by any of these forms can be covered by standard endorsements?

How can you use what you will learn?

Examine several commercial package policies, noting the endorsements applicable to the commercial property coverage part. Identify insureds that might benefit from certain additional coverage endorsements.

- Why would you recommend such endorsements for these insureds?

Chapter 3
Commercial Property Insurance, Part II

This chapter continues the discussion of commercial property insurance that began in Chapter 2. The chapter covers the following topics:

1. The commercial property causes-of-loss forms
2. The Builders Risk Coverage Form, used for insuring buildings during construction
3. Coverage forms for insuring condominium associations and condominium unit owners
4. Endorsements that can be used with commercial property policies
5. The Commercial Property Conditions, which are included in every commercial property coverage part
6. Commercial property rating

CAUSES-OF-LOSS FORMS

The first insurance policies covering buildings in colonial America covered loss by fire only. In time, lightning was added as an insured cause of loss, as well as some other perils.

In the 1930s several additional perils (windstorm, civil commotion, smoke, hail, aircraft, vehicles, explosion, and riot) were grouped into an endorsement known as "extended coverage." This endorsement was added to fire insurance policies to provide a combination known as "fire and extended coverage." Extended coverage was followed by "broad form" coverage, which added even more perils, and "special form" coverage, which covered all perils except those specifically excluded. Fire and extended coverage has been superseded by "basic form" coverage, which includes the fire and extended coverage perils plus a few others.

Even though only a handful of insurers still use it, the extended coverage endorsement still has some importance. Older mortgages, leases, and contracts (and even some recent ones) call for extended coverage as part of the insurance requirements. The basic, broad, or special form is an acceptable substitute.

The perils covered in a contemporary commercial property policy are specified in any of three causes-of-loss forms:

- Causes of Loss—Basic Form
- Causes of Loss—Broad Form
- Causes of Loss—Special Form

Although the special form is by far the most widely used of the three causes-of-loss forms, learning the differences between the three forms is easier if you start with the basic form and work up to the special form.

Causes of Loss—Basic Form

Causes of Loss—Basic Form
Form that covers fire, lightning, explosion, windstorm, hail, smoke, aircraft, vehicles, riot, civil commotion, vandalism, sprinkler leakage, sinkhole collapse, and volcanic action.

The **Causes of Loss—Basic Form** (or simply "basic form") consists principally of two sections:

- Section A, a listing of several covered causes of loss (also known as *perils*), which are subject to some definitions and limitations expressed within that listing
- Section B, a set of exclusions that further limit the application of the covered perils

When trying to determine whether a particular cause of loss is covered, you need to consider those two sections equally. A cause of loss that seems to be covered because it is listed as such in section A may not actually be covered because of a more specific exclusion in section B. For example, assume that a steam boiler exploded in the basement of an apartment building and extensively damaged the boiler and the building. Although "explosion" is listed as a covered cause of loss in section A, section B contains an exclusion of *steam boiler* explosion. Thus, the building owner's commercial property policy would not cover this loss. (Steam boiler explosion is usually insured under separate equipment breakdown forms, discussed in Chapter 6.)

Covered Causes of Loss

The causes of loss covered by the basic form are listed in Exhibit 3-1 and described below.

Fire and Lightning

Although the form does not define fire, the courts generally have held that fire insurance covers only damage by "hostile fire" (fire that is not in a place where fire is intended to be). Therefore, the policy would not cover damage caused by a fire in a stove (a "friendly fire"), but it would cover damage caused by a fire that escaped from a stove.

Lightning, also not defined in the form, is a naturally occurring electrical discharge between clouds or between a cloud and the earth. The peril of lightning does not include artificially generated electrical current.

EXHIBIT 3-1

Covered Causes of Loss in Basic and Broad Forms

Both Forms Cover:

1. Fire
2. Lightning
3. Explosion
4. Windstorm or hail
5. Smoke
6. Aircraft or vehicles
7. Riot or civil commotion
8. Vandalism
9. Sprinkler leakage
10. Sinkhole collapse
11. Volcanic action

Broad Form Also Covers:

12. Falling objects
13. Weight of snow, ice, or sleet
14. Water damage
15. Collapse caused by certain perils (provided as an additional coverage)

Explosion

The basic form contains no formal definition of explosion. However, the form states that the term includes the explosion of gases in a furnace or flue (called "combustion explosion") but does not include either of the following:

- The rupture of pressure relief valves
- The rupture of a building (such as a grain storage shed) resulting from the expansion or swelling of its contents caused by water absorption

Certain exclusions, discussed later in this chapter, place further limitations on the types of explosions covered.

Windstorm or Hail

Covered wind or hail damage does not include damage caused by frost, cold weather, ice (other than hail), snow, or sleet, even if driven by wind. Also, damage by rain, snow, sand, or dust to the interior of a building or property inside the building is not covered unless the building first sustains exterior damage by wind, and the rain, snow, sand, or dust enters through the damaged part.

Smoke

Covered smoke damage must be sudden and accidental. There is no coverage for damage by smoke from agricultural smudging or industrial operations.

Aircraft or Vehicles

In order to be covered, damage caused by aircraft must result from actual physical contact with the aircraft or objects falling from it. Spacecraft and self-propelled missiles are considered to be aircraft, but the war exclusion (discussed below) would eliminate coverage for damage by missiles in time of war. To be covered, vehicle damage must result from accidental physical contact with a vehicle or an object thrown by a vehicle. There is no coverage for damage caused by vehicles owned by the insured or operated in the insured's business.

Riot or Civil Commotion

The basic form does not define riot and civil commotion. In most states, a riot is defined by law as a violent public disturbance by three or more persons. However, the policy states that riot or civil commotion includes acts by striking workers while occupying the insured premises as well as looting occurring at the time and place of a riot or civil commotion.

Vandalism

Vandalism means the willful or malicious damage to or destruction of property. The vandalism peril does not cover loss by theft, but damage to the building caused by the entry or exit of burglars is covered.

Sprinkler Leakage

Sprinkler leakage means the escape of any substance from an automatic fire protection or extinguishing system. The system need not be a water sprinkler system. It could use carbon dioxide or any other extinguishing agent. The collapse of a tank constituting a part of such a system is covered, as is the cost of repairing damage to the system if the damage results in the sprinkler leakage or if the damage is caused by freezing. Also covered is the cost to tear out and replace any part of the building or structure to repair damage to the automatic sprinkler system.

Sinkholes

Sinkholes result from underground water dissolving limestone and creating an empty space or cavern under the ground. When the roof of the cavern gets too close to the ground surface, the surface collapses, causing damage to buildings or other property located over or near the resulting sinkhole. Damage to buildings or other property is covered, but the cost of filling the sinkhole is not. Collapse into other underground openings, such as mineshafts, is not covered.

Volcanic Action

The volcanic action peril covers damage caused by lava flow, ash, dust, particulate matter, airborne volcanic blast, or airborne shock waves resulting from a volcanic eruption. Because such losses may occur over a relatively long period of time, the basic form stipulates that all eruptions that occur within any 168-hour period are considered a single occurrence and thus subject to only one deductible and one policy limit. The cost to remove ash, dust, or particulate matter is not covered except for the ash, dust, or particulate matter that caused loss to insured property.

Exclusions

Covered causes of loss are further defined or limited by the exclusions applying to the basic causes-of-loss form. The basic form exclusions are described below.

Ordinance or Law

To promote public welfare and safety, municipalities regularly upgrade the building codes that set the standards for new construction or significant remodeling. For example, a building code might require that elevators be provided in multi-story buildings or that heavier gauge electric wiring be used. Furthermore, in some cities building codes require that new buildings in certain areas be fire resistive. Old buildings that do not comply with the codes may continue to be used without change. However, if a building that does not comply with the code sustains damage by fire or another peril, the building code may require that the restoration meet the new standards. In some cases, a building ordinance or law may require that a partially damaged building be totally demolished, changing what would have been a partial loss to a total loss.

The ordinance or law exclusion eliminates coverage for these additional consequential losses that result from the enforcement of building ordinances or laws. The excluded losses can be covered by an endorsement, to be discussed later, for an additional premium.

Earth Movement

The basic form provides no coverage for damage caused by earth movement, other than sinkhole collapse. Earth movement includes earthquake, landslide, mine subsidence, and similar movements. Damage by fire or explosion caused by earth movement is covered.

Earthquake coverage can be added for an additional premium. When it is added to the policy, it also covers land shocks and movement resulting from volcanic eruption (which are not covered by the volcanic action peril).

Governmental Action

Seizure or destruction of property by governmental action is not covered. This exclusion does not apply to the destruction of property by governmental order to stop the spread of a covered fire. In that event, the policy provides coverage.

Nuclear Hazard

The basic form excludes loss caused by nuclear reaction, radiation, or radioactive contamination. Loss by fire resulting from these causes is covered. Some coverage for radioactive contamination can be provided by endorsement.

Utility Services

The basic form excludes loss caused by power failure or failure of other utility service if the damage causing such failure occurs away from the described premises. However, loss from a covered peril resulting from power failure is covered. Coverage for off-premises service interruption caused by an insured cause of loss is available by endorsement.

War and Military Action

The war and military action exclusion eliminates coverage for loss caused by war, revolution, insurrection, or similar actions.

Water

Loss caused by flooding and related perils is difficult to insure. Depending on their locations, some insureds have a much greater likelihood than others of suffering a flood loss. Moreover, the consequences of a flood can be catastrophic. Insurers therefore exclude flood losses from commercial property forms. The water exclusion eliminates coverage for damage caused by the following:

- Flood, surface water, tides, and tidal waves
- Mudslide or mudflow
- Backing up of sewers, drains, or sumps
- Underground water pressing on, or flowing or seeping through, foundations, walls, doors, windows, or other openings

However, damage by fire, explosion, or sprinkler leakage caused by any of the foregoing is covered. The exclusions listed above apply whether or not the loss event results in widespread damage or affects a substantial area.

Other Exclusions

The basic form also excludes loss or damage caused by the following:

1. Artificially generated electric currents. However, if a fire results, the resulting fire damage is covered.
2. Rupture or bursting of water pipes unless caused by a covered cause of loss, but this exclusion does not apply to sprinkler leakage.
3. Leakage of water or steam from any part of an appliance or system containing water or steam (other than an automatic sprinkler system), unless caused by a covered cause of loss.
4. Explosion of steam boilers, steam pipes, steam turbines, or steam engines owned by, leased to, or operated by the insured. However, if such an explosion causes a fire or a combustion explosion, the damage caused by fire or combustion explosion is covered. (For a definition of "combustion explosion," see the earlier discussion of the explosion peril.)
5. Mechanical breakdown, including rupture or bursting caused by centrifugal force.
6. Loss resulting from the neglect of the insured to use all reasonable means to save and preserve property at and after the time of loss. This exclusion reinforces the insured's duty to protect covered property after a loss. (This duty is expressed in the loss conditions of the BPP and other commercial property coverage forms.)

Some of these excluded exposures can be insured under equipment break-down insurance, which will be discussed in Chapter 6.

Causes of Loss—Broad Form

The **Causes of Loss—Broad Form** (or simply "broad form") covers all of the perils covered under the basic form plus (1) falling objects, (2) weight of snow, ice, or sleet, and (3) water damage (see Exhibit 3-1). In addition, collapse resulting from specified perils is covered as an "additional coverage" of the broad form.

Causes of Loss—Broad Form
Form that covers basic form perils plus falling objects; weight of snow, ice, or sleet; water damage; and (as additional coverage) collapse caused by certain perils.

Falling Objects

The coverage for falling objects does not include damage to personal property in the open. The peril also does not include damage inside a building unless the roof or an outside wall is first damaged by a falling object.

Weight of Snow, Ice, or Sleet

The coverage for damage caused by the weight of snow, ice, or sleet does not cover damage to personal property in the open.

Water Damage

The water damage peril covers loss from leakage of water or steam resulting from the breaking apart or cracking of a plumbing, heating, air conditioning, or other system or appliance that is located on the described premises and contains water or steam.

If the building is covered property, the form also covers the cost to tear out and replace any part of the building to repair damage to the appliance or system that leaked.

The water damage peril specifically excludes the following:

1. The cost to repair any defect that caused the loss or damage.
2. Gradual damage that occurs over a period of fourteen days or more.
3. Discharge or leakage from an automatic sprinkler system. (The sprinkler leakage peril would cover such damage.)
4. Discharge or leakage from a sump, including overflow because of sump pump failure.
5. Discharge or leakage from roof drains, gutters, downspouts, or similar fixtures or equipment.

The water damage peril also does not cover damage resulting from freezing unless the insured has made a reasonable effort to heat the building or, if the building was not heated, unless the system has been drained and the water supply shut off.

Additional Coverage—Collapse

Under this additional coverage, the insurer agrees to pay for loss resulting from collapse of a building or any part of a building if the collapse is caused by one or more of the following:

• Any of the covered causes of loss under the broad form.

• Hidden decay, unless such decay is known to an insured before the collapse occurs.

• Hidden insect or vermin damage, unless such damage is known to an insured before the collapse occurs.

• Weight of people or personal property.

• Weight of rain that collects on a roof.

• Use of defective materials or construction methods if the collapse occurs during the course of construction. (Collapse of a *completed* building caused by defective materials or construction is covered only if it is caused in part by a cause of loss listed above.)

Collapse is specifically and narrowly defined. It means an abrupt falling down or caving in of a building or part of a building that, as a result, can no longer be occupied for its intended purpose. It does not include a building that is in danger of falling down or caving in, nor one that is standing but shows evidence of cracking, bulging, sagging, bending, leaning, settling, shrinkage, or expansion. A part of a building that is standing is not considered to be in a state of collapse even if it has separated from another part of the building.

The additional coverage for collapse also covers loss to property caused by the collapse of *personal property* inside a building (such as storage racks in a warehouse) if the collapse is a result of one of the causes listed above.

Certain types of property—primarily outdoor property such as awnings, yard fixtures, outdoor swimming pools, fences, and roadways—are covered for collapse only if the damage is the result of the collapse of an insured building caused by one of the causes listed above.

Glass Coverage

Before the ISO commercial property forms were revised in 2000, they included only limited glass breakage coverage. The restrictions on glass breakage coverage were removed in the 2000 revision of commercial property forms. Glass that is covered property is now covered up to the policy limit for all covered perils, including vandalism. Glass breakage, like any other loss, is subject to the policy deductible, thus eliminating most small losses.

With the inclusion of glass coverage in the causes-of-loss forms, ISO withdrew its separate Glass Coverage Form. The need for separate glass coverage continues, however. Some non-ISO commercial property policies continue to place restrictions on glass coverage, and many leases require the tenant to provide full glass coverage, without any deductible. Separate glass coverage is available from insurers.

Causes of Loss—Special Form

The **Causes of Loss—Special Form** (or simply "special form"), instead of listing the perils covered, states that it covers "risks of direct physical loss," subject to the exclusions and limitations expressed in the form. Moreover, use of the term "risks" requires that loss or damage be accidental and unforeseen by the insured in order to be covered.

This type of coverage has long been known as "all-risks." However, the possibility of court decisions making the term "all-risks" broader than intended resulted in a switch to the current terminology, "risks of direct physical loss." Policies that take this open-ended approach to stating what perils are covered are known by several different terms, including "open perils policies." This text refers to them as "special-form policies."

The special form offers the following advantages to the insured:

- Certain causes of loss that are omitted or excluded under the broad form are not excluded—and are therefore covered—under the special form. Most significantly, the special form covers theft of covered property under a wide variety of circumstances, subject to some exclusions and limitations described below. The basic and broad forms cover theft by looting at the time of a riot or civil commotion but in no other circumstances.

- By covering any risk of loss other than those that are specifically excluded, the special form covers losses that the insured might not have anticipated.

- The special form shifts the "burden of proof" from the insured to the insurer. Under a named perils form, such as the basic or broad form, the insured must prove that the loss was caused by a covered cause. Under the special form, an accidental loss is presumed to be covered unless the insurer can prove that it was caused by an excluded peril.

Exclusions and Limitations

The special form contains most of the exclusions of the basic and broad forms, including many (but not all) of the limitations expressed in the descriptions of the basic and broad covered causes of loss. In those instances in which the special form does not contain an exclusion or a limitation equivalent to any of those contained in the basic and broad forms, it provides broader coverage. Two examples are given below:

1. The vehicle peril in both the basic and broad forms excludes loss or damage caused by or resulting from vehicles owned by the named insured or operated in the course of the named insured's business. The special form, in contrast, does not contain a similar exclusion. So, for example, the special form covers such loss or damage to an insured building when an employee accidentally drives a truck owned by the insured through the building's garage wall.

Causes of Loss—Special Form
Form that covers "risks of direct physical loss," subject to the form's exclusions and limitations. (Traditionally known as "all-risks" coverage.)

2. The windstorm peril in both the basic and broad forms excludes damage to the interior of a building by rain, snow, sleet, ice, sand, or dust, unless the roof or walls of the building are first damaged by a covered cause of loss. The special form contains the same exclusion, but with an additional exception: The special form exclusion does not apply if loss results from the melting of ice, sleet, or snow on the building or structure. Thus, unlike the basic and broad forms, the special form covers loss caused by water that enters a covered building because of "ice dam" in the building's gutters.

Exclusions Unique to the Special Form

Because the special form covers more causes of loss than the broad form, it contains some exclusions and limitations that are not needed in the broad form. The special form, as explained above, covers any risks of loss other than those that are specifically excluded. Thus, many hard-to-insure perils that are not covered under the basic and broad forms (because they are not named as covered causes of loss in those forms) must be specifically excluded in the special form. Examples of perils that the special form specifically excludes are as follows:

- Wear and tear
- Rust, corrosion, fungus, decay, or deterioration
- Smog
- Settling, cracking, shrinking, or expansion
- Infestations and waste products of insects, birds, rodents, or other animals
- Damage to personal property by dampness or dryness of atmosphere, changes or extremes in temperatures, or marring or scratching

However, the insurer will pay losses caused by a "specified cause of loss" that results from the excluded peril. The special form defines "specified causes of loss" to include all of the causes of loss insured under the Causes of Loss—Broad Form. For example, a basement wall of an insured building might crack because soil has settled beneath the foundation. The special form excludes such cracking damage. However, if the settling and cracking cause a natural gas pipe in the building to rupture, resulting in an explosion (a "specified cause of loss"), the resulting explosion damage will be covered even though the special form excludes the initial cause of loss (settling).

The special form also excludes loss caused by the following:

1. Weather conditions that contribute to other excluded causes of loss. If, for example, covered property is damaged by flood waters that were driven in part by high winds, the flood damage will not be covered even though windstorm is not otherwise excluded.

2. Acts or decisions, including the failure to act or decide, of any person, group, organization, or governmental body. Thus, for example, if flooding occurs because municipal authorities fail to take proper flood control measures, the flood exclusion cannot be overcome by the insured's claim that the municipality's failure to act was the cause of the loss.

3. Faulty or inadequate planning, zoning, surveying, siting, design, specifications, workmanship, repair, construction, renovation, remodeling, grading, compaction, materials, or maintenance.

If one of these excluded causes of loss results in a covered cause of loss, the insurer will pay the loss resulting from the covered cause. For example, the failure of a city's fire department to take necessary measures might allow a fire to spread and burn down several adjoining row houses. Even though the fire department's failure to act contributed to the destruction of the adjoining row houses, they were destroyed by fire, a covered cause of loss. Thus, the loss would be covered.

Another noteworthy exclusion that is unique to the special form eliminates coverage for the release, discharge, or dispersal of pollutants. However, the exclusion does not apply to any release of pollutants caused by any of the "specified causes of loss," nor does it apply to chemicals applied to glass.

Loss to the following kinds of property is covered only if it is caused by "specified causes of loss":

1. Valuable papers and records
2. Animals, and then only in the event of their death
3. Fragile articles if broken, such as glassware, statuary, marble, chinaware, and porcelain (but not including building glass, containers of property held for sale, and lenses)
4. Builders' machinery and equipment owned or held by the insured unless on or within 100 feet of the described premises

Theft-Related Exclusions

The special form does not contain a general exclusion of theft, and thus it covers any theft of covered property that is not specifically excluded.

The special form excludes dishonest acts of the insured or of partners, members, officers, managers, directors, or employees of the insured. Losses resulting from employees' dishonest acts can be covered under separate crime coverage forms, discussed in Chapter 5.

The special form also excludes the voluntary surrendering of possession of property as the result of a fraudulent scheme or trickery. If, for example, a thief posing as an honest customer tricks the insured's salesperson into *voluntarily* allowing the thief to remove merchandise from the insured's store, the resulting theft loss will not be covered. Similarly, the special form excludes loss of property transferred outside the described premises on the basis of unauthorized instructions.

Loss by theft of construction materials not attached as part of the building is excluded unless the materials are held for sale by the named insured. Moreover, the special form excludes loss of property that is simply missing without explanation or that is evidenced only by an inventory shortage.

The special form imposes limits on theft loss of certain kinds of property that are especially attractive to thieves. Such property can be insured for higher limits under separate crime or inland marine forms. The special form's theft limits are as follows:

- $2,500 for furs and garments trimmed with fur
- $2,500 for jewelry, watches, and precious metals, but the limit does not apply to jewelry or watches valued at $100 or less per item
- $2,500 for patterns, dies, molds, and forms
- $250 for stamps, tickets, and letters of credit

The special form does not provide any coverage for theft of *money*, which is the type of property most attractive to thieves. This is because money is not covered property under any of the commercial property coverage forms (such as the Building and Personal Property Coverage Form) to which the causes-of-loss forms are attached. Separate crime coverage forms are available to cover loss of money. A theft exclusion endorsement can be attached to the policy to eliminate theft coverage when the underwriter feels that the risk is unacceptable or when the insured wants to reduce the policy premium.

Additional Coverage—Collapse

The special form contains an additional coverage for collapse that is essentially the same as the additional coverage for collapse under the broad form.

Additional Coverage Extensions

Two additional coverage extensions extend the policy to cover two kinds of losses that would not otherwise be covered: loss to property in transit and certain repair costs related to damage caused by water or other specified substances.

Property in Transit

The property in transit extension provides up to $5,000 of additional protection for loss to the insured's property in transit. The property must be in or on a motor vehicle owned, leased, or operated by the insured and cannot be in the custody of the insured's sales personnel. It covers only those losses that occur within the coverage territory.

The transit extension does not provide special-form coverage. The perils insured against are fire, lightning, explosion, windstorm, hail, riot, civil commotion, vandalism, upset or overturn of the conveying vehicle, collision of the conveying vehicle with another vehicle or an object other than the roadbed, and theft. The coverage for theft is limited to theft of an entire bale, case, or package by forced entry into a securely locked body or compartment of the vehicle, evidenced by marks of the forced entry.

Since the property in transit coverage extension is limited in terms of both the limit of coverage provided and the perils covered, insureds who have property in transit should consider covering such property under an inland marine or ocean marine policy, which will be discussed in Chapter 7.

Cost of Tearing Out and Replacing

A clause titled Water Damage, Other Liquids, Powder or Molten Material Damage extends coverage to pay for the cost of tearing out and replacing any part of a building necessary to repair an appliance or a system from which water or another liquid—or even powder fire-extinguishing agents or molten materials—escaped. The extension does not pay for the repair of any defect that resulted in the leakage. It will pay for repairs to fire extinguishing equipment if the damage results in the discharge of any substance from an automatic fire protection system or is directly caused by freezing.

OTHER COMMERCIAL PROPERTY COVERAGE FORMS

The Building and Personal Property Coverage Form (BPP), which was described in Chapter 2, is intended to meet the needs of the vast majority of organizations that wish to insure their buildings and business personal property. More specialized commercial property coverage forms for insuring buildings or business personal property or both are available for those that need them. Three such ISO forms, described below, are the Builders Risk Coverage Form, the Condominium Association Coverage Form, and the Condominium Commercial Unit-Owners Coverage Form.

Builders Risk Coverage Form

The BPP provides some protection for new buildings while under construction. However, that coverage is limited and is intended only as incidental protection. Buildings under construction are insured more appropriately under the **Builders Risk Coverage Form**. The discussion that follows describes the ISO builders risk form in terms of its notable *differences* from the BPP.

Builders Risk Coverage Form
Form that covers buildings in the course of construction, including additions or alterations to existing buildings.

Eligible Property and Insureds

The builders risk form may be used to insure any building in the course of construction, including buildings (such as farm buildings and dwellings) that will not be eligible for coverage under the BPP when construction is completed. By using special endorsements, the builders risk form can also be adapted for covering additions or alterations to existing buildings. The parties that can be insured by a builders risk policy include the building owner and the building contractor.

Covered Property

The property covered by the builders risk form is the building described in the declarations while in the course of construction, including the following:

- Foundations
- If not covered by other insurance, temporary structures built or assembled on site, such as scaffolding or concrete forms
- Property intended to become part of the building—such as lumber, uninstalled windows, doors, sinks, and furnaces—while located within 100 feet of the described premises

The builders risk form does *not* cover land or water; outside radio or television antennas, including satellite dishes; or outdoor signs not attached to the building.

Coverage Extensions

The builders risk form contains all of the additional coverages found in the BPP except for increased cost of construction, but the builders risk form contains only two coverage extensions. The first builders risk coverage extension provides up to $5,000 at each covered location for damage to building materials or supplies owned by others, such as a plumbing or roofing subcontractor. In order to be covered, the materials must be in the insured's care, custody, or control; must be located in or on the building or within 100 feet of its premises; and must be intended to become a permanent part of the building. The $5,000 limit can be increased by showing a higher limit in the declarations.

The second extension covers loss of or damage to sod, trees, shrubs, and plants outside of buildings on the described premises, but only if the loss or damage is caused by fire, lightning, explosion, riot, civil commotion, or aircraft. The most the insurer will pay under the extension is $1,000 per occurrence, subject to a sublimit of $250 for any one tree, shrub, or plant.

The builders risk form does not contain the BPP coverage extension for non-owned detached trailers. This omission can be important because a leased trailer is frequently used as a construction office or storage facility at a job site.

Causes of Loss

Like the BPP, the builders risk form must be combined with a basic, broad, or special causes-of-loss form. Some especially important points about the causes-of-loss forms, as they apply to builders risks, are described below.

Collapse During Construction

The broad and special causes-of-loss forms cover collapse of a building caused by certain named perils, including defective materials or faulty construction, if the collapse occurs during construction. However, the builders risk form specifically excludes collapse occurring during construction. For an additional premium, collapse coverage can be added to a builders risk policy by using the Builders Risk—Collapse During Construction Endorsement.

Theft of Building Materials

Uninstalled building materials at construction sites are a target for thieves. Thus, owners and contractors usually want theft coverage, but insurers are understandably cautious in providing it.

As discussed earlier in this chapter, the basic and broad causes-of-loss forms do not cover theft. Although the special form covers theft, it excludes theft of building materials and supplies not attached as part of the building or structure. Thus, even with the special form, the builders risk form does not cover theft of uninstalled building materials. However, the excluded exposure can be insured by adding an optional endorsement, titled Builders Risk—Theft of Building Materials, Fixtures, Machinery, Equipment. This approach allows the insurer to provide coverage for an additional premium.

Need for Adequate Insurance

Builders risk insurance is usually written on a completed-value basis. That is, the amount of insurance is set equal to the expected value of the completed building. Since the insured value increases during construction from nil to the completed value, the rate is reduced to reflect the reduced exposure during most of the policy term. To be sure that the insured is complying with the completed-value requirement, a condition in the builders risk form titled Need for Adequate Insurance replaces the coinsurance provision found in the BPP.

In effect, the Need for Adequate Insurance condition is a 100 percent coinsurance clause, with one exception. The condition requires the insured to carry insurance in an amount that is at least equal to the actual cash value of the building *on completion*. In contrast, a 100 percent coinsurance clause would require insurance equal to 100 percent of the value of the building *on the date of loss*.

Before subtracting the deductible, the amount of loss payment under the builders risk form is calculated by the following formula:

$$\text{Loss payment} = \left(\frac{\text{Limit of insurance}}{\text{Actual cash value of building on completion}} \times \text{Loss} \right) - \text{Deductible}.$$

Builders risk insurance can also be provided on a reporting basis; policy premiums are determined on the basis of periodic reports of value rather than on an estimate of the completed value. The reporting approach is seldom used because of the difficulty of making timely and accurate reports of value.

When Coverage Ceases

Coverage under the builders risk form terminates upon the earliest of the following:

1. The expiration date shown in the declarations
2. The date of cancellation

3. The date when the property is accepted by the purchaser
4. When the insured's interest in the property ceases
5. When the insured abandons construction with no intention to complete it
6. Unless the insurer indicates otherwise in writing:
    (a) Ninety days after the construction is completed or
    (b) Sixty days after the building is occupied in whole or in part or is put to its intended use

Other Provisions

In addition to the provisions discussed above, the builders risk form includes provisions relating to the limits of insurance, deductible, abandonment, appraisal, duties in the event of loss or damage, loss payment, recovered property, and mortgageholders. These provisions are essentially the same as the corresponding clauses in the BPP. The valuation clause is much shorter than that of the BPP. It merely says that the covered property will be valued at actual cash value at the time of loss. There is little difference between actual cash value and replacement cost for most buildings under construction because they usually experience little, if any, depreciation.

Condominium Coverage Forms

Condominiums involve the separate ownership of individual units in a multiple-unit building or buildings. In a condominium, each unit owner is the owner of that condominium unit and has an undivided interest with all other unit owners in the jointly owned "common elements" of the building. A condominium association is formed by unit owners to manage the condominium and to own the common elements.

The precise dividing line between the condominium unit (owned by the unit owner) and the common elements (owned by the association) depends on the terms of the particular condominium association agreement, also referred to as the master deed, declarations, or bylaws. State laws can also specify the division of property ownership. Whenever insurance is arranged for a condominium unit owner or association, the pertinent documents and laws must be reviewed carefully in order to ascertain insurance needs.

The unique legal characteristics of condominiums make it necessary to use specialized forms for insuring the respective interests of condominium associations and unit owners. There are two commercial property condominium forms: one for condominium associations and another for owners of *commercial* condominium units.

Two other forms of community ownership, the cooperative corporation and the planned unit development (also called a "homeowners association"), are in many respects similar to condominiums. In each case there is joint ownership of some property. Insurers often use condominium forms to insure cooperative corporations and planned unit developments.

Condominium Association Coverage Form

Like the BPP, the ISO **Condominium Association Coverage Form** provides coverage for property in three categories:

1. Building
2. Business personal property of the named insured (which is the association of unit owners)
3. Personal property of others

The discussion that follows highlights the fundamental differences between the condominium association form and the BPP. These differences, which principally concern the building and business personal property items, are due to the unique nature of condominium property ownership.

Condominium Association Coverage Form
Form that covers buildings and business personal property of condominium associations.

Building Coverage

The building coverage of the condominium association form closely resembles the building coverage of the BPP. However, a significant difference relates to the following types of property contained within individual units of a condominium building:

- Fixtures, improvements, and alterations
- Appliances, including (but not limited to) those used for refrigerating, ventilating, cooking, dishwashing, laundering, or housekeeping

The condominium building coverage applies to the above items only if the condominium association agreement requires the association to insure them. Otherwise, such property items are not included in the association's building coverage. As will be explained in more detail below, the unit owner's coverage picks up where the association's coverage leaves off, and vice versa.

Business Personal Property

Many condominiums have community clubhouses, health clubs, and the like. The furnishings and equipment of these facilities can be covered as business personal property. As in the case of building coverage, the condominium association coverage form clarifies the dividing line between personal property insured by the association and that insured by individual unit owners:

- Business personal property is covered if it is owned by the association or if it is indivisibly owned by all unit owners.
- Business personal property is not covered if it is owned only by a unit owner.

Other Provisions

Most of the conditions of the condominium association form are the same as those of the BPP. Some of the more notable variations from the BPP are described below.

The condominium association form provides that it is primary as to any loss covered by both that form and the condominium commercial unit owners form. The unit owners form is excess in such situations.

The condominium association form also includes a provision waiving the insurer's right to recover from a unit owner for any loss the insurer has paid to the condominium association. If, for example, the condominium building burned down because of a fire that resulted from a unit owner's negligence, the insurer, after paying the loss, would not be able to exercise its usual right to recover damages from the unit owner.

If the division of ownership between the association and the unit owners (as determined by the condominium association agreement or by state law) differs from the division indicated in the policy form, an endorsement can be used to adapt the policy to meet such requirements. Standard endorsements are provided by ISO to comply with most applicable state laws, but manuscript endorsements may be needed to comply with some condominium association agreements.

Condominium Commercial Unit-Owners Coverage Form

Condominium Commercial Unit-Owners Coverage Form
Form that covers business personal property and building property exposures of commercial (nonresidential) condominium units.

Commercial condominium units are used for offices, stores, and other business activities. The ISO **Condominium Commercial Unit-Owners Coverage Form** is used for insuring owners of such *commercial* condominium units only. Owners of *residential* condominium units should purchase coverage under homeowners policies designed for unit owners.

Covered Property

The unit-owners form covers only "your business personal property" and personal property of others. These coverages are basically the same as in the BPP. Fixtures, improvements, and alterations that are part of the building and owned by the unit owner are included in the definition of "your business personal property" in the unit-owners form.

An exclusion in the unit-owners form coordinates that coverage with the condominium association's coverage. Fixtures, improvements, alterations, and appliances (such as those used for refrigerating, cooking, and so on) are not covered by the unit owner's policy if the condominium association agreement requires the association to insure them. If the agreement requires the association to insure such property but the association fails to do so, the unit owner's policy still does not apply. Another policy provision makes unit-owners coverage excess over the coverage of any association insurance covering the same property.

Optional Coverages

Two optional coverages that are often needed by condominium unit owners are available in a single endorsement that can be attached to the unit-owners coverage form.

One of these optional coverages is **loss assessment coverage**, which covers the unit owner's share of any assessment made by the association against all unit owners because of physical loss or damage to condominium property caused by a covered cause of loss. Typically, a condominium association has the right to assess all unit owners for uninsured losses that the association incurs. These uninsured losses can result, for example, from a large deductible on the association's property policy.

The other optional coverage is **miscellaneous real property coverage**, which extends the unit-owners form to cover real property items that pertain only to the named insured's condominium unit or that the named insured has a duty to insure according to the condominium association agreement. An example of property insurable under this endorsement is a storage or garage building owned by the association but used solely by the unit owner.

> **Loss assessment coverage**
> Coverage for a commercial condominium unit-owner's share of any assessment made by the association against all unit-owners because of physical loss to condominium property caused by a covered cause of loss.

> **Miscellaneous real property coverage**
> Coverage for real property (such as a storage shed or garage building) that pertains only to the named insured's condominium unit or real property that the named insured has a duty to insure under the condominium association agreement.

> **Insurance for highly protected risks (HPR)**
> Property insurance that covers large property risks with superior loss protection characteristics; has broader coverage than most commercial property policies and usually a lower premium rate.

Insurance for Highly Protected Risks

Insurance for highly protected risks, commonly known as **HPR insurance**, is used to insure large, well-protected properties. HPR insurance originated with New England textile manufacturers who, in the early 1830s, formed mutual insurance companies (factory mutuals) to obtain lower insurance rates for their mills. They felt that lower rates were justified by the mills' heavy-timber construction and the extensive fire protection equipment installed.

HPR coverages are broader in many respects than standard forms, and HPR rates are often considerably lower than most insurers' standard commercial property rates. But not every insured can qualify for HPR insurance, and not every insurer is able to provide it. The insured must have a proactive management determined to control the risk of property loss; fire-resistive, noncombustible, or heavy timber construction; loss prevention systems such as automatic sprinkler systems; adequate water supply and pressure; and, adequate fire protection. The insurer must provide the specialized engineering services needed to implement a highly effective loss prevention plan for the insured's property.

Most HPR insurance is written by pools of insurance companies and by a few large insurers. Each pool or individual insurer offering HPR insurance develops its own policy forms. Generally speaking, HPR policies contain a broader definition of property covered, cover more perils, and provide more supplementary coverages than the ISO commercial property forms. ISO forms are sometimes amended to provide coverage similar to that of HPR policies.

ENDORSEMENTS

One of the strengths and challenges of commercial property coverage is the large number of endorsements that are available to modify coverage. Endorsements are useful in many ways. They can do any of the following:

- Enhance coverage that some insureds may want but that others either do not feel they need or cannot afford
- Eliminate coverage for certain exposures thereby enabling underwriters to accept applications that they would otherwise decline

- Change policy provisions to match the specific characteristics of certain industries or insureds
- Amend the policy to comply with state insurance regulations

The ISO portfolio of commercial property forms contains over 130 multi-state forms and endorsements and almost twice that many state-specific endorsements. In addition, many insurers use independently developed endorsements, or they draft manuscript endorsements to suit special requirements. A handful of endorsements are described below to illustrate the diversity that is available. A few other endorsements were discussed in Chapter 2 or will be mentioned in later chapters. In this chapter, we'll briefly review the following endorsements:

- Ordinance or Law Coverage
- Spoilage Coverage
- Manufacturers' Consequential Loss Assumption
- Brands and Labels
- Flood Coverage
- Earthquake and Volcanic Eruption Coverage

Ordinance or Law Coverage

Ordinance or Law Coverage Endorsement
Endorsement that covers three types of losses due to the enforcement of building ordinances or laws: (1) the value of undamaged property that must be demolished, (2) the cost to demolish the building's undamaged portion and remove its debris, and (3) the increased cost to rebuild the property.

The **Ordinance or Law Coverage Endorsement** provides three coverages for losses resulting from the enforcement of building ordinances or laws.

- Coverage A covers the value of the undamaged portion of the building that must be demolished. For example, an entire structure may have to be totally demolished if it is a frame building in an area where only fire-resistive construction is now permitted. Demolishing the undamaged parts of the building changes what would have been a partial loss to a total loss.
- Coverage B covers the cost to demolish the undamaged portion of a building and remove its debris when demolition is required by the building code.
- Coverage C covers the increased cost to repair or rebuild the property resulting from the enforcement of a building, zoning, or land use law. Building codes may require that reconstruction of damaged property meet higher standards, such as heavier electrical service, elevators to upper floors, and fire-resistive stairwells. Coverage C pays the added expense for these improvements.

The unendorsed forms exclude these losses except for the additional coverage for increased cost of construction, which adds a small amount of coverage for the types of loss insured by Coverage C of the endorsement.

Spoilage Coverage

Spoilage Coverage Endorsement
Endorsement that covers damage to perishable stock due to power outages; on-premises breakdown; or contamination of the insured's refrigerating, cooling, or humidity control equipment.

The **Spoilage Coverage Endorsement** is available to cover damage to perishable stock caused by power outage or on-premises breakdown or contamination of the insured's refrigerating, cooling, or humidity control apparatus or equipment. The power outage must be caused by conditions beyond the insured's control.

The maximum amount of insurance available under this endorsement is $50,000. The coverage is not subject to coinsurance and cannot be blanketed. For a smaller insured, such as a small restaurant or food store, the spoilage endorsement may provide sufficient coverage. The $50,000 limit, however, would probably be inadequate for a business with a potentially large spoilage loss, such as a milk bottling plant. Equipment breakdown insurance, to be discussed in Chapter 6, can provide higher coverage limits for spoilage.

Manufacturers' Consequential Loss Assumption

Many manufacturing firms can suffer a reduction in the value of undamaged items as a result of a loss to other property. This is an example of what in insurance terminology is called consequential loss. For example, if the fronts of skirts that have been cut but not stitched are damaged, the remaining parts of the skirts are worth little more than rags unless the fronts can be replaced. A new supply of cloth that is of a slightly different color or shade may frustrate attempts to match the original, causing a reduction in value of the undamaged parts.

The **Manufacturers' Consequential Loss Assumption Endorsement** provides coverage for these situations. When damage to parts of stock in the process of manufacture at the described premises causes a reduction in value to the remaining parts of the stock, coverage is provided for the reduction in value wherever the remaining, undamaged parts may be located.

Manufacturers' Consequential Loss Assumption Endorsement
Endorsement that covers reduction in value of undamaged property due to physical loss to other property.

Brands and Labels

When the insurer pays for loss to covered property, it has the right to take any salvaged property, such as smoke-damaged merchandise, and sell it to the public at a reduced price. That situation can pose a problem for an insured that bases its marketing appeal on a brand name with a reputation for high quality, because the salvaged material that the insurer sells to the public might not meet the insured's quality standards.

To help protect the reputation of the insured's goods when the insurance company takes any part of the property as salvage, the **Brands and Labels Endorsement** permits the insured to take the following actions:

A. Stamp "salvage" on the merchandise or its containers, if the stamp will not physically damage the merchandise; or

B. Remove the brands or labels, if doing so will not physically damage the merchandise.

Brands and Labels Endorsement
Endorsement that permits the insured, when the insurer takes damaged merchandise as salvage, to stamp the word "salvage" on the merchandise or to remove its brands or labels before sale.

The insurance company will pay the reasonable costs involved as part of the loss subject to the limit of insurance. The brands and labels endorsement is available to cover only the original manufacturer of the goods.

Flood Coverage

In the United States, losses from flooding accompany hurricanes, heavy rains, and melting snows. Collapsing dams can also cause floods. Any of these events can cause catastrophic losses. Because of the movable nature of the property they insure, auto physical damage insurance and many inland marine forms include flood as an insured peril. However, insurers are reluctant to write flood insurance on property at fixed locations, such as buildings and their contents, and that is why all three of the causes-of-loss forms exclude flood.

Flood insurance for buildings and their contents is available through the National Flood Insurance Program (NFIP), which provides insurance for properties located in eligible communities. The NFIP is administered by the Federal Insurance Administration, part of the Federal Emergency Management Agency (FEMA). For commercial properties, the maximum NFIP limit is $500,000 per building and $500,000 for the contents of a building. Although the demand for flood insurance is greatest from insureds in the most hazardous flood zones, NFIP provides coverage in all areas. Most private insurers are unwilling to provide flood coverage for commercial properties located in zones that have more than a once-in-100-years flooding probability risk (shown in NFIP flood maps as Zone A).

For properties located outside the high-hazard flood zones, private insurers often write flood coverage by endorsement to the insured's commercial property policy, subject to a substantial deductible (often $25,000 or more). The ISO commercial property program includes a Flood Coverage Endorsement for use with the ISO commercial property coverage forms. In some cases, insurers will only provide excess flood coverage that applies in addition to the maximum limit available from NFIP.

Earthquake and Volcanic Eruption Coverage

Earthquake and volcanic eruption, like flooding, present potentially catastrophic loss exposures. Consequently, earthquake insurance is expensive and limited in availability in areas with a high probability of severe earthquake damage, principally in parts of California and locations near the New Madrid Fault, which extends into portions of Arkansas, Illinois, Indiana, Kentucky, Mississippi, Missouri, and Tennessee. In other areas, earthquake insurance is generally available but is often overlooked. Overlooking the earthquake exposure can be a costly mistake. In the past 100 years, earthquakes have occurred in 39 of the 50 states.[1] One of the most severe earthquakes in U.S. history was centered in Charleston, South Carolina.

Insurers can use either of two ISO endorsements to add earthquake and volcanic eruption as covered perils under a commercial property coverage part. Independently filed earthquake endorsements are also available from some insurers. The two ISO endorsements are as shown below:

- Earthquake and Volcanic Eruption Endorsement
- Earthquake and Volcanic Eruption Endorsement (Sub-Limit Form)

Both endorsements extend commercial property coverage to include earthquake and volcanic eruption. The first endorsement includes coverage for the full policy limit and contains a coinsurance clause. The second endorsement includes earthquake and volcanic eruption coverage subject to a sublimit that is lower than the regular policy limit, and it does not contain a coinsurance clause.

COMMERCIAL PROPERTY CONDITIONS

One of the documents required to make up a commercial property coverage part is the Commercial Property Conditions as discussed in Chapter 2. The nine conditions expressed in this form apply in addition to the common policy conditions, described in Chapter 1. The commercial property conditions are listed in the box below and explained in the paragraphs following the box.

Commercial Property Conditions

- Concealment, misrepresentation, or fraud
- Control of property
- Insurance under two or more coverages
- Legal action against the insurance company
- Liberalization
- No benefit to bailee
- Other insurance
- Policy period, coverage territory
- Transfer of rights of recovery against others

Concealment, Misrepresentation, or Fraud

The commercial property coverage part is void if the insured commits any fraudulent act related to the coverage. (A void contract is one that never legally existed.) Submission of a fraudulent claim, for example, would void the coverage part.

The coverage part is also void if the insured conceals or misrepresents any material fact pertaining to (1) the coverage part, (2) the covered property, or (3) the insured's interest in the covered property. A **misrepresentation** is an active misstatement of a fact. For example, assume that John Doe, who has previously been convicted of arson, applies for fire insurance. If the application specifically asks whether the applicant has ever been convicted of arson and Doe responds that he has not, his answer would be a misrepresentation.

Misrepresentation
A misstatement of a fact.

Concealment
A failure to disclose a fact.

Concealment does not involve an active misstatement of fact. A **concealment** is a passive failure to disclose a material fact. In the example, if the application does not ask about past convictions for arson and Doe simply remains silent about his conviction, this could be considered concealment.

Misrepresentation or concealment does not always void coverage. Only *material* misrepresentation or concealment voids coverage. A fact is material if knowledge of it would cause the insurer to charge a higher premium or decline to write the coverage. For example, an insured might state that his or her building is painted red when in fact it is painted yellow. This misstatement would have no bearing on the insurance and would therefore not be material.

Control of Property

The control of property condition consists of two parts. The first part states that coverage under the policy will not be affected by acts or omissions of persons other than the insured if the others are not acting under the direction or control of the insured. The second part of the condition says that a violation of a policy condition at one location will not affect coverage at any other location.

To illustrate how this clause might apply, assume that a liquor store's policy is endorsed to require that its burglar alarm system be maintained in working order at all insured locations. Assume also that the insured leases these locations from other parties. The first part of the clause would protect the insured if the system was disconnected by a building owner, providing the owner was not under the insured's control.

The second part of the control of property condition can be important to the insured if the policy provides coverage at more than one location. In the absence of this part of the control clause, the insured's failure to maintain the alarm system at one location might suspend coverage at all locations, even though the alarm systems are properly maintained at the other locations. Under this provision, only the coverage at the location with the deficient alarm system would be affected.

Insurance Under Two or More Coverages

This policy condition is necessary because some property might be covered under two or more of the coverage parts that can be included in a single commercial package policy. This clause prevents double recovery by the insured in such instances. The total payment under all applicable coverage parts is limited to the actual amount of the loss. Duplication, or "stacking," of the limits is avoided.

Legal Action Against the Insurance Company

This condition spells out two requirements the insured must meet before legal action can be brought against the insurance company to enforce the policy.

First, the insured must have complied with all conditions of the policy, including those in the coverage part and the common policy conditions, as well as the applicable loss conditions. Second, the action must be brought within two years after the date on which the direct physical loss occurred.

Liberalization

If the insurance company adopts any revision that would broaden the coverage under the commercial property coverage part and for which there is no additional premium charge, the broader coverage is extended automatically to outstanding policies. This automatic coverage applies only if the broadening amendment is adopted during the policy term or within forty-five days before the effective date of the policy. Liberalization applies only to amendments that broaden coverage and not to those that restrict coverage.

The liberalization clause is beneficial to insureds because it provides them with the broadened coverage automatically and immediately upon adoption, even if they are not aware of the broadening amendment. However, it applies only to broadening amendments for which there is no additional premium charge.

The liberalization clause is beneficial to producers because it relieves them from having to search their client files to find insureds who would benefit from adding the amendments. In addition, insurance companies are relieved of the cost of issuing numerous individual endorsements to add the broader coverage to outstanding policies.

No Benefit to Bailee

A *bailee* is a person or business organization that has temporary custody of the property of another. Examples are dry cleaners, television repair shops, laundries, and fur storage firms. Bailees may be liable to *bailors* (the owners of the property) for damage to the property they hold. Bailees sometimes try to limit their liability by contractual provisions stating that the bailee is not liable for damage if the damage is recoverable under insurance carried by the bailor. The "no benefit to bailee" clause is intended to defeat such provisions in the bailment contract and to reinforce the insurance company's right of subrogation against the bailee. (The "Transfer of Rights of Recovery Against Others" section that appears below explains subrogation.)

Other Insurance

An insured may have more than one policy covering a given loss. In keeping with the principle of indemnity, the other insurance condition limits the total recovery from all applicable insurance to an amount not in excess of the actual loss sustained.

If the other insurance is provided by another policy subject to the same plan, terms, and conditions, then each policy pays in the proportion its policy limit bears to the total policy limits of all applicable policies. If the other insurance is not subject to all of the conditions of the ISO commercial property coverage part, then the policy subject to the commercial property coverage part is excess coverage and pays only to the extent the covered loss exceeds that amount due from the other policy. Exhibit 3-2 provides illustrations of these loss-sharing procedures.

The proration of coverage between dissimilar policies is often complicated by the presence of an excess provision in the other policy or policies. When each policy provides that it is excess, the courts generally disregard the excess provisions and require each company to share in the loss.

EXHIBIT 3-2

Application of the Other Insurance Clause

Insurance on Building

• Insurance Company A	$100,000
• Insurance Company B	$150,000
Total insurance of	$250,000

$$\text{Company A's share of insurance} = \frac{\$100,000}{\$250,000} = 0.40 = 40\%.$$

$$\text{Company B's share of insu rance} = \frac{\$150,000}{\$250,000} = 0.60 = 60\%.$$

If both policies are subject to the same plan, terms, and conditions:

- Insurance Company A pays 40 percent of loss = $20,000
- Insurance Company B pays 60 percent of loss = $30,000

If Insurance Company B used ISO Commercial Property

Coverage Part and Insurance Company A did not:

A. Covered loss $50,000

- Insurance Company A pays as primary — payment of $50,000
- Insurance Company B pays as excess — payment of $0

B. Covered loss $200,000

- Insurance Company A pays as primary — $100,000
- Insurance Company B pays as excess — $100,000

Note: These examples ignore any coinsurance, deductible, or other clauses that might otherwise apply.

Policy Period, Coverage Territory

The commercial property conditions state that coverage begins on the effective date and ends on the expiration date shown in the common declarations. The declarations state that the beginning and ending time is 12:01 A.M., determined by standard time at the insured's mailing address as shown in the common declarations, even though some or all of the insured property may be located in a different time zone. The insured property is covered only while it is located within the United States of America (including its territories and possessions), Puerto Rico, or Canada.

Transfer of Rights of Recovery Against Others

This policy condition enables the insurance company, after it has paid a loss under the policy, to recover the amount paid from any party (other than the insured) who caused the loss or is otherwise legally liable for the loss. This process is known as **subrogation**, though that term is not used in the policy.

If the insured takes any action that eliminates the insurer's right of recovery (other than those actions specifically authorized by the policy), the insurer may not be required to pay the loss. The policy specifically permits the insured to waive the right of recovery against any other party, provided the waiver is made in writing and before the loss occurs.

Waiver of recovery may be given by the insured *after* loss only to (1) another party insured under the same policy, (2) a parent or subsidiary company, or (3) a tenant of the insured property. Any other waiver given by the insured after loss has occurred may impair the insured's right to collect from the insurer for the loss.

Subrogation
The process by which an insurer can, after it has paid a loss under the policy, recover the amount paid from any party (other than the insured) who caused the loss or is otherwise legally liable for the loss.

RATING COMMERCIAL PROPERTY COVERAGE

A **rate** is the price per exposure unit for insurance coverage—for example, $1.00 per $100 of insurance coverage. **Rating** is the process of applying a rate to a particular exposure and performing any other necessary calculations to determine the policy premium for that exposure.

Thus, as a simplified example, if the applicable rate for a particular coverage is $.50 per $100 of insurance and the limit of the coverage is $100,000, the premium for the coverage would be calculated as follows:

$$\frac{\$.50}{\$100} \times \$100,000 = \$500.$$

In reality, rating is usually more complicated; additional calculations are often needed. For example, the rate or the premium must often be multiplied by additional factors to account for territorial differences in theft losses (if theft is a covered cause of loss), to reduce the premium when the insured has

Rate
The price per exposure unit for insurance coverage; rate multiplied by number of exposure units equals premium.

Rating
The process of applying a rate to a particular exposure and performing any other necessary calculations to determine the policy premium for that exposure.

selected a higher deductible, to increase the premium when a coverage option has been added, and so on.

Commercial Lines Manual (CLM)
An ISO publication that includes rules and rating procedures for nine major lines of commercial insurance.

The primary source of information for rating ISO coverages is the ***Commercial Lines Manual (CLM)*** published by ISO. (Similar information is provided by the American Association of Insurance Services on behalf of its member companies for rating AAIS coverage forms.) The CLM contains nine divisions, titled as follows:

1. Automobile
2. Boiler and Machinery
3. Crime and Fidelity
4. Farm
5. Fire and Allied Lines
6. General Liability
7. Professional Liability
8. Inland Marine
9. Multiple Line

Loss costs
The portion of the rate that covers projected claim payments and loss adjusting expenses.

Division 5 contains rating procedures and loss costs for the ISO commercial property coverages. **Loss costs** are the portion of the rate that covers projected claim payments and loss adjusting expenses. To convert these loss costs to complete rates that can be used to rate a policy, each insurer calculates a loss cost multiplier to cover other expenses that the insurer will incur (such as underwriting, marketing, and taxes). In addition, a charge is usually added to allow for possible errors in the insurer's predictions. An allowance for insurer profit may also be added.

Most insurers that provide commercial property insurance follow the CLM rating procedures in applying their own rates. Because these rating procedures are many and detailed, the discussion that follows does not attempt to describe the actual mechanics of rating. Rather, the discussion focuses on the rating factors that principally affect the premium for commercial property coverage on buildings and business personal property. The factors that affect the premium are information that the producer often needs to transmit to the underwriter and the rater. Understanding those factors is also fundamental to reducing the cost of insurance, since many of the factors are within the insured's control.

Some of the factors affecting commercial property premiums are various aspects of coverage expressed in the commercial property coverage part. Other factors—such as the type of building construction and the type of business occupying the building—exist independently of the coverage being provided.

Aspects of Coverage

The aspects of coverage that affect the premium are the limit of insurance being provided, the causes-of-loss form that applies, the applicable coinsurance requirement, the amount of the deductible, and any optional coverages that apply to the commercial property coverage part.

Aspects of Coverage Affecting Commercial Property Premiums

- Limit of insurance
- Covered causes of loss
- Coinsurance percentage
- Deductible amount
- Optional coverages

Limit of Insurance

The limit of insurance applicable to the coverage is an important component of the final premium since that is the "exposure" against which the applicable rate is multiplied to calculate the premium. Given the same rate, doubling the limit of insurance doubles the premium for property insurance.

Causes of Loss

The premium for the causes of loss—basic form consists of a Group I premium (for fire, lightning, explosion, vandalism, and sprinkler leakage) and a Group II premium (for all other causes of loss covered under the basic form). The broad form premium consists of the basic form (Group I and Group II) premium plus a premium for the cost of covering the additional perils covered by the broad form. The same approach is used with the special form except that the additional premium is higher than the additional premium that applies to the broad form.

Coinsurance

The rates ordinarily used for insuring buildings and personal property are calculated with the assumption that they will be used with an 80 percent coinsurance clause in the policy. These rates are therefore called the "80 percent coinsurance rates." When a policy contains a higher coinsurance percentage, the 80 percent coinsurance rate is lowered to reflect the reduced likelihood that a loss will exceed 80 percent of the value of the property and to encourage the purchase of higher limits. For 90 percent coinsurance, the 80 percent coinsurance rate is multiplied by 0.95, and for 100 percent coinsurance, the 80 percent coinsurance rate is multiplied by 0.90. Thus, with 90 or 100 percent coinsurance, the insured must buy a greater amount of insurance to comply with the coinsurance requirement, but the rate is reduced. When the coinsurance requirement is less than 80 percent, the rate is increased.

Deductibles

Commercial property rates are developed with the assumption that the policy will be subject to a base deductible of $500. Many policyholders are willing and able to retain a larger deductible. Because raising the deductible reduces the insurer's loss payments, rates are reduced accordingly in return for the insured's acceptance of a higher deductible. If the deductible is reduced to $250, rates are increased.

Optional Coverages

Adding optional coverages to the BPP or another coverage form ordinarily increases the policy premium.

In some cases, the optional coverage increases the premium only because the limit of insurance must be increased to cover the additional property values being insured. For example, replacement cost insurance does not involve a higher rate, but the amount of insurance needed to meet the coinsurance requirement on a replacement cost basis may be considerably higher than the amount needed on an actual cash value basis.

In other cases, the charge for a coverage option is a separate rate applied to the amount of insurance. For example, a grocery store that wishes to buy optional spoilage coverage under its BPP will pay an additional premium.

Other Factors

Apart from the terms of coverage, factors that affect commercial property premiums are the building's construction, occupancy, protection, exposure, and location. The first four factors are referred to by the acronym COPE. To a large extent, the COPE factors relate to fire, which is often the most significant cause of loss in a commercial property policy.

Other Factors Affecting Commercial Property Premiums

- **C**onstruction
- **O**ccupancy
- **P**rotection
- **E**xposure
- Location

Construction

Some types of buildings resist fire better than others, thus lessening the fire risk for both the buildings and their contents. Although buildings can be classified in many ways, the system used to classify buildings for purposes of rating commercial property insurance is based on resistance to fire.

The six construction classes used for purposes of rating commercial property insurance are (1) frame, (2) joisted masonry, (3) noncombustible, (4) masonry noncombustible, (5) modified fire resistive, and (6) fire resistive. Frame construction, which uses wood or other combustible material in the exterior walls of a building (even if covered by brick veneer or stucco), is the most susceptible to fire damage. Fire-resistive construction uses materials with a fire-resistance rating of at least two hours and is the least susceptible to fire damage.

Occupancy

Occupancy refers to the type of activity conducted inside the building. Some occupancies are riskier than others. To cite an extreme example, a building, if used for manufacturing fireworks, will face a greater explosion and fire risk than if the same building were used for storing bottled water. Accordingly, commercial property rates are higher for buildings with more hazardous occupancies.

Protection

Fire protection can be either internal (such as a sprinkler system) or external (the local fire department). For purposes of rating commercial property insurance, external protection is graded on a scale of 1 (the best protection) to 10 (the worst), with the assigned number indicating the availability of firefighting personnel and equipment. For internal protection, buildings classified as "sprinklered" receive rate reductions. In contrast, buildings that have certain fire hazards (such as unsafe heating or cooking devices or inadequate electrical wiring) are charged higher premiums than if these hazards did not exist.

Exposure

In addition to hazards arising from a building's construction and occupancy, other properties adjacent to the building can increase the probability of loss to the insured building and its contents. In the example above, a fire or explosion in the fireworks plant could damage the building and contents of the adjacent bottled water storage building. Underwriters use the term "exposure" for the hazard posed by surrounding properties. Insurers include a charge for exposure only when a "specific rate" is calculated for a particular location. Specific rating is further discussed below.

Location

The risk of loss caused by windstorm, theft, earthquake, and other perils varies depending on the location of the insured property. For example, buildings along the coastline of the southeastern United States are more exposed to hurricane damage than buildings in other areas. Thus, different rates apply to different areas, or the rates are modified by "territorial multipliers" that account for the differences.

Class Rates and Specific Rates

At one time, commercial buildings were inspected individually by rating bureau representatives, and rates reflecting the exposure to loss of a particular business were published. This approach to developing rates is known as **specific rating.**

Specific rating
A rating approach that bases a building's property insurance rate on inspecting and evaluating that particular building.

As the gathering of loss statistics became more sophisticated, insurance companies were better able to generalize about the probabilities of loss within large groups of similar risks and to formulate rates that reflected the average probability of loss for businesses within these groups. With this approach, known as **class rating**, a building and its contents can be rated without inspecting the building and developing a specific rate.

Class rating
A rating approach that uses rates reflecting the average probability of loss for businesses within large groups of similar risks; the predominant method used for rating commercial properties.

Large businesses, along with certain other businesses with operations involving unusual or increased exposures to loss, are still specifically rated. However, class rating is the rule for the majority of commercial insureds.

SUMMARY

Three causes-of-loss forms are available for a commercial property policy: the basic form, the broad form, and the special form.

The basic form covers fire, lightning, explosion, windstorm, hail, smoke, aircraft, vehicles, riot, civil commotion, vandalism, sprinkler leakage, sinkhole collapse, and volcanic action.

The broad form covers the same causes of loss as the basic form plus falling objects; weight of snow, ice, or sleet; and water damage. Collapse is covered as an "additional coverage."

The special form covers risks of direct physical loss except those specifically excluded. Although not spelled out by name, the perils covered by the special form include all the perils covered by the broad form plus additional, possibly unanticipated perils. Theft is one major peril that is covered by the special form but not by the other two forms.

All three causes-of-loss forms exclude building ordinance or law requirements, earth movement, governmental action, interruption of off-premises utility services, war, flood, electrical disturbances, steam boiler explosion, and mechanical breakdown. The special form contains several additional exclusions.

In addition to the BPP, several other commercial property forms are available for insuring special exposures.

The Condominium Association Coverage Form can be used to insure a condominium association against loss to its buildings, its personal property, and the personal property of others. The form covers fixtures, improvements, alterations, and appliances within condominium units if the condominium association agreement requires the association to insure them.

The Condominium Commercial Unit-Owners Coverage Form provides business personal property coverage for commercial (not residential) unit owners. The form provides essentially the same coverage for the insured's business personal property as the BPP. To dovetail with the condominium association form, the unit-owners form covers fixtures, improvements, alterations, and appliances owned by the insured unless the condominium association agreement requires the association to insure them.

The Builders Risk Coverage Form is designed to insure the interests of owners or contractors (or both) in buildings or other structures during construction. The form covers the building under construction and building materials and temporary structures located at the building site. The builders risk form is usually issued with a limit equal to the projected value of the completed building.

Hundreds of endorsements can be used to modify commercial property coverage. Examples of the exposures that can be covered by endorsement include building ordinance or law, spoilage, consequential loss, brands and labels, flood, and earthquake.

The commercial property conditions form must be included in every commercial property coverage part. The commercial property conditions address various matters that could affect any commercial property coverage form.

Commercial property policy premiums are affected by the following factors: the limit of insurance, the causes of loss covered, the applicable coinsurance rate, deductible levels, the presence of optional coverages, and the building's construction, occupancy, protection, exposure, and location.

CHAPTER NOTE

1. Ruth Gastel, ed., "Earthquakes: Risk and Insurance Issues," *Insurance Issues Update* (New York: Insurance Information Institute, October 2000), p. 10.

Chapter 4

Direct Your Learning

OUTLINE

Business Income Loss Exposure

Business Income Coverage Forms

Other Forms and Endorsements

Rating Business Income Coverage

Summary

Business Income Insurance

After learning the content of this chapter, you should be able to:

- ■ Describe the business income loss exposure.

- ■ Given a case about a business income loss, explain whether coverage applies and determine the amount, if any, the insurer will pay for the loss.

  - Describe the coverage provided by the Business Income (and Extra Expense) Coverage Form.

  - Explain how the Business Income (Without Extra Expense) Coverage Form differs from the Business Income (and Extra Expense) Coverage Form.

  - Describe the exclusions appearing in the causes-of-loss forms that apply specifically to business income coverage.

  - Describe the loss conditions of the business income coverage form.

- ■ Explain how each of the four optional coverages affects business income coverage.

- ■ Describe the Extra Expense Coverage Form and the types of businesses for which this form would be appropriate.

- ■ Describe the purpose of each of the following endorsements:

  - Business Income From Dependent Properties

  - Ordinary Payroll Limitation or Exclusion

  - Power, Heat, and Refrigeration Deduction

  - Ordinance or Law—Increased Period of Restoration

- ■ Briefly explain how business income coverage is rated.

Develop Your Perspective

What are the main topics covered in the chapter?

This chapter examines business income and extra expense losses, and the commercial property forms and endorsements that can be used to insure these losses.

Consider the reasons why three separate coverage forms are available for business income and extra expense insurance.

- Identify a business operation that might prefer each.

Why is it important to learn about these topics?

Business income and extra expense loss exposures are often overlooked, but they can result in monetary losses exceeding the amount of the physical losses that cause them. Part of the service that insurance professionals provide is educating customers to the need for this insurance and arranging coverage to meet a customer's specific exposures.

Imagine that one of your customers selected business income and extra expense insurance but wants to avoid any possibility of a coinsurance penalty.

- Where could you find more information about eliminating coinsurance?

How can you use what you will learn?

Examine the operations of an organization you know well.

- What information might you gather from this organization to estimate the amount of business income and extra expense insurance it needed to cover its loss exposures?

Chapter 4
Business Income Insurance

The two previous chapters described coverage for buildings and personal property that may be damaged or destroyed by insured perils. However, the loss in value of the property and the expense of restoring it are not the only losses that a business may sustain. Almost all of a commercial firm's property is acquired because of the income that it will generate or facilitate. It is this income that can also be lost when property is damaged or destroyed.

Consider the following example. Dynamic Insurance Agency (DIA) owns a two-story building. DIA occupies the second floor, and the first floor is rented to Toys Unlimited, a single-location toy store. A fire damaged the building and personal property of both the building's occupants. Restoration of the building took six months. The losses resulting from the fire consisted of the following:

1. The cost of repairing the building and removing debris
2. The cost of replacing and restoring the contents of the agency office and the toy store
3. The loss of income that the toy store would have earned from sales during the six months that it was closed due to the restoration
4. The loss of the rental income that DIA would have received from Toys Unlimited
5. The extra expenses that DIA incurred in renting and equipping a temporary office nearby and in reconstructing its records. (By quickly relocating and advertising its new location, DIA believed that it did not lose any sales.)

Properly arranged building and personal property coverage would cover the losses described in items 1 and 2. The losses described in items 3, 4, and 5 could be insured by business income insurance, the topic of this chapter.

Simply described, **business income insurance** covers the reduction in an organization's income when operations are interrupted by damage to property caused by a covered peril. Because the severity of a business income loss is directly related to the length of time required to restore the property, business income coverage is called a "time element" coverage. It is also referred to as "business interruption" coverage, because the loss of business income results from the interruption of the insured's business.

Business income insurance
Insurance that covers the reduction in an organization's income when operations are interrupted by damage to property caused by a covered peril.

To examine business income insurance in more detail, Chapter 4 will first analyze the business income loss exposure then review the standard policy provisions for covering this exposure.

BUSINESS INCOME LOSS EXPOSURE

Evaluating business income loss exposures requires an understanding of how business income losses can be measured, how expenses are affected during a business interruption, and the property and perils that can be involved in business income losses.

Measurement of Business Income Losses

Net income
Excess of revenues over expenses; revenues less expenses.

Business income losses can be measured in terms of net income. **Net income** is the difference between revenues (such as money received for goods or services) and expenses (such as money paid for merchandise, rent, and insurance). The definition of net income can be expressed by the following formula:

Revenues – Expenses = Net income.

Profit
Net income that results when revenues exceed expenses.

Net loss
Net income that results when expenses exceed revenues.

When a firm's revenues exceed its expenses, the resulting net income is called a **profit**. When a firm's expenses are greater than its revenues, the result is called a **net loss**, which is indicated by placing the amount of net loss in parentheses. The reduction in a firm's net income because of accidental damage to property is the loss exposure covered by business income insurance. The amount of a business income loss can be calculated by subtracting the amount of net income that a firm actually earned in a period of interruption from the amount of net income that the firm could reasonably have been expected to earn for the same period.

The following simplified example illustrates the concepts discussed above. Sam's Hardware Store suffered a partial fire loss and was closed for three months until the building could be repaired and the personal property replaced. During the three-month interruption, Sam's revenue was reduced to nil; some ordinary expenses (payroll, electricity, and so on) were temporarily reduced or eliminated; and Sam's also incurred some additional expenses (such as overtime labor and express freight on merchandise) to reopen the store as soon as possible.

The "Expected" column below shows the revenue, expenses, and profit that could reasonably have been expected to occur during the three-month period if no business interruption had occurred. The "Actual" column shows the revenue, expenses, and net loss (indicated by parentheses) that actually did occur during the three-month period of interruption.

	Expected	Actual
Revenue	$300,000	$ –0–
Expenses	240,000	120,000
Net profit (or loss)	$ 60,000	($120,000)

Sam's business income loss is the $180,000 difference between the $60,000 profit the store had been expected to experience and the $120,000 net loss that it did experience during the period of interruption. The loss amount can also be calculated by adding the $60,000 net income that Sam's would have earned to the $120,000 expenses that Sam's actually incurred during the period of interruption.

For the sake of simplicity, this example assumes that Sam's revenue returned to its normal level as soon as the store reopened, which is seldom the case. In reality, Sam's business income loss could have continued for several months after the store reopened.

Changes in Expenses During Business Interruption

During a business interruption, some of the firm's expenses (called **continuing expenses**) will continue, and other expenses (called **noncontinuing expenses**) will not continue. A business can also incur extra expenses during a business interruption. All resulting changes in expenses must be considered when measuring a business income loss.

Continuing expenses
Expenses that continue to be incurred during a business interruption.

Noncontinuing expenses
Expenses that cease during a business interruption.

Continuing Expenses

If business is interrupted only for a short time, payroll of key employees, debt repayments, taxes, insurance, and many other expenses will continue during the interruption. If a longer interruption of business occurs, many expenses can be reduced or eliminated. Workers can be laid off, taxes are reduced, and insurance premiums are smaller. It is often difficult to predict which expenses will continue and which will not.

Any reduction in expenses during a business interruption lessens the severity of the resulting business income loss. Nevertheless, continuing expenses can be, and ordinarily are, a significant part of business income losses. If, for example, a firm's revenues are reduced to nil during a business interruption, the firm's business income loss will be its lost profit for the period of interruption, plus the *continuing* expenses for that period, plus any extra expenses. In many cases, a company's continuing expenses are greater than the profit that the company would have earned.

Extra Expenses

Extra expenses are expenses that an organization would not have incurred if the business interruption had not occurred. Examples of extra expenses are as follows:

Extra expenses
Expenses that an organization only incurs if business is interrupted.

- In order to reopen an assembly line that had been shut down because of an explosion, the factory owner paid the additional costs of overtime labor and overnight air shipment of needed repair parts.

- After sustaining fire damage to its warehouse, a wholesale distributor rented a similar warehouse and was able to continue its operations within two weeks instead of shutting down entirely for several months.

- To continue classes while an elementary school building was being rebuilt following hurricane damage, a school district rented mobile classrooms and situated them on the school's playground.

Extra expense measures often pay for themselves. For example, the extra cost of overtime labor and air freight of needed parts might have been considerably less than the income that would have been lost if such measures had not been taken. Such measures actually reduce the business income loss, and most organizations will readily undertake measures that reduce loss.

Some organizations will even incur extra expenses that they know will actually increase the business income loss. For example, after a property loss occurs, a hospital might incur substantial extra expenses to maintain essential services for its patients even though such expenses will increase the business income loss. The decision to incur such extra expenses depends on the organization's objectives. For some organizations, maintaining continuous service to its customers may be more important than reducing the business income loss.

Property and Perils Involved in Business Income Losses

Business income losses typically result from physical damage to the affected organization's own buildings or personal property. A tenant's operations can be interrupted by damage to the building in which the tenant is located even though the part of the building the tenant occupies has not been damaged. For example, an explosion that knocks out heating, air conditioning, and ventilating equipment makes offices in modern, sealed high-rise buildings uninhabitable in very hot or very cold weather even though the offices themselves are not damaged.

In some cases, a physical loss at one location can cause a business interruption elsewhere. For example, a business may be shut down because of damage to off-premises property providing utilities, such as electricity, water, or communications. Or one business may depend on another property either as a major customer or as a sole supplier. It is also possible that a business is dependent simply because it is near a key facility or "magnet" property, such as a major department store in a shopping mall. If any of these other properties is damaged, the effects could include a business income loss at a location where no physical damage occurred.

For business income losses associated with property exposures, the causes of loss are typically the same as those for physical damage losses. Thus, a fire or a windstorm that damages property may also cause a business income loss. A business income loss can also result when there has been no physical damage to buildings or personal property. The closing of a road or a labor strike can cause a business income loss, although such risks are generally not insurable. Any number of other events that are not covered by business income insurance can cause a reduction in an organization's net income. In order for business income insurance to apply, the following must occur:

- An interruption of operations . . .
- caused by property damage from a covered peril . . .
- to property at locations or situations described in the policy . . .
- resulting in a loss of business income and/or extra expense.

Business Income Insurance for Nonprofit Organizations?

This chapter makes frequent use of terms such as "business income," "business interruption," and "profit." Although many kinds of organizations (such as nonprofit organizations and public entities) do not use these labels, they, too, have revenues and expenses that govern their financial existence and make them similar, for insurance purposes, to profit-making enterprises. Thus, although this chapter uses terms that relate more directly to for-profit business organizations, the insurance applies equally to nonprofit and governmental entities.

BUSINESS INCOME COVERAGE FORMS

Insurance for most business income exposures can be provided under either of two ISO forms.

- The **Business Income (and Extra Expense) Coverage Form** covers both business income loss and extra expense losses.
- The **Business Income (Without Extra Expense) Coverage Form** covers business income loss but only covers extra expenses to the extent that they reduce the business income loss.

Either business income coverage form (BIC) can be included in a commercial property coverage part, with or without another commercial property coverage form such as the BPP. The causes of loss covered for business income coverage can be designated by either the same causes-of-loss form that applies to other coverage forms or by a different causes-of-loss form that applies to business income coverage only.

Because the two versions of the BIC are similar in all respects except extra expense coverage, the discussion that follows applies equally to both forms unless otherwise specified.

Coverage

The business income insuring agreement, four additional coverages, and a coverage extension are set forth in the initial section of the BIC entitled Coverage.

Business Income Insuring Agreement

The insurer agrees to pay the actual loss of business income sustained by the named insured because of the necessary suspension of the named insured's

Business Income (and Extra Expense) Coverage Form
Form that covers both business income and extra expense losses (even if the extra expenses do not reduce the business income loss).

Business Income (Without Extra Expense) Coverage Form
Form that covers business income loss but only covers extra expenses to the extent that they reduce the business income loss.

"operations" during the "period of restoration." The suspension must result from direct physical loss or damage to real or personal property caused by a covered cause of loss and occurring at the premises described in the declarations. If the insured is a tenant, the definition of "premises" is broadened to include "any area within the building or on the site . . . if that area services, or is used to gain access to, the described premises." Thus, if fire damaged the elevator motors in the basement of a building, a tenant on the thirtieth floor would be covered for any resulting business income loss even if there was no damage above the first floor. The covered causes of loss are specified in the causes-of-loss form entered in the declarations and attached to the policy.

Business income

The sum of (1) net profit or loss that would have been earned or incurred if operations had not been suspended plus (2) normal operating expenses, including payroll, that continue during the suspension.

Business income, for the purposes of this coverage, means the sum of (1) net profit or loss that would have been earned or incurred if the suspension had not occurred and (2) normal operating expenses, including payroll, that continue during the suspension. For manufacturing risks, net income includes the net sales value of production. The amount of profit or loss that would have been earned or incurred if the suspension had not occurred must be estimated based on past and prospective performance of the business. The continuing expenses can be determined during the suspension. Those expenses might include salaries of key employees, property taxes, and interest expenses.

The terms "operations," "period of restoration," and "suspension" are defined in a separate section of the form. The operations of the insured are (1) the business activities of the insured that occur at the premises described in the declarations or (2) in the case of rental value coverage, the tenantability of the described premises.

Period of restoration

The period during which business income loss is covered under the BIC forms; begins seventy-two hours after the physical loss occurs and ends when the property is (or should have been) restored to use with reasonable speed. (With regard to extra expense coverage, begins immediately after the physical loss occurs.)

Period of restoration also has a split definition. For business income coverage, it is the period of time that begins seventy-two hours after the time of direct physical loss or damage; for extra expense coverage, it begins immediately after the loss. In both cases, the period of restoration ends when the property should be restored with reasonable speed and similar quality or when the business is resumed at a new, permanent location. Thus, for business income coverage, there is no coverage for the first three days following the physical loss. The seventy-two hour deductible can be reduced to twenty-four hours or eliminated entirely by endorsement for an additional premium.

The period of restoration does not include any additional time that might be required to repair or reconstruct the building in order to comply with any building code or law, unless the policy has been specifically endorsed to cover such additional time. (The endorsement used for this purpose is separate from the ordinance or law endorsement discussed in Chapter 3.) The period of restoration also does not include any increased period required by ordinance or law to respond to or assess the effects of pollutants.

"Suspension" means the slowdown or cessation of business activities or, in the case of rental value coverage, that a part of the premises is rendered untenantable.

Additional Coverages and Coverage Extension

Each version of the BIC contains four additional coverages and one coverage extension to insure several sources of business income loss that would not otherwise be covered. The additional coverages and coverage extensions of both forms are identical except that the "extra expense" additional coverage in the Business Income (and Extra Expense) Coverage Form is replaced with "expenses to reduce loss" in the Business Income (Without Extra Expense) Coverage Form. The additional coverages and coverage extensions of the two BIC forms are listed in Exhibit 4-1 and discussed in more detail in the sections that follow.

EXHIBIT 4-1

BIC Additional Coverages and Coverage Extension	
Business Income (and Extra Expense) Coverage Form	**Business Income (Without Extra Expense) Coverage Form**
Additional Coverages	**Additional Coverages**
• Extra expense	• Expenses to reduce loss
• Civil authority	• Civil authority
• Alterations and new buildings	• Alterations and new buildings
• Extended business income	• Extended business income
Coverage Extension	**Coverage Extension**
• Newly acquired locations	• Newly acquired locations

Extra Expense

The **extra expense coverage** of the Business Income (and Extra Expense) Coverage Form provides coverage for extra expenses incurred by the named insured to avoid or minimize the suspension of operations. Examples of extra expenses to avoid or minimize the suspension of business are expenses to move to a temporary location, increased rent at the temporary location, rental of substitute equipment (furniture, fixtures, and machinery), and the cost of substitute services such as data processing. The Business Income (and Extra Expense) Coverage Form covers such expenses in full, subject to the policy limit.

However, extra expenses *to repair or replace property* are treated differently. They are covered only to the extent that they actually reduce the business income loss. For example, a businessowner might pay a contractor at an overtime rate to work around the clock to repair damaged property so that the business can reopen promptly. The additional cost paid to do so would be payable as extra expense, but only to the extent that it actually reduced the business income loss. Thus, if reopening earlier reduced the business income

Extra expense coverage
Coverage for extra expenses incurred by the named insured to avoid or minimize the suspension of operations; additional coverage of the business income and extra expenses coverage form.

loss by $20,000, the insurer would pay the overtime charges up to that amount (and subject to the limit of insurance).

Expenses To Reduce Loss

Instead of extra expense coverage, the Business Income (Without Extra Expense) Coverage Form contains an additional coverage titled Expenses To Reduce Loss.

Expenses to reduce loss
Coverage for necessary expenses incurred by the named insured to reduce business income loss; the expenses are covered only to the extent they actually reduce the business income loss.

Under the **expenses to reduce loss** coverage, the insurer agrees to pay any necessary expenses incurred by the named insured (except the cost of extinguishing a fire) to reduce the business income loss. Thus, the insured can incur the same types of expenses as covered under the extra expense coverage, but they are covered only to the extent that they reduce the business income loss.

A danger of the business income *without extra expense* form is that the insured can incur more extra expenses than the resulting reduction in the business income loss. A large, uninsured extra expense loss can result. The business income *and extra expense* form greatly reduces that possibility. Since the rate for the business income and extra expense form is close to the rate for the business income without extra expense form, many businesses opt for the broader coverage form.

Civil Authority

Civil authority additional coverage
Coverage for loss of business income that results when access to the insured's premises is prohibited by civil authority because of damage to property other than the insured's.

In almost all cases, a loss covered under the BIC results from damage to property at the insured's premises. However, the **civil authority additional coverage** provides limited coverage if access to the insured's premises is prohibited by civil authority because of damage to other property. For example, fire damage to another building may make it unsafe for customers to go to the insured's premises. If the damage to the other premises resulted from a cause of loss covered by the insured's policy, the resulting income loss at the insured's premises would be covered for the period of suspension, beginning seventy-two hours after the time of the action by civil authority, up to a maximum of three consecutive weeks after the time of the action. The maximum period of coverage can be increased to 60, 90, or 180 days by endorsement. If the seventy-two hour elimination period in the definition of period of restoration is reduced or eliminated, the endorsement makes the same change in the civil authority additional coverage.

Alterations and New Buildings

In most cases, business income losses result from the interruption of operations that are already underway. However, the form also provides coverage for loss of income resulting from a delay in beginning operations if the delay results from damage at the described premises by a covered cause of loss to any of the following:

1. New buildings or structures, either completed or under construction
2. Alterations or additions to existing buildings

3. Machinery, equipment, supplies, or building materials located on or within 100 feet of the described premises (provided they are used in the construction, alterations, or additions or are incidental to the occupancy of new buildings)

The period of restoration for losses to new or altered buildings begins on the date that operations would have begun if the damage had not occurred. The business income and extra expense form specifically states that this additional coverage includes necessary extra expense.

Extended Business Income

Business income coverage ceases when the period of restoration ends, that is, on the date "when the property at the described premises should be repaired, rebuilt or replaced with reasonable speed and similar quality." However, all of the insured's former customers may not return immediately, especially if the interruption has been long. The **extended business income (EBI) additional coverage** provides coverage for the resulting reduction in earnings. For example, if a restaurant is closed because of fire damage, its regular diners will patronize other restaurants, and it will take time for the restaurant to rebuild its business after the repairs are made. The EBI coverage begins when the damaged property has been restored and ends when the insured's business returns to normal, subject to a maximum period of thirty days.

However, EBI does not apply to loss of business income as a result of unfavorable business conditions caused by the effect of the covered cause of loss in the insured's area. This limitation would apply, for example, after a severe hurricane, when an insured's hotel has been repaired but still suffers a reduction in income after reopening because of damage to beaches or other recreational facilities in the area.

Concerning loss of rental value, the form specifies that the coverage ends thirty days after the property has been restored or, if earlier than thirty days, on the date on which tenant occupancy could be restored, with reasonable speed, to the level that would have existed had no loss occurred. This makes clear that the thirty-day period does not apply to loss of rental value for property that might, for example, have been unrented even if no loss had occurred.

The thirty-day period can be extended for an additional premium. This coverage option, called "extended period of indemnity," is described in more detail later in this chapter.

Newly Acquired Locations

If coinsurance of 50 percent or more is shown in the declarations, the coverage may be extended, at the option of the insured, to property at premises newly acquired during the policy period (other than property at fairs or exhibitions). The coverage at any newly acquired location is limited to $100,000. This coverage is an additional amount of insurance above the limit stated in the declarations and is not subject to the coinsurance clause. An

Extended business income (EBI) additional coverage
Coverage for business income losses that continue after the period of restoration ends; the coverage begins when the damaged property has been restored and ends when the insured's business returns to normal, subject to a maximum of thirty days.

additional premium is charged for the automatic coverage from the date of acquisition of the new property. The coverage terminates on the earliest of (1) the expiration date of the policy, (2) the date on which the insured reports the acquisition to the insurer, or (3) thirty days after the date of acquisition. This extension is intended to be temporary coverage, providing protection until the insured obtains permanent coverage.

Exclusions

The business income forms themselves contain no exclusions labeled as such. However, the exclusions in the applicable causes-of-loss form apply to the BIC. In addition to the exclusions discussed in Chapter 3, the causes-of-loss forms contain six exclusions that apply specifically to business income coverage. These six exclusions are listed in Exhibit 4-2 and discussed in the sections that follow.

EXHIBIT 4-2

BIC Exclusions in Causes-of -Loss Forms

- Off-premises services interruption
- Finished stock
- Antennas

- Delay
- Loss of privilege
- Other consequential losses

Off-Premises Services Interruption

The first exclusion applies to any loss caused by a power failure or loss of utility service, however caused, *if the failure occurs outside of a covered building.* Thus, loss of business income caused by a fire at a public utility's electric generating plant or by a windstorm that knocks down telephone lines outside a covered building would not be covered. Power failures can cause severe business income losses. In 1993, a fire in an electric utility's generating station in Lower Manhattan shut down electric service to portions of New York City's financial district for up to ten days. The resulting loss of business income for some firms exceeded $1 million. The unendorsed policy excludes such losses. Coverage for this excluded exposure, which is significant for some organizations, can be added by endorsement.

If a covered cause of loss occurs at the described premises because of a power or utility service failure (such as freezing of plumbing), causing a reduction in business income, business income coverage applies—but only for loss of business income resulting from the damage caused by the covered peril.

Finished Stock

The second exclusion provides that the policy does not cover any loss caused by or resulting from damage to or destruction of finished stock or the time required to reproduce finished stock. Finished stock is not defined in the causes-of-loss forms, but it is defined in the BIC as stock manufactured by the named insured. Finished stock does not include stock manufactured by the insured and held for sale at a retail location insured under the same coverage part. If a coinsurance percentage is shown in the declarations, finished stock also does not include alcoholic beverages held for aging.

The exclusion of finished stock means that the BIC does not insure any loss of business income resulting from damage to or destruction of finished stock of manufacturers. Loss of profit on finished stock can be covered by insuring such stock for its selling price under the Building and Personal Property Coverage Form by adding the Manufacturer's Selling Price (Finished Stock Only) Endorsement. This endorsement amends the valuation basis for finished stock covered by the BPP to selling price less discounts and unincurred expenses.

Antennas

The third exclusion eliminates coverage for any income loss resulting from damage to or destruction of radio or television antennas, including satellite dishes, or their lead-in wiring, masts, or towers. Coverage for this type of property, as in the case of a television or radio station, may be complex, and the insurer would likely want to consider it separately. However, when the insurer is willing to extend coverage, this exclusion can be eliminated by attaching the appropriate endorsement.

Delay

The fourth exclusion has two parts. The first part excludes any increase of loss resulting from a delay in rebuilding, repairing, or replacing property or resuming operations if such a delay is caused by the interference of strikers or others at the location of the rebuilding, repairing, or replacing. The interference must be at the premises where the restoration is in progress. The exclusion would not apply, for example, to a delay in rebuilding a store caused by a strike at a steel mill that prevented the insured from rebuilding because of a lack of steel.

The second part of the exclusion provides that the insurer will not pay for any increase of loss resulting from the suspension, lapse, or cancellation of any license, lease, or contract. However, if the suspension, lapse, or cancellation results from the suspension of operations, the insurer will cover the loss of business income during the period of restoration, plus any extension provided by the EBI additional coverage (already discussed) or the extended period of indemnity optional coverage (to be discussed later in this chapter).

Loss of Privilege

The fifth exclusion applies only to extra expense insurance. It excludes any extra expenses arising from the suspension, lapse, or cancellation of any license, lease, or contract if such expenses are incurred after the end of the period of restoration. For example, if the insured's lease is canceled because fire damage makes the leased premises unusable, any increase in rent at substitute facilities will not be covered after the period of restoration at the damaged premises. The increased rent would be paid under the extra expense coverage *during* the period of restoration. A leasehold interest coverage form can be used to cover the increase in rent to the original expiration date of the canceled lease.

Other Consequential Losses

The final exclusion simply says that the insurer will not pay for "any other consequential loss." *Black's Law Dictionary* (6th ed.) defines consequential loss as "losses not directly caused by damage, but rather arising from results of such damage." Loss of business income is, by that definition, itself a consequential loss. This exclusion reinforces the insurer's position that no other consequential losses are covered. Examples of such losses might be the loss of goodwill or market share by failing to supply or serve customers because of damage to the insured's building.

Limits of Insurance

With the exception of coverage for newly acquired locations, the limit stated in the declarations is the maximum amount the insurer will pay for the total of loss and expenses in any one occurrence. The coverage for a newly acquired location is an additional amount of insurance, but the additional coverages for alterations and new buildings, civil authority, extra expense, and extended business income do not increase the limit of insurance.

Loss Conditions

The loss conditions in the BIC are similar to those under the BPP. The BIC loss conditions are discussed below.

Appraisal

The appraisal clause allows appraisal of losses in disputes regarding the amount of loss, but not in disputes as to coverage.

Duties in the Event of Loss

The duties of the insured after loss are similar to the duties specified in the BPP. The BIC imposes one additional duty on the insured: to resume operations, in whole or in part, as quickly as possible (if the insured intends to resume operations).

Limitation—Electronic Media and Records

Coverage for a business income loss due *solely* to damage to or destruction of electronic media or records is limited to a maximum of sixty days from the initial date of loss. If other property is also damaged or destroyed, the covered loss is limited to a maximum of (1) sixty days or (2) the period required to restore *the other property* with reasonable speed and similar quality, whichever is longer. This limitation does not apply to an extra expense loss.

Examples of Business Income Coverage for Electronic Media and Records

Example 1:

A covered cause of loss on June 1 damages a computer and the data and media used with it. It takes until September 1 to replace the computer and until October 1 to restore the lost data. The insurer will pay only for business income loss sustained during the period June 1 to September 1. Loss during the period September 1 to October 1 is not covered since loss resulting from damage to electronic media and records is covered only for either sixty days (in this case, until July 31) or the time it takes to restore the other property (in this case, until September 1), whichever is longer.

Example 2:

A covered cause of loss results in the loss of data processing programming records on August 1. The records are replaced on October 15. All other property is restored by September 1. The insurer will pay only for the business income loss sustained during the period August 1 through September 29—sixty consecutive days.

Electronic media include tapes, films, discs, drums, or cells used in conjunction with computers to store data and computer programs. Electronic records consist of the data and programs stored on such media. The sixty-day limitation does not apply to damage to the computer, but only to damage to the media and records used with the computer. The period of indemnity for business income loss resulting from damage to the computer continues until the computer is restored with reasonable speed. The 60-day limit can be increased to 180 days or extended indefinitely for an additional premium.

Loss Determination

The amount of a business income loss can never be known precisely, so the form sets forth the items to be considered in estimating it. The business income loss is determined on the basis of the following:

1. The net income of the business before the loss occurred

2. The probable net income of the business if no loss had occurred

3. The operating expenses that must continue during the period of restoration to permit the insured to resume operations with the quality of service that existed prior to loss

4. Other relevant sources of information

Continuing expenses would include payroll and might, depending on the insured's circumstances, include taxes, interest payable on loans, and similar items. "Other relevant sources of information" could include the insured's financial and accounting records, bills, invoices, notes, deeds, liens, and contracts.

The BIC states that the amount of loss will *not* be based on the net income that might have been earned as a result of an increase in business due to favorable business conditions caused by the effect of the covered cause of loss. This change was motivated by questions that arose following Hurricane Andrew in 1992. Insurers felt that the proper measure of damages for a hotel, for example, would be the room rentals that they would normally have earned had Andrew not occurred. Since Andrew struck in late August, the occupancy rate would normally have been about 60 percent. Insured hotel owners, however, argued that the loss should be based on 100 percent occupancy because their hotels, if they had not been damaged by the storm, would have been filled to capacity. They pointed out that hotels twenty or more miles away from the area were fully occupied by construction workers, claim adjusters, and others involved in estimating or restoring hurricane damage. This change makes it clear that the increase in business resulting from a catastrophe will not be included when estimating the likely net income.

The loss determination condition also reinforces the insured's obligation to resume operations as soon as practical. If the insured can resume operations in whole or in part and fails to do so, the business income loss payment will be reduced to the amount of loss that would have been incurred if operations had been resumed as quickly as possible. The extra expense loss may also be reduced if the insured could have returned to normal operations, without the continuing need for the extra expense, and failed to do so. If the insured does not resume operations, the period of restoration will be based on the time it would have taken to resume operations as quickly as possible.

Loss Payment

The insurer agrees to pay for a covered loss within thirty days after the date on which the amount of loss is agreed to (or an appraisal award is made). The insured must have complied with all policy conditions, including filing a sworn statement of loss.

Coinsurance

The coinsurance provision for business income coverage is expressed as an additional condition. The coinsurance percentage may be 50, 60, 70, 80, 90, 100, or 125 percent. The policy may also be written with no coinsurance. The loss payment is calculated by the same procedure used under the coinsurance clause in the BPP. The denominator of the fraction (the amount of insurance required) is found by multiplying the coinsurance percentage by the sum of (1) the insured's net income plus (2) all operating expenses (less certain expenses specified in the form, as shown in Exhibit 4-3) that would have been incurred in the absence of a loss. Both the profit (or loss) and expenses are for the twelve-month period beginning at the inception or latest anniversary date of the policy.

Although the method is similar to that used for the BPP, the coinsurance basis used for business income insurance is significantly different. For other property coverages, the coinsurance basis is the same as the property covered. That is, if a building is the covered property, the coinsurance basis is the value of the building. This is not the case with business income insurance. The item covered in business income insurance is net income plus *continuing* operating expenses; the coinsurance basis is the projected net income and *all* operating expenses except for certain deductible items.

Another difference between the item covered and the coinsurance basis is the period of time used in computing the values. For coverage purposes, the time covered is the period of restoration plus thirty days of EBI coverage. For coinsurance purposes, it is the estimated net income and expense for one year starting with the policy inception or anniversary. This makes the calculation of the amount of insurance needed to satisfy coinsurance more complicated for business income than for other property coverages. To assist insureds in making the necessary calculations, ISO publishes a Business Income Report/ Work Sheet.

EXHIBIT 4-3

Expenses Excluded When Calculating Operating Expenses for the BIC Coinsurance Condition

a. Prepaid freight—outgoing

b. Returns and allowances

c. Discounts

d. Bad debts

e. Collection expenses

f. Cost of raw stock and factory supplies consumed (including transportation charges)

g. Cost of merchandise sold (including transportation charges)

h. Cost of other supplies consumed (including transportation charges)

i. Cost of services purchased from outsiders (not employees) to resell that do not continue under contract

j. Power, heat, and refrigeration expenses that do not continue under contract (if they have been excluded by endorsement)

k. Ordinary payroll expenses excluded by endorsement

l. Special deductions for mining properties

An added complication in selecting a coinsurance percentage is the availability of two endorsements: (1) ordinary payroll limitation and (2) power, heat, and refrigeration deduction. These endorsements reduce both the insured's coverage and coinsurance basis. They are discussed later in the chapter.

The variety of coinsurance percentages that the insured may choose reflects the fact that the probable maximum loss for a given insured seldom equals exactly the projected net income and operating expenses for twelve months. An insured should carry, at a minimum, an amount of insurance equal to its probable maximum loss in order to be properly protected. **Probable maximum loss (PML)** is the largest loss that an insured is likely to sustain.

Probable maximum loss (PML)
The largest loss that an insurer is likely to sustain.

For some insureds, PML may be only a small fraction of the coinsurance basis. For example, a retail store operating in an area where there are numerous empty stores might be able to relocate and be in full operation within three months if its present location was totally destroyed. In contrast, a manufacturer that uses sophisticated, special-order machinery might be shut down for eighteen months waiting for replacement equipment if it sustained extensive physical damage. The retail store might need an amount of insurance equal to less than half its coinsurance basis and could thus choose a 50 percent coinsurance clause; the manufacturer might need an amount of insurance much greater than its coinsurance basis. It could select a 125 percent coinsurance clause, which would lower the rate since higher coinsurance percentages receive lower rates.

An insured must consider other factors in addition to the maximum length of time it will take to restore the property when calculating PML. These factors include the following:

- The effect of peak seasons. Some retailers do as much as 50 percent of their annual business in December.
- Seasonal variations in construction. Construction work is slow, if not impossible, during the winter months in many parts of the country.
- Changes in income and expenses during the period of restoration. The period of restoration can begin at the end of the policy year. A rapidly changing business may have a very different profit and loss picture at that time.
- Noncontinuing expenses. Even though they are included in the coinsurance basis, certain expenses, such as rent, might stop and are therefore not part of the PML.
- Extended business income and extra expense. While not part of the coinsurance basis, these items are part of the PML.

Optional Coverages

The BIC includes four optional modifications of the basic coverage: maximum period of indemnity, monthly limit of indemnity, agreed value, and extended period of indemnity. Each of the options can be activated by an entry in the declarations. No endorsements are necessary to add these coverages.

> ### BIC Optional Coverages
> - Maximum period of indemnity
> - Monthly limit of indemnity
> - Agreed value
> - Extended period of indemnity

Maximum Period of Indemnity

The **maximum period of indemnity coverage option** is not an additional coverage. It is a restriction of the period of restoration provided by the form, but it has the advantage of voiding the coinsurance clause. If this option is selected, it limits the loss payment to the lesser of (1) the amount of loss sustained during the 120 days immediately following the beginning of the period of restoration or (2) the policy limit. The coinsurance provision does not apply at any location to which the maximum period of indemnity is applicable. This option should be used only when the insured feels certain that any suspension of operations will last no more than four months.

Maximum period of indemnity coverage option
Option that deletes the coinsurance clause while limiting loss payment to the lesser of (1) the amount of loss sustained during the 120 days following the beginning of the period of restoration or (2) the policy limit.

Monthly Limit of Indemnity

The **monthly limit of indemnity coverage option** is activated by inserting a fraction in the appropriate space in the declarations. The fraction may be $1/6$, $1/4$, or $1/3$. The fraction is the maximum portion of the policy limit that the insured can recover for any period of thirty consecutive days of interrupted operations. For example, if the fraction shown in the declarations is $1/4$ and the policy limit is $100,000, the maximum amount that the insured would recover for loss during any period of thirty consecutive days would be $25,000. The claim payment would be the lesser of the actual loss sustained or $25,000 for the applicable thirty-day period.

Monthly limit of indemnity coverage option
Option that deletes the coinsurance clause while limiting the amount recoverable during any month of business interruption to a stipulated fraction (1/6, 1/4, or 1/3) of the insurance amount.

The first period would start with the beginning of the period of restoration. Remember that the period of restoration begins seventy-two hours after the time of direct physical loss. Thus the "three-day deductible" would apply to these optional coverages in the same manner that it applies to the standard business income coverage. As previously mentioned, the seventy-two-hour period can be reduced to twenty-four hours or eliminated by endorsement.

The coinsurance clause does not apply to any location at which the monthly limit of indemnity is applicable. This option is sometimes chosen because the insured does not want to disclose financial information to prove compliance with the coinsurance clause or because the coinsurance clause requires more insurance than the insured deems necessary.

Agreed Value

Agreed value coverage option
Option that suspends the coinsurance clause as long as the insured carries an amount of business income insurance that is equal to the value agreed on by the policyholder and the insurer.

The **agreed value coverage option** is another method of avoiding the possibility of a coinsurance penalty. Two steps are necessary to activate the agreed value option.

First, the insured must furnish to the insurer a completed business income report/worksheet showing the following:

- The insured's actual financial data for the most recent twelve months' accounting period before the date of the worksheet
- Estimated financial data for the twelve months immediately following the inception of the coverage

Second, the agreed value must be entered in the declarations. The agreed value must be at least equal to the product obtained by multiplying the coinsurance percentage shown in the declarations by the estimated net income and operating expenses shown on the worksheet for the twelve months following the inception of the optional coverage.

The agreed value is effective for a period of twelve months or until the expiration of the policy, whichever comes first. A new worksheet must be filed every twelve months to keep the agreed value option in force.

The coinsurance clause is suspended while the agreed value option is in force. However, during this period, the insured must carry an amount of insurance equal to the agreed value if losses are to be paid in full. The coinsurance clause is automatically reinstated if the agreed value option is permitted to lapse. This could happen, for example, if a policy is renewed but a new worksheet is not submitted by the insured.

To illustrate the operation of this option, assume that ABC Corporation carries a business income policy with an agreed value of $200,000. If ABC carries insurance of $200,000 or more, its covered losses will be paid in full up to the amount of insurance. However, if ABC carries only $150,000 of insurance, only three-fourths of its covered losses will be paid (calculated as $150,000/$200,000 = $^3/_4$).

Extended Period of Indemnity

Extended period of indemnity coverage option
Option that extends the duration of EBI coverage for up to two years.

The **extended period of indemnity coverage option** extends the EBI additional coverage to include business income losses that continue for more than thirty days after the property is restored. The period of indemnity can be extended up to 730 days. The actual number of days selected depends on the insured's estimate of the amount of time it would take for revenues to return to normal after the property is restored. Many insureds, such as restaurants and clothing stores, depend on repeat business and would have a hard time returning to normal income levels within thirty days after reopening following a severe loss. For such insureds, this optional coverage can be very attractive.

OTHER FORMS AND ENDORSEMENTS

The BIC meets the needs of most organizations. Several more specialized forms and endorsements are available for organizations that have unusual needs.

Extra Expense Coverage Form

Service businesses and organizations such as banks, hospitals, newspapers, and insurance agencies must continue to operate after a property loss, even if the cost of continuing operations is very high. Although such organizations can (and many do) cover *both* their extra expense exposure and their business income exposure under the Business Income (and Extra Expense) Coverage Form, some of these organizations have a minimal business income exposure and therefore wish to buy only extra expense insurance. In such cases, the **Extra Expense Coverage Form** is available.

The coverage provided by this form is essentially the same as the extra expense coverage under the Business Income (and Extra Expense) Coverage Form, with one major exception. The extra expense form restricts the amount that can be recovered for a relatively short period of restoration. For example, recovery may be limited as follows:

Period of Restoration	Maximum Recovery as Percent of Insurance
30 days or less	40 percent
31–60 days	80 percent
over 60 days	100 percent

Extra Expense Coverage Form
Form that covers the same extra expenses incurred as does the Business Income (and Extra Expense) Coverage Form, with the exception that this form limits maximum recovery based on the period of restoration.

The following example illustrates the use of these percentage limitations.

County Bank has an extra expense form with the above limitations and a $100,000 limit of insurance. Following a direct damage loss, County Bank paid extra expenses of $90,000 to remain in operation during a period of restoration of forty-five days. Because the period of restoration was more than thirty days and less than sixty days, only 80 percent of the limit of insurance ($80,000) will be paid. The remaining $10,000 will not be covered.

The limitations shown above are used frequently, but other percentages and other periods of restoration can be used to meet the needs of the insured. For most businesses, the extra expense coverage provided by the business income and extra expense form, which does not contain percentage limitations, is a better alternative.

Business Income From Dependent Properties

An insured may be so dependent on a single supplier or single customer that damage to the operations of the supplier or customer may interrupt the insured's operations. For example, a manufacturer may use a raw material that is available from only one supplier. If the supplier's factory is destroyed, the manufacturer cannot continue to make its products. The unendorsed BIC does not cover this loss exposure because the loss of business income must result from direct damage to the insured's property.

Two endorsements are available to provide coverage. They are the Business Income From Dependent Properties—Broad Form and the Business Income From Dependent Properties—Limited Form. These endorsements cover the insured's loss of income resulting from physical damage to property at *other* locations. The *broad form* endorsement extends the BIC to include loss from damage to property at other locations, subject to the BIC's regular limit of insurance. The *limited form* is used to provide different limits for dependent property exposures.

Dependent property exposures usually result when the insured has a business relationship with one of the following:

- A *contributing* location, which furnishes materials or services to the insured

- A *recipient* location, which purchases materials or services from the insured

- A *manufacturing* location, which manufactures products for delivery to the insured's customers

- A *leader* location, which attracts customers to the insured's location (a major department store at a shopping center, for example)

Ordinary Payroll Limitation or Exclusion

The BIC coinsurance clause requires an amount of insurance based on net income plus operating expenses, including payroll. Some insureds have unskilled workers who can be laid off during a prolonged interruption of operations and recalled when operations are resumed. For these insureds, the coinsurance clause may require an amount of insurance substantially greater than they need to cover their income and continuing expenses.

The **Ordinary Payroll Limitation or Exclusion Endorsement** provides a solution to their problem. The endorsement identifies the job classes considered to be *ordinary payroll* and either limits coverage for such payroll expenses to a specified number of days following direct property loss or excludes such expenses from coverage. The amount of payroll thus limited or excluded from coverage can be deducted from operating expenses in calculating the amount of insurance needed to comply with the coinsurance clause. The insured can thus carry a lower limit of insurance without incurring a coinsurance penalty in the event of loss.

Power, Heat, and Refrigeration Deduction

Many manufacturers incur large expenses for power, heat, and refrigeration. These expenses may not continue when operations are shut down. The

Dependent property exposures
The possibility of incurring business income loss because of physical loss occurring on the premises of an organization that the insured depends on for materials, products, or sales.

Ordinary Payroll Limitation or Exclusion Endorsement
Endorsement that limits coverage for ordinary payroll expenses to a specified number of days or excludes such expenses altogether; allows the insured to satisfy the coinsurance requirement with a lower amount of insurance, thus reducing the policy premium.

Power, Heat, and Refrigeration Deduction Endorsement enables manufacturers to adjust their insurance accordingly. It eliminates these expenses from both the definition of business income and the coinsurance computation and thus enables the insured to carry a lower limit of insurance and still satisfy the coinsurance requirement.

Care must be exercised in selecting this endorsement. Some firms are subject to minimum "energy" charges even if they are shut down. Moreover, there may be no savings in premium unless the excluded energy expenses are a substantial portion of the insured's operating expenses, because the rate for business income coverage is increased when this endorsement is added.

Ordinance or Law—Increased Period of Restoration

The BIC does not cover any increase in the period of restoration resulting from compliance with building ordinances or laws. For example, a store might be located in a frame building in an area where all new buildings must be fire resistive. If the frame building is severely damaged, the law may require that it be demolished and replaced with a fire-resistive building. The business income policy would cover only the decrease in net income during the period required to repair the frame building with reasonable speed and like quality. It would not cover lost business income during the additional time required to demolish the frame building and build a fire-resistive building. For example, sixty days might be enough time to repair the frame building, but 180 days would be needed to demolish the remains of the frame building and to build a fire-resistive building. The unendorsed business income form would cover loss of business income for only sixty days. The **Ordinance or Law—Increased Period of Restoration Endorsement** can be used to cover business income loss during the additional time required to reconstruct the building.

Other Endorsements

Several other endorsements are available to meet the specialized needs of some insureds. Three examples of such endorsements are summarized below.

- The *Business Income Premium Adjustment Endorsement* (like the Value Reporting Form described in Chapter 2) allows the insured to carry a limit of insurance set high enough to cover the highest anticipated fluctuation in business income values while paying premium based on the amount of insurance actually required.

- The *Business Income Changes—Educational Institutions Endorsement* adapts the policy to meet the needs of schools.

- The *Utility Services—Time Element Endorsement* extends the policy to cover loss of earnings resulting from off-premises interruptions of utilities and communications services.

Power, Heat, and Refrigeration Deduction Endorsement
Endorsement that eliminates power, heat, and refrigeration expenses from coverage and from the coinsurance calculation; allows insured to satisfy the coinsurance requirement with a lower limit of insurance.

Ordinance or Law—Increased Period of Restoration Endorsement
Endorsement that covers business income loss during the additional time required to comply with building ordinances or laws.

RATING BUSINESS INCOME COVERAGE

Rating business income coverage is closely related to rating property coverage, because the same perils that damage covered property also cause the business income loss. Rating business income coverage begins with the base rate for building coverage written at 80 percent coinsurance. This base rate is multiplied by rating factors that reflect the type of coverage provided. The three aspects of coverage that modify the base rate are as follows:

1. The type of business being insured
2. The coinsurance percentage at which the business income coverage is being written
3. The coverage options the insured has chosen

The final premium for business income coverage can be calculated after the business income rate, including all modifications for optional coverages, has been determined. The rate is applied to the desired limit of insurance to arrive at the final premium.

SUMMARY

A business income loss is measured as the reduction in the insured's net income—the difference between expected net income had no loss occurred and actual net income after the loss. The causes of loss are often the same as for direct property losses. A business income loss can sometimes be more devastating for an insured than the associated property loss.

Two ISO business income forms are available: (1) the Business Income (and Extra Expense) Coverage Form and (2) the Business Income (Without Extra Expense) Coverage Form. These forms differ only with respect to their coverage for extra expense coverage. The business income and extra expense form covers certain extra expenses regardless of whether they reduce the business income loss. The business income without extra expense form covers extra expenses only to the extent that they reduce the business income loss.

Either business income coverage form (BIC) can be included in a commercial property coverage part. The BIC pays the actual loss of business income because of a suspension of "operations" during a "period of restoration."

The period of restoration begins seventy-two hours after the start of the direct physical loss—in effect, a "three-day deductible." This waiting period can be reduced to twenty-four hours or eliminated by endorsement. The suspension must have resulted from direct physical loss or damage to real or personal property caused by a covered cause of loss and occurring at the insured premises.

Business income, as defined in the form, is the net profit or loss that would have been earned or incurred if the suspension had not happened plus any normal operating expenses that must continue. Certain extra expenses may also be covered. The additional coverage for extended business income (EBI) lengthens the period of recovery to up to thirty days after the property is restored.

The amount of a business income loss is determined based on (1) the net income of the business before the loss, (2) the probable net income if no loss had occurred, (3) continuing operating expenses, and (4) other relevant sources of information that may be developed.

Four optional coverages are contained within the form and can be activated by an entry on the declarations page. The four coverages are maximum period of indemnity, monthly limit of indemnity, agreed value, and extended period of indemnity. The first three options allow the insured to avoid the coinsurance provisions of the form. The extended period of indemnity option allows the insured to extend EBI coverage to up to 730 days. In addition to the coverage options, many endorsements are available to modify the coverage to suit the exposures of the insured.

Rating business income coverage is similar to rating direct damage property insurance. The 80 percent coinsurance building rate is modified by business income rating factors that reflect (1) the type of business insured, (2) the coinsurance percentage chosen, and (3) any options or endorsements selected.

Chapter 5

Direct Your Learning

Commercial Crime Insurance

After learning the content of this chapter, you should be able to:

■ Explain whether a described loss would be covered under the ISO Commercial Crime Coverage Form.

- Identify the causes of loss, types of property, and locations that can be covered by the Commercial Crime Coverage Form and related endorsements.

- Describe the crime exclusions discussed in this assignment.

- Explain (1) when a loss must occur and (2) when a loss must be discovered in order for it to be covered under each of the following:

  - A "loss sustained" crime form

  - A "discovery" crime form

OUTLINE

ISO Commercial Crime Program

Financial Institution Bonds

Summary

Develop Your Perspective

What are the main topics covered in the chapter?

The main subject of this chapter is commercial crime coverage as designed for commercial and governmental entities other than financial institutions. The specialized crime forms that are used to insure banks, credit unions, and similar businesses are also described.

Consider the crime loss exposures facing businesses such as stores, manufacturers, and contractors.

- Which causes of crime loss are covered by the basic insuring agreements of the ISO Commercial Crime Coverage Form?

Why is it important to learn about these topics?

Crime losses take a huge financial toll on businesses. Many commercial property forms (such as the BPP) exclude money losses entirely, and the causes-of-loss forms exclude most criminal acts. Knowing which commercial crime coverage to choose and the coverage provided will help you understand why this coverage is an effective method of managing crime exposures.

Determine the crime loss exposures for two different types of businesses you know well.

- Identify the crime insuring agreements that address each loss exposure.
- How should crime coverage differ for each business based on the dissimilar loss exposures each faces?

How can you use what you will learn?

Examine several claim files for crime losses.

- Consider how each of the losses could have been prevented.
- If a loss was not covered under the policy, identify a crime insuring agreement that could have been used to cover the loss.

Chapter 5
Commercial Crime Insurance

The Federal Bureau of Investigation's Index of Crime shows that over 10 million crimes against property were reported in 1999. According to the U.S. Chamber of Commerce, employers may be losing $40 billion annually to employee theft. Other studies suggest this figure may be as high as $60 billion to $120 billion.[1] Clearly, crime is a serious exposure for individuals and businesses.

A *crime* is a violation of law punishable by government authority. To cope with the many criminal acts (such as vandalism or theft) that result in loss of or damage to property, organizations use a number of strategies. Among these strategies are loss avoidance (for example, paying employees by check or direct deposit instead of in cash), loss control (for example, burglar alarms and window gates), and insurance. This chapter will only discuss insurance, but other risk management techniques are important in managing crime exposures.

Many types of insurance provide coverage against some property losses resulting from criminal acts. For example, the basic, broad, and special causes-of-loss forms cover vandalism, riot, and civil commotion; the special causes-of-loss form covers theft; automobile insurance policies cover vehicle theft; and many forms of inland marine insurance cover theft. Nevertheless, insurance companies prefer to insure certain types of crime-related property loss under separate crime insurance forms. Insurers often prefer to underwrite (and rate) these exposures separately from other property exposures. Because crime loss exposures can vary significantly among policyholders and can involve specialized underwriting skills, insurers have devised specialized commercial crime insurance forms that allow an organization to cover many crime exposures that are not insured under its other insurance policies.

This chapter describes **commercial crime insurance**, using the ISO Commercial Crime Coverage Form and related endorsements as examples of these coverages. The chapter also briefly discusses financial institution bonds, which are used to insure banks, stockbrokers, insurance companies, and other financial institutions.

Commercial crime insurance
Insurance that covers (1) money and securities against numerous perils (not limited to crime perils) and (2) property other than money and securities against crime perils, such as employee theft, robbery, theft by outsiders, and extortion.

ISO COMMERCIAL CRIME PROGRAM

The ISO commercial crime program includes crime coverage forms that can be added to a commercial package policy and crime policy forms that can be written as monoline crime policies. The principal difference between the coverage forms and the policy forms is that the policy forms include the conditions contained in the Common Policy Conditions form (discussed in Chapter 1), thus eliminating the need to attach that form to a monoline crime policy.

Discovery form
Form that covers losses discovered during the policy period even though they may have occurred before the policy period.

Each coverage form and policy form comes in two versions: a "discovery form" and a "loss sustained form." Basically, a **discovery form** covers losses that are discovered during the policy period (even though they may have occurred earlier), and a **loss sustained form** covers losses that are actually sustained during the policy period and discovered no later than one year after the policy expires.

Loss sustained form
Form that covers losses actually sustained during the policy period and discovered no later than one year after policy expiration.

The ISO commercial crime coverage forms and policy forms are designed for insuring any type of nongovernment commercial or nonprofit entity other than financial institutions. A separate set of ISO government crime coverage forms and policy forms are used to insure government entities, such as states, counties, public utilities, fire districts, transit authorities, state universities, school districts, and boards of education. The ISO crime program also includes employee theft and forgery forms for insureds that wish to buy only (1) employee theft coverage or (2) forgery or alteration coverage or both. This chapter primarily discusses the loss sustained version of the Commercial Crime Coverage Form, which is the most commonly used of the ISO crime forms. (The declarations page of the Commercial Crime Coverage Form is shown in Exhibit 5-1.) The other forms and policies provide similar coverages. The differences between the loss sustained forms and the discovery forms and between the commercial and government forms are noted later in this chapter.

Basic Crime Insuring Agreements

The commercial crime form and policy are self-contained forms that contain seven insuring agreements. The insured may select one or more of these insuring agreements—or none at all, if the insured only wants coverage under another insuring agreement that is added by endorsement. The phrase "Not Covered" is inserted on the declarations page for those coverages that are not included. The seven insuring agreements are as follows:

1. Employee Theft
2. Forgery or Alteration
3. Inside the Premises—Theft of Money and Securities
4. Inside the Premises—Robbery or Safe Burglary of Other Property
5. Outside the Premises
6. Computer Fraud
7. Money Orders and Counterfeit Paper Currency

EXHIBIT 5-1

Advisory Commercial Crime Coverage Part Declarations

POLICY NUMBER:

COMMERCIAL CRIME
CR DS 01 03 00

ADVISORY COMMERCIAL CRIME COVERAGE PART
DECLARATIONS

The Commercial Crime Coverage Part consists of this Declarations Form and the Commercial Crime Coverage Form.

EMPLOYEE BENEFIT PLAN(S) INCLUDED AS NAMED INSUREDS: _____

_____

INSURING AGREEMENTS, LIMITS OF INSURANCE AND DEDUCTIBLES:

INSURING AGREEMENTS	LIMIT OF INSURANCE Per Occurrence	DEDUCTIBLE AMOUNT Per Occurrence
1. Employee Theft	$	$
2. Forgery Or Alteration		
3. Inside The Premises - Theft Of Money And Securities		
4. Inside The Premises - Robbery Or Safe Burglary Of Other Property		
5. Outside The Premises		
6. Computer Fraud		
7. Money Orders And Counterfeit Paper Currency		
If Added by Endorsement, Insuring Agreement(s):	$	$

If "Not Covered" is inserted above opposite any specified Insuring Agreement, such Insuring Agreement and any other reference thereto in this policy is deleted.

ENDORSEMENTS FORMING PART OF THIS COVERAGE PART WHEN ISSUED:

CANCELLATION OF PRIOR INSURANCE: By acceptance of this Coverage Part you give us notice cancelling prior policy Nos. _____

the cancellation to be effective at the time this Coverage Part becomes effective.

COUNTERSIGNED _____ BY: _____
(Date)   (Authorized Representative)

The sections that follow discuss all seven insuring agreements.

Employee Theft

Employee theft coverage
Coverage for the theft of money, securities, or other property committed by an insured's employee.

In general terms, **employee theft coverage** insures an employer against theft of the employer's property by its own employees. Exhibit 5-2 summarizes the key elements of employee theft coverage, and the discussion that follows provides a more complete description of the coverage.

EXHIBIT 5-2	
Summary of Employee Theft Coverage	
Cause of Loss	"Theft" committed by any "employee"
Property Covered	"Money," "securities," and "other property"
Where Coverage Applies	U.S. (including its territories and possessions), Puerto Rico, and Canada, plus ninety-day worldwide travel extension

The terms in quotation marks in Exhibit 5-2 are defined in the policy. These definitions are key to understanding the scope of coverage.

"Theft"

Theft
The unlawful taking of money, securities, or other property to the insured's deprivation.

The policy defines **theft** as follows:

> "Theft" means the unlawful taking of "money", "securities" or "other property" to the deprivation of the insured.

An unlawful act is one that is not authorized by law or is a violation of a civil or criminal law. A common misconception about the definition of employee theft is that proof of unlawful taking requires that the employee be convicted of a crime. In reality, the ISO forms do not even require that employee theft claims be reported to the police. The act must be unlawful, but the proof does not have to meet the standards needed to obtain a criminal conviction.

"Employee"

The policy definition of "employee" is much longer than the definition of "theft" and is only summarized here. According to the definition, a person must meet all three of the following criteria in order to be considered an employee.

1. The person must be currently employed by the insured or an ex-employee whose employment ended in the past thirty days.
2. The person must be compensated by the insured by salary, wages, or commissions.
3. The person must be subject to the control and direction of the insured.

The definition also includes "temps" (temporary personnel) furnished to the insured either to substitute for permanent employees who are on leave or to meet seasonal or short-term work load conditions. However, such temporary personnel are excluded while having care and custody of property outside the insured's premises.

The definition of employee specifically excludes leased employees. Leased employees are regular workers who are nominally employed by a labor-leasing firm but subject to day-to-day control by the insured firm that leases the workers. Also excluded are "any agent, broker, . . . factor, commission merchant, consignee, independent contractor or representative of the same general character." Standard endorsements are available to broaden the definition of employee to include leased employees, agents and their employees, noncompensated officers, volunteer workers, and others. Adding coverage for such individuals can be very important for some firms.

The definition of employee excludes the insured's corporate directors, managers (if the insured is a limited liability company), or trustees except while performing duties usual to an employee. Corporate officers who meet the criteria described above are employees.

Employee Dishonesty Versus Employee Theft

A number of crime coverage forms other than the ISO forms are used to cover commercial, non-profit, and government entities. For the most part, the forms are similar to the ISO forms discussed in this chapter. One important exception is employee dishonesty coverage. The prior crime program of ISO and the Surety Association of America, current American Association of Insurance Services (AAIS) forms, and many independently developed forms cover employee *dishonesty* instead of employee *theft*.

Employee dishonesty forms cover loss resulting from an employee's dishonest act. In and of itself, a "dishonest act" encompasses a broader range of offenses than "theft" as defined in the current ISO crime forms. To reduce this broad scope of coverage, employee dishonesty forms require that the employee must have acted with "manifest intent" (i.e., evident intent) to (1) cause a loss to the insured and (2) obtain financial benefit for the employee or for another person or entity that the employee wants to receive the benefit. This other person or entity might be a friend, a relative, or a favorite charity. The financial benefit must be something other than wages, commissions, or other employee benefits. Sometimes referred to as a "dual trigger," both elements of manifest intent must be present in order for coverage to apply. Because of the manifest intent requirement, the resulting coverage in the employee dishonesty forms is substantially the same as in employee theft forms.

"Money," "Securities," and "Other Property"

The employee theft insuring agreement covers loss of or damage to "money," "securities," and "other property." The policy definitions of these terms are paraphrased below.

- *Money* is defined as currency, coins, and bank notes in current use and having a face value; and travelers checks, register checks, and money orders held for sale to the public.

- *Securities* are defined as negotiable and nonnegotiable instruments or contracts representing either "money" or other property. Examples of securities include stocks, bonds, tokens, tickets, stamps in current use (including unused value in a postage meter), and evidences of debt issued in connection with charge or credit cards other than cards issued by the insured.

- *Other property* is defined as all tangible property, other than money and securities, that has intrinsic value and that the coverage form or policy does not otherwise exclude. "Tangible" is an important qualification. Dictionaries define tangible to mean "possible to touch." Copyrights, patents, intellectual property, and other intangible items can be very valuable and they are "property," but they are not *tangible* property, so they are not included as part of covered property.

Limit of Insurance

The most that the insurer will pay under the employee theft insuring agreement depends on the Limit of Insurance provision and the policy definition of "occurrence." For purposes of employee theft coverage, the definition of occurrence is "all loss caused by, or involving, one or more 'employees', whether the result of a single act or series of acts." According to the Limit of Insurance provision, the most that the insurer will pay for loss in any one occurrence is the limit of insurance shown in the declarations for employee theft. Thus, if the applicable limit of insurance is $50,000, the most the insurer would be required to pay for one embezzlement—regardless of how many employees might have been involved in the crime—is $50,000.

Note that the limit of liability applies to a single act *or a series of acts*. In one case, the bookkeeper of a small insurance agency embezzled $190,000 by pocketing cash receipts and inserting her name as payee on customers' checks in over 100 separate incidents. The agency had employee theft coverage with a limit of only $10,000. It claimed that the limit should be applied to each act, which would have enabled the agency to collect the full loss because no one incident involved more than $10,000. The insurer contended that it was all one series of acts and that the $10,000 limit was the most the insurer was liable to pay. The court sided with the insurer.[2]

Special Conditions

Two of the conditions contained in the commercial crime form are chiefly (if not exclusively) applicable to the employee theft insuring agreement. These two conditions are titled Cancellation as to Any Employee and Employee Benefit Plan(s). The commercial crime form also contains a territory condition that applies only to the employee theft insuring agreement. These three conditions are described below.

Cancellation as to Any Employee   This condition contains two distinct parts. The first part provides *automatic* cancellation of coverage with respect to any employee who has previously committed a dishonest act known to the insured or any partner, officer, director, or limited liability company (LLC) member or manager. This provision does not apply to knowledge possessed by partners, officers, directors, or LLC members or managers who are in collusion with the dishonest employee. The second part of the condition gives the insurer the right to cancel coverage with respect to any employee by providing thirty days' advance notice to the insured.

Employee Benefit Plans   This condition explains how employee theft coverage will apply when the policy includes one or more employee benefit plans as insureds under the employee theft insuring agreement. The condition eliminates the need for attaching the Employee Retirement Income Security Act of 1974 (ERISA) compliance endorsement to the policy to satisfy the fidelity bonding requirement of ERISA. To provide coverage, the plan must be named as an insured.

Territory   The employee theft insuring agreement is subject to a special extension of the coverage territory. This extension provides coverage for loss caused by any employee while temporarily outside the regular policy territory (the United States including its territories and possessions, Puerto Rico, and Canada) for a period of not more than ninety days. The many firms that have employees permanently located in other parts of the world must make special arrangements to obtain coverage, using either the standard endorsement, Amend Territorial Limits, or a nonstandard policy that provides the desired coverage territory.

Underinsured Employee Theft Losses

The difficulty of determining an adequate amount of employee theft insurance can result in insureds being severely underinsured for that exposure. Many insureds have an "It can't happen to me" attitude about employee theft and fail to appreciate the catastrophic loss potential. Case histories that involve firms large and small, for-profit and not-for-profit, may focus attention on the problem and help insureds realize the need for stringent controls and high limits for employee theft.

In one four-month period, newspapers carried the following stories:

- Just a week after a bookkeeper admitted stealing $150,000 from the Ohio Division of the American Cancer Society, the chief administrative officer was arrested and charged with fraud. He had wired $6.9 million from the Society's bank to his own account in Austria. (*The Columbus Dispatch*, June 9, 2000)

- A thirty-year employee of Harris Publishing Company was charged with stealing over $10 million by altering the payee on checks. She was a beloved figure in her hometown, known for her generosity to local charities. (*The New York Times*, August 5, 2000, p. B3)

Continued on next page.

- Starbucks lost $3.7 million to an employee who had worked for them for less than a year. She approved payments to a fictitious consulting firm that she and her husband had created. (*The Wall Street Journal*, September 20, 2000, p. B2)

- A church in Forest Hills, New York, is trying to find out what its retired priest did with $2 million that he apparently took from the weekly collections. Auditors became suspicious when they noticed that ledger records of the total amount collected had been erased and rewritten. (*The New York Times*, October 6, 2000, p. B1)

Forgery or Alteration

The forgery or alteration insuring agreement covers loss sustained by the insured because of:

> "forgery" or alteration of checks, drafts, promissory notes, or similar written promises, orders or directions to pay a sum certain in "money" that are

> **(1)** Made or drawn by or drawn upon you;

> **(2)** Made or drawn by one acting as your agent;

> or that are purported to have been so made or drawn.

The coverage responds to losses resulting from forgery or alteration of the *insured's* checks, drafts, etc., not to losses resulting from the insured's acceptance of forged checks, etc., of *others*. Forgery or alteration coverage is summarized in Exhibit 5-3.

EXHIBIT 5-3	
Summary of Forgery or Alteration Coverage	
Causes of Loss	"Forgery" and alteration
Property Covered	Checks, drafts, promissory notes, or similar instruments made or drawn by the insured or the insured's agent
Where Coverage Applies	Worldwide

Forgery
Signing the name of another person with intent to deceive.

Alteration
Something done to a written instrument that changes its meaning or terms without the consent of all parties to the instrument.

The form defines **forgery** as follows:

> "Forgery" means the signing of the name of another person or organization with intent to deceive; it does not mean a signature which consists in whole or in part of one's own name signed with or without authority, in any capacity, for any purpose.

Alteration is not defined in the policy and therefore takes its ordinary meaning: something that has been done to a written instrument that changes its meaning or terms without the consent of all parties to the instrument. An example of alteration is changing the amount of a check from $100 to $1,000.

Forgery or alteration coverage does not apply to loss resulting from dishonest acts of the insured, its partners, members, directors, trustees representatives, or employees. The employee theft insuring agreement will cover forgery or alteration committed against the insured by the insured's employees because it would be an unlawful taking to the detriment of the insured.

Endorsements are available for covering forgery or alteration of credit, debit, or charge cards; personal accounts of specified persons; and warehouse receipts and withdrawal orders.

Inside the Premises—Theft of Money and Securities

The insuring agreement titled Inside the Premises—Theft of Money and Securities covers money and securities inside the "premises" or a "banking premises" against an extremely broad scope of perils stated as **theft, disappearance, and destruction.**

Theft, disappearance, and destruction
A combination of covered causes of loss in some crime insuring agreements that provides an extremely broad scope of coverage.

The policy definition of theft, as discussed above, includes any type of "unlawful taking" of covered property "to the deprivation of the insured." Hence, an insured loss (subject to exclusions) can be caused by burglary, robbery, observed or unobserved theft, or any other unlawful taking of money or securities.

The addition of the words "disappearance and destruction" increases the scope of the coverage to include losses even when there is no unlawful act. For example, coverage is provided for money and securities that are destroyed in a fire. Disappearance is covered whether it is mysterious or not, and whether or not theft appears to be the cause of the disappearance. This broad scope of coverage is subject to several exclusions, described below. Inside the premises coverage for money and securities is summarized in Exhibit 5-4.

The insuring agreement covers loss of money and securities from within either the "premises" or "banking premises." "Premises" means the interior of that portion of any building the named insured occupies in conducting its business. "Banking premises" means the interior of that portion of any building occupied by a banking institution or similar safe depository.

The insuring agreement provides two extensions of the money and securities coverage, which apply to loss or damage to (1) the premises, if the insured is the owner or is liable for the damage, and (2) containers holding covered property caused by safe burglary or attempted safe burglary. These extensions are not additional amounts of insurance; any payment the insurer makes under these extensions is subject to the applicable limit of insurance.

EXHIBIT 5-4

Summary of Inside the Premises—Theft of Money and Securities Coverage

	Basic Coverage	Extension for Damage to Premises	Extension for Containers
Covered Causes of Loss	"Theft," disappearance, destruction	Actual or attempted "theft" of "money" or "securities"	Actual or attempted "theft" or unlawful entry
Covered Property	"Money," "securities"	The "premises" or their exterior	Locked safe, vault, cash register, cash box, or cash drawer
Where Coverage Applies	Inside the "premises" or "banking premises"	At the "premises"	Inside the "premises"

Inside the Premises—Robbery or Safe Burglary of Other Property

The fourth insuring agreement is titled Inside the Premises—Robbery or Safe Burglary of Other Property. Insuring agreement 3, discussed above, covers *money and securities* inside the premises; this insuring agreement covers *other property* inside the premises. Not only are different types of property covered by each insuring agreement, but the perils insured against by each insuring agreement are also different. Insuring agreement 3, covering money and securities, insures against theft, disappearance, or destruction, whereas the agreement for other property insures against only robbery and safe burglary. Inside the Premises—Robbery or Safe Burglary of Other Property coverage is summarized in Exhibit 5-5. Insureds that carry special-form property coverage do not need this coverage because the special form covers insured property against these and other perils.

Covered Causes of Loss

The covered causes of loss are (1) actual or attempted "robbery" of a "custodian" and (2) actual or attempted "safe burglary." These two perils are described below.

"Robbery" of a "Custodian"   The policy definition of **robbery** is as follows:

"Robbery" means the unlawful taking of property from the care and custody of a person by one who has:

a. Caused or threatened to cause that person bodily harm; or

b. Committed an obviously unlawful act witnessed by that person

Robbery
The unlawful taking of property from the care and custody of a person by one who has caused or threatened to cause that person bodily harm; includes situations in which the thief commits an obviously unlawful act that is witnessed by the custodian of the stolen property (such as an observed "smash and grab" theft from a shop window).

The taking of property is considered robbery if the person taking the property has caused or threatened to cause bodily harm to the person having care or custody of the property or if the custodian witnesses an obviously unlawful act, for example, seeing someone run out of the store with property that has not been paid for.

EXHIBIT 5-5

Summary of Inside the Premises—Robbery or Safe Burglary of Other Property Coverage

	Basic Coverage	Extension for Damage to Premises	Extension for Containers
Covered Causes of Loss	Actual or attempted "robbery" of a "custodian" or "safe burglary"	Actual or attempted "robbery" or "safe burglary" of "other property"	Actual or attempted "robbery" or "safe burglary"
Covered Property	"Other property"	The "premises" or their exterior	Locked safe or vault
Where Coverage Applies	Inside the "premises"	At the "premises"	Inside the "premises"

To be covered, the property must also be taken from someone who meets the policy definition of **custodian**, defined as follows:

> "Custodian" means you, or any of your partners or "members", or any "employee" while having care and custody of property inside the "premises", *excluding* [emphasis added] any person while acting as a "watchperson" or janitor.

A custodian may, for example, be a salesperson or cashier working inside the insured's store. The definition of custodian excludes any person while acting as a "watchperson" or janitor. The policy definition of watchperson is "any person you retain specifically to have care and custody of property inside the 'premises' and has no other duties." A janitor includes either a doorkeeper or a person who cleans or maintains the premises. Robbery of a watchperson can be added by endorsement.

Safe Burglary

The policy definition of **safe burglary**, the other peril covered by the insuring agreement, is as follows:

> "Safe burglary" means the unlawful taking of:
> a. Property from within a locked safe or vault by a person unlawfully entering the safe or vault as evidenced by marks of forcible entry upon its exterior; or
> b. A safe or vault from inside the "premises".

Custodian
The named insured, any of the named insured's partners or members, or the named insured's employee while having care and custody of the property inside the premises; excludes any person while acting as a watchperson or janitor.

Safe burglary
The unlawful taking of property from within a locked safe or vault by a person who unlawfully and forcibly enters the safe or vault; includes the unlawful taking of the entire safe or vault from inside the premises.

Marks of forcible entry into the *premises* are not required. The burglar might have hidden within the premises or entered into the premises through an unlocked door or window—but that has no bearing on coverage as long as the burglar leaves marks of forcible entry into the *safe or vault*. However, the insurer can add an endorsement that also requires visible signs of forcible entry to the premises if it feels that such a restriction is necessary to meet underwriting standards.

Coverage Extensions

The insuring agreement is subject to two coverage extensions. The first extension covers damage to the premises or their exterior resulting from actual or attempted robbery or safe burglary of "other property." The second extension covers loss of or damage to a locked safe or vault located inside the premises resulting from actual or attempted robbery or safe burglary. These extensions are not additional amounts of insurance; any payment the insurer makes under these extensions is subject to the applicable limit of insurance.

Special Limit of Insurance

Inside the Premises—Robbery or Safe Burglary of Other Property is subject to a special limit of $5,000 per occurrence for the following types of property:

(1) Precious metals, precious or semiprecious stones, pearls, furs, or completed or partially completed articles made of or containing such materials that constitute the principal value of such articles; or

(2) Manuscripts, drawings, or records of any kind or the cost of reconstructing them or reproducing any information contained in them.

Outside the Premises

The outside the premises insuring agreement covers money, securities, and other property while outside the premises and in the care and custody of either a "messenger" or an armored vehicle company. The policy definition of **messenger** is as follows:

Messenger
The named insured, a relative of the named insured, any of the named insured's partners or members, or any of the named insured's employees while having care and custody of property outside the insured premises.

> "Messenger" means you, or a relative of yours, or any of your partners or "members", or any "employee" while having care and custody of property outside the premises.

The principal difference between a custodian and a messenger is as follows:

• A custodian has care and custody of property *inside* the premises.

• A messenger has care and custody of property *outside* the premises.

A watchperson or janitor can be a messenger, but not a custodian. An employee taking cash and checks to the bank for deposit in the insured's account is an example of a messenger.

The perils insured against by the outside the premises insuring agreement vary with the type of property involved. Money and securities are covered against theft, disappearance, or destruction. Other property is covered against actual or attempted robbery.

Outside the premises coverage is subject to the same $5,000 special limit of insurance for certain types of property that applies to Inside the Premises—Robbery or Safe Burglary of Other Property, described above.

Even insureds who carry special-form property coverage and have no insurable money or securities exposure may need this coverage since the Building and Personal Property Coverage Form provides very little coverage for property away from the insured's premises. Exhibit 5-6 summarizes outside the premises coverage.

EXHIBIT 5-6

Summary of Outside the Premises Coverage

	Coverage for "Money" and "Securities"	Coverage for "Other Property"
Covered Causes of Loss	"Theft," disappearance, destruction	Actual or attempted "robbery"
Where Coverage Applies	Outside the "premises" while in care or custody of a "messenger" or an armored car company and inside the U.S. (including its territories and possessions), Puerto Rico, and Canada	Outside the "premises" while in care or custody of a "messenger" or an armored car company and inside the U.S. (including its territories and possessions), Puerto Rico, and Canada

---

Computer Fraud

The almost universal use of computer systems by businesses has increased the opportunities for using computers to commit fraud and other criminal acts. The computer fraud insuring agreement provides a way for organizations to insure against loss of money, securities, and other property caused by:

> the use of any computer to fraudulently cause a transfer of that property from inside the "premises" or "banking premises":
>
> a. To a person (other than a "messenger") outside those "premises"; or
> b. To a place outside those "premises".

Computer fraud coverage is summarized in Exhibit 5-7.

Computer fraud coverage
Coverage for loss of covered property due to using a computer to fraudulently transfer covered property to the wrongdoer.

EXHIBIT 5-7

Summary of Computer Fraud Coverage

Covered Cause of Loss	Use of a computer to fraudulently cause a transfer of covered property
Covered Property	"Money," "securities," and "other property"
Where Coverage Applies	The property must be transferred from inside the "premises" or a "banking premises" to a person or place anywhere else in the world

The insuring agreement does not require that the computers used to commit the fraud be the property of the insured or even that they be located on the insured's premises. Coverage would apply if a nonemployee, using his or her own computer, gained access to the insured's computer system and, for example, directed shipments of property to unauthorized parties or made unauthorized transfers from the insured's bank accounts by gaining access to the bank's computer system. The computer fraud insuring agreement does not cover computer-related theft committed by the insured's own employees because that exposure is insured under the employee theft insuring agreement.

Computer fraud coverage is subject to a $5,000 per occurrence sublimit for loss of or damage to manuscripts, drawings, or records of any kind, including the cost of reconstructing them. The cost of reproducing data stored on computer media can be insured for higher limits under an electronic data processing (EDP) equipment policy (discussed in Chapter 7).

Money Orders and Counterfeit Paper Currency

The money orders and counterfeit paper currency insuring agreement covers loss due to the insured's good-faith acceptance of the following:

- a. Money orders issued by any post office, express company or bank that are not paid upon presentation; or
- b. "Counterfeit" paper currency that is acquired during the regular course of business.

The insured must have accepted the money orders or counterfeit currency in exchange for merchandise, money, or services. Money orders and counterfeit paper currency coverage is summarized in Exhibit 5-8.

Many firms omit insuring agreement 4 (Inside the Premises—Robbery or Safe Burglary of Other Property) because they have comparable coverage in their special-form commercial property coverage. Many firms also prefer to retain their exposure to money orders and counterfeit paper currency instead of selecting insuring agreement 7. Of course, some firms may want these and other coverages available in the commercial crime insurance program.

EXHIBIT 5-8

Summary of Money Orders and Counterfeit Paper Currency Coverage

Covered Cause of Loss	Good-faith acceptance of: (1) money orders that are not paid upon presentation or (2) "counterfeit" paper currency
Covered Property	Money orders issued by any post office, express company, or bank; and "counterfeit" paper currency acquired during the regular course of business
Where Coverage Applies	U.S. (including its territories and possessions), Puerto Rico, and Canada

Crime Coverages for a Typical Firm

Many organizations do not buy all seven of the coverages that are included in the Commercial Crime Coverage Form. A typical firm might select the following crime coverages:

Coverage	Comments
Insuring Agreement 1: Employee Theft	Employee theft is a serious exposure for almost every firm.
Insuring Agreement 2: Forgery or Alteration	Forgery and alteration occur infrequently. However, because of its low cost, this coverage is almost always selected when employee theft coverage is purchased.
Insuring Agreement 3: Inside the Premises—Theft of Money and Securities	Almost all firms have some exposure to theft, disappearance, or destruction of money and/or securities within the premises.
Insuring Agreement 5: Outside the Premises	Insuring agreement 5 complements insuring agreement 3 by covering property outside the premises.
Insuring Agreement 6: Computer Fraud	The widespread use of computer networks has greatly increased the need for this coverage.
Fund Transfer Fraud Endorsement	Almost every firm of any size moves money between bank accounts by phone, fax, or other types of instructions and needs this coverage for fund transfer fraud committed by nonemployees. (Insuring agreement 1 covers employee fraud.) The fund transfer fraud endorsement is discussed later in this chapter.

Exclusions

The basic insuring agreements discussed above are subject to many exclusions. In these forms, the exclusions are divided into different groups depending on whether they apply to all insuring agreements or only to some insuring agreements. The exclusions are discussed below in the same groupings used in the forms.

General Exclusions

The seven exclusions described below are applicable to any of the crime insuring agreements.

Acts Committed by You, Your Partners or Your Members

The exclusion eliminates coverage for loss resulting from theft or any other dishonest act committed by the named insured, the named insured's partners, or (if the named insured is a limited liability company) the named insured's members, whether acting alone or in collusion with other persons.

Acts of Employees, Managers, Directors, Trustees or Representatives

Only the employee theft insuring agreement covers acts of employees. Other crime insuring agreements exclude theft or other dishonest acts committed by the named insured's employees, managers, directors, trustees, or authorized representatives. Consequently, the crime forms each contain an exclusion of such losses. The exclusion applies (1) whether such person was acting alone or in collusion with others and (2) while such person is performing services for the named insured or otherwise.

Government Action

Like virtually any policy covering property loss, the ISO crime forms exclude loss resulting from seizure or destruction of property by order of government authority.

Indirect Loss

The exclusion eliminates coverage for three types of loss that are not physical loss of or damage to covered property: (1) business income losses; (2) payment of damages for which the insured is legally liable (other than compensatory damages arising directly from a loss covered by the policy); and (3) expenses incurred in establishing either the existence or the amount of loss under the policy.

Legal Expenses

The policy excludes expenses related to any legal action, except when covered under the forgery and alteration insuring agreement.

Nuclear

The exclusion eliminates coverage for loss resulting from nuclear reaction, nuclear radiation, or radioactive contamination.

War and Similar Actions

The policy excludes war in all its various forms, declared or not, including insurrection, rebellion, or revolution.

Exclusions Applicable Only to Employee Theft

The exclusions described below apply only to the employee theft insuring agreement.

Employee Canceled Under Prior Insurance

The insurer will not pay for loss caused by an employee who was canceled under any similar prior insurance and not reinstated since that last time of cancellation.

Inventory Shortages

The insurer will not pay for any loss that depends on inventory or profit-and-loss calculations to prove either the existence or the amount of the loss. This exclusion is commonly referred to as the inventory shortages exclusion. An inventory shortage is the difference between a physical inventory and the inventory shown in the insured's books and records. The courts in many states have refused to enforce the part of the inventory shortages exclusion pertaining to the amount of loss. Accordingly, the current ISO inventory shortages exclusion states that "where you establish wholly apart from such computations that you have sustained a loss, then you may offer your inventory records and actual physical count of inventory in support of the amount of loss claimed."

Trading

The policy definition of theft might be held to include an employer's losses resulting from an employee's *unauthorized* trading in stocks, bonds, futures, commodities, or other similar items. Such losses can be catastrophic, and the rates for employee theft coverage do not contemplate them. Therefore, the ISO crime forms exclude "loss resulting directly or indirectly from trading, whether in [the named insured's] name or in a genuine or fictitious account." Coverage for trading losses that meet the criteria for employee theft can be added by endorsement.

Warehouse Receipts

The warehouse receipts exclusion eliminates coverage for "[l]oss resulting from fraudulent or dishonest signing, issuing, canceling or failing to cancel, a warehouse receipt or any papers connected with it." Such a loss might occur, for example, when an employee releases merchandise without canceling the receipt or issues a receipt without having received the merchandise. The customer could then make a claim for missing goods based on the erroneous receipts. Such claims would not be covered because of this exclusion.

Exclusions Applicable to Inside the Premises and Outside the Premises

The eight exclusions discussed below apply specifically to the following insuring agreements:

- Inside the Premises—Theft of Money and Securities
- Inside the Premises—Robbery or Safe Burglary of Other Property
- Outside the Premises

Accounting or Arithmetical Errors or Omissions

There is no coverage for losses resulting from accounting or arithmetical errors or omissions. Although many losses of this type are within the policy deductible, some losses could be sizable. The exposure falls within the general category of business risks that can be addressed by loss control measures, with any losses retained by the business.

Exchanges or Purchases

Loss due to giving or surrendering property in an exchange or purchase is excluded. Thus, a fraudulent transaction or confidence scam that involves the loss of money, securities, or other property is not covered.

Fire

The three insuring agreements do not cover loss resulting from fire, regardless of how the fire may be caused. However, the exclusion does not apply to fire damage to a safe or vault. The exclusion also does not apply (under "inside the premises" coverage for money and securities) to money or securities damaged or destroyed by fire. Nearly all organizations have commercial property insurance to cover the fire losses that the crime form excludes.

Money Operated Devices

Loss of property from money operated devices (such as vending machines, amusement devices, or change machines) is not covered *unless* a continuous recording instrument inside the machine keeps track of the amount of money deposited. In the absence of a recording device, establishing the amount of the loss would be difficult or impossible.

Motor Vehicles or Equipment and Accessories

There is no coverage for loss of or damage to motor vehicles, trailers, or semi-trailers; or equipment and accessories attached to them. Theft of automobiles and related equipment can be insured under automobile physical damage coverage, and theft of mobile equipment can be insured under inland marine forms.

Transfer or Surrender of Property

This exclusion addresses two exposures that involve transfer or surrender of property to someone outside the premises.

- The first exposure involves transfer or surrender of property to someone on the basis of unauthorized instructions.
- The second exposure involves surrendering property as the result of a threat to do bodily harm to a person or to damage or destroy property, sometimes referred to as kidnapping or extortion.

Unauthorized instructions losses that involve computer fraud can be insured under the computer fraud insuring agreement. Some extortion losses can be covered by endorsement.

Vandalism

As noted earlier, coverage extensions cover (1) damage to the premises and their exterior and (2) loss of or damage to various types of receptacles containing covered property, if directly caused by a covered peril. However, the vandalism exclusion eliminates coverage for damage to those types of property by vandalism or malicious mischief. Commercial property forms normally include coverage for damage to such property by vandalism or malicious mischief, including building damage caused by the breaking in or exiting of burglars.

Voluntary Parting With Title to or Possession of Property

The purpose of the voluntary parting exclusion is to eliminate coverage when the insured or an agent of the insured is tricked into *voluntarily* handing over property to a thief. For example, suppose a businessowner tells the firm's cashier that a bank messenger is to pick up money at a given time each day. If a wrongdoer impersonates the messenger and succeeds in getting the cashier to hand over the money *voluntarily*, the loss would not be covered by Inside the Premises—Theft of Money and Securities.

Crime Policy Conditions

The crime form includes numerous policy conditions that apply to all insuring agreements. Not all of the conditions are discussed in this chapter. Concealment, misrepresentation or fraud; legal action against us; liberalization; and loss covered under more than one coverage of this insurance are identical to the conditions with the same titles that were discussed in previous chapters. Two of the conditions—Cancellation as to Any Employee and Employee Benefit Plans—were discussed in the section dealing with employee theft. Other conditions apply only to certain insuring agreements; where pertinent, these conditions have been mentioned in the discussion of those insuring agreements. The remaining conditions, although listed alphabetically in the form, are presented here in logical order to facilitate discussion and understanding.

Interests Insured

The following conditions help to clarify issues concerning the interests insured under a crime policy.

Ownership of Property—Interests Covered

The insurance applies only to property owned or held by the named insured or for which the named insured is legally liable, but there is no legal liability coverage for property within a client's premises. Coverage for theft by the insured's employee of property within clients' premises may be added by endorsement. The insurance is for the benefit of the named insured only.

Joint Insured

The joint insured condition appoints the first named insured as agent for all other insureds with regard to all transactions under the policy. It also provides that an employee of any insured is considered to be an employee of every insured and that knowledge possessed by any insured or any partner, officer, or LLC member of any insured is considered to be known to all insureds.

Consolidation—Merger

If the insured acquires additional employees or premises by consolidation or merger, policy coverage will be extended automatically to the new employees or premises. The insured must notify the insurer of the acquisition within ninety days and pay the appropriate additional premium.

Where Coverage Applies

Many of the crime insuring agreements limit coverage to occurrences that take place inside the premises described in the policy. When coverage is not restricted to the premises, the "territory" provision defines the geographical scope of coverage. This provision limits coverage for all insuring agreements to acts committed or events occurring within the United States (including its territories and possessions), Puerto Rico, and Canada. The territorial provision for employee theft coverage is extended to include coverage for loss caused by employees temporarily outside the coverage territory for not more than ninety days; this was discussed in the employee theft section.

When Coverage Applies

Several conditions, described below, are principally concerned with determining when a loss must occur in order to be covered under the loss sustained version of the Commercial Crime Coverage Form.

Loss Sustained and Extended Period to Discover Loss

Under the loss sustained form, the insurer will pay for loss that the named insured sustains through acts committed or events occurring during the policy period. Moreover, coverage applies only to acts discovered during the policy period or within the period that ends one year after the policy is terminated or cancelled. However, the **extended period to discover loss** terminates immediately upon the effective date of any other insurance that the insured obtains that replaces coverage in whole or in part.

> **Extended period to discover loss**
> A specified period following policy expiration providing coverage for loss first discovered during this period if the loss occurred before policy expiration.

Discovery Form

As mentioned earlier, all of the ISO crime forms come in loss sustained and discovery versions. The loss sustained coverage trigger was just discussed. To recap, the loss sustained form covers loss that occurs during its policy period and is discovered within the one-year discovery period that applies to the loss sustained form. In contrast, the discovery form covers losses no matter when they occurred if they are first discovered during the policy period or during the sixty-day discovery period that applies to most claims under the discovery form. (The discovery form allows a one-year discovery period for losses to employee benefit plans.)

To limit the broad coverage for prior occurrences that discovery forms provide, the insurer may attach a **retroactive date endorsement**. This endorsement provides that coverage is limited to losses the insured sustains through acts committed or events occurring after the retroactive date shown in the policy schedule. In order for coverage to apply, the loss must still be discovered during the policy period or the extended loss discovery period.

> **Retroactive date endorsement**
> Endorsement that modifies the discovery form by limiting coverage to losses the insured incurs because of acts committed or events occurring after the policy's retroactive date.

Loss Sustained During Prior Insurance

Some losses occurring before the current policy period of a loss sustained crime policy may be covered by the policy currently in effect. Under the Loss Sustained During Prior Insurance condition, which is found in the loss sustained form but not in the discovery form, the insurer agrees to pay a loss that meets all of the following criteria:

1. The loss occurred while prior insurance was in effect.
2. The insured could have recovered the loss under the prior insurance except that the discovery period in that policy has expired.
3. The current insurance became effective when the prior insurance was canceled or terminated.
4. The loss would have been covered by the present insurance if the insurance had been in force at the time of loss.

If all four of these requirements are met, the insurer will pay the *lesser* of the amount recoverable under (1) the present insurance or (2) the prior insurance, if it had remained in effect.

Loss Covered Under This Insurance and Prior Insurance Issued by Us or Any Affiliate

Sometimes a covered loss occurs over a period of time that spans more than one policy period. This is especially common with employee theft losses, in which an employee may embezzle funds for several years before the employer discovers the loss. The condition under discussion states that if any loss is covered partly by this insurance and partly by prior cancelled or terminated insurance issued by the same or an affiliated insurer, the most that the insurer will pay is the larger amount recoverable under the current or prior insurance. *No limit of insurance accumulates from year to year.* A policy in force ten years with a $50,000 limit will pay a maximum of $50,000 for any one covered loss, not ten times $50,000. This condition is important to consider when selecting the amount of insurance for employee theft coverage. A dishonest employee often steals smaller amounts on numerous occasions spread over many years that, in total, add up to serious losses. This condition is found in the loss sustained form only; it is not needed in the discovery form because the discovery form covers loss, regardless of when it occurred, that is discovered during the current policy period.

Claims Provisions

The provisions described below set forth the procedures and practices to be used following a loss involving covered property.

Duties After Loss, Records

The insured's duties after loss under a crime policy are essentially the same as under other property policies. After discovering a loss or a situation that may result in a loss, the insured must do the following:

1. Notify the insurer as soon as possible and, except for employee theft and forgery and alteration losses, notify the police if the insured believes that the loss involves a violation of law.
2. Submit to examination under oath if requested by the insurer.
3. Submit a detailed, sworn proof of loss within 120 days.
4. Cooperate with the insurer in its investigation of the loss.

The separate Records condition requires the insured to keep sufficient records to enable the insurer to verify the amount of loss.

Valuation—Settlement

The value of a covered loss is determined differently for each of the three categories of covered property:

- Money is valued at its face value. If foreign money is lost, the insurer has the option of paying for the loss at the face value of the money or at its equivalent U.S. value on the date the loss is discovered.
- Securities are valued as of the close of business on the day the loss is discovered. In many cases, duplicate securities can be issued if the insured

posts a bond. The insurer will pay the cost of the bond as part of the loss. The insurer has the option of paying the value of lost securities or replacing them in kind. If securities are replaced, the insured must assign to the insurer all rights, title, and interest in the lost securities.

- If property other than money and securities is lost or damaged, the insurer has the option of paying the replacement cost of the property, repairing the property, or replacing it. If the property is not promptly repaired or replaced as soon after the loss or damage as possible, the insurer will pay the loss on an actual cash value basis.

Recoveries

The Recoveries condition specifies how any subrogation or salvage recoveries will be divided between the insurer and the insured. First the insurer is entitled to the expense of recovery from the recovered property. Then, the insured is reimbursed for any loss greater than the limit of insurance plus the deductible. If any amount of the recovery is left, it goes to the insurer until the insurer has recovered all that it paid. Finally, any remaining value goes to the insured to reimburse it for the deductible amount.

Transfer of Your Rights Against Others

Like most insurance policies, the crime general provisions include a subrogation provision. For any loss the insurance company pays to the insured, the insured must transfer its rights of recovery against others to the insurance company. Moreover, the insured must do nothing *after* loss to impair those rights. (The insured is permitted to waive its rights of action against other parties if the waiver is made *before* loss occurs.)

Other Insurance

The Other Insurance provision states that the insurance will apply as excess coverage over any other insurance available to the insured to cover a loss. Often the other policy will have a similar clause. When two or more policies cover a loss and all policies purport to be excess over other insurance, the courts usually require the insurers to contribute on a pro rata basis if the insurers are unable to agree on a mutually acceptable method.

Endorsements

ISO has filed numerous endorsements for use with its commercial crime forms. The previous ISO/Surety Association of America (SAA) commercial crime program used many more coverage forms, designated by letters A through R. For example, Form A was employee dishonesty, Form F was computer fraud, and Form R was money orders and counterfeit paper currency. Except for employee dishonesty coverage, which was replaced by employee theft coverage, endorsements in the new program can provide coverage similar to all the other coverages in the previous program that are not among the seven insuring agreements in the new coverage form. In addition, some of the endorsements in the new program provide options that were not previously available.

A few of the more important endorsements available in the ISO program are listed and briefly described in Exhibit 5-9. Refer to the forms for complete terms and conditions.

Government Crime Forms

Because of the differing exposures of government units and coverage requirements imposed by some state or local laws, ISO has developed separate government crime forms. They are very similar to the commercial crime forms except that they have eight insuring agreements instead of seven. The additional insuring agreement is a second employee theft insuring agreement offering "per employee coverage." Some of the differences are summarized below.

- Each government crime form contains two employee theft insuring agreements. One of these insuring agreements provides "per loss coverage," and the other provides "per employee coverage." With per loss coverage, the applicable limit of insurance applies *per loss*; with per employee coverage, the limit applies *per employee*.

- The government crime forms contain two additional exclusions that are not included in the commercial crime forms. These exclusions eliminate coverage for loss caused by (1) any employee required by law to be individually bonded or (2) any treasurer or tax collector. Some insurers will eliminate these exclusions by endorsement. Coverage is also available under surety bonds designed specifically for public officials.

- Faithful performance of duty coverage can be added to government crime policies by endorsement. The endorsement broadens employee theft coverage to include loss "resulting directly from the failure of any 'employee' to faithfully perform his or her duties as prescribed by law."

- In the government crime forms, the policy territory for employee theft coverage does not include Canada except for coverage under the ninety-day worldwide travel extension for employee theft.

- The condition dealing with cancellation as to any employee is modified in the government forms. In those forms, insurance for any employee who has committed theft or any other dishonest act is canceled immediately upon discovery of the theft or other dishonest act by the insured *or any official or employee authorized to manage, govern, or control the insured's employees*.

- The government crime forms contain an indemnification condition, not found in the commercial crime forms. The indemnification condition states that the insurer will indemnify any of the insured's officials who are required by law to provide faithful performance bonds against loss resulting from theft committed by employees who serve under these officials.

EXHIBIT 5-9

Commercial Crime Form Endorsements

Endorsement Title	Description and Comments
Employee Theft—Name or Position Schedule	Covers employee theft by only those employees who are specifically identified by name (John Wilson) or by position (bookkeeper). This coverage is obviously more restricted than insuring agreement 1. It is sometimes used by smaller firms or those that feel that only a few employees pose an employee theft risk.
Inside the Premises—Theft of Other Property	Covers theft of property other than money and securities inside the premises. This endorsement provides broader coverage than insuring agreement 4, which provides only robbery and safe burglary coverage.
Inside the Premises—Robbery or Safe Burglary of Money and Securities	Covers loss of money and securities by robbery or safe burglary. This is more restrictive coverage than the "theft, disappearance or destruction" coverage provided by insuring agreement 3.
Inside the Premises—Robbery or Burglary of Other Property	Covers loss of property other than money and securities by robbery of a watchperson or by burglary of the premises. The policy defines **burglary** as the taking of property from inside a building by unlawful entry into or unlawful exit from the building, evidenced by visible signs of forcible entry or exit.
Clients' Property	Covers theft, committed by the insured's employees, of clients' property within clients' premises. A useful coverage for cleaning services and other firms that have employees who work within clients' premises.
Funds Transfer Fraud	Covers loss of money and securities by fraudulent electronic, telephonic, telefacsimile, telegraphic, cable, or teletype instructions from the insured's account at a financial institution.
Extortion—Commercial Entities	Covers loss due to surrender of money, securities, or other property as a result of (1) a threat of bodily harm to an employee, director, trustee, partner, member, manager, or proprietor; or (2) a threat to do damage to the insured's premises. (Similar coverage is also available for governmental organizations.)

Burglary
The taking of property from inside a building by unlawful entry into or exit from the building; signs of forcible entry or exit must be visible.

FINANCIAL INSTITUTION BONDS

Financial institution bond
A policy that covers the crime loss exposures of financial institutions such as banks, savings and loan institutions, and insurance companies.

Few industries have crime loss exposures equal to those faced by financial institutions. Insurance for those exposures is provided by **financial institution bonds** developed by the Surety Association of America (SAA). These insurance policies are called "bonds" because one of the key coverages that they provide is employee dishonesty insurance, which was traditionally called a "fidelity bond."

Although banks may readily come to mind as an example of financial institutions, other entities—such as savings and loan associations, credit unions, stockbrokers, finance companies, and even insurance companies—are also eligible to be insured under financial institution bonds. Entities eligible for financial institution bonds are not eligible for the ISO forms discussed earlier in this chapter.

The most widely used financial institution bond is Standard Form No. 24, used to insure banks and savings and loan associations. For many years, this form was called the "bankers blanket bond," a name that is still often used informally to refer to this coverage. Form 24 includes six insuring agreements, as listed below. Agreements D and E are optional. Several additional coverages, such as computer fraud, can be added by endorsement.

A. Fidelity
B. On Premises
C. In Transit
D. Forgery or Alteration
E. Securities
F. Counterfeit Currency

The forms used for the other types of financial institutions are similar to Form 24.

SUMMARY

A *crime* is a violation of law punishable by government authority. Property loss or damage caused by crimes can be insured under many types of policies. However, crime insurance is the principal source of coverage for loss of money and securities and losses caused by employee theft. Crime insurance policies can also provide coverage for losses caused by other perils, such as robbery, burglary, and theft.

Numerous versions of crime insurance are available, but all cover essentially the same exposures. This chapter has primarily looked at ISO crime forms, which can be used in either monoline or commercial package policies.

ISO has filed a commercial crime form (used for all entities, including nonprofits, other than governmental organizations and financial institutions) and a government crime form. In addition, a separate employee theft and forgery form is available for firms that want only those coverages. All three forms exist in stand-alone policy and modular form formats as well as in discovery and loss sustained versions.

The ISO commercial crime coverage form contains seven insuring agreements, as listed below. Reviewing the exhibits in this chapter that summarize these insuring agreements will help you to remember the causes of loss, the types of property, and the locations covered.

1. Employee Theft
2. Forgery or Alteration
3. Inside the Premises—Theft of Money and Securities
4. Inside the Premises—Robbery or Safe Burglary of Other Property
5. Outside the Premises
6. Computer Fraud
7. Money Orders and Counterfeit Paper Currency

Numerous endorsements can be added to the policy, including the following: Employee Theft—Name or Position Schedule; Inside the Premises—Theft of Other Property; Inside The Premises—Robbery or Safe Burglary of Money and Securities; Inside The Premises—Robbery or Burglary of Other Property; Clients' Property; Funds Transfer Fraud; and Extortion.

ISO government crime forms resemble the commercial crime forms. However the government forms include two employee theft insuring agreements, one providing per employee coverage, the other providing per loss coverage. A number of other provisions are slightly changed to reflect the differences in governmental organizations or to conform to state and local laws.

For both commercial and governmental insureds, loss sustained forms are the most commonly used. Loss sustained forms require that the loss occur during the policy period and be discovered no later than one year after the termination of coverage. In order to provide continuity of protection, the policy covers loss sustained during prior insurance if certain conditions are met.

A discovery form covers losses no matter when they occurred if they are first discovered during the policy period or during the sixty-day discovery period of this form. (A one-year discovery period applies to employee benefit plans.) A retroactive date endorsement can limit coverage to losses that occurred after a certain date.

Financial institutions—such as banks, stockbrokers, and insurance companies—are insured under financial institution bonds developed by SAA. The most widely used is Form 24, which insures banks and savings and loan associations. The forms used for the other types of financial institutions are similar.

CHAPTER NOTES

1. Joan Jakel, "Fraud in the Workplace: Eliminate Employee Theft From Your Bottom Line," *Looking Fit*, April 2000. http://www.lookingfit.com/articles/041feat4.html.

2. American Commerce Insurance Brokers, Inc. v. Minnesota Mutual Fire and Casualty Co., Minn. Ct App. NoC 9-94-499, 8/1/95. The court ruled that the claim should be treated as two series of acts, one being the theft of cash receipts and the other being the altering of the checks. The important point is that the agency had a $190,000 loss involving over 100 separate acts but collected only $20,000 because of the series-of-acts limitation.

Direct Your Learning

OUTLINE

Insuring Agreements

Exclusions

Limits of Insurance

Conditions

Summary

Equipment Breakdown Insurance

After learning the content of this chapter, you should be able to:

■ Explain whether a described loss would be covered under the Equipment Breakdown Protection Coverage Form.

- Explain why equipment breakdown insurance is often needed in addition to building and personal property insurance.

- Describe the coverages that can be provided in an equipment breakdown policy.

- Describe the types of exclusions typically found in equipment breakdown policies.

- Explain the conditions unique to equipment breakdown policies.

Develop Your Perspective

What are the main topics covered in the chapter?

This chapter describes equipment breakdown insurance, which covers the various types of loss (physical damage, loss of business income, extra expense, and so forth) that can result from the accidental breakdown of covered equipment.

Imagine that you are the owner of an apartment building or a small retail store.

- How might you benefit from equipment breakdown insurance?

Why is it important to learn about these topics?

Equipment breakdown insurance covers exposures that are excluded from commercial property causes-of-loss forms. Knowing the coverages available under equipment breakdown insurance will help you understand how this type of insurance supplements the commercial property causes-of-loss forms, why many organizations need this form of insurance, and what types of loss exposures this insurance covers.

Review the categories of equipment included in the definition of "covered equipment."

- In addition to the "covered equipment" itself, what other property does an equipment breakdown policy cover?

How can you use what you will learn?

Tour your office or office building and identify all the equipment.

- Which items would be considered "covered equipment" under an equipment breakdown policy?

- Analyze the severity of loss—slight, moderate, or high—that could result from a breakdown to each piece of equipment you identified. (Do not overlook business income!)

Chapter 6
Equipment Breakdown Insurance

Equipment breakdown insurance—traditionally called boiler and machinery insurance—covers loss resulting from the accidental breakdown of almost any type of equipment that operates under pressure or that controls, transmits, transforms, or uses mechanical or electrical power. Some common examples of such equipment are steam boilers and other pressure vessels; electrical generating and transmitting equipment; pumps, compressors, turbines, engines; air conditioning and refrigeration systems; production machinery used in manufacturing operations; and all types of electrically powered office equipment such as copiers, computers, and telephone systems.

The types of equipment listed above are covered property under the Building and Personal Property Coverage Form (BPP), but the BPP covers the equipment only with regard to the perils insured against by the causes-of-loss forms used with the BPP. The commercial property causes-of-loss forms exclude electrical breakdown, mechanical breakdown, and steam boiler explosion, all of which can damage such equipment and sometimes the other property around it. Equipment breakdown insurance can be used to fill this gap, covering physical damage to both the covered equipment and other property of the insured that results from the accidental breakdown of covered equipment. Equipment breakdown insurance can also be used to cover business income, extra expense, and other consequential losses resulting from such physical damage. Exhibit 6-1 provides examples of equipment breakdown losses.

Although a relatively small line of insurance, equipment breakdown insurance is important for businesses of all sizes. Few insurers have the expertise to underwrite and provide risk control services for equipment breakdown coverage independently, but many insurers provide it in their package policies through reinsurance arrangements with insurers that specialize in equipment breakdown coverage.

The inspection and risk control services provided by equipment breakdown insurers are an important part of the insurer's services. It is not unusual for an insurer's inspection expenses for equipment breakdown coverage to equal or exceed its loss payments.

Insurance Services Office and the American Association of Insurance Services both file equipment breakdown coverage forms for the use of their member insurers. The development of the ISO and AAIS forms was influenced by the forms used by the Hartford Steam Boiler Group (HSB), a member of the American International Group, which writes the largest share of the equipment

Equipment breakdown insurance
Insurance that covers loss due to the accidental breakdown of almost any type of equipment that operates under pressure or that controls, transmits, or uses mechanical or electrical power.

breakdown market in the United States. The other leading writers of equipment breakdown coverage use forms that they have developed independently, but that are generally similar. The discussion that follows is based on the ISO Equipment Breakdown Protection Coverage Form.

EXHIBIT 6-1

Examples of Equipment Breakdown Losses

Steam boiler explosions can cause extensive damage not only to the boiler itself but to the building that houses it. In one case, a heating boiler in a telephone company switching office exploded and tore through the roof, leaving the building looking as if it had been struck by a missile.

Boilers can sustain serious damage as a result of malfunction even when they don't explode. Severe overheating of a boiler in a factory, caused by low-water conditions in the boiler, resulted in damage to the furnace tubes and a portion of the rear tube sheet. The physical damage loss was $27,000, and the business income loss was $30,000.

Although boiler explosions provided the original impetus for equipment breakdown coverage, other types of equipment can suffer serious damage in many other ways. Some examples follow.

- A short-circuit in the aluminum bus (an electrical conductor) in an apartment building caused extensive damage to the building's electrical cables and wiring. Residents were temporarily relocated. The physical damage loss was $120,000, and the extra expense loss was $72,000.

- The rotating cylinder door assembly of a 400-pound commercial washing machine opened during the extract cycle, damaging the basket and inner and outer shells. The cost to repair the physical damage amounted to $61,000.

- A portion of an air conditioning compressor became detached and fell into the evaporator, puncturing several tubes. The cooling water from the tubes contaminated the refrigerant and caused severe damage to the driving motor windings. The loss amounted to $45,000.

- Voltage fluctuation caused two terminal boards in an office building's phone computer to short-circuit. The resulting loss amounted to $52,000.

These loss examples are adapted, with permission, from *Whistle Stop*, a publication of The Hartford Steam Boiler Inspection and Insurance Company, Hartford, Conn.

INSURING AGREEMENTS

The ISO Equipment Breakdown Protection Coverage Form contains ten insuring agreements. The coverages that apply in a particular policy are those that are indicated on the declarations page by either a limit of insurance or the word "included." If neither a limit nor "included" is shown, then that coverage does not apply. Several of the coverage agreements might be more aptly described as coverage extensions rather than basic coverages.

The covered cause of loss in the Equipment Breakdown Protection Coverage Form is a "breakdown" to "covered equipment." The prior ISO Boiler and Machinery Equipment Coverage Form and some independently developed equipment breakdown policies use the terminology "accident" to an "object" instead of "breakdown" to "covered equipment." Despite the difference in wording, the coverage definitions of these alternative terms are similar.

The ISO equipment breakdown form defines **breakdown** to mean direct physical loss that causes damage to covered equipment and necessitates its repair or replacement as a result of any of the following:

Breakdown
A direct physical loss to covered equipment that necessitates its repair or replacement due to failure of pressure equipment, mechanical failure, or electrical failure.

- Failure of pressure or vacuum equipment
- Mechanical failure including rupture or bursting caused by centrifugal force
- Electrical failure, including arcing

Various exclusions apply to the definition of "breakdown," such as leakage, defects, or viruses in computer equipment and programs, damage to vacuum or gas tubes, and damage to foundations or structures supporting the equipment.

The policy definition of **covered equipment** is very broad, and includes the following types of equipment:

Covered equipment
Includes pressurized equipment, electrical or mechanical equipment, communication and computer equipment, and other specified equipment.

- Equipment built to operate under internal pressure or vacuum
- Electrical or mechanical equipment used in the generation, transmission, or utilization of energy
- Communication and computer equipment

This definition is broad enough to encompass all of the types of property listed in the introduction to this chapter, as well as some additional types that insurers are generally not willing to insure under equipment breakdown policies. Accordingly, the definition excludes various types of property that are outside the intended scope of coverage. The list of excluded property includes, but is not limited to, the following: computer media; vehicles, aircraft, and vessels (including any attached equipment); excavation or construction equipment; parts and tools subject to periodic replacement (such as brake pads); medical diagnostic equipment; and equipment manufactured by the named insured for sale.

Each of the ten insuring agreements of the ISO equipment breakdown form is listed below and described in the sections that follow.

Ten Insuring Agreements of the ISO Equipment Breakdown Form

- Property damage
- Expediting expenses
- Business income and extra expense
- Spoilage damage
- Utility interruption
- Newly acquired premises
- Ordinance or law
- Errors and omissions
- Brands and labels
- Contingent business income and extra expense

Property Damage

Under property damage coverage, the insurer agrees to pay for direct damage to "covered property." The policy definition of covered property differs from, and is much broader than, the policy definition of covered equipment. Covered property means (1) property that the named insured owns or (2) property that is in the named insured's care, custody, or control and for which the named insured is legally liable. In either case, the property must be situated at a location described in the declarations.

Thus, breakdown property damage coverage insures loss to a much broader description of property than "covered equipment." The purpose of equipment breakdown coverage is not merely to cover damage to the covered equipment but also to cover damage to other property that results from accidents to the covered equipment. For example, as illustrated in Exhibit 6-2, a steam boiler explosion might not only destroy the steam boiler but also damage the building in which the steam boiler is contained and the contents of the building. The commercial property causes-of-loss forms would cover none of this damage because they all exclude damage resulting from steam boiler explosion.

EXHIBIT 6-2

Building Damage Caused by Boiler Explosion

Courtesy of The Hartford Steam Boiler Inspection and Insurance Company, Hartford, Conn.

Covered Equipment Versus Covered Property

"Covered equipment" and "covered property," two terms that are key to understanding equipment breakdown insurance, can be easily confused. Covered property is a much broader classification than covered equipment. All covered equipment is covered property.

Breakdown to covered *equipment* triggers coverage for damage to covered *property*. The covered property damaged might include items that are specifically excluded from the definition of covered equipment. However, breakdown to items that are not covered equipment does not trigger any coverage under an equipment breakdown policy.

Equipment breakdown insurance also fills a gap with respect to property of others in the insured's care, custody, or control for which the insured is legally liable. Although most insureds have commercial general liability (CGL) coverage, the CGL form *excludes* liability for damage to (1) personal property in the insured's care, custody, or control and (2) real or personal property that the insured rents or occupies. Equipment breakdown coverage fills this gap when the liability for such property arises out of equipment breakdown at a location described in the declarations.

Unlike commercial property forms, the ISO equipment breakdown form does not include any coinsurance provision applicable to property damage coverage; a coinsurance provision is only found in the business income and extra expense coverage discussed below. Some non-ISO equipment breakdown forms do provide the option for coinsurance to apply to coverages other than business income and extra expense, but that option is seldom used.

Equipment breakdown policies generally do not contain a separate provision dealing with debris removal. Debris removal is covered as part of the property damage limit.

Explosion of Pressure Vessel—What's Covered?

The violent explosion of a steam boiler in Acme Manufacturing Company's factory caused the following losses:

1. Destruction of the boiler
2. Damage to Acme's building
3. Damage to Acme's business personal property
4. Damage to a customer's patterns in Acme's possession
5. Damage to the building of a neighboring firm
6. Bodily injury to some of Acme's employees

Because the explosion was an "accident" to "covered equipment," Acme's equipment breakdown insurance would cover items 1, 2, 3, and 4.

Continued on next page.

Acme's equipment breakdown insurance would not cover damage to the neighboring firm's building (item 5). Equipment breakdown insurance does not cover property of others unless it is in the insured's care, custody, or control at a described location.

Acme's equipment breakdown insurance also would not cover item 6, because such insurance does not cover bodily injury of any kind. Instead, Acme's responsibility for injury to its own employees would be covered under Acme's workers compensation insurance.

Expediting Expenses

Expediting expenses coverage
Coverage for the reasonable extra cost to make temporary repairs in order to speed up (expedite) permanent repairs or replacement of covered property.

Under **expediting expenses coverage**, the insurer agrees to pay the reasonable extra cost to make temporary repairs and expedite (speed up) permanent repairs or replacement of covered property. An example of expediting expenses is the payment of overtime wages in order to speed up repairs. If the insured also carries the extra expense coverage available through another insuring agreement of the form, coverage for expediting expenses overlaps to some degree. However, expediting expenses coverage is not as broad as extra expense coverage. For example, the cost of renting substitute facilities in order to continue operations could be covered as extra expense but not as expediting expenses. For expenses that come within both coverages, the insured can collect under either one, but not both. This would be advantageous to an insured that has exhausted the limits under one coverage but not the other.

Business Income and Extra Expense

Chapter 4 discussed the need for business income and extra expense insurance and described the forms and endorsements that provide time element coverages for the perils covered by the commercial property causes-of-loss forms. Many firms have a similar need for time element coverage in connection with equipment breakdown perils not covered by commercial property forms. The breakdown of equipment (and resulting damage to covered property in addition to the covered equipment) can interrupt operations and cause the insured to lose business income, incur extra expenses, or both. Accordingly, equipment breakdown policies normally offer business income and extra expense coverage.

In the business income and extra expense agreement of the ISO form, the insurer agrees to pay for the insured's actual loss of business income during the "period of restoration" because of equipment breakdown. The period of restoration begins at the time of the breakdown or twenty-four hours before the insurer receives notice of loss, whichever is later. It ends five days after the date when damaged property is repaired or replaced. The replacement property must be of similar quality, and the repairs or replacement must be completed with reasonable speed. The five-day period can be changed by an entry in the declarations. In addition, the insurer will pay the insured's actual loss of business income or extra expenses up to $25,000 during the thirty-day period that follows the period of restoration. The $25,000 limit can be increased by an entry in the declarations.

The insurer will also pay the extra expense the insured necessarily incurs to operate its business during the period of restoration. This extra expense coverage applies even when the expenditure does not reduce the loss of business income. However, the expenditure must have been necessary to continue operations. By appropriate entry in the declarations, the coverage can be amended to cover extra expenses only.

The only coinsurance provision in the ISO form is applicable to business income and extra expense coverage. It does not work in the same manner as the coinsurance provision contained in the Business Income (and Extra Expense) Coverage Form, discussed in Chapter 4.

At policy inception, the insured specifies the estimated business income annual value, which is entered in the declarations. Thereafter, the insured is required to submit annual reports of business income values within three months of the report date shown in the declarations. The insurer will then calculate the amount of earned premium. If the amount calculated is more than the premium already charged, the insured must pay the difference. If it is less, the insurer will refund the excess, but the return premium will not exceed 75 percent of the original premium.

The coinsurance condition only applies if the insured has not submitted the required report within the time period specified. If the report has not been submitted on time, the amount that the insurer will pay is equal to the estimated annual business income value shown in the declarations divided by the actual annual value times the loss. This calculation is similar to the coinsurance provision discussed in Chapter 3. It can be summarized as follows:

$$\left(\frac{\text{Estimated}}{\text{Actual}} \times \text{Business income loss} \right) - \text{Deductible} = \text{Amount payable.}$$

Spoilage Damage

The purpose of spoilage coverage is to pay for loss caused by the spoilage of perishable goods as a result of a breakdown to covered equipment. If, for example, the insured is a meat processor and its refrigeration system fails, perishable goods coverage would pay for the resulting spoilage of food. The spoilage must be due to the lack or excess of power, light, heat, steam, or refrigeration.

The insurer will also pay for expenses to reduce the amount of the loss to the extent that they do not exceed the amount that would otherwise have been payable.

Utility Interruption

Utility interruption coverage extends the business income and extra expense coverage to include loss caused by breakdown of equipment owned by a utility or other supplier that has contracted to provide the insured with any of the following services: electricity, communications, air conditioning, heating, gas, sewer, water, or steam. The list of services can differ in the forms used by other insurers. Some include additional services, such as air, refrigeration, or on-line service providers. Others omit one or more, such as sewer services.

To illustrate how utility interruption coverage might apply, suppose that a utility's electrical transformer is destroyed by a breakdown at a substation, shutting off all electrical power to an insured's premises for several days. Utility interruption coverage purchased by the insured will cover the insured's resulting loss of business income.

To eliminate coverage for small losses, utility interruption coverage only applies to an interruption that lasts more than the number of hours specified in the declarations.

Newly Acquired Premises

The newly acquired premises coverage extends all of the equipment break-down coverages to property situated at newly acquired locations that the insured has purchased or leased after policy inception. The coverage begins when the insured acquires the property and continues for a period not exceeding the number of days shown in the declarations for newly acquired premises coverage. The insured must notify the insurer in writing of a newly acquired location as soon as practicable.

This coverage is automatically included in equipment breakdown policies; the word "included" is preprinted in the declarations for this coverage.

Ordinance or Law

Chapter 3 discussed the loss exposures created by ordinances or laws that regulate the repair or construction of buildings. The same types of loss can occur when equipment breakdown damages a building. The insured may be required by law to demolish undamaged portions of the building and replace the entire building for a cost that exceeds what it would have cost to replace only the damaged portion of the building. In less severe cases, the insured may not be required to demolish any undamaged parts of the building but may still be required to make certain upgrades in the building as part of the repairs, such as installing an elevator to accommodate people with disabilities.

The ordinance or law coverage pays for such demolition costs, the loss in value of the undamaged portion of the building that must be demolished, and increased costs of construction. If the insured has purchased business income and extra expense coverage under the equipment breakdown form, the ordinance or law coverage agreement extends those coverages to include time element losses resulting from the extra time required to comply with a building ordinance or law.

Errors and Omissions

The ISO equipment breakdown form includes an agreement for **errors and omissions (E&O) coverage,** which provides protection similar to what risk managers and knowledgeable insureds and producers often request to be included in their property insurance policies. This coverage commits the insurer to pay for loss or damage not covered because of any of the following:

- Any error or unintentional omission in the description or location of the property insured
- Any failure through error to include any premises owned or occupied by the insured
- Any error or unintentional omission by the insured that results in cancellation of coverage for any premises insured under the policy

The error or omission must be unintentional, and the insured must pay the additional premium from the date that coverage would have been applicable had no error or omission occurred. Not all insurers include an errors and omissions provision in their equipment breakdown forms.

Brands and Labels

The equipment breakdown form includes a brands and labels coverage agreement that is similar to the brands and labels endorsement for commercial property policies that was discussed in Chapter 3. However, a separate limit of insurance, shown in the declarations, applies to this coverage in the equipment breakdown form.

Contingent Business Income and Extra Expense

The agreement for **contingent business income and extra expense coverage** extends the business income and extra expense coverage to cover the insured's loss as a result of equipment breakdown occurring at a location, shown in the declarations, that is not owned or operated by the insured. This coverage is similar to dependent properties coverage discussed in Chapter 4. "Contingent business income" was the name given to dependent properties coverage in previous versions of ISO commercial property forms.

EXCLUSIONS

The exclusions contained in equipment breakdown policies can be classified as follows:

1. Exclusions that duplicate exclusions contained in commercial property policies
2. Exclusions that eliminate coverage for perils covered under other policies
3. Exclusions that are unique to equipment breakdown forms

The sections that follow provide examples of exclusions from each of these three categories. For a full list of the exclusions, see the coverage form itself.

Errors and omissions (E&O) coverage
Coverage for loss or damage that would otherwise not be covered because of certain unintentional errors or omissions made in arranging the insurance, such as incorrectly describing an insured building's location.

Contingent business income and extra expense coverage
Coverage for business income and extra expense loss due to equipment breakdown occurring at a location, shown in the declarations, that the insured does not own or operate.

Another Approach to Insuring Equipment Breakdown

Although most equipment breakdown insurance is provided by separate policies or by separate coverage forms attached to a package policy, some insurance companies have come up with a less complicated solution: integrating equipment breakdown coverage into their commercial property forms. They do this by omitting the customary property coverage exclusions such as mechanical breakdown, artificially generated electrical currents, and steam boiler explosion. Some insurers also add other clauses that mirror separate equipment breakdown coverage.

The result is a commercial property form that provides essentially the same coverage as a separate equipment breakdown policy. In addition to the advantage of having one policy replace two, the potential for coverage disputes under two policies, often written by different insurers, is avoided. Whether the loss falls into the property coverage or the equipment breakdown coverage, the same insurer will pay the loss, subject to the same terms and limits.

Exclusions That Duplicate Commercial Property Exclusions

Equipment breakdown policies contain exclusions that are comparable to the commercial property exclusions of ordinance or law; nuclear hazard; war or military action; water; and neglect to preserve property from further damage. However, some of the exclusions are subject to special exceptions.

Exclusions That Exclude Perils Covered Under Other Policies

The equipment breakdown form excludes fire, windstorm or hail, explosion (other than explosion of a steam boiler, piping, turbine or engine; electric steam generator; or gas turbine), war, earth movement, regardless of whether the insured has other insurance covering these perils. Almost all of the other perils covered by the Causes of Loss—Broad Form are excluded if the insured has other insurance covering such perils.

Exclusions Unique to Equipment Breakdown Policies

An example of an exclusion unique to equipment breakdown policies is the testing exclusion. Equipment breakdown policies exclude certain types of testing because it can pose significantly increased risk of loss. For example, the ISO form excludes damage to covered equipment undergoing a pressure or electrical test. When such testing occurs in a newly constructed building, it is often covered by endorsement to the builders risk policy covering the entire construction project. Some insurers do not exclude testing in their equipment breakdown forms.

LIMITS OF INSURANCE

Equipment breakdown insurance is written subject to one overall limit, which is the most that the insurer will pay for all loss or damage resulting from any one breakdown. If a separate limit is shown for an individual coverage agreement, that is the most that the insurer will pay under that coverage agreement for any one breakdown, and this limit is included in the overall limit. When the word "Included" is shown for an individual coverage agreement, that coverage agreement is subject to the overall limit for each breakdown.

The limits of insurance section also provides for sublimits under the following headings: Ammonia Contamination, Hazardous Substance, Water Damage, Consequential Loss, and Data and Media. Unless a higher limit or the word "Included" is shown in the declarations, $25,000 is the most that the insurer will pay for direct damage due to breakdown to covered equipment for each of the categories, which are described below.

Some insurers refer to these provisions as coverage extensions, but ISO includes them in the section on limitations. Remember that in all cases, the damage must result from a breakdown to covered equipment.

Ammonia Contamination

Ammonia is used as a refrigerant in some equipment. The ammonia contamination sublimit applies to the spoilage of covered property contaminated by ammonia as the result of a covered breakdown, including any salvage expense.

Hazardous Substance

Cleaning up hazardous substances poses difficult challenges to insureds and insurers. For example, old electrical transformers contain PCBs (polychlorinated biphenyls), which are now believed to cause diseases and mutations. An electrical breakdown that releases PCBs into a building could require extensive and expensive cleanup operations. The hazardous substance provision applies to the additional expenses the insured incurs to clean up, repair, replace, or dispose of covered property that is contaminated by a hazardous substance as a result of equipment breakdown. "Hazardous substance" is defined to mean any substance, other than ammonia, declared to be hazardous to health by a government agency. (Ammonia contamination is covered under the preceding sublimit).

Consequential Loss

Consequential loss covers the reduction in value of undamaged parts of a product that becomes unmarketable as a result of physical loss or damage to another part of the product. Examples of consequential loss were discussed in Chapter 3.

Water Damage

The ISO equipment breakdown form excludes most types of water damage, such as flooding, backup of sewers, and discharge from a sprinkler system or domestic water system. The water damage sublimit applies to water damage losses that are not otherwise excluded. An example of water damage that would be covered is damage to the insured's merchandise resulting from leakage of water from a steam boiler as the result of a breakdown. The water damage sublimit restricts the amount that the insured could collect for this loss.

Data and Media

The definition of "covered equipment" excludes computer media. Therefore, breakdown to computer media is not a covered cause of loss. However, the definition of "covered property" does not exclude computer media or the data contained on such media. Therefore, loss to computer media and data because of breakdown to covered equipment (a boiler explosion, for example) is covered—*subject to the data and media sublimit.* This sublimit applies to the expense to research, replace, or restore damaged data or media, including the cost to reprogram instructions used in any computer. "Media" includes films, tapes, discs, drums or cells. "Data" means programmed and recorded material stored on media and programming records used for electronic data processing or electronically controlled equipment.

Debris Removal Coverage in Equipment Breakdown Policies

Most equipment breakdown forms do not discuss debris removal except in connection with the ordinance or law and hazardous substance coverages. When the form is silent on this subject, debris removal that is necessary because of a breakdown to covered equipment is considered part of the loss to covered property.

Commercial property coverage forms generally contain a coverage extension dealing with debris removal for two reasons: (1) to limit debris removal coverage to 25 percent of the amount of the loss and (2) to provide some additional coverage for debris removal in the event the limit of insurance is exhausted.

CONDITIONS

Most of the general conditions contained in equipment breakdown policies are comparable to those contained in other property insurance policies and are therefore not discussed here. The sections that follow describe only those conditions that distinguish equipment breakdown policies from commercial property policies.

Suspension

If the insurer or its representative finds that an item of covered equipment is in a dangerous condition, the **suspension condition** allows the insurer or any of its representatives to immediately suspend the insurance on losses arising from an accident to that item of equipment. The insurer can suspend coverage by delivering or mailing a written notice of coverage suspension to the named insured. Once coverage for that item of equipment has been suspended, coverage can be reinstated only by endorsing the policy.

The suspension condition may seem harsh, but it is reasonable when one considers the enormous loss potential involved in some equipment breakdown exposures. The condition allows a boiler inspector or another representative of the insurer to take action when there is imminent danger of an accident. Most insureds want a loss-free operation and willingly cooperate when a dangerous situation is discovered. The suspension provision is seldom invoked. However, it serves as a last resort that the insurer can use when the insured cannot or will not cooperate in remedying or repairing a dangerous condition.

Suspension condition
Condition that allows the insurer to immediately suspend equipment breakdown insurance on an item of equipment that the insurer determines to be in a dangerous condition.

Valuation

The valuation provisions answer the question "How will the insurer determine how much to pay?" The section also contains the annual reporting and coinsurance provisions applicable to business income and extra expense. These conditions were discussed previously in connection with the business income provisions.

Subject to several exceptions that will be noted separately below, covered property under the Equipment Breakdown Protection Coverage Form is valued on a replacement cost basis. The insurer agrees to pay the smallest of the following amounts for a covered loss: (1) the cost to repair the damaged property with property of the same kind, capacity, size, or quality; (2) the cost to replace the damaged property on the same site or another site; or (3) the amount the insured actually spends that is necessary to repair or replace the damaged property. However, the insurer will not pay for damaged property that is obsolete or useless to the insured.

If the insured does not repair or replace the damaged property within twenty-four months after the date of the accident, the insurer will pay no more than (1) what it would have cost to repair the property at the time of loss or (2) the property's actual cash value at the time of loss, whichever amount is less.

Separate valuation procedures apply to property held for sale by the named insured, data and media, and property covered for spoilage:

- Property manufactured by and held for sale by the insured is valued at its selling price, less any discounts and expenses the insured otherwise would have had, if it cannot be replaced before its anticipated sale.
- Computer media that are mass-produced and commercially available are valued at replacement cost. All other media are valued at the cost the insured actually spends to reproduce the records on blank materials.

- For spoilage damage, raw materials will be valued at replacement cost; property-in-process will be valued at the labor expended plus the proper proportion of overhead charges; and finished products will be valued at selling price.

Finally, special provisions apply to certain types of equipment upgrades or improvements and to property protected by extended warranties or service contracts.

The insurer will pay the additional cost to replace covered equipment with equipment that is better for the environment, safer, or more efficient than the equipment being replaced. The most that the insurer will pay under this extension is an additional 25 percent of the property damage amount that would have been paid. Many, but not all, independently developed forms include this coverage extension.

If any damaged property is protected by an extended warranty or service contract that becomes void or unusable because of a covered breakdown, the insurer will reimburse the insured for the unused costs of non-refundable, non-transferable warranties or contracts.

Deductibles

The insurer will not pay for any loss or damage until the covered amount for any one breakdown exceeds the deductible shown in the declarations for each applicable coverage agreement. The deductible applies separately to each coverage agreement unless (1) a deductible is shown as "combined" for two or more coverage agreements, in which case the insurer will subtract the combined deductible from the aggregate amount of loss to which the combined deductible applies; or (2) more than one item of covered equipment is involved in a single breakdown, in which case only the highest deductible is applied.

Any of four different types of deductibles may be used: dollar deductible, time deductible, multiple of daily value deductible, and percentage of loss deductible.

- A dollar deductible is shown in the declarations as a dollar amount. After the deductible has been satisfied, the remaining amount of loss is payable up to the full limit of insurance.
- A time deductible (such as forty-eight hours or three days) is frequently used with the business income, extra expense, and service interruption coverages. When a time deductible applies, the insurer will not pay for any loss occurring during the specified number of hours or days immediately following the accident.
- A multiple of daily value (MDV) deductible is sometimes used instead of a time deductible for the business income, extra expense, and service interruption coverages. An MDV deductible is expressed as a particular number (such as 3) times what the insured's average daily business income

This transformer fire was caused by the breakdown of a turbine inside the building. The turbine experienced an accident (covered by equipment breakdown insurance) that broke a turbine blade, throwing the blade through the turbine casing and the building wall, ultimately causing the transformer fire (covered by commercial property insurance). This loss illustrates how a single incident can involve both equipment breakdown insurance and commercial property insurance. Photo courtesy of The Hartford Steam Boiler Inspection and Insurance Company, Hartford, Conn.

for the location where the loss occurred would have been during the period of restoration (had no loss occurred).

- A percentage of loss deductible may also be used. If an insured with a 2 percent deductible experiences a $100,000 loss, the amount of the deductible for this loss would be $2,000.

In the case of the multiple daily value and the percentage of loss deductibles, minimum and maximum dollar amounts can apply if shown in the declarations. In that case, no matter what the calculated deductible is, the deductible will be no less than the minimum (such as $1,000) nor more than the maximum (such as $10,000).

Joint or Disputed Loss Agreement

When different insurers provide an organization's equipment breakdown insurance and its commercial property insurance, coverage disputes may occur when the cause of loss is uncertain. For example, the insurers may disagree on whether an explosion was an explosion in the pressurized chambers of a steam boiler (covered by the equipment breakdown policy) or an explosion in the firebox that heats the boiler (covered by the commercial property policy). Disputes may also occur when fire breaks out following an "accident" to covered equipment. The insurers may disagree on how much of the damage was caused by the accident and how much by the fire.

Joint or disputed loss agreement
Condition that addresses claim situations in which the insured's equipment breakdown insurer and the insured's commercial property insurer disagree on which insurer covers a loss; each insurer pays half the loss to quickly indemnify the insured; insurers then resolve their differences.

If these or other coverage disputes arise, the insured may receive no payment until the insurers settle their differences. The **joint or disputed loss agreement** contained in the equipment breakdown form provides a way for the insured to receive prompt payment. In order for the agreement to work, however, the commercial property policy must contain a similar provision with substantially the same conditions as the loss adjustment agreement.

When both policies contain the joint or disputed loss agreement or its equivalent, each insurer will (after receiving a written request from the insured) pay the entire amount of loss that each agrees is covered under its own policy plus one-half of the amount in dispute. In this way, the insured is fully paid without having to wait for the insurers to reach agreement on their respective liabilities. In addition to setting forth this loss procedure for the benefit of the insured, the loss adjustment agreement also requires the insurers to settle their differences through arbitration.

Jurisdictional Inspections

Many states and municipalities require that boilers and other pressure vessels be inspected by a qualified inspector. The inspectors working for equipment breakdown insurers are usually licensed to perform these inspections, which are often referred to as "jurisdictional inspections." Some insurers' equipment breakdown policies state that the insurer will make jurisdictional inspections for their insureds. The ISO form does not contain such a statement, but most insurers arrange for the required inspections for their equipment breakdown insureds whether or not the form includes a jurisdictional inspection provision.

SUMMARY

Equipment breakdown insurance (traditionally known as boiler and machinery insurance) covers "breakdown" (such as mechanical breakdown, electrical arcing, or steam pressure explosion) to "covered equipment."

Covered equipment encompasses a wide range of equipment including electrical equipment, mechanical equipment, air conditioning and refrigerating equipment, boilers and pressure vessels, and even office equipment such as copiers, fax machines, and computers.

Equipment breakdown coverage extends not only to the insured equipment but also to other covered property damaged by a breakdown to covered equipment. The other property covered includes any real or personal property owned by the insured as well as property of others in the insured's care, custody, or control for which the insured is legally liable.

Equipment breakdown insurance is needed by most insureds because commercial property policies exclude loss caused by perils such as mechanical breakdown and steam boiler explosion. The inspection and risk control services provided by equipment breakdown insurers are an important part of equipment breakdown insurance.

The leading writers of equipment breakdown insurance use their own forms; ISO and AAIS forms were influenced by independent forms. All forms can provide substantially similar coverage. Under the ISO form, the insured may select any or all of nine coverages:

- Property damage
- Expediting expenses
- Business income and extra expense
- Spoilage damage
- Utility interruption
- Ordinance or law
- Errors and omissions
- Brands and labels
- Contingent business income and extra expense

A tenth coverage, newly acquired premises, is included automatically.

Many of the exclusions in equipment breakdown policies duplicate exclusions found in commercial property policies; others exclude perils covered under commercial property policies; and still others exclude certain losses unique to equipment breakdown exposures, such as hazardous types of equipment testing.

Important general conditions of equipment breakdown coverage that distinguish it from commercial property insurance include the following: suspension, valuation, deductibles, and joint or disputed loss agreement.

Chapter 7

Direct Your Learning

Inland and Ocean Marine Insurance

After learning the content of this chapter, you should be able to:

■ Given a case, recommend inland marine coverages that are appropriate for insuring an organization's loss exposures.

- Describe inland marine loss exposures.

- Identify the property that is ordinarily insured under each of the inland marine coverages discussed in the text.

- Describe important provisions of the inland marine coverages discussed in the text.

■ Given a case, describe ocean marine loss exposures.

■ Given a case about an ocean marine loss, explain whether coverage applies.

- Describe the causes of loss covered by cargo insurance and by hull insurance.

- Describe the types of property covered by cargo insurance and by hull insurance.

- Explain what the collision liability clause of a hull policy covers.

- Identify the sources of liability claims for which protection and indemnity (P&I) insurance provides coverage.

OUTLINE

Development of Inland Marine Insurance

Inland Marine Exposures

Inland Marine Insurance

Ocean Marine Exposures

Ocean Marine Insurance

Summary

Develop Your Perspective

What are the main topics covered in the chapter?

This chapter surveys inland and ocean marine loss exposures and the coverages that are available for insuring those exposures. Roughly thirty different policies or coverage forms are described.

Consider the reasons why an organization that does not own any vessels would carry ocean marine insurance.

Why is it important to learn about these topics?

Inland and ocean marine insurance policies provide a way to cover property in transit and property that is often used away from the insured's own premises. Typically, these loss exposures are not adequately covered by commercial property forms. Understanding the coverages provided by inland and ocean marine insurance will help you decide when a loss exposure requires the additional coverage provided under these types of insurance.

Imagine that you are the risk manager for an oil company constructing a 1,000-mile pipeline.

- What is the main advantage of being able to insure the project under a nonfiled inland marine policy?

How can you use what you will learn?

Consider an organization with several inland and/or ocean marine loss exposures.

- Analyze these exposures and recommend specific coverages for insuring them.

- Why did you choose these particular coverages?

Chapter 7
Inland and Ocean Marine Insurance

Ocean marine insurance covers waterborne exposures—most commonly, damage to vessels and their cargoes, as well as liability arising out of the operation of vessels. Although relatively few organizations own vessels, many organizations are involved in either importing or exporting goods and thus need ocean marine insurance. Almost all organizations are exposed to loss that can be insured through *inland* marine insurance. Inland marine insurance, which evolved from ocean marine insurance, encompasses a far wider range of risks than inland transportation and is thus more prevalent than ocean marine insurance. Both inland and ocean marine insurance are discussed in this chapter because of their logical and historical relationships.

DEVELOPMENT OF INLAND MARINE INSURANCE

What is called "ocean marine insurance" in the United States is known simply as **marine insurance** in the rest of the world. Marine insurance is the oldest and most traditional type of insurance, originating in the Middle Ages. For historical reasons that will be explained below, marine insurance took on a broader definition within the United States and was divided into two branches—inland and ocean.

Marine insurance
Insurance that, in the U.S., includes both ocean and inland marine coverage and in the rest of the world is limited to insurance for vessels and cargo.

Inland marine insurance developed in the early 1900s, when American insurers were restricted to writing one of the following general kinds of insurance:

1. Fire (which included insurance against fire and some other causes of property loss)
2. Casualty (liability insurance and miscellaneous lines such as burglary, glass, and steam boilers)
3. Marine (ships and their cargoes)

Although fire insurers could insure buildings and their contents against fire and allied perils, they were not permitted to insure against most crime perils. In addition, they were generally not interested in providing "fire and allied" coverage on property in transit or on valuable property such as jewelry.

In contrast with fire insurers, marine insurers were accustomed to covering ocean cargoes of all types against many different causes of loss, including theft, while the property was either at sea or ashore. Accordingly, marine insurers were willing to provide broad perils or "all-risks" coverage on the types of property that fire insurers avoided. The inventories of jewelry stores, property while in the course of inland transit, tourists' baggage, and even bridges were typical inland properties insured by marine insurers in the early 1900s. Thus, the insurance came to be known as *inland* marine insurance.

By the 1930s, inland marine insurance had grown to include so many types of property that fire insurers believed that marine insurers were encroaching on their territory. To resolve the conflict, the National Association of Insurance Commissioners adopted in 1933 a **Nationwide Marine Definition** that restricted the underwriting powers of marine insurers to specified types of property.

Nationwide Marine Definition
A statement used mainly to determine whether a particular coverage is marine insurance (inland or ocean).

Following legislation in the 1950s that permitted a single insurer to offer fire, casualty, and marine coverages, the definition was no longer needed for restrictive purposes. However, many states continue to use an updated definition to determine whether a particular coverage is marine insurance (either inland or ocean) under their form and rate filing laws. Typically, inland and ocean marine insurance is subject to less rate and form regulation than other lines. The current Nationwide Marine Definition includes the types of property shown in Exhibit 7-1.

EXHIBIT 7-1

Summary of Nationwide Marine Definition

A. Imports

B. Exports

C. Domestic shipments

D. Instrumentalities of transportation and communication, such as bridges, tunnels, piers, wharves, docks, pipelines, power and telephone lines, radio and television towers and communication equipment, and outdoor cranes and loading equipment.

E. Various types of property owned or used by individuals, such as jewelry, furs, musical instruments, silverware, coin collections, and stamp collections.

F. Various types of property pertaining to a business, a profession, or an occupation. Examples of such property include mobile equipment, builders risks, property in the custody of bailees, live animals, property at exhibitions, and electronic data processing equipment.

INLAND MARINE EXPOSURES

Inland marine loss exposures are surveyed below in terms of (1) the items subject to loss, (2) causes of loss, and (3) the economic or financial effect of loss.

Items Subject to Loss

Inland marine insurance covers the types of property designated in the Nationwide Marine Definition except imports and exports, which are covered under ocean marine insurance. The sections that follow examine distinctive categories of inland marine loss exposures.

Inland marine insurance
Insurance that covers many different classes of property that typically involve an element of transportation.

Goods in Domestic Transit

Domestic shipments by rail, motor truck, or aircraft, or while in the custody of the U.S. Postal Service, are exposed to loss while in transit. The exposure can be faced by the originator (shipper), the transporter (carrier), or the recipient (consignee), depending on the type of carrier and the terms of sale of the goods being shipped.

Type of Carrier

Carriers of goods are classified as common, contract, or private. **Common carriers** are airlines, railroads, or trucking companies that furnish transportation to any member of the public seeking their offered services. **Contract carriers** do not serve the general public but furnish transportation for shippers with which they have contracts. **Private carriers** haul their own goods.

Because private carriers mainly transport their own goods, loss of or damage to such goods is a property exposure, not a liability exposure. In contrast, common carriers and contract carriers transport property of others and, depending on the circumstances, can be held legally liable to pay the shipper or consignee for loss of or damage to the cargo. Occasionally, some private carriers haul property of others, in which case the carrier's status changes from private carrier to common carrier or contract carrier, depending on the circumstances. The cargo liabilities of common carriers and contract carriers differ as described below.

Common carriers
Airlines, railroads, trucking companies, and other entities that furnish transportation services to the public.

Contract carriers
Carriers that furnish transportation services to shippers with whom they have contracts.

Private carriers
Organizations that transport their own goods.

Liability of Common Carriers

Common carriers are liable to shippers for the safe delivery of cargo entrusted to them except for losses arising from the following:

- "Acts of God," meaning natural phenomena such as floods, hurricanes, tornadoes, or earthquakes
- Acts of public enemies (meaning war risks)
- Acts of public authority
- Neglect or fault on the part of the shipper
- Inherent vice in the cargo itself

When the common carrier is liable for goods damaged in transit, the amount of the liability may be limited by the **bill of lading**, which is the contract between the shipper and the carrier. A *straight* bill of lading fixes no limit on the amount of recovery. A *released value* bill of lading limits recovery to a specified amount. The released amounts of liability are generally low and are

Bill of lading
The contract between the shipper and the carrier, which may limit the shipper's recovery for cargo loss.

usually quoted as dollar limits per pound or parcel. The shipper has the option to pay an additional charge and declare a value for the shipment, thereby increasing the limit of the carrier's liability.

Liability of Contract Carriers   The liability of contract carriers is defined by the contract between the carrier and the shipper. Such contracts often release the carrier from substantial liability except in the case of extreme negligence. However, a contract carrier is generally unable to totally avoid liability to the shipper.

Terms of Merchandise Sale

In ocean marine insurance, "F.O.B." means "free on board" and indicates that the shipper (seller) is responsible for arranging to have the cargo delivered on board the vessel. Once this has been accomplished, both the title (ownership) to the goods and the responsibility for them change hands from the seller to the buyer. In domestic transactions, "F.O.B." is used more loosely to indicate the point at which ownership and exposure to loss shift from seller to buyer. For example, a contract of sale might stipulate "F.O.B. shipper's loading dock." In that case, the transit exposure would be the buyer's once the goods are on the shipper's loading dock. Many other terms of sale exist, each with specific points at which the exposure shifts from the seller to the buyer.

Property in the Possession of Bailees

Bailment
The temporary possession by one party (the bailee) of personal property owned by another party (the bailor) for a specific purpose, such as cleaning or repair.

Bailor
The owner of the personal property in a bailment.

Bailee
The party temporarily possessing the personal property in a bailment.

A **bailment** exists when goods are left to be held in trust for a specific purpose and returned when that purpose has ended. The **bailor** is the owner of the goods, and the **bailee** is the one in possession of the goods. There are three basic categories of bailments, as follows:

1. Bailment for the benefit of the bailor ("Please keep my dog for the weekend.")
2. Bailment for the benefit of the bailee ("May I borrow your lawn mower?")
3. Bailment for the mutual benefit of bailor and bailee ("Fix my watch. I'll pick it up Friday and pay you for your work.")

Bailments for the mutual benefit of bailor and bailee are also called "commercial bailments." In commercial bailments, the bailor ordinarily pays the bailee to clean, repair, or perform some other service on the bailor's personal property. Examples of commercial bailees are laundries, TV repair shops, furniture upholsterers and refinishers, and industrial equipment repair facilities. As a general rule, a commercial bailee is legally responsible for damage to a customer's property that results from the bailee's negligence. Even if a bailee cannot be held legally liable for damage to a customer's property, the customer is likely to expect the bailee to pay for the loss. Thus, many bailees want to buy insurance that will pay for damage to customers' property regardless of whether the bailee is legally liable.

Movable Equipment and Unusual Property

A wide variety of property is eligible for inland marine insurance. In most cases, such property is subject to frequent movement from place to place or is simply an unusual kind of property. The box that follows shows some examples.

Examples of Movable Equipment and Unusual Property

- Agricultural equipment, such as tractors and cultivators

- Mobile equipment used by contractors, such as cranes and backhoes

- Physicians' and surgeons' equipment

- Computer equipment

- Farm animals

- Fine arts

- Buildings under construction (builders risks)

- Patterns, molds, and dies

- Partially completed products while at another location for processing

- Property on exhibition

- Sales samples while in the custody of sales representatives

- Valuable papers and records

- Records of accounts receivable

- Theatrical property

- Signs

- Cameras

- Musical instruments

Property of Certain Dealers

One of the first inland marine policies offered was the jewelers block policy, so named because it covered a jeweler's unique "block" of exposures, including the jeweler's merchandise in the store or in transit, other property of the jeweler (such as furniture and fixtures), and property of others in the jeweler's care, custody, or control.

In time, inland marine dealers policies were developed for insuring furriers, fine art dealers, coin and stamp dealers, camera dealers, musical instrument dealers, and dealers in mobile or agricultural equipment. The Nationwide Marine Definition permits an inland marine dealers policy to be written for dealers in any type of property that, in the hands of the final consumer, can be insured under an inland marine form.

Instrumentalities of Transportation and Communication

Property used in transportation such as bridges, tunnels, and pipelines can be insured using inland marine insurance. Inland marine insurance can also cover instrumentalities of communication such as television towers and transmission equipment.

Causes of Loss

Because the kinds of property eligible for inland marine insurance are diverse, the causes of loss to which such property is exposed are also diverse. However, the common thread that runs through most inland marine policies is an "all-risks" approach, also referred to as a special-form approach. Often the unique situation or high value of the property exposes it to different causes of loss than property that is generally at a fixed location and insured under commercial property coverage. Even if the property is not exposed to different causes of loss, the degree of exposure to loss may be different.

For example, the merchandise of a jeweler is exposed to fire, but it is more likely that a loss will be from theft. Compact, high-valued property like jewelry or furs is more vulnerable to theft than bulky items of low value like concrete or lumber. The probability of loss from the perils of transportation, particularly breakage and theft, is high when the property is in transit. Property in the custody of a bailee may be exposed to processing damage. Electronic data processing equipment is subject to electrical injury and mechanical breakdown. Mobile equipment and agricultural equipment are exposed to the elements, including earthquake and flood, and can be found at hazardous work sites. Instrumentalities of communication and transportation may be more likely to collapse than other types of stationary property. For inland marine loss exposures, each item subject to loss must be examined separately to determine the causes of loss that may damage or destroy it.

Economic or Financial Effect of Loss

The economic or financial effect of loss to property covered by inland marine policies is no different from the effect of loss to property covered by commercial property forms, with one exception: bailments (discussed below). Lost property must be valued, and the loss value may include the loss of use of the property.

The valuation of the property itself can be at replacement cost, actual cash value, or agreed value. For certain situations, such as goods in transit, valuation based on selling price or invoice price is most appropriate. Another technique (more common in ocean marine than inland marine) is to add a percentage of the value (such as 10 percent) to the invoice value to cover other costs associated with the loss.

The financial effect of loss of use of the property must also be considered. For instance, damage to a contractor's mobile equipment may necessitate the temporary rental of substitute equipment, and loss of use of a computer can cause extra expenses. Damage to the merchandise of a jeweler or an equipment dealer can also interrupt business.

In bailment situations, the financial effect of the loss will more resemble a liability loss than a property loss. The financial effect of the loss could be set by statute, contract, or the common-law rules of negligence.

There may be a statutory obligation, like regulations that mandate the liability of a common carrier to the shipper. Such laws could limit liability to a specific dollar amount per pound or per parcel for certain kinds of property, and this would be the extent of the loss to the common carrier. However, the loss to the shipper or the consignee could be much greater.

A contract between the parties in a bailment situation could stipulate the amount owed. A common carrier that accepts goods for transportation under a released bill of lading can tell in advance the amount owed the shipper if there is damage. Furriers, as another example, usually have their customers declare a value on furs before they are taken in for repair or storage. The measure of the loss of a customer's fur garment is the value set by the customer and agreed to by the furrier.

In other cases, the financial effect on the bailee may be determined by common law through the courts. This would be the case if a laundry was found negligent and thus became obligated to pay damages to customers for their goods destroyed in a fire.

INLAND MARINE INSURANCE

There are many kinds of inland marine policies covering many "classes of business" (such as contractors equipment, builders risk, motor truck cargo, and so on). Insurance regulatory authorities have recognized this diversity by dividing inland marine classes of business into two categories: filed and nonfiled.

The **filed classes** are those for which the policy forms and rates must be filed with the state insurance department. Filed classes are characterized by (1) a large number of potential insureds and (2) reasonably homogeneous loss exposures. Examples are policies that cover musical instruments and photographic equipment.

Filed class
The class of inland marine business for which policy forms and/or rates must be filed with the state insurance department.

The **nonfiled classes** are those for which neither policy forms nor rates are filed with the state insurance department. Nonfiled classes are characterized by a relatively small number of potential insureds, diverse loss exposures, or both. The contractors equipment floater is a good example. The property covered might range from simple hand tools and small power equipment to very large cranes and earthmovers. The property might be used in a desert, in a rain forest, or on the arctic tundra. It might be used to build roads, buildings, pipelines, or other structures. Policies must be drafted, rates calculated, and underwriting keyed to all of these variables. The fact that these policies do not need to be filed with state regulators allows insurers the flexibility needed to determine appropriate policy provisions and rates for individual risks.

Nonfiled class
The class of inland marine business for which neither policy forms nor rates must be filed with the state insurance department.

Nonfiled Inland Marine Coverages

The largest classes of inland marine business (as measured by premiums written) are nonfiled. Historically, each insurer has developed its own forms although AAIS and ISO have both developed standardized nonfiled forms for use by their member companies. The forms may range from preprinted forms and endorsements that the insurer uses for most insureds to a one-of-a-kind manuscript policy drafted for an unusual risk. Some important nonfiled policies are described below, though there are many other nonfiled inland marine policies.

Contractors Equipment

Contractors equipment floater
Policy that covers mobile equipment or tools while anywhere in the coverage territory.

Contractors equipment is the largest class of commercial inland marine business. The equipment used by contractors may include cranes, earthmovers, tractors, stone crushers, bulldozers, mobile asphalt plants, portable offices, and scaffolding. All such equipment can be insured under a **contractors equipment floater**. (The term "floater" is often used to denote an inland marine policy that covers property that is moved between different locations, i.e., "floating" property.)

The property eligible for a contractors equipment floater is not limited to that used by contractors. For example, contractors equipment floaters are used to insure mobile equipment used in mining and lumbering operations as well as snow removal and road repair equipment owned by municipalities.

A contractors equipment floater for a small or medium-sized contractor with perhaps two or three dozen pieces of equipment normally contains a schedule listing each piece of equipment with its own limit of insurance. A policy may also provide blanket coverage on unscheduled hand tools and miscellaneous equipment.

It is difficult, if not impossible, to keep an up-to-date insurance schedule of all items when several hundred pieces of equipment are used by an insured. A large contractor may therefore obtain blanket coverage applying to all equipment, whether owned, rented, or borrowed by the contractor.

Coverage may be on a special-form ("all-risks") basis or for named perils. When coverage is on a named perils basis, the following perils are commonly included: fire, lightning, explosion, windstorm, hail, vandalism, theft, earthquake, flood, collision, overturn, and collapse of bridges and culverts.

Contractors equipment floaters frequently include rental reimbursement coverage, which pays the cost of renting substitute equipment when covered property has been put out of service by a covered cause of loss. Rental reimbursement coverage is comparable to the extra expense coverage provided by the Business Income (and Extra Expense) Coverage Form.

Builders Risk

Builders risk policy
Policy that covers a building in the course of construction, including building materials and supplies while on or away from the building site.

Although there is an ISO Builders Risk Coverage Form that can be issued as a component of a commercial property coverage part, buildings or other structures in the course of construction can also be insured under a nonfiled inland marine **builders risk policy**. The nonfiled approach is often preferred by both insureds and insurers because it allows more flexibility in coverage and rating.

Inland marine builders risk policies typically cover the structure being built, temporary structures at the building site, and building materials that have not yet become part of the building. Building materials are covered while on the insured location, in transit, or in storage at another location. Business income coverage may be provided as part of the policy.

Inland marine builders risk policies usually cover on a special-form basis, and many insurers will provide coverage for losses that are usually excluded under standard commercial property forms, such as the following:

- Flood
- Earthquake
- Theft of building materials that have not been installed

Many insurers that write inland marine builders risk policies offer an endorsement providing "soft costs" coverage. **Soft costs coverage** insures various incidental expenses that may result from a physical loss by a covered peril to a building project, such as the following:

1. Additional interest on funds borrowed to finance reconstruction or repairs
2. Additional real estate taxes
3. Additional advertising expenses
4. Additional costs and commissions from having to renegotiate leases

Closely related to the builders risk policy is the installation floater. An **installation floater** usually insures a contractor's interest in building supplies or in fixtures that the contractor has been hired to install. It does not cover the entire building, as in the case of a builders risk policy.

Transit

Transit insurance, also called transportation insurance, covers owners of property against damage to their property while in the course of transit by carriers. This coverage is desirable for shippers because their property may be damaged in circumstances under which a common or contract carrier has no legal obligation to pay the shipper's loss. Transit policies may also cover property being transported on the insured's own vehicles.

Two basic types of transit insurance are available. The **trip transit policy**, purchased by occasional shippers, covers the particular shipment of goods specified in the policy. The **annual transit policy**, designed for frequent shippers, covers all shipments made or received by the insured throughout a one-year policy period. The provisions typically found in annual transit policies are summarized below.

Any annual transit policy excludes certain types of property. Contraband, for example, is not insurable as a matter of public policy, and most insurance policies make this clear by excluding it. Other types of property are commercially insurable, but they are especially attractive to thieves and therefore expensive to insure. Examples are precious metals, furs, jewelry, and money

Soft costs coverage
Coverage for various incidental expenses that might result from a physical loss to a building project, such as additional interest, advertising expenses, or real estate taxes; can be added to a builders risk policy.

Installation floater
Policy that covers a contractor's interest in building supplies or fixtures that the contractor has been hired to install.

Trip transit policy
Policy that covers a particular shipment of goods specified in the policy.

Annual transit policy
Policy that covers all shipments made or received by the insured throughout a one-year policy period.

and securities. Most annual transit policies exclude these items. If coverage for such items is wanted and the insured is willing to pay an additional premium, the exclusions can be deleted or modified to provide coverage. (Coverage might also be obtained under another policy, such as a jewelers or furriers block policy or a crime policy covering money and securities.)

Most annual transit policies cover on a special-form basis. However, an annual transit policy typically does not contain as many exclusions as the Causes of Loss—Special Form and thus covers a broader scope of perils. For example, flood and earthquake are usually covered.

Many annual transit policies cover only within the continental United States, Alaska, and Canada, including airborne shipments between those places. The "continental United States" does not include Hawaii, Puerto Rico, or any overseas possessions. Such wording precludes the insurer from having to cover air or water shipments to or from overseas locations. Overseas shipments by plane or ship (even between places within the coverage territory) are usually insured under ocean marine cargo policies.

Property covered under an annual transit policy is usually valued at the amount of invoice (including freight charges) if the property is being transported between buyer and seller. When no invoice applies (such as when a company is shipping its own property between its own locations), the property may be valued at actual cash value.

Motor Truck Cargo Liability

As discussed earlier, a motor carrier, whether operating as a common carrier or a contract carrier, can be held liable for damage to the property it is transporting in certain circumstances. A motor carrier can cover this exposure by purchasing a **motor truck cargo liability policy**.

Motor truck cargo liability policy
Policy that covers a trucker's liability for damage to cargo of others being transported by the trucker.

This form of insurance applies only to cargo damage for which the motor carrier is legally liable. It is not direct property insurance for the benefit of the cargo owner. For example, a cargo loss may have resulted from an "act of God" (such as a hurricane) without any negligence on the part of the motor carrier. The motor carrier would not be liable under such circumstances, and the insurance would not cover the loss.

In addition to limiting coverage to losses for which the insured is legally liable, some policies also limit coverage to losses caused by specified perils. Other forms cover any loss for which the insured is liable as long as the loss is not subject to any of the exclusions expressed in the form.

The description of covered property is usually broad enough to encompass most property accepted by the insured for transportation. However, as in transit policies certain types of valuable property likely to be targeted by thieves are commonly excluded, such as precious metals, jewelry, and fine arts. Some policies exclude liquor and cigarettes, two other commodities that attract hijackers. A carrier that transports such commodities can usually have the exclusions deleted in return for an additional premium.

The property is covered only while in or on a land vehicle operated by the insured (including connecting carriers) or while located at the insured's terminal. Terminal coverage, however, is usually limited to a certain number of hours, such as seventy-two. The insurer will usually extend the duration of terminal coverage for an additional premium.

Difference in Conditions

A **difference in conditions (DIC) policy** can serve a variety of needs. Its basic purpose is to fill in gaps left by the insured's commercial property insurance. Originally, a DIC policy was a means of providing "all-risks" coverage to insureds whose basic policy provided only named perils coverage. DIC policies are still used for that purpose, but with the widespread availability of special-form commercial property policies, the purposes for buying DIC policies now include the following:

Difference in conditions (DIC) policy
Policy that covers on an "all-risks" basis to fill gaps in the insured's commercial property coverage, especially gaps in flood and earthquake coverage.

1. To provide coverage for flood and earthquake exposures not covered by basic policies
2. To provide excess limits over flood and earthquake coverages included in basic policies
3. To cover loss exposures not covered in basic policies, such as property in transit or loss of business income resulting from theft or transit losses
4. To cover property at overseas locations

DIC policies are a nonfiled class of inland marine insurance in most states. Thus, insurers have great flexibility in arranging the insurance to address the specific needs or exposures of their insureds.

Electronic Data Processing Equipment

"Electronic data processing equipment" basically means "computer equipment." Although such equipment is covered as business personal property in the Building and Personal Property Coverage Form and other commercial property forms, an inland marine **electronic data processing (EDP) equipment floater** can provide added benefits. Many EDP equipment floaters cover special perils such as mechanical or electrical breakdown. They may also insure covered property while in transit or at unlisted locations. Moreover, since EDP equipment is a nonfiled class of inland marine in most states, an EDP equipment floater can be tailored to meet the individual needs of insureds.

Electronic data processing (EDP) equipment floater
Policy that covers computer equipment, software, and electronic data.

An EDP floater typically covers equipment, data, and media owned by the insured, as well as similar property of others in the insured's care, custody, or control. The policy definition of "equipment" usually includes (but is not limited to) mainframe computers, minicomputers, microcomputers, terminals, monitors, printers, disk drives, and modems. The term "data" includes both computer programs (which direct the processing of data) and data files (which store processed data, such as a customer mailing list). "Media," such as disks and tapes, are the materials used to store data.

Coverage for extra expenses incurred as the result of covered loss is usually included in an EDP policy. Business income coverage can often be added when the insured requests it.

Coverage is usually on an "all-risks" basis but without all the exclusions found in the Causes of Loss—Special Form. In addition, breakdown coverage can usually be added to an EDP policy. Subject to a separate deductible, breakdown coverage insures loss to equipment resulting from such perils as mechanical failure, electrical disturbance, and changes in temperature resulting from breakdown of air conditioning equipment.

Equipment and data are usually subject to separate valuation methods. Equipment may be valued at its actual cash value, replacement cost, or upgraded value. Upgraded value is the cost to replace the property with the latest, comparable, state-of-the-art equipment available. For data and media, property can be valued at the actual cost of reproduction or for an agreed dollar amount.

Some EDP floaters exclude loss of or damage to covered property while in transit. Because it is fairly common to transport computers to repair shops, many insureds may wish to have the floater amended to cover the property while in transit and while at other locations.

Bailees

Insurers use two basic approaches to insuring bailees for the property in their custody.

1. One approach covers loss to customers' goods only if the insured bailee is legally liable for the loss. A common example of this type of coverage is a **warehouse operators legal liability policy**, which covers warehouse operators against liability for damage to the property of others being stored in their warehouses.

2. The other approach covers damage to customers' goods regardless of whether the insured bailee is legally liable for the loss. An inland marine policy that takes this approach is called a **bailees' customers policy**. Because this type of policy allows the bailee to pay customers' losses even when the bailee is not legally obligated to do so, it can preserve customer goodwill under circumstances when a legal liability policy would not cover the loss. Bailees' customers policies are written for many different types of bailees, including dry cleaners, laundries, furriers, tailors, upholsterers, and appliance repair shops.

Instrumentalities of Transportation and Communication

Property essential to transportation or communication can be insured under an inland marine policy. The major types of properties in this class are bridges, tunnels, pipelines, and radio and television broadcasting equipment.

Warehouse operators legal liability policy
Policy that covers warehouse operators against liability for damage to the property of others being stored in operators' warehouses.

Bailees' customers policy
Policy that covers damage to customers' goods while in the possession of the insured, regardless of whether the insured is legally liable for the damage.

Filed Inland Marine Coverages

ISO and AAIS file inland marine coverage forms, endorsements, manual rules, and loss costs for several classes of inland marine business. These forms and endorsements can be used to make up a commercial inland marine coverage part. The coverage part can be included in a commercial package policy or issued as a monoline policy.

The ISO commercial inland marine coverage forms are briefly described below. Comparable AAIS forms are also available. The ISO forms cover on a special-form basis. Valuation is typically on an actual cash value basis. However, ISO manual rules permit the valuation clause to be modified to provide for any other basis of valuation to which the insurer and the insured might agree.

Commercial Articles

The **Commercial Articles Coverage Form** covers photographic equipment and musical instruments used commercially by photographers, motion picture producers, professional musicians, and others. It is not intended for dealers of these types of property. Coverage can be provided on a scheduled or blanket basis.

Commercial Articles Coverage Form
Form that covers photographic equipment and musical instruments used commercially by photographers, motion picture producers, professional musicians, and others.

Camera and Musical Instrument Dealers

The **Camera and Musical Instrument Dealers Coverage Form** covers the stock in trade of dealers in cameras and musical instruments. Similar property of others in the insured's care, custody, or control is also covered. Coverage can be provided by endorsement for other types of equipment while it is on the insured's premises.

Camera and Musical Instrument Dealers Coverage Form
Form that covers the stock in trade (inventory) of camera dealers or musical instrument dealers; also covers similar property of others in the insured's care, custody, or control.

Equipment Dealers

The **Equipment Dealers Coverage Form** is intended primarily to cover the stock in trade of dealers in agricultural or construction equipment. Customers' equipment in the care, custody, or control of the named insured is also covered. Coverage under a reporting form is available.

Equipment Dealers Coverage Form
Form that covers the stock in trade of dealers that sell agricultural or construction equipment; also covers customers' equipment in the insured's care, custody, or control.

Physicians and Surgeons Equipment

The **Physicians and Surgeons Equipment Coverage Form** is used to insure the professional equipment, materials, supplies, and books of physicians, surgeons, and dentists and, at the insured's option, similar property of others used by the insured in his or her profession. Coverage is also provided for the insured's office equipment, including furniture and fixtures, and for improvements and betterments if the insured does not own the building. Coverage can be added by endorsement for (1) office equipment while off premises for no more than thirty consecutive days, (2) extra expenses following a covered loss, (3) money and stamps on premises, (4) personal effects of the insured or others while on premises, and (5) valuable records.

Physicians and Surgeons Equipment Coverage Form
Form that covers the professional equipment, materials, supplies, and books of physicians, surgeons, and dentists; also covers the insured's office equipment and (if the insured is a tenant) improvements and betterments that the insured has made to the building.

Signs

Signs Coverage Form
Form that covers neon, fluorescent, automatic, or mechanical signs.

The **Signs Coverage Form** is used to insure neon, fluorescent, automatic, or mechanical signs. The covered signs must be scheduled with a limit of insurance shown for each item. The signs form is used by many businesses because commercial property forms exclude or severely limit coverage for signs.

Theatrical Property

Theatrical Property Coverage Form
Form that covers stage scenery, costumes, and similar property used in theatrical productions.

The **Theatrical Property Coverage Form** covers stage scenery, costumes, and other similar personal property used in theatrical productions. It covers similar property of others in the insured's care as well as property owned by the insured. The insured must have used or must intend to use the property in a production stated in the declarations.

Film

Film Coverage Form
Form that covers exposed motion picture film and magnetic tapes or videotapes, including related soundtracks or sound records.

The **Film Coverage Form** insures exposed motion picture film and magnetic tapes or videotapes, including related soundtracks or sound records. The amount of insurance reflects the cost of reshooting the film if it is lost or damaged.

Floor Plan

Floor Plan Coverage Form
Form that covers merchandise being held for sale and that the dealer has financed under a floor plan.

A floor plan is a financing technique in which a manufacturer or finance company holds title to merchandise but permits a dealer to display and sell the merchandise. It is used extensively for agricultural equipment, construction equipment, major home appliances, and similar merchandise. The **Floor Plan Coverage Form** may be used to insure (1) the interest of the dealer in floor-planned property, (2) the interest of the manufacturer or finance company, or (3) both interests. Coverage is written on a reporting form basis.

Jewelers Block

Jewelers Block Coverage Form
Form that covers the merchandise of retail jewelers, including similar property of others in the insured's care, custody, or control.

The **Jewelers Block Coverage Form** was designed to meet the needs of small retail jewelers. This filed coverage form covers damage to the insured's stock of jewelry, precious and semiprecious stones, watches, precious metals, and similar merchandise, along with other stock used in the insured's business. Similar property of others in the insured's care, custody, or control is also covered.

Nonfiled jewelers block policies are used to insure (1) retailers with average inventories exceeding $250,000, (2) jewelry wholesalers, and (3) jewelry manufacturers.

Mail

Mail Coverage Form
Form that covers a financial institution against loss of securities and other negotiable instruments while in transit through specified types of mail.

The **Mail Coverage Form** is written for banks, trust companies, insurance companies, investment brokers, and similar firms that frequently ship securities by mail. It covers securities and other negotiable instruments while in transit by first-class mail, certified mail, express mail, or registered mail.

Accounts Receivable

Many businesses would be unable to collect their accounts receivable if the records of those accounts were destroyed. This exposure can be significant, but it is easily overlooked during the process of identifying loss exposures.

The **Accounts Receivable Coverage Form** covers the insured's records of accounts receivable. In the event of loss, the insurer pays the amount of accounts receivable the insured is unable to collect because of the destruction of records. The form also covers the cost to reconstruct accounts receivable records, interest on loans made necessary by an inability to collect accounts receivable, and increased collection costs resulting from loss of records. Coverage may be written on either a reporting or nonreporting form.

Because many businesses keep backup (duplicate) copies of all their computer records, including records of accounts receivable, at a secure off-premises location, they do not buy accounts receivable insurance. However, insurers frequently include a certain amount of accounts receivable coverage in their package policies. The inland marine form might be used when an insured wants a higher coverage limit than the insurer is willing to include in a package policy.

Accounts Receivable Coverage Form
Form that covers losses (including uncollectible accounts) due to destruction of the insured's records of accounts receivable.

Valuable Papers and Records

The **Valuable Papers and Records Coverage Form** is used to insure against loss to valuable papers and records. Such valuable papers might include prescription records in a drug store, plans and blueprints belonging to an architectural or engineering firm, and similar records. The policy covers the cost of necessary research to reconstruct the records. Irreplaceable records, such as valuable manuscripts, are scheduled with an agreed value shown for each item.

Valuable Papers and Records Coverage Form
Form that covers valuable papers and records, such as an architect's blueprints and plans.

Rating Inland Marine Coverage

Rating methods for the filed commercial inland marine forms discussed in this chapter are based on rate factors, loadings, and credits contained in the ISO *Commercial Lines Manual (CLM)*. In most cases, loss costs for these filed lines are derived from the contents loss costs that apply to standard commercial property coverage and are increased or decreased for use in inland marine premium determination.

The CLM does not contain rating methods for the nonfiled classes of inland marine insurance. However, many nonfiled inland marine policies are so widely written that both their coverage provisions and rates have become standardized to an extent. Motor truck cargo liability insurance, for example, is a common form of inland marine coverage, and the rates for it are based on many years of loss experience. Insurance companies active in insuring truck shipments have developed their own manuals and rate schedules for this coverage.

In other cases, the property being insured under a nonfiled policy may be so unusual or the coverage terms so specialized that there is not enough previous loss information to give the insurance company a statistically accurate idea of what the coverage should cost. What is a fair price for transporting a priceless painting from one museum to another for a special exhibit? How much should be charged for coverage on a one-of-a-kind piece of machinery that could be damaged as it is custom-fitted and installed in a new factory? How do you rate coverage on a drawbridge?

Judgment rating
Rating used by underwriters to rate one-of-a-kind risks.

When faced with questions like these, inland marine underwriters must rely on their best judgment to set rates. **Judgment rating** (as opposed to manual rating, the method used to determine the premium for filed lines of insurance) requires a thorough knowledge of the class of business for which coverage is being written. An underwriter might have to draw on expertise in any of several specialized fields—fine arts, heavy equipment, construction, communications—to determine an adequate rate for the unique risks that are eligible for inland marine coverage.

OCEAN MARINE EXPOSURES

Overseas trade by oceangoing vessels creates several loss exposures. These loss exposures exist not only for the owners of the cargo being shipped, such as manufacturers, importers, and exporters, but also for the owners of the vessels in which the cargo is being transported. (The owner of a vessel that transports property of others may operate as either a common carrier or a contract carrier.)

For the owners of the cargo there is the possibility of loss to the cargo while it is in the course of transit, either aboard the vessel or on land between the vessel and the cargo's point of origin or destination. For the owners of the vessels there is the chance of loss of or damage to their vessels by largely the same perils that can damage or destroy the cargo they carry. These perils include the action of wind and waves, striking of rocks or other vessels, shifting of cargo, fire, war, and breakage of machinery.

Freight
The compensation a carrier receives for transporting cargo.

A carrier that is prevented by an accident from delivering the cargo aboard its ship may face an additional exposure, called loss of **freight** (the compensation the carrier receives for transporting cargo). If the cargo cannot be delivered as promised, the carrier may lose the freight that the cargo owner (also called the "shipper") would otherwise have paid. More frequently, however, the shipper guarantees that freight charges will be paid whether the cargo is delivered or not, provided the failure to deliver the cargo results from causes beyond the carrier's control. When freight is guaranteed, it is the shipper, and not the carrier, who is primarily exposed to loss of freight.

Finally, a vessel owner faces the exposure to legal liability for damage to cargo, damage to other property, and bodily injury to crew members, passengers, and other persons. If, for example, an oil tanker operator's negligence resulted in a collision with another vessel, the operator could become liable to the cargo owner for loss of oil being carried; to the owner of the struck ship for damage to the ship and its cargo; to persons on either vessel injured in the accident; and for the costs of cleaning up a resulting oil spill.

Summary of Ocean Marine Loss Exposures

Vessel Owner (Carrier)

- Loss of or damage to vessel
- Loss of use of vessel
- Loss of non-guaranteed freight
- Liability for:
  - Loss to cargo of others
  - Injury to crew, passengers, or others
  - Damage to other vessels (collision, etc.)
  - Oil spills

Cargo Owner (Shipper)

- Loss of or damage to cargo
- Loss of guaranteed freight

OCEAN MARINE INSURANCE

Ocean marine insurance is used to insure the exposures described above. To a large degree, the same coverages are used to insure commercial vessels and cargoes on rivers, lakes, and other inland waterways and even yachts and pleasure craft. Miscellaneous forms of ocean marine insurance are used to cover boat dealers, marina operators, shipbuilders, ship repairers, stevedores, wharf operators, and other maritime businesses.

Ocean marine insurance is written using a variety of forms. Because there can be considerable variation from one ocean marine policy to another, this discussion is limited to the general characteristics of the three most common types of ocean marine policies: (1) cargo, (2) hull, and (3) protection and indemnity.

Ocean marine insurance
Insurance that covers vessels and their cargos, including various vessel-related liability exposures.

Cargo Insurance

There are two basic types of ocean marine cargo policies. A **voyage policy** (like the inland marine *trip* transit policy) covers cargo for a single trip described in the policy. In contrast, an **open cargo policy** (like the inland marine *annual* transit policy) is essentially a reporting form policy that covers all goods shipped or received by the insured during the term of the policy. The insured periodically pays premiums to the insurer based on reports from the insured of covered shipments. The open cargo policy is well suited to the needs of an insured who frequently ships or receives goods overseas. Open cargo policies are often extended to cover air shipments as well as ocean shipments.

The open cargo policy also permits the insured to prepare "special policies" or certificates of insurance as may be required in ocean commerce. A special policy is a complete insurance policy that is sometimes required to accompany a shipment of cargo and is assignable to anyone having an insurable interest in the property during the course of transit. In some transactions, a

Voyage policy (cargo)
Policy that covers cargo for a single trip specified in the policy; comparable to an inland marine trip transit policy.

Open cargo policy
Policy (ocean marine) that covers all goods shipped or received by the insured during the policy's term; comparable to an inland marine annual trip transit policy.

shorter form of the special policy, called a certificate, is used. In either case, the insured with an open cargo policy is ordinarily permitted to prepare and issue the document without having to obtain the insurer's consent.

Valuation of Property

If a policy covers only one particular voyage, the property can be insured for a specific agreed value. It would be impractical, however, for an open cargo policy to list an individual valuation for every shipment made under that policy, especially if the insured makes many shipments each year. Consequently, the usual practice is to value a shipment of cargo by a formula typically including the amount of invoice, all freight charges, and a stated percentage to cover additional expenses. The stated percentage varies depending on the circumstances, but 10 percent is often used. Thus, a typical valuation of an ocean shipment is as shown below:

Amount of invoice + Freight + 10%.

Open cargo policies are ordinarily subject to a maximum limit of insurance for cargo shipped on any one vessel. There may also be a separate (lower) limit for "on deck" shipments, because they present a greater hazard than cargo stowed under deck. Open cargo loss payments are usually subject to a dollar deductible.

Warehouse to Warehouse Clause

Warehouse to warehouse clause
Clause in open cargo policies that covers the insured cargo during the ordinary course of transit (including land transit) from the time the cargo leaves the point of shipment until it is delivered to its final destination.

Many importers and exporters are not located in a seaport. Consequently, their overseas shipments may be exposed to loss while in transit by truck or railcar to the port facility, while aboard the cargo ship, and while being transported again by land to the final destination. To accommodate shippers' needs for continuous coverage during the entire course of transit, including inland transportation, ocean cargo policies usually contain a **warehouse to warehouse clause**. This clause provides that the insured cargo is covered during the ordinary course of transit from the time the cargo leaves the point of shipment until it is delivered to its final destination. If the cargo is discharged at the final port and not delivered to an inland destination, coverage ceases after a stipulated number of days.

The warehouse to warehouse clause is often supplemented by the marine extension clauses, which expand the coverage to include (1) unavoidable deviations from the ordinary course of transit or (2) delays caused by natural disasters, orders of civil authorities, or strikes of port workers. For example, a ship may become damaged and have to dock for repairs at an unintended port. If the cargo owner arranges for transshipment of the cargo by another carrier to the final destination, the policy will cover the remainder of the trip. The insured must pay the additional premium required by the insurer.

Covered Causes of Loss

Traditionally, ocean cargo policies insured against specified causes of loss. Today, most ocean cargo policies use the "all-risks" approach. When cargo insurance is written on an "all-risks" basis, the insurer covers any unexpected or fortuitous loss not specifically excluded. Typically, an "all-risks" open cargo policy excludes loss caused by delay, inherent vice, war, strikes, riots, or civil commotion. Coverage for loss caused by strikes, riots, or civil commotion is reinstated in virtually every open cargo policy by means of the strikes, riots, and civil commotion (SR&CC) endorsement. Loss caused by war can usually be insured under a separate cargo war risk policy issued at the same time as the ocean cargo policy.

Sue and Labor Expenses

Virtually every cargo policy contains a **sue and labor clause**. In the event of loss to the covered property, the sue and labor clause requires the insured to take reasonable measures to protect the property from further damage. In return, the insurer agrees to pay expenses the insured incurs in carrying out this duty.

Sue and labor clause
Clause that covers the cost of reasonable measures that the insured is required to take to protect property from damage at the time of loss.

General Average and Salvage Charges

Cargo policies specifically cover the insured's liability for general average and salvage charges. In marine terminology, "average" means partial loss, and **general average** is partial loss that is to be shared by all parties to the venture. **Particular average**, in contrast, is partial loss that is borne by only one party (such as a cargo owner).

General average
Partial loss that must, according to maritime law, be shared by all parties to a voyage (cargo owners and vessel owner).

General average situations arise when some of the ship's cargo is jettisoned (thrown overboard) or otherwise sacrificed in order to save the entire venture. Under maritime law, all parties to the venture, including the shipowner and all cargo owners, are required to share the losses of the owners whose property was sacrificed. Similarly, if the shipowner incurs certain expenses (such as the cost of being towed to a port of refuge) in order to ensure the safety of a voyage following a collision or other casualty, the shipowner and all owners of cargo aboard the vessel will be required to share the expenses.

Particular average
Partial loss that is borne by only one party to a voyage (such as a cargo owner).

"Salvage" refers to situations in which owners of cargo aboard a ship that falls in distress become liable to pay awards to those who put themselves at risk to rescue the ship.

Hull Insurance

A "hull" is the body of a vessel. **Hull insurance** covers damage to or loss of an insured vessel's structure. Also covered are machinery, boilers, and fuel supplies owned by the insured. Equipment installed for use on board the insured vessel that the insured does not own is usually covered as well, if the insured has assumed responsibility for its safety. Hull insurance also covers

Hull insurance
Insurance that covers physical damage to vessels, including their machinery and fuel but not their cargo.

provisions and stores for the operation of the ship. Hull policies ordinarily exclude any cargo on board the vessel, as well as personal effects of passengers and crew.

Covered Causes of Loss

Hull insurance policies usually cover on a specified perils basis rather than an "all-risks" basis. The following causes of loss are typically covered:

Perils of the seas
Accidental causes of loss that are peculiar to the sea and other bodies of water.

- *Perils of the seas.* **Perils of the seas** are accidental causes of loss that are peculiar to the sea and other bodies of water. Examples include abnormally high winds and rough seas, strandings, groundings, and collision with other vessels or objects.
- *Fire, lightning, earthquake.* The inclusion of earthquake provides coverage for the possibility that a vessel might be damaged by earthquake while docked.
- *Barratry.* Barratry is serious misconduct by the vessel's master or crew that is contrary to the owner's interest, such as a fraudulent or criminal act that causes damage to the vessel.
- *All other like perils.* "All other like perils" refers to perils *similar* to the perils specifically listed in the policy. The phrase does not provide "all-risks" coverage.

In addition to the basic perils listed above, many hull policies include an additional perils clause covering losses caused by several other perils, such as electrical breakdown, bursting of boilers, breakage of shafts, latent defects, and negligence of the crew.

Hull policies exclude loss caused by war, piracy, strikes, riots, and virtually any situation in which the vessel is taken by another party. Coverage for many of the excluded perils can be added to the policy by endorsement.

Types of Policies

Hull insurance can be written as either a voyage policy or a time policy. A voyage policy covers a specified voyage "at and from" the port named, with coverage typically ending after the ship has moored safely at its destination for twenty-four hours. Voyage policies are primarily used for ships taking hazardous voyages or operating irregularly and without established routes.

A time policy covers the insured vessel(s) for a specified period of time, typically a year. It may cover voyages anywhere in the world or restrict coverage to certain areas. Time policies are often written for fleets of ships, in which case the policy may be arranged to cover all ships owned or acquired by the insured, including nonowned ships that the insured charters. Most time policies stipulate that if the policy expires while an insured vessel is at sea, in distress, or at a port of refuge or a port of call, the insurance will continue in effect until the vessel reaches its port of destination; however, the insured must notify the insurer and pay any additional premium required.

Other types of hull policies include port risk policies and builders risk policies. Port risk policies are used to insure vessels that are confined to port and not subject to navigation hazards. Builders risk policies are written to insure vessels during the course of construction.

Valuation of Property

A vessel is normally insured for a value agreed on by the insurer and the insured. If the vessel sustains a total loss caused by a covered cause of loss, the insurer pays the "agreed value" stated in the policy. In the event of a partial loss, the insurer pays the cost of repairs.

Underwriters consider several factors in determining the value of a vessel. These factors include the vessel's replacement cost, its age and condition, the current market value if the vessel could be sold, the freight the vessel could earn during its remaining useful life, and its scrap value at the end of its useful life. A relatively new ship may be valued at close to its replacement cost, while an older vessel for which there is little demand may be valued at its present market value, which may be only a small fraction of its replacement cost.

Types of Loss Covered

Ordinarily, a hull policy applies to both partial and total losses, including general average, salvage, and sue and labor charges, subject to a flat deductible. However, some hull policies are written to cover total loss only. A total-loss-only policy might be used for an older ship chartered for a single voyage or for a ship that is engaged in a hazardous undertaking.

Collision Liability Clause

Most hull policies contain a **collision liability clause** (also known as a "running down clause"), which covers the insured's liability for collision damage to other ships and their cargoes, including resulting loss of freight charges and loss of use of the other owner's ship. Collision liability coverage is a separate amount of insurance ordinarily equal to the amount of insurance on the hull. The costs of defending a suit alleging covered damages are also covered, and such costs do not reduce the amount of insurance available for paying damages.

Collision liability clause
Clause that covers the insured's liability for collision damage to other ships and their cargoes.

The collision liability clause does not cover liability for bodily injury, nor does it cover property damage resulting from some cause other than collision. Usually, it also does not apply to liability for collision damage to any property besides other ships and their cargoes. For these reasons and because an insured may want higher collision liability limits than the amount of insurance on the hull, shipowners usually purchase an additional form of liability insurance, called protection and indemnity.

Protection and Indemnity

Protection and indemnity (P&I) insurance
Insurance that covers shipowners against various liability claims due to operating the insured vessel.

Protection and indemnity (P&I) insurance covers shipowners against various liability claims resulting from operating the insured vessel. P&I insurance is usually provided in a separate policy. Some of the important sources of liability claims that may be covered by P&I insurance are as follows:

1. Damage to bridges, piers, wharves, and other structures along waterways
2. Injury to passengers, crew, and other persons on the ship
3. Injury to persons on other ships
4. Damage to cargo of others aboard the insured vessel

P&I policies cover several miscellaneous exposures as well, such as expenses incurred to remove the wreck of an insured vessel, the costs of entering an unscheduled port to obtain medical assistance for a passenger or crew member, and fines resulting from the violation of laws. Some P&I policies do not cover the insured's liability for discharging pollutants. Separate pollution liability insurance for shipowners is available from underwriting syndicates or industry pools.

Although conventional insurers write P&I insurance, a significant portion of P&I insurance is issued by P&I "clubs." A P&I club is a mutual insurer, owned by the shipowner policyholders, that writes P&I insurance exclusively for its owners.

Rating Ocean Marine Insurance

There is no advisory organization that computes ocean marine loss costs. Moreover, ocean marine insurance is generally not subject to rate filing laws in the various states. Thus, each insurer writing ocean marine insurance develops its own ocean marine rates, guided by the judgment of its underwriters and the forces of competition in the marine insurance market.

A marine underwriter's judgment in rating may be influenced by many factors. For example, a cargo underwriter usually considers past loss experience, the product being shipped, the type of packing, the trade route over which the product is to be shipped, the volume of shipments, port conditions, the ocean and inland carriers, and, significantly, the shipper's reputation and quality of management. Hull and P&I underwriters consider past loss experience; the size, type, and age of the insured vessel; the area of navigation; the trade in which the vessel is employed; the nation in which the vessel is registered (the loss experience of ships registered under one flag may differ dramatically from ships under another flag); and the vessel owner's reputation and quality of management.

SUMMARY

Inland marine insurance evolved from ocean marine insurance in the early 1900s to meet consumers' needs in an inflexible regulatory environment. Inland marine insurance covers a broad range of exposures and is needed by most insureds. Ocean marine insurance is needed by owners of vessels and by importers and exporters.

Some common inland marine exposures are goods in domestic transit, property in the possession of bailees, movable equipment and unusual property, property of certain dealers, and instrumentalities of communication and transportation. These items of property may be subject to unusual perils. Financial effects of inland marine losses include a decrease in value, extra expenses, loss of business income, and bailee liability.

Some inland marine policies are "filed," and others are "nonfiled." Filed policies must be filed with state regulators. Nonfiled policies do not have to be filed and thus allow more flexibility for insuring unusual exposures. ISO and AAIS file various forms on behalf of their members. However, the largest classes of inland marine insurance are nonfiled and include contractors equipment, builders risk and installation, transit, motor truck cargo, difference in conditions, and electronic data processing equipment.

Loss costs for filed inland marine policies are derived from the insurer's commercial property loss costs, which are increased or decreased according to certain factors, loadings, and credits. Nonfiled policies, in contrast, must be judgment rated when there are insufficient statistics to support a manual rating approach.

The principal ocean marine loss exposures can be summarized as follows:

- Loss to cargo being carried on vessels
- Loss to vessels
- Legal liability for various accidents arising out of the operation of vessels

These exposures can be insured by three basic types of marine insurance: (1) cargo insurance, (2) hull insurance, and (3) protection and indemnity (P&I) insurance.

The open cargo policy covers all goods shipped or received by the insured during the term of the policy. The policy is often extended to cover air shipments as well. Property is usually valued at invoice cost plus freight plus a stated percentage of the invoice value (such as 10 percent). Shipments are covered on a "warehouse to warehouse" basis, including transit by water and land. Coverage is usually on an "all-risks" basis. Although excluded by the open cargo form, strikes, riots, and civil commotion are usually covered by endorsement. War is also excluded but can be covered in a companion war risk cargo policy. Open cargo policies also cover sue and labor expenses and the insured's liability for general average and salvage charges.

Hull insurance covers the vessel, its machinery, fuel, and supplies. Although a hull policy can be written to cover a specified voyage, the more common approach is a time policy covering the insured's vessels for a one-year term. Each vessel is usually insured for an amount agreed on by the insured and the insurer. In the event of a total loss, the agreed value is paid. For partial losses, the insurer pays the cost of repairs. Hull policies typically cover "perils of the seas" and several other named perils. Coverage for loss caused by war, piracy, or seizure of the vessel can be added by endorsement. The hull policy also provides collision liability coverage, which covers the insured's liability for damage to other vessels and their cargoes resulting from collision with the insured vessel.

Protection and indemnity (P&I) insurance covers shipowners against various liability claims resulting from the operation of the insured vessel. Some of the liability exposures commonly covered by P&I include the following:

- Injury to crew members, passengers, or other persons on the vessel
- Injury to persons on other vessels
- Damage to cargo of others being carried on the vessel
- Damage to piers, docks, and other property

Each insurer writing ocean marine insurance develops its own rates, guided by the judgment of its underwriters and the forces of competition in the marine insurance market.

Direct Your Learning

Commercial General Liability Insurance, Part I

After learning the content in this chapter, you should be able to:

■ Describe the liability loss exposures faced by a business or another organization.

■ Given a case about a liability loss, explain whether CGL coverage applies.

- • Explain what is covered and what is limited or excluded under Coverages A, B, and C of the CGL coverage form.

- • Describe the supplementary payments addressed in the CGL coverage form.

OUTLINE

Liability Loss Exposures

Overview of Commercial General Liability Insurance

Coverage A: Bodily Injury and Property Damage Liability

Coverage B: Personal and Advertising Injury Liability

Supplementary Payments

Coverage C: Medical Payments

Summary

Develop Your Perspective

What are the main topics covered in the chapter?

This chapter introduces liability loss exposures and one of the most fundamental commercial insurance forms for insuring them, the Commercial General Liability Coverage Form (CGL).

Read your regular newspaper or online news service.

- Identify stories involving liability claims.
- Would a CGL policy cover these claims?

Why is it important to learn about these topics?

All organizations are exposed to the types of liability losses covered by the CGL, and most have liability loss exposures that are *not* covered by the CGL. Knowing whether or not the CGL covers a particular loss exposure will help you know when to recommend additional coverage forms to cover loss exposures.

Identify the principal liability loss exposures facing one of your organization's customers.

- Classify each exposure under the proper coverage of the CGL policy.

How can you use what you will learn?

Obtain and analyze the facts surrounding a liability claim.

- Is the claim covered under any of the CGL insuring agreements?
- Do any exclusions apply?
- If the facts of the claim were different, would there be coverage under the policy?
- What facts would need to change?

Chapter 8
Commercial General Liability Insurance, Part I

The preceding chapters of this text have focused on property loss exposures and the corresponding types of commercial insurance. This chapter describes *liability* loss exposures and begins the examination of **commercial general liability insurance**, the foundation of liability insurance protection for most organizations. The examination of commercial general liability insurance continues in Chapter 9. Policies covering other types of liability exposures, such as automobile liability and workers compensation obligations, will be discussed in later chapters.

Commercial general liability insurance
Insurance that covers many of the common liability loss exposures faced by an organization, including its premises, operations, and products.

LIABILITY LOSS EXPOSURES

All businesses and other organizations face liability loss exposures. A liability loss exposure is the possibility of experiencing a liability loss. A **liability loss** includes all costs to a person or an organization as the result of a specific legal claim or suit against that person or organization.

Liability loss
All costs to a person or an organization due to a legal claim or suit against that person or organization.

For example, Speedy Convenience Store could be sued for injuries resulting from a dangerous condition (such as a slippery floor) on its premises. The possibility that such a suit could occur is a liability loss *exposure*. If Debbie, one of Speedy's customers, slips and falls on Speedy's floor and sues Speedy to recover for her medical expenses and lost wages resulting from the accident, the store will experience a liability loss. At the very least, the store's liability loss will include the costs of investigating and defending against the suit. If Debbie wins her suit, the store's liability loss will include the cost of paying damages to compensate Debbie for her medical expenses, lost wages, and perhaps even pain and suffering. Investigation and defense costs and damages are covered under general liability policies. Other consequences of liability claims, which are generally *not* covered, include the following:

- Costs incurred by the sued organization to reduce the chance of additional, related losses in the future. For example, a business that has been sued because of injuries occurring on its property may adopt several new loss control measures.

- Hidden costs, including the time consumed in defending against a claim and the adverse publicity that comes from being sued.

To be able to identify, analyze, and properly handle an organization's liability loss exposures, one must understand (1) the concept of legal liability and (2) the common sources of liability loss exposures. Both topics are explored below.

Legal Liability

Legal liability
A legally enforceable obligation of a person or an organization to pay a sum of money (called damages) to another person or organization.

Legal liability describes a legally enforceable obligation of a person or an organization to pay a sum of money (called damages) to another person or organization. When a person or an organization becomes legally obligated to pay damages, the person or organization suffers a liability loss. Anyone who wishes to evaluate an organization's liability loss exposures must understand the various ways in which the organization could become legally liable.

As illustrated in the example above, an organization can experience a liability loss even if it is not held legally liable. All that the other party (called the "claimant") must do is *allege* that the organization is legally liable to pay damages. The accused organization (or its liability insurer) must then incur expenses to investigate and defend against the claimant's allegation of legal liability. Even if the claim is eventually found to be invalid, the organization (or its insurer) will have incurred a liability loss. If the claimant succeeds in proving legal liability, the loss will be increased by the amount that must be paid as damages.

A liability insurance policy typically obligates the insurance company to defend the insured against allegations that, if true, would be covered under the policy. In addition, the policy obligates the insurance company to pay damages for which the insured is legally liable. Most liability claims never go to court. If the insurer believes that its policyholder is legally liable, the insurer ordinarily attempts to settle the claim (by offering to pay a certain amount of damages to the claimant) and avoid the additional expense of going to court. Thus, being able to determine whether the insured would, in all likelihood, be held legally liable if the case went to court is a required skill for liability claim personnel.

Civil Law and Criminal Law

Civil law
The branch of the law that provides a means to settle disputes between parties.

Criminal law
The branch of the law that imposes penalties for wrongs against society.

Legal liability can be imposed by civil law, criminal law, or both. **Civil law** provides a means to settle disputes between parties, whereas **criminal law** imposes penalties for wrongs against society. Liability insurance responds to liability imposed by civil law. Insurance is not available for criminal liability. Such insurance would be against public policy and is prohibited by law.

The same conduct can constitute both a civil wrong and a crime. For example, if a driver causes the death of a pedestrian, government authorities may charge the driver with vehicular homicide, a criminal act. The driver may also be subject to a civil action by the estate of the deceased pedestrian for medical bills, funeral expenses, loss of support, and other damages that the law allows.

Insurance coverage would not respond to the criminal charges. It could, however, provide payment for the civil claims.

Civil liability can be based on torts, contracts, or statutes. The bases for legal liability are summarized in Exhibit 8-1 and discussed in more detail in the sections that follow.

EXHIBIT 8-1

Bases for Legal Liability

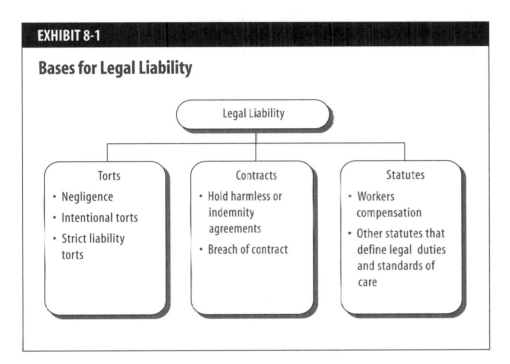

Legal Liability Based on Torts

A **tort** is a civil wrong against another person other than a breach of contract. Most of the claims covered by liability insurance are based on the law relating to torts (tort law). Tort law protects the rights of individuals. These legally protected rights originally included the rights to security of person, property, and reputation. Over the years, legal changes have established other rights of individuals, such as the right to privacy. Where there is a right, there is also a duty on the part of others to respect that right and to refrain from any act or omission that would impair or damage that right. Any wrongful invasion of legally protected rights entitles the injured party to bring an action against the wrongdoer for damages.

Tort
A civil wrong, other than a breach of contract, against another person.

The numerous types of torts recognized by law can be classified into three broad types: (1) negligence, (2) intentional torts, and (3) strict liability torts.

Negligence

The tort of **negligence** is based on four elements: (1) a duty owed to another person, (2) a breach of that duty, (3) the occurrence of injury or damage, and

Negligence
A tort that occurs when a person exposes others to an unreasonable risk of harm because of failure to exercise the required degree of care.

(4) a close causal connection between the negligent act and the resulting harm. Negligence occurs when a person exposes others to an unreasonable risk of harm because of failure to exercise the required degree of care. For example, negligence exists when a motorist drives at an unsafe and excessive speed and, as a result, causes an accident that injures another motorist.

Intentional Torts

Intentional tort
A tort committed by a person who foresees (or should be able to foresee) that his or her act will harm another person.

If a person foresees (or should be able to foresee) that his or her act will harm another person, the act is classified as an **intentional tort.** The act does not necessarily have to be performed with malicious or hostile intent. An example of an intentional tort is libel, the publication of a false statement that damages a person's reputation.

Strict Liability Torts

Strict liability
Liability that is imposed even though the defendant acted neither negligently nor with intent to cause harm; for example, liability for injury caused by wild animals or dangerously defective products.

In various situations, tort liability can be imposed when the defendant acted neither negligently nor with intent to cause harm. This type of legal liability is commonly referred to as **strict liability** (or absolute liability). Common examples of strict liability include liability for abnormally dangerous instrumentalities (such as wild animals), ultrahazardous activities (such as blasting), and dangerously defective products.

The term "strict liability" is also used to describe liability imposed by certain statutes, such as workers compensation laws. Strict liability imposed by statute, as opposed to strict liability based on tort, is described in a separate section below.

Legal Liability Based on Contracts

Contract
A legally enforceable agreement between two or more parties in which each party makes some promise to the other.

In addition to torts, contracts are another basis for imposing legal liability. A **contract** is a legally enforceable agreement between two or more parties in which each party makes some promise to the other. If one party fails to honor the promise, the other may go to court to enforce the contract. Liability based on contracts can arise out of either a breach of contract or an agreement to assume the liability of another party.

Breach of Contract

Breach of contract
Failure to fulfill one's contractual promise.

A common type of **breach of contract** involves the promise (called a warranty) made by a seller regarding its product. If the product fails to live up to the promise, the warranty has been breached, and the buyer can make claim against the seller. The warranty may be either expressly stated or implied by law. For example, the law implies a warranty that every product is fit for the particular purpose for which it is sold. If the product is unfit for its intended purpose and the buyer is injured as a result, the seller may be held legally liable for damages.

Liability for injury or damage resulting from a seller's breach of warranty is commonly insurable. Other consequences of breach of contract are not insurable. For example, if a builder fails to complete a new store by the completion date promised, the store owner's claim for loss of revenue is normally not insurable under the builder's general liability insurance.

Assumption of Liability

Many contracts contain a provision that obligates one of the parties to assume the legal liability of another party. Such a provision is often called a **hold harmless agreement** because it requires one party to "hold harmless and indemnify" the other party against liability arising from the activity or product that is the subject of contract.

For example, a lease on a building may obligate the tenant to hold the landlord harmless against any liability claims made against the landlord by any person injured on the leased premises. The tenant, in this case, is agreeing by contract to pay claims for which the tenant would not otherwise have been legally liable. This type of liability—often called **contractual liability** or assumed liability—is commonly covered under liability insurance policies.

Hold harmless agreement
A contractual provision that obligates one of the parties to assume the legal liability of another party.

Contractual liability
Liability assumed through a hold harmless agreement.

Legal Liability Based on Statutes

In addition to torts and contracts, statutes are a third major basis for imposing legal liability. A **statute** is a written law passed by a legislative body, at either the federal or state level. Written laws at the local level are usually referred to as ordinances. Statutes and ordinances can modify the duties that persons owe to others. Thus, the duties imposed by statute or ordinance may be used as evidence of a person's duty of care in a tort action. Apart from playing that role in tort actions, a statute can also impose legal liability on certain persons or organizations regardless of whether they acted negligently, committed any tort, or assumed liability under a contract.

Statute
A law passed by a state or federal legislative body.

In other words, a statute can give certain persons or organizations an absolute legal obligation to compensate other persons if certain events occur. This type of obligation is a form of strict liability, like that discussed earlier, except that it is based entirely on requirements imposed by statute rather than on tort law. An important example of liability imposed by statute is the workers compensation system, which requires employers to pay prescribed benefits for occupational injuries or illness of their employees. The employer must pay these benefits even if an employee's injury or illness did not result from the employer's negligence. (The workers compensation system will be discussed in Chapter 12.)

Sources of Liability Exposures

A wide range of exposures, arising from various sources, can spawn liability losses. One major source of liability exposures is the operation of automobiles. Another major source of liability exposures is employees, since most employers are obligated by workers compensation laws to pay for occupational injuries of their employees. Those two sources of liability exposures will be examined in later chapters. The present chapter focuses on liability exposures covered under commercial general liability (CGL) insurance. CGL insurance provides coverage primarily for liability losses arising from premises, operations, products, and completed operations, although it also covers other exposures.

Premises Liability Exposure

Premises liability exposure
Exposure to liability for injury or damage due to the ownership, occupancy, or use of premises.

The **premises liability exposure** exists when there is ownership, occupancy, or use of property (the premises). The standard of care imposed on an owner-occupant, a landlord, or a tenant is that the property be maintained as a reasonable and prudent person would maintain it. For example, a reasonable and prudent person would be expected to keep floors dry and free of objects that might cause injury to another person.

Operations Liability Exposure

Operations liability exposure
Exposure to liability for injury or damage due to activities in addition to the ownership, occupancy, or use of premises; for example, a building contractor's liability exposure while constructing a house.

The **operations liability exposure** relates to activity in addition to the occupancy of property. The operations could be those of any kind of business, but this exposure is generally associated with manufacturers, processors, or contractors. For example, a contractor paving a road has an operations liability exposure. If a member of the public is injured as a result of negligent construction activity while the project is underway, any resulting liability claim against the contractor will be said to have arisen out of the operations liability exposure.

Products Liability Exposure

Products liability exposure
Exposure to liability for injury or damage due to products sold or distributed by the exposed party.

The **products liability exposure** of an organization is the possibility that a member of the general public might be injured by a product manufactured, sold, or distributed by the organization. If, for example, a child is injured by a dangerously defective toy, the injury can be said to have arisen out of the toy manufacturer's products liability exposure. Products liability can be imposed on a manufacturer, seller, or distributor of products under several different legal theories, including negligence, breach of contract, and strict liability in tort.

Completed Operations Liability Exposure

Completed operations liability exposure
Exposure to liability for injury or damage due to work completed by the exposed party.

Although the **completed operations liability exposure** is traditionally linked with the products liability exposure, the two exposures are distinguishable in liability insurance. The products liability exposure is associated with any items or goods sold by an organization, which might be the manufacturer, the wholesaler, or the retailer of the goods. The completed operations liability exposure typically relates to an organization's liability for work it has performed and finished, including any materials provided by the organization doing the work.

For example, a furnace sold by its manufacturer to a heating contractor is within the manufacturer's *products* liability exposure. After the contractor who bought the furnace has installed it in a customer's home, the furnace and all labor and parts included in the installation job are within the contractor's *completed operations* liability exposure.

The word "completed" is important. If an injury had occurred because of the contractor's negligence during the course of the work (before the work was *completed*), the claim would be said to have arisen out of the contractor's operations liability exposure, not its *completed* operations liability exposure.

Principal Loss Exposures Covered by CGL

Exposure	Example
Premises liability	Customer slips on a spill in the insured's store and breaks ankle.
Operations liability	Employee of the insured plumbing contractor accidentally sets customer's house on fire while soldering pipes.
Products liability	Defective gas range manufactured by the insured causes explosion that damages buyer's home.
Completed operations liability	Building constructed by the insured collapses after being put to use by its owner.

Other CGL Exposures

Other liability exposures covered by the CGL policy include liability assumed under certain contracts and liability for some intentional torts (such as libel and slander). These additional exposures, as well as those described above, will become more apparent as the corresponding provisions of commercial general liability insurance are described in the remainder of this chapter.

OVERVIEW OF COMMERCIAL GENERAL LIABILITY INSURANCE

Most organizations have, at the least, premises or operations liability exposures and therefore commonly purchase commercial general liability (CGL) insurance to cover those exposures. CGL insurance can therefore be viewed as the foundation for most organizations' liability insurance programs. Additional types of liability insurance, such as automobile liability insurance, are frequently added to this foundation in order to insure exposures that the CGL policy excludes.

The most commonly used standard form for providing CGL insurance is the Commercial General Liability Coverage Form of Insurance Services Office (ISO). This coverage form can be combined with CGL declarations and any applicable endorsements to form a CGL coverage part. Like the other ISO coverage parts, this one can be either included in a commercial package policy or issued as a monoline policy.

The CGL coverage form comes in two versions: the occurrence form and the claims-made form. "Occurrence" and "claims-made" refer to the events that trigger coverage under the forms (a point that will be explained in more detail later in this chapter). The two forms differ only in their provisions respecting these coverage triggers. Because the occurrence form is much more widely used than the claims-made form, it is described first. The claims-made form will be discussed in the next chapter.

Both versions of the CGL coverage form provide three separate coverages:

- Coverage A—Bodily Injury and Property Damage Liability
- Coverage B—Personal and Advertising Injury Liability
- Coverage C—Medical Payments

This chapter describes the insuring agreements and applicable exclusions for each of these coverages as found in the 2001 edition of the CGL coverage form.

COVERAGE A—BODILY INJURY AND PROPERTY DAMAGE LIABILITY

Coverage A insures against claims arising out of the premises, operations, products, completed operations, and contractual liability exposures described earlier. The main provisions for Coverage A consist of a broad insuring agreement that is limited by several exclusions. If a claim against an insured meets all of the criteria of the insuring agreement and does not come within the scope of any of the exclusions, it is covered, subject to policy limits and conditions.

Coverage A Insuring Agreement

The Coverage A insuring agreement consists of two distinct promises made by the insurer: (1) a promise *to pay damages* on behalf of the insured and (2) a promise *to defend* the insured against claims or suits seeking damages covered under the policy.

Insurer's Duty To Pay Damages

The insuring agreement imposes several conditions on the insurer's duty to pay damages. All of the following conditions must be fulfilled:

1. The insured must be legally obligated (legally liable) to pay damages.
2. The damages must result from "bodily injury" or "property damage" as defined in the policy (see below).

3. The policy must apply to the bodily injury or property damage.
4. The bodily injury or property damage must be caused by an "occurrence" (see definition below).
5. The occurrence must take place in the "coverage territory."
6. The bodily injury or property damage must occur during the policy period. (The claims-made form contains a different provision in this regard.)

1. Legally Obligated To Pay Damages

Whether the insured is legally obligated to pay damages is a question that can be settled either in court or by the insurer's claim investigation. Often, the insurer's investigation reveals that the insured is legally liable. If the insurer also believes that the policy covers the claim, it will usually attempt to negotiate with the third-party claimant and try to arrange an out-of-court settlement.

The basic types of damages that a court might award consist of the following:

- Special damages, for such out-of-pocket costs as medical expenses and loss of earnings
- General damages, for such intangibles as pain and suffering
- Punitive damages, awarded to punish or make an example of the wrongdoer

Although the insurer promises to pay all damages for which the insured is liable, a few states do not recognize the concept of punitive damages, and some other states do not permit insurers to pay punitive damages on behalf of an insured. Even in states that do allow insurers to pay punitive damages, insurers are not likely to pay them in an out-of-court settlement.

2. "Bodily Injury" and "Property Damage"

The CGL coverage form broadly defines **bodily injury** as "bodily injury, sickness or disease sustained by a person, including death resulting from any of these at any time." The insuring agreement contains a statement that damages because of "bodily injury" include damages for care, loss of services, or death resulting at any time from the "bodily injury." Damages for pain and suffering are part of "bodily injury."

Bodily injury (as defined in the CGL)
Bodily injury, sickness, or disease sustained by a person, including death resulting from any of these at any time.

The policy definition of **property damage** includes both of the following:

- *Physical injury to tangible property, including resulting loss of use of that property.* An example of physical injury is the destruction of a customer's building by fire caused by the insured contractor's negligence. "Resulting loss of use" would include the loss of income sustained by the customer until the building could be rebuilt.

- *Loss of use of tangible property that is not physically injured.* An example is loss of business income suffered by a stock brokerage firm because utility services were interrupted for several hours as a result of utility company negligence.

Property damage
Physical injury to tangible property, including resulting loss of use of that property and loss of use of tangible property that is not physically injured.

The definition of "property damage" (beginning in the 2001 edition of the CGL forms) also states that for purposes of the definition, electronic data is not tangible property. The policy defines "electronic data" broadly to include "information, facts, or programs stored as or on, created or used on, or transmitted to or from computer software" or any type of electronic medium or device. This exclusion of electronic data was added after courts in some states held that electronic data was tangible property and therefore a liability claim for loss of electronic data could be covered under a CGL policy. The exclusion clarifies that the CGL does not cover such claims. Coverage for this exposure can be added to the CGL form by endorsement. The Electronic Data Liability Endorsement redefines "property damage" to include loss of electronic data. The endorsement also imposes a "loss of electronic data limit," which restricts the amount the insurer will pay for loss of electronic data in any one occurrence.

3.   Injury or Damage to Which the Insurance Applies

The insurer is not obligated to pay damages if any of the Coverage A exclusions applies to the claim or if the claim is not covered for any other reason. The Coverage A exclusions are described in a later section of this chapter.

4.   Caused by an "Occurrence"

Occurrence
An accident, including continuous or repeated exposure to substantially the same general harmful conditions.

To be insured, the bodily injury or property damage must be caused by an "occurrence." The policy definition of **occurrence** is "an accident, including continuous or repeated exposure to substantially the same general harmful conditions."

The term "accident" is not defined in the policy. However, the intent is to provide coverage for any adverse condition that continues over a long period and eventually results in bodily injury or property damage, as well as for an event that happens suddenly and results in immediate bodily injury or property damage. In either case, the bodily injury or property damage would be caused by an "occurrence."

Unintended results of intentional acts generally qualify as accidents. For example, in using a propane torch to thaw out a customer's frozen water pipe (an intentional act), a plumber might accidentally set the building on fire. The fire, because it was an unintended result, would qualify as an accident. In contrast, if a plumber intentionally set a customer's house on fire, perhaps to get back at a customer who refused to pay for the plumber's services, the fire (an example of arson) would not be considered an accident or, by extension, an "occurrence."

5.   "Coverage Territory"

Coverage A applies only to occurrences that take place in the "coverage territory" defined in the policy. The coverage territory that applies to most claims is the United States (including its territories and possessions), Puerto Rico, and Canada. International waters and international airspace are included in the coverage territory if the injury or damage occurs in the course of travel or transportation between places included in the basic coverage territory described above.

The coverage territory also includes the entire world with respect to the following:

- Goods or products made or sold by the named insured in the basic coverage territory described above

- Activities of a person whose home is in the basic coverage territory but who is away for a short time while pursuing the named insured's business

In either case, the insured's liability for damages must be determined either in a suit filed in the basic coverage territory (the United States, its territories or possessions, Puerto Rico, or Canada) or in a settlement to which the insurer agrees.

6. Injury or Damage Occurring During the Policy Period

The occurrence version of the CGL coverage form requires that, in order for a claim to be covered, the bodily injury or property damage must occur during the policy period. This requirement is the so-called **occurrence coverage trigger.** In other words, the policy that applies to a particular claim is the one that is in effect when the bodily injury or property damage occurs. This is so even if the claim is not made until many years after the policy period ends.

Occurrence coverage trigger
Bodily injury or property damage that occurs during the policy period; what triggers coverage under the "occurrence" version of the CGL coverage form.

In the 2001 revision of CGL forms, a trigger-related provision was added to the occurrence CGL coverage form. The provision reinforces the idea that if any insured became aware of injury or damage before the policy took effect, the injury or damage will be deemed to have occurred before the current policy period and thus will not be covered under the current policy. This provision was developed in response to a California court case in which the court adopted a "continuous injury trigger." The continuous injury trigger holds that injury or damage is deemed to occur continuously over time as long as an injury continues, thus triggering coverage under all occurrence-based policies in effect while the injury was ongoing. The provision is referred to as either the continuous or progressive injury provision or the Montrose provision (after the name of the plaintiff in the court case referred to above).

The claims-made version of the CGL coverage form contains a different coverage trigger. Basically, the *claim* for bodily injury or property damage must be first made during the policy period. However, several additional conditions apply. The claims-made form will be described in more detail in Chapter 9.

Insurer's Duty To Defend

The Coverage A insuring agreement also expresses the insurer's right and duty to defend the insured against any suit seeking damages for bodily injury or property damage to which the insurance applies. The policy defines the word "suit" to include arbitration or other alternative dispute resolution proceedings, as well as formal lawsuits.

Courts frequently describe the insurer's duty to defend as being broader than its duty to pay damages. The insurer must defend its insured whenever a claimant alleges a wrongful act or omission of the insured that could conceivably fall within the coverage of the policy. The duty to defend exists even if the allegations are later proved to be groundless, false, or fraudulent. In many cases, a plaintiff will allege various acts or omissions, some of which may be clearly outside the scope of coverage. However, as long as at least *one* of the alleged acts or omissions is conceivably covered, the insurer is usually obligated to defend the insured against the entire complaint.

Coverage A Exclusions

Fifteen exclusions, labeled *a* through *o* in the CGL coverage form, apply to Coverage A. Many of these exclusions contain exceptions that restore coverage for certain types of claims.

Many of the exclusions eliminate coverage for exposures (such as automobile liability, workers compensation, and pollution liability) that are customarily insured under other policies or that can be insured, for an additional premium, under endorsements to the CGL coverage form. A smaller number of exclusions deal with exposures (such as intentional injury or product recall) that are uninsurable or, at best, difficult to insure.

Expected or Intended Injury

Exclusion *a* eliminates coverage for bodily injury or property damage expected or intended by the insured. Thus, there would be no coverage if the insured intentionally injured the claimant. However, the exclusion does not apply to bodily injury resulting from the use of reasonable force to protect persons or property. For example, a store owner might use *reasonable* force to restrain a customer from defacing merchandise. This act of protecting property would be covered even though the store owner intentionally used force. Acts undertaken to protect persons or property are not covered if *excessive* force is used.

Contractual Liability

Exclusion *b* eliminates coverage for liability assumed by the insured under a contract. This exclusion applies only if the liability would not have existed in the absence of the contract. That is, if liability for a claim could have been imposed by tort law, the exclusion will not apply even though the insured might also have assumed liability for the claim under a hold harmless agreement.

More significantly, the exclusion also does not apply to liability assumed under an "insured contract" if the bodily injury or property damage occurs after the contract or agreement is executed. Therefore, the CGL form *covers* liability assumed under any contract that meets the policy definition of "insured contract"—as long as the bodily injury or property damage occurs after the contract is executed.

Definition of "Insured Contract"

The policy definition of **insured contract** includes the following:

1. A lease of premises, but not that portion of a lease of premises that indemnifies another party for fire damage to premises rented to or temporarily occupied by the insured

2. A railroad sidetrack agreement

3. Any easement or license agreement, except in connection with construction or demolition within fifty feet of a railroad

4. An obligation to indemnify a municipality if required by ordinance, except in connection with work performed for the municipality

5. An elevator maintenance agreement

6. Any other contract or agreement pertaining to the insured's business under which the insured assumes the *tort* liability of another

Item 6 above covers contracts not specifically listed in items 1 through 5. Thus, for example, if the insured assumed the tort liability of another party under a hold harmless agreement in a construction contract, such an agreement would be an "insured contract."

However, the following types of contracts are specifically excluded from the definition of "insured contract" and therefore are not covered:

1. Contracts to indemnify a railroad for bodily injury or property damage arising from construction or demolition operations within fifty feet of a railroad property and affecting any railroad bridge or trestle, tracks, roadbeds, tunnel, underpass, or crossing

2. Contracts to indemnify architects, engineers, or surveyors for their errors or omissions in performing their professional duties

3. Contracts under which architects, engineers, or surveyors assume liability for injury or damage arising from their errors and omissions in performing their professional duties

Defense Costs Assumed Under Contract

In many cases, a hold harmless agreement will obligate the insured to pay the other party's defense costs in addition to its damages. Earlier versions of the CGL policy did not specifically address defense costs assumed under contract. Although some insurers paid such costs under their CGL policies, other insurers held that CGL contractual liability coverage applied only to damages and not to defense costs.

Insured contract
A contract under which liability assumed by the insured is covered in the CGL; includes a lease of premises, a sidetrack agreement, an easement or license agreement, an obligation (as required by ordinance) to indemnify a municipality, an elevator maintenance agreement, or that part of any other contract pertaining to the insured's business under which the insured assumes the tort liability of another party.

The current edition of the CGL coverage form obligates the insurer to pay reasonable attorney fees and necessary litigation expenses assumed by the insured under an insured contract. However, such expenses paid by the insurer are treated as "damages" and thus are subject to the policy limits. In contrast, the insurer is obligated to pay regular defense costs (those incurred in defending the insured against direct claims) *in addition* to policy limits.

Liquor Liability

Exclusion *c* applies only to insureds who are in the business of manufacturing, distributing, selling, serving, or furnishing alcoholic beverages. It eliminates coverage if liability arises from causing or contributing to the intoxication of any person, from furnishing alcoholic beverages to a person under the legal drinking age, or otherwise violating the laws governing the sale and distribution of such beverages. The liquor liability exclusion does not apply to the casual or occasional distribution of alcoholic beverages, such as at an annual company picnic or holiday office party, as long as the insured is not in the alcoholic beverage business.

Workers Compensation and Employers Liability

Exclusions *d* and *e* deal with injuries to any employee of the insured. Exclusion *d* eliminates coverage for obligations of the insured under any workers compensation, disability benefits, unemployment compensation, or similar law.

Exclusion *e* eliminates coverage for bodily injury to any employee of the insured if the injury arises out of and in the course of employment. The exclusion applies regardless of whether the insured is liable in a capacity other than as an employer. It also applies to obligations to share damages with someone else or to repay someone who has paid damages. However, the exclusion does not apply to liability assumed by the insured under an insured contract.

The CGL coverage form defines "employee" to include a "leased worker." Thus, exclusion *e* applies to both normal employees and leased workers as defined. A "leased worker" is a worker leased to the insured by a labor-leasing firm to perform duties related to the insured's business. Many businesses use leased workers in an attempt to reduce record keeping and paperwork, provide better employee benefits at lower cost, and achieve other savings. A temporary worker—that is, a worker furnished to the insured to substitute for a permanent employee on leave or to meet seasonal or short-term workload conditions—is excluded from the definitions of "employee" and "leased worker." Thus, exclusion *e* does not apply to injuries to temporary workers.

Pollution

Exclusion *f* eliminates coverage for pollution liability claims related to the insured's premises and operations. The exclusion is worded very broadly in order to encompass the many ways pollutants might enter the environment. It deals with bodily injury and property damage resulting from pollution and with the cost or expense involved with the cleanup of pollutants.

The exclusion is virtually absolute with regard to the insured's premises, sites, or locations (past and present) as well as premises, sites, or locations used by the insured for the handling, storage, disposal, processing, or treatment of waste. The exclusion expresses several exceptions, which provide coverage for the following:

- Bodily injury sustained in a building and caused by smoke, fumes, vapor, or soot from the building's heating equipment.
- Bodily injury or property damage caused by heat, smoke, or fumes from a hostile fire. A hostile fire is a fire that becomes uncontrollable or breaks out from where it was intended to be.
- Bodily injury or property damage resulting from the escape of fuels, lubricants, or other operating fluids needed to perform the normal functions of mobile equipment. The fuels, lubricants, or operating fluids must escape from a vehicle part designed to hold them, and the escape must be accidental.
- Bodily injury or property damage sustained in a building and caused by the release of gases, fumes, or vapors from materials brought into that building in connection with operations being performed by the named insured or on the named insured's behalf by a contractor or subcontractor.

By inference from the wording of the exclusion, the exclusion does not apply to bodily injury or property damage resulting from pollution caused by the insured's products or completed operations away from the insured's premises. For example, a family might be taken ill by chemical vapors emanating from carpeting sold by the insured. The family's claim for bodily injury would not be excluded.

By inference, the exclusion also does not apply to work being performed away from the insured's premises by the insured or by a contractor or subcontractor working on the insured's behalf as long as the following are true:

1. The pollutants are not brought onto the site by the insured, the contractor, or the subcontractor.
2. The operations do not in any way involve testing for, monitoring, or cleaning up pollutants.

To illustrate, the insured, an excavation contractor, might accidentally run a bulldozer into another contractor's oil storage tank at a work site. As long as the insured did not bring the oil onto the site, any liability that the insured might have for resulting bodily injury or property damage would be covered under the insured's CGL policy.

Aircraft, Auto, and Watercraft

Auto
A land motor vehicle, trailer, or semitrailer designed for travel on public roads, including attached machinery or equipment, but excluding mobile equipment.

Loading or unloading
The handling of property (1) after it is moved from the place where it is accepted for movement onto an aircraft, watercraft, or auto; (2) while on any such vehicle; or (3) while being moved from such vehicle to the place where it is finally delivered. Does not include movement by means of a mechanical device (other than a hand truck) that is not attached to the vehicle.

Exclusion *g* eliminates coverage for bodily injury and property damage arising from the ownership, maintenance, or use of any aircraft, "auto," or watercraft. As defined by the form, an **auto** is a land motor vehicle, trailer, or semitrailer designed for travel on public roads, including any attached machinery or equipment. However, any land motor vehicle that is included within the definition of "mobile equipment" (discussed below) is not an "auto."

The exclusion also applies to the **loading or unloading** of aircraft, autos, and watercraft. As defined in the coverage form, loading or unloading occurs when property is handled during the following periods:

- After it is moved from the place where it is accepted for movement into or onto an aircraft, auto, or watercraft
- While it is on such a conveyance
- While it is being moved from the conveyance to the place where it is finally delivered

Loading or unloading includes the movement of property by a hand truck but not the movement of property by any other mechanical device that is not attached to the conveyance.

To illustrate the definition of loading or unloading, assume that an appliance store sold a deep freezer to a customer and agreed to deliver the freezer to the customer's home and place it in the basement. The store employees delivering the freezer accidentally gouged wood trim and wallboard while moving the freezer down the basement stairs. According to the definition, the damage occurred during loading or unloading (that is, while the freezer was being moved from the store's truck "to the place where it is finally delivered"). Thus, the customer's claim for property damage will not be covered under the store's CGL policy. It will, however, be covered under the store's auto liability insurance as long as the delivery truck is a covered auto.

Some coverage for claims involving aircraft, autos, and watercraft is provided through the following exceptions to exclusion *g*:

1. Claims arising from watercraft while ashore on the insured's premises are covered.
2. Claims arising out of nonowned watercraft are covered if the craft is less than twenty-six feet long and is not being used to carry persons or property for a fee.
3. Liability assumed under an insured contract for the ownership, maintenance, or use of aircraft or watercraft (but not autos) is covered.
4. The operation of certain types of equipment (such as a cherry picker) attached to autos is covered.
5. Claims arising from parking an auto on or next to the insured's premises are covered if the auto is not owned by, rented to, or loaned to any insured.

The last exception listed above primarily benefits organizations that provide valet parking service. If, for example, a restaurant employee, while parking a patron's car in the restaurant's parking lot, negligently struck another car and injured its driver, the restaurant's CGL policy would cover the damage to the other car and the injury to its driver. Damage to the customer's auto would not be covered by the CGL, however, because of exclusion j, discussed below. Liability for damage to customers' autos in the insured's care, custody, or control can be covered through garagekeepers insurance, discussed in Chapter 10.

Mobile Equipment

The only CGL exclusion that specifically applies to mobile equipment is exclusion h, which applies only in narrow circumstances. Thus, the CGL form generally covers liability arising out of the ownership, maintenance, or use of mobile equipment.

The mobile equipment exclusion eliminates coverage for the following:

1. The transportation of "mobile equipment" by an auto that is owned, operated, rented, or borrowed by an insured

2. The use of mobile equipment in a prearranged racing, speed, or demolition contest or in a stunting activity

The policy definition of **mobile equipment** includes a variety of motorized land vehicles and any machinery or equipment attached to them. The types of vehicles included in the definition of "mobile equipment" are presented in Exhibit 8-2. The exhibit also lists the types of equipment that are considered "autos." Although most claims involving autos are excluded from CGL coverage, claims arising from the operation of "mobile equipment" as defined are covered as long as they are not excluded by exclusion h.

Note that a truck can be classified as mobile equipment if it is used solely on or next to the insured's premises. Thus, an accident involving a truck used only to move beams around the storage yard of an iron and steel wholesaler would be covered under the wholesaler's CGL policy.

Mobile equipment
Various types of vehicles designed for use principally off public roads, such as bulldozers and cranes.

EXHIBIT 8-2

Distinction Between "Mobile Equipment" and "Autos" in the CGL Coverage Form

"Mobile Equipment"

The following types of land vehicles, including attached equipment:

a. Bulldozers, farm machinery, forklifts and other vehicles designed for use principally off public roads

b. Vehicles maintained for use solely on or next to premises owned or rented by the named insured

---

Continued on next page.

c. Vehicles that travel on crawler treads

d. Vehicles (self-propelled or not) maintained primarily to provide mobility to permanently mounted power cranes, shovels, loaders, diggers, drills, or road construction or resurfacing equipment such as graders, scrapers, or rollers

e. Vehicles that are not self-propelled and are maintained primarily to provide mobility to permanently attached equipment of the following types: air compressors, pumps, and generators (including spraying, welding, building cleaning, geophysical exploration, lighting, or well servicing equipment) and cherry pickers and similar devices used to raise or lower workers

f. Vehicles not described above that are maintained primarily for purposes other than transportation of persons or cargo

"Autos"

Land motor vehicles, trailers, or semitrailers designed for travel on public roads, including any attached machinery or equipment

Self-propelled vehicles with the following types of permanently attached equipment:

- Snow removal

- Road maintenance (not construction or resurfacing)

- Street cleaning

- Cherry pickers and similar devices mounted on automobile or truck chassis and used to raise or lower workers*

- Air compressors, pumps, and generators, including spraying, welding, building cleaning, geophysical exploration, lighting, and well servicing

* The operation of these types of attached equipment is covered under the CGL. However, the operation of the vehicles to which the equipment is attached is *not* covered by the CGL.

War

It is unlikely that an insured would be held directly liable for bodily injury or property damage resulting from war. However, an insured might become obligated under an "insured contract" for some war-related claims. Consequently, exclusion *i* of the CGL form excludes liability resulting from war if the liability is assumed under a contract or other type of agreement.

Damage to Property

Exclusion *j* eliminates coverage for damage to any of the following:

1. Property owned, rented, or occupied by the named insured

2. Premises the named insured has sold, given away, or abandoned if the damage arises out of any part of such premises

3. Property loaned to the named insured

4. Personal property in the care, custody, or control of an insured

5. That particular part of any real property on which work is being done by the named insured or any contractor or subcontractor working for the named insured if the damage arises from the work

6. That particular part of any property that must be restored, repaired, or replaced because the named insured's work was incorrectly performed on it

It is usually possible to purchase other policies to cover many of the excluded items. The insured's property, excluded by item 1, can be insured by the Building and Personal Property Coverage Form or by another property insurance form. Other property in the insured's custody, excluded by items 1, 3, and 4, can be covered in a property insurance form or in various inland marine forms.

An exception to exclusion *j* provides limited coverage for property damage (other than damage by fire) to premises, including contents of such premises, rented to the named insured for seven or fewer consecutive days. This coverage is subject to the Damage to Premises Rented to You limit shown in the policy declarations. *Fire* damage to premises rented to or occupied by the named insured is covered separately by an additional provision discussed later in this chapter under the heading "Fire Legal Liability Coverage." Fire legal liability coverage is also subject to the Damage to Premises Rented to You limit.

Item 2 does not apply to premises that are the named insured's work if they were never occupied, rented, or held for rental by the insured. This exception provides coverage for a builder who constructs a building for sale and later becomes liable for damage to the building after it has been sold. Furthermore, since the exclusion applies only to property damage, bodily injury arising out of premises the named insured has sold, given away, or abandoned would be covered.

Items 5 and 6 often cause confusion. Item 5 excludes only "that particular part" of *real property* on which the named insured is working. The exclusion does not, therefore, apply to *personal property* under any circumstances, and it applies only to "that particular part" of real property on which the insured is working. To illustrate, say that the insured is an electrician who is installing electrical components in a building under construction. If, while working on an electrical control panel, the electrician negligently causes a fire that burns down the entire building, item 5 will only exclude damage to "that particular part" on which the insured was working. "That particular part" would presumably be limited to the control panel. Damage to the rest of the building would be covered.

Item 6 applies to "that particular part" of either real property or personal property that must be repaired or replaced because the insured's work on it was done incorrectly. In other words, the insurer will not pay the cost of redoing the insured's faulty work. The insurer will, however, pay for damage to property other than "that particular part" that must be redone.

To illustrate the application of item 6, assume that a remodeling contractor installed a faulty roof on a home addition that he was constructing. Before the addition was completed, rainwater entered the addition and damaged the inside of the addition, and the owner made claim against the contractor for resulting damages. Item 6 under the contractor's CGL policy would exclude the cost of repairing the roof, but it would not exclude the cost of repairing the other parts of the building that were damaged because of the faulty roof.

Insured's Products and Work

Four CGL exclusions (*k* through *n*) relate directly to the insured's products and work. In general, they exclude claims for damage to the insured's products or to work performed by or on behalf of the insured if the damage arises from defects in the insured's products or work. The primary purpose of this group of exclusions is to prevent the insurer from having to pay for failures of the insured's products or work—other than bodily injury or damage to property besides the insured's own product or work. The CGL form contains detailed definitions of "your product" and "your work," which will not be restated here.

Damage to Your Product

Exclusion *k* eliminates coverage for any damage to the insured's product if the damage results from a defect in any part of the product. For example, if cabinets that the insured manufactured collapse because of a defect in the cabinets, the damage to the cabinets would not be covered. However, the insured's CGL policy would cover claims for breakage of the contents of the cabinets.

Damage to Your Work

Exclusion *l* is similar to exclusion *k*, but it applies to claims for property damage to the insured's work rather than to the insured's products. The exclusion applies only to completed work—not to work that is still being performed when the property damage occurs. (Damage to property being worked on is addressed by exclusion *j*.)

Exclusion *l* does not apply to claims if either the damaged work or the work from which the damage arose was performed for the insured by a subcontractor. For example, assume that defective plumbing caused extensive damage to a house built by Miller Construction Company but not owned by Miller at the time of the damage. If Miller did all of the work, including the plumbing, there would be no coverage for any claim based on damage from the plumbing. If a subcontractor did the plumbing, then claims against Miller for damage caused by the work of the plumbing subcontractor would be covered.

Damage to Impaired Property or Property Not Physically Injured

Exclusion *m* eliminates coverage for claims for property damage to "impaired property" or property that has not been physically injured if the damage arises from (1) a defect in the insured's product or work or (2) failure of the insured or anyone acting on behalf of the insured to complete a contract or agreement in accordance with its terms.

The form defines "impaired property" as tangible property other than the insured's product or work that cannot be used or is less useful because (1) it includes the insured's defective product or defective work or (2) the insured has failed to fulfill a contract or agreement.

To illustrate the application of the exclusion to impaired property, assume that BC Company manufactures small electric motors that are incorporated in drills produced by other companies. If the BC motors are defective and must be replaced so that the drills will function properly, the drills would be "impaired property." Accordingly, BC's CGL policy would not cover claims against BC for the loss in value of the drills or for the cost of replacing the motors.

The exclusion also applies to property damage to "property that has not been physically injured." Remember that the definition of "property damage" includes loss of use of property that has not been physically injured. However, the exclusion under consideration eliminates coverage for such loss-of-use claims when the cause is a defect in the insured's product or work or the insured's failure to perform a contract.

To illustrate this aspect of the exclusion, suppose that Acme Heating Company installed a furnace in a new office building. However, the furnace was defective and did not provide sufficient heat for the building. Consequently, occupancy of the building was delayed for several weeks while a new furnace was ordered and installed. The building owner sustained a loss of income because the building could not be occupied. The owner might have a valid legal claim against Acme, but it would not be covered under Acme's CGL policy because of exclusion m: the loss of use of the building (which was not physically injured) resulted from a defect in Acme's product.

However, the exclusion contains an important exception. The exclusion does not apply if loss of use of property other than the insured's product or work arises out of *sudden and accidental damage* to the insured's product or work after it has been put to its intended use.

Returning to the example of Acme Heating Company, suppose that the building opening was delayed because the furnace had been suddenly and accidentally damaged by an explosion inside its firebox. In this case, the impaired property exclusion would not apply, and Acme's CGL policy would cover the building owner's claim for the resulting loss of use of the building. (Damage to the furnace itself would still be excluded, because of the "damage to your product" exclusion.)

Recall of Products, Work, or Impaired Property

Exclusion n eliminates coverage for any loss, cost, or expense resulting from loss of use, withdrawal, recall, inspection, repair, replacement, adjustment, removal, or disposal of (1) the insured's product, (2) the insured's work, or (3) impaired property.

Manufacturers must often recall products that are found to pose a risk of serious injury to users or others. Even though such a recall may avoid claims that would be covered by the policy, the CGL policy does not (because of exclusion n) cover the cost of the recall. Such recalls can be extremely expensive. Johnson & Johnson spent over $100 million removing Tylenol from store shelves after the deaths of seven persons who ingested cyanide-contaminated capsules.[1]

Personal and Advertising Injury

The final exclusion under Coverage A eliminates coverage—under Coverage A only—for bodily injury arising out of "personal and advertising injury." Bodily injury resulting from a "personal and advertising injury" offense (such as bodily injury caused by a security guard's false arrest and detention of a store customer) is covered under Coverage B—Personal and Advertising Injury Liability of the CGL policy.

Fire Legal Liability Coverage

An exception to exclusions c through n at the end of the Coverage A exclusions grants coverage for fire damage to premises rented to or temporarily occupied by the named insured. This coverage, widely known as **fire legal liability coverage,** insures claims that would otherwise be excluded by exclusion j, which applies to property that the named insured rents or occupies.

To illustrate the application of fire legal liability coverage, assume that the insured occupies, under lease, part of a multi-tenant building. Assume also that the insured's negligence causes a fire in its own part of the building. In this case, the insured's liability to the building owner for fire damage to that part of the building would be covered by the fire legal liability coverage in the insured's CGL policy; that is, the exclusion of damage to property rented or occupied by the insured would not apply. This coverage is subject to the Damage to Premises Rented to You limit shown in the policy declarations.

The insured's liability for damage to any *other* parts of the building would also be covered, regardless of the fire legal liability coverage, since the other parts of the building are not rented or occupied by the insured. A claim for damage to such other parts of the building would not be subject to the Damage to Premises Rented to You limit. Instead, it would primarily be subject to the each occurrence limit, which is normally set higher than the Damage to Premises Rented to You limit. CGL policy limits will be discussed in more detail in Chapter 9.

Fire legal liability coverage
Coverage for fire damage to premises rented to or temporarily occupied by the named insured.

COVERAGE B—PERSONAL AND ADVERTISING INJURY LIABILITY

Coverage B of the CGL form insures against claims based on torts such as libel, slander, and wrongful eviction. The provisions relating to Coverage B, like those relating to Coverage A, consist of an insuring agreement and several exclusions.

Coverage B Insuring Agreement

The Coverage B insuring agreement parallels the Coverage A insuring agreement in several ways. The insurer agrees to pay those sums that the insured becomes legally obligated to pay as damages. In addition, the insurer agrees to defend the insured against any suit seeking such damages. However, instead of responding to claims for bodily injury and property damage, Coverage B responds to claims for "personal and advertising injury" to which the insurance applies.

The CGL policy defines **personal and advertising injury** to include several specific offenses. The policy definition is reproduced in Exhibit 8-3.

Personal and advertising injury
Injury that is covered by Coverage B of the CGL. Includes injury resulting from numerous offenses such as false detention, malicious prosecution, wrongful eviction, slander, libel, use of another's advertising idea, and copyright infringement.

EXHIBIT 8-3

CGL Policy Definition of "Personal and Advertising Injury"

"Personal and advertising injury" means injury, including consequential "bodily injury", arising out of one or more of the following offenses:

a. False arrest, detention or imprisonment;

b. Malicious prosecution;

c. The wrongful eviction from, wrongful entry into, or invasion of the right of private occupancy of a room, dwelling or premises that a person occupies, committed by or on behalf of its owner, landlord or lessor;

d. Oral or written publication, in any manner, of material that slanders or libels a person or organization or disparages a person's or organization's goods, products or services;

e. Oral or written publication, in any manner, of material that violates a person's right of privacy;

f. The use of another's advertising idea in your "advertisement"; or

g. Infringing upon another's copyright, trade dress* or slogan in your "advertisement".

* The term "trade dress" refers to the overall appearance and image of a product.

Although the CGL form does not define "injury," it states that injury includes consequential bodily injury. In its usual and ordinary sense, the word "injury" has a broad meaning and can include not only physical harm or impairment but also mental anguish, mental injury, fright, shock, humiliation, and loss of reputation. Courts can award damages for any of the above types of harm that result from the offenses included in the CGL definition of "personal and advertising injury."

To be covered, a personal and advertising injury offense must be committed within the CGL "coverage territory." The policy definition of "coverage territory" was discussed earlier in connection with Coverage A of the CGL. One part of the definition, which was not discussed earlier, applies only to personal and advertising injury. The coverage territory includes worldwide coverage for personal and advertising injury offenses that take place through the Internet or similar electronic means of communication. This does not mean that the CGL form covers all Internet-related liability for personal and advertising injury liability. In fact, some of the Coverage B exclusions directly exclude some Internet loss exposures.

Under the occurrence CGL coverage form, the coverage trigger for Coverage B is a covered offense committed during the policy period. That is, the policy in effect when the insured committed the offense is the policy that covers any damages resulting from that offense (even if claim is not made until after the policy has expired).

Coverage B Exclusions

Coverage B is subject to fourteen exclusions, designated *a* through *n*. These exclusions eliminate coverage for the following:

a. Injury caused by or at the direction of the insured with the knowledge that the act would violate the rights of another person and inflict personal and advertising injury. Example: The insured knowingly uses a competitor's advertising ideas in its own advertisements.

b. Injury arising out of oral or written publication of material, if done by or at the direction of the insured with knowledge of its falsity. Example: The insured knowingly makes false statements about a competitor.

c. Injury arising out of publication of material whose first publication took place before the beginning of the policy period. Example: an advertisement used by the insured in late 2001 and early 2002 caused injury to a competitor; the insured's CGL policy whose inception date was January 1, 2002, would not cover any injury resulting from this advertisement. (In the claims-made CGL coverage form, this exclusion applies to material whose first publication took place before the policy's retroactive date, if any.)

d. Injury arising out of a criminal act committed by or at the direction of the insured. Example: The insured paid an individual to spray-paint defamatory graffiti on a competitor's building. Because the spray-painting was a criminal act (vandalism), the insured's CGL policy would not cover a resulting suit against the insured for personal or advertising injury resulting from the criminal act.

e. Injury for which the insured has assumed liability in a contract or agreement (other than liability that the insured would have in the absence of the contract or agreement). Example: In a contract with a provider of security services, the insured, a department store, assumes liability for all "personal injury" occurring on its premises. After an employee of the security firm detains a customer suspected of shoplifting, the customer sues the security firm for false imprisonment, and the security firm demands that the insured provide a defense.

f. Injury arising out of a breach of contract. Example: The insured fails to deliver goods to a buyer in accordance with a sales contract. The buyer alleges that the insured had advertised "an abundant supply" of the goods in question.

g. Injury arising out of the failure of goods, products, or services to conform with any statement of quality or performance made in the named insured's advertisement. Example: A buyer of the insured's "wrinkle cream" sued the insured, alleging that the cream did not "get rid of those old crow's-feet" as promised in the insured's advertising.

h. Injury arising out of the wrong description of the price of goods, products, or services stated in the named insured's advertisement. Example: The insured, an auto dealer, advertised a new car for $2,399 instead of its actual price of $23,999. When the insured refused to sell the advertised car for that amount, several potential buyers sued for the $21,600 difference between the actual price and the advertised price.

i. Injury arising out of the infringement of copyright, patent, trademark, trade secret, or other intellectual property rights. This exclusion does not apply to infringement, *in the named insured's advertisement,* of copyright, trade dress, or slogan. Example: The insured manufactured a product that infringed upon another organization's patent.

j. Injury committed by an insured whose business is any of the following: advertising, broadcasting, publishing, or telecasting; designing or determining the content of Web sites for others; or an Internet search, access, content, or service provider. However, this exclusion does not apply to paragraphs a., b., and c. of the definition of "personal and advertising injury" (see Exhibit 8-2). Furthermore, the exclusion states that the placing of frames, borders or links, or advertising, for the named insured or others anywhere on the Internet, is not considered the business of advertising, broadcasting, publishing, or telecasting. Because of this exclusion, organizations that engage in the businesses listed above need to obtain special policies covering personal or advertising injury arising out of their activities. Example: The insured, a publishing company, was sued for libelous statements that appeared in a book published by the insured.

k. Injury arising out of an electronic chatroom or bulletin board that the insured hosts, owns, or controls. Example: The insured, a public interest group, posted a newspaper editorial on its electronic bulletin board. The editorial falsely accused a public official of criminal behavior. The public official sued the insured for libel.

l. Injury arising out of the unauthorized use of another organization's name or product in the named insured's e-mail address, domain name, or metatag, or any other similar tactics to mislead the potential customers of another organization. Example: An organization picked a domain name that was deceptively similar to the principal competitor's name, and the competitor sued for unauthorized use of its name.

m. Injury arising out of the actual, alleged, or threatened discharge of pollutants at any time. Unlike the pollution exclusion under Coverage A, this pollution exclusion has no exceptions.

n. Any loss, cost, or expense arising out of (1) any request, demand, or order to test for, monitor, or clean up pollutants or (2) any claim or suit by or on behalf of a governmental authority for damages because of testing for, monitoring, or cleaning up pollutants.

SUPPLEMENTARY PAYMENTS

The CGL coverage form contains a section titled "Supplementary Payments," which supplements the insuring agreements for Coverages A and B. Both of those insuring agreements obligate the insurer to defend any claim or suit seeking damages if such damages would be covered under the policy. The supplementary payments section describes the specific items that the insurer will pay (in addition to damages).

The supplementary payments are payable in addition to the limits of insurance that apply to CGL coverage. However, the insurer's obligation to pay these supplementary payments ends as soon as the applicable limit of insurance has been used up in paying damages for judgments or settlements. The supplementary payments consist of the following:

*   All expenses incurred by the insurer, such as fees for attorneys, witness fees, cost of police reports, and similar items.

*   Up to $250 for the cost of bail bonds required because of accidents or traffic law violations involving any covered vehicle (typically mobile equipment).

*   The cost of bonds to release any property of the insured's held by a plaintiff to ensure payment of any judgment that may be rendered against the insured. The insurer is not required to provide either of the bonds described above; its only obligation is to pay the premium.

*   Reasonable expenses incurred by the insured at the insurer's request, including loss of earnings (up to $250 a day) if the insured must miss work to testify, attend court, or otherwise assist in the defense.

*   Court costs or other costs (other than actual damages) assessed against the insured in a suit.

- Interest on judgments awarded against the insured. In some cases, courts will award either prejudgment interest or post-judgment interest, or both, to a plaintiff. Prejudgment interest is interest that accrues on the amount of a judgment before entry of the judgment. Post-judgment interest is interest that accrues after the judgment is entered but before the judgment is paid to the plaintiff. Under the CGL coverage form, the insurer agrees to pay either type of interest. However, if the insurer offers to pay the applicable limit of insurance to a third-party claimant, the insurer will not pay any prejudgment interest for the period of time after the offer is made.

The supplementary payments of the 1996 and later editions of the CGL coverage form contain an additional provision, relating to the costs of defending a person or organization (called an "indemnitee") that the insured has agreed to hold harmless or indemnify under an "insured contract."

As discussed earlier in this chapter, the contractual liability exclusion states that any defense costs paid to an indemnitee under an insured contract are payable *within policy limits*. In contrast, the supplementary payments provision states that the insurer will pay an indemnitee's defense costs *in addition to policy limits* if an indemnitee and an insured are both named as parties in the same suit.

This supplementary payment applies only if the insured has assumed the obligation to defend the indemnitee under an insured contract and no conflict appears to exist between the interests of the insured and the interests of the indemnitee. Moreover, the indemnitee must cooperate with the insurer in the defense and perform essentially the same duties as any other insured would have to perform. The insurer's duty to defend ends when the insurer has paid the applicable limit of insurance.

COVERAGE C—MEDICAL PAYMENTS

Medical payments coverage is not liability insurance, because it pays regardless of whether the insured is legally liable. However, the coverage provides a modest amount of insurance for settling minor injury cases without having to make a determination of liability. In that sense, the coverage provides a means of making prompt settlements, satisfying potential liability claimants, and avoiding possibly larger liability claims.

Coverage C Insuring Agreement

The insurer agrees to pay medical expenses (including, by definition, funeral expenses) for bodily injury caused by an accident occurring on or next to premises that the insured owns or rents. Bodily injury caused by an accident that occurs away from the insured's premises or next to them is covered if the accident results from the named insured's operations.

The accident must occur in the CGL coverage territory and during the policy period. The medical expenses must be incurred and reported to the insurer within one year after the date of the accident. An injured person who wishes to receive medical payments coverage must agree to be examined by a physician designated by the insurance company.

Coverage C Exclusions

CGL medical payments coverage does not apply to bodily injury to the following persons:

- Any insured (other than a volunteer worker of the named insured)
- Anyone hired to do work for an insured or for a tenant of an insured
- A person injured on that part of the named insured's premises which the person normally occupies
- A person entitled to workers compensation benefits for the injury
- A person injured while taking part in athletics

Medical payments coverage also does not apply to bodily injury included within the products-completed operations hazard, bodily injury excluded under Coverage A, or bodily injury caused by war.

SUMMARY

A liability loss exposure is the possibility of experiencing a liability loss. A liability loss includes all costs to an organization as the result of a specific legal claim or suit against that organization.

The person making claim or suit against the organization (the claimant) ordinarily attempts to prove that the organization is legally liable to pay damages. Anyone who wishes to evaluate an organization's liability loss exposures must understand the various ways in which the organization could become legally liable. Broadly speaking, civil liability (in contrast with criminal liability) can be based on torts, contracts, or statutes.

- Torts, which are civil wrongs, consist of negligence and various intentional torts.
- A contract is a legally enforceable agreement between two or more parties. Legal liability can result from breach of contract or from a "hold harmless" agreement.
- A statute is a written law. Statutes can either modify the duties that persons owe to others, or, as in the case of workers compensation statutes, they can create obligations to pay benefits to other persons regardless of fault.

Liability exposures covered under commercial general liability (CGL) insurance are commonly categorized as premises, operations, products, and completed operations. Other liability exposures covered by CGL insurance include liability assumed under contract and liability for some torts such as libel and slander.

The CGL coverage form provides three basic coverages:

1. Coverage A—bodily injury and property damage liability
2. Coverage B—personal and advertising injury liability
3. Coverage C—medical payments

The Coverage A insuring agreement expresses the insurer's promise to (1) pay damages for which the insured is legally liable and (2) defend the insured against claims or suits alleging bodily injury or property damage covered under the policy. The bodily injury or property damage must be caused by an occurrence, and the occurrence must take place in the coverage territory. Moreover, under the occurrence version of the CGL form, the bodily injury or property damage must occur during the policy period.

Coverage A is subject to several exclusions that further define the coverage. Subject to some exceptions, the exclusions eliminate coverage for the following:

- Injury or damage expected or intended by the insured
- Liability assumed under contract (other than an "insured contract")
- Liquor liability if the insured is in the business of selling or serving alcoholic beverages
- Injury to employees of the insured
- Liability arising from the release of pollutants
- Liability for aircraft, autos, and watercraft
- Mobile equipment while being transported by an auto or used in racing
- Damage to property owned, rented, or borrowed by the insured or to personal property in the insured's care, custody, or control
- Damage to that particular part of real property on which the insured is working
- Damage to the named insured's products or work
- Damage to "impaired property" or property not physically injured
- The cost of recalling the named insured's products or work
- Bodily injury arising out of personal and advertising injury

Coverage B of the CGL form covers claims for "personal and advertising injury" as defined in the form. This coverage insures against liability for various torts, such as libel, slander, and wrongful eviction.

Coverage C of the CGL form pays for medical expenses of persons injured on the insured's premises or as a result of the insured's operations. Coverage does not apply to bodily injury to any insured (other than a volunteer worker), to anyone who is entitled to workers compensation benefits for the same injury, or to bodily injury excluded under Coverage A.

CHAPTER NOTE

1.   Brian O'Reilly, "J & J is on a Roll," *Fortune Magazine*, December 26, 1994, p. 192.

Chapter 9

Direct Your Learning

OUTLINE

Who Is an Insured?

Limits of Insurance

Claims-Made CGL
Coverage Form

CGL Endorsements

Rating CGL Coverage

Miscellaneous Liability
Coverage Forms

Summary

Commercial General Liability Insurance, Part II

After learning the content of this chapter, you should be able to:

■ Given a case about a liability loss, explain whether coverage applies and determine the amount, if any, the insurer will pay for the loss.

- Identify the persons and organizations that may be insured by an unendorsed CGL coverage form.

- Identify the various limits of insurance in the CGL coverage form and explain how they apply.

■ Describe the CGL conditions.

■ Explain how the claims-made coverage trigger makes the claims-made CGL form differ from the occurrence CGL form.

■ Explain how the retroactive date affects the coverage provided by the claims-made CGL coverage form.

■ Describe the purpose of extended reporting periods in a claims-made form.

■ Describe the nature and purpose of the following CGL endorsement types:

- State endorsements
- Classification endorsements

- Exclusion endorsements
- Miscellaneous endorsements

■ Explain how the premium for commercial general liability coverage is determined.

■ Describe the purpose of each of the following:

- Liquor Liability Coverage Form

- Products/Completed Operations Liability Coverage Form

- Owners and Contractors Protective (OCP) Liability Coverage Form

- Railroad Protective Liability Coverage Form

Develop Your Perspective

What are the main topics covered in the chapter?

This chapter discusses the CGL policy provisions that address such questions as "Who is an insured?" and "How much will the policy pay?" This chapter also explains how the "claims-made" CGL form differs from the more common "occurrence" form, how the CGL can be modified by endorsement, and how the process of rating works with CGL coverage.

Review some of the CGL policies handled by your organization.

- Identify the various limits of insurance that apply to a CGL policy.

- What are the usual dollar limits?

Why is it important to learn about these topics?

The CGL provisions discussed in this chapter will help you determine whether a claim is covered under the policy and, if so, for how much. Understanding coverage and rating will enable you to recommend appropriate CGL endorsements and explain how CGL coverage is priced.

Locate the named insured(s) on a CGL form.

- What other individuals or organizations are also insureds under the CGL form?

- Under what circumstances might these other parties ask to be named as additional insureds under another CGL policy?

- How can they be added to the policy?

How can you use what you will learn?

Review a liability claim that would be covered under at least one of the CGL coverage agreements.

- What additional CGL provisions would you need to consider in determining whether the claim involved an "insured" and how much would be payable for the claim?

Chapter 9
Commercial General Liability Insurance, Part II

The preceding chapter described Coverage A (bodily injury and property damage liability), Coverage B (personal and advertising injury liability), and Coverage C (medical payments) of the Commercial General Liability (CGL) Coverage Form. This chapter continues the discussion of the CGL coverage form and covers the following topics:

- Who is an insured
- Limits of insurance
- CGL conditions
- Claims-made provisions
- CGL endorsements
- Rating CGL coverage

This chapter also describes several miscellaneous liability coverage forms developed by Insurance Services Office (ISO). These forms are used to cover special situations or loss exposures.

WHO IS AN INSURED?

Depending on the circumstances, many different persons or organizations may be insured under the CGL coverage form. These persons and organizations are discussed under the following three categories:

1. Named insured
2. Employees of the named insured
3. Other persons and organizations

Named Insured and Related Parties

The named insured may be an individual, a partnership, a joint venture, a corporation, a limited liability company, or a trust.

If the named insured is an individual, both the named insured and his or her spouse are insureds. However, coverage applies only to claims arising from the conduct of a business owned solely by the named insured. The named insured and spouse are not covered for their nonbusiness activities.

If the named insured is a partnership or joint venture, the named partnership or joint venture and all partners or members and their spouses also are insureds, but only for liability claims arising out of the conduct of the business of the partnership or joint venture.

If the named insured is a limited liability company (an entity that in some ways resembles a partnership and in other ways resembles a corporation), the named company is an insured, as are the following:

1. The "members" of the company (the persons who receive the company's income), but only with respect to the conduct of the named insured's business
2. The managers of the company, but only with respect to their duties as managers of the named insured

If the named insured is an organization other than a partnership, joint venture, or limited liability company (for example, a corporation, a school district, a municipality, or an association), then all executive officers, directors, and stockholders are insureds, but only with respect to their liability as officers, directors, or stockholders.

If the named insured is a trust (a legal entity created for the benefit of designated beneficiaries), the named trust is an insured. The named insured's trustees are also insureds, but only with respect to their duties as trustees.

Employees and Volunteer Workers of the Named Insured

Employees and volunteer workers of the named insured are covered for liability claims arising from their duties as such. However, an employee or volunteer worker is not an insured for the following:

*   Bodily injury or personal and advertising injury to the named insured, to the named insured's partners or members (if the named insured is a partnership or joint venture), or to a co-employee or other volunteer worker while in the course of his or her duties as such
*   Bodily injury or personal and advertising injury arising out of the employee's or volunteer worker's providing or failing to provide professional health-care services (for example, a doctor employed by the named insured who provides improper medical treatment to a co-employee or a guest visiting the named insured's place of business)
*   Property damage to property owned, occupied, or used by any of the following: the named insured, the named insured's employees, the named insured's volunteer workers, or the named insured's partners or members

Other Persons and Organizations

In addition to the named insured and the named insured's employees, several other persons and organizations are insureds under certain circumstances. These other persons and organizations include the following:

1. Real estate managers
2. Legal representatives
3. Mobile equipment operators
4. Newly acquired organizations

Real Estate Managers

Any person (other than an employee or a volunteer worker) or organization acting as real estate manager for the named insured is an insured. Coverage applies only while the person or organization is serving as real estate manager for the named insured.

Legal Representatives

If the named insured dies, any person or organization having proper temporary custody of the named insured's property is an insured under the CGL until a legal representative is appointed. The coverage for a temporary custodian applies only to liability arising out of the maintenance or use of the property. The appointed legal representative is also an insured, but only with respect to his or her duties as legal representative.

Mobile Equipment Operators

The insureds described above would be covered while operating mobile equipment in most circumstances. In addition, the CGL coverage form insures certain additional persons or organizations for liability claims arising from operating mobile equipment registered in the name of the named insured under any motor vehicle registration law. Those additional insureds are the following:

1. Any person while driving the named insured's mobile equipment along a public highway with the permission of the named insured
2. Any other person or organization responsible for the conduct of the driver

However, coverage applies only if liability arises from operating the equipment and only if no other insurance is available to the person or organization. Coverage does not apply to bodily injury to a co-employee of the driver. It also does not apply to damage to property owned by, rented to, in the charge of, or occupied by the named insured or the employer of the driver.

Newly Acquired Organizations

Any subsidiary or affiliated organization of the named insured that is in existence at or before the inception of the CGL policy must be shown in the declarations as a named insured in order to be covered. If the named insured acquires or forms a new organization during the policy period, the new organization qualifies as a named insured and is covered for ninety days or to the end of the policy period, whichever comes first. This provision does not extend to partnerships, joint ventures, or limited liability companies that are not named in the policy.

Moreover, Coverage A does not apply to bodily injury or property damage occurring before the organization was acquired or formed, and Coverage B does not apply to personal and advertising injury arising out of any offense committed before the organization was acquired or formed.

LIMITS OF INSURANCE

CGL coverage is subject to the following limits of insurance:

1. General aggregate limit
2. Products-completed operations aggregate limit
3. Personal and advertising injury limit
4. Each occurrence limit
5. Damage to premises rented to you limit
6. Medical expense limit

The dollar amount of each limit is shown on the CGL declarations page. How these limits apply is explained below and illustrated in Exhibit 9-1.

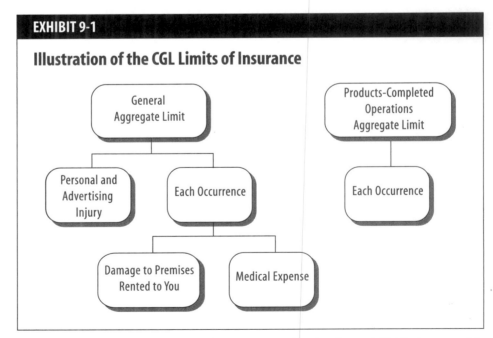

EXHIBIT 9-1

Illustration of the CGL Limits of Insurance

Adapted with permission from International Risk Management Institute, Inc., *Commercial Liability Insurance*, vol. 1, p. IV.E.14. Copyright © 1994.

Aggregate Limits

An aggregate limit is the most the insurer will pay under a policy for the sum of covered claims during the policy period (usually one year beginning on the effective date of the coverage part). When an aggregate limit is exhausted by payment of applicable claims, the insurer is no longer obligated to pay damages or defend claims subject to that aggregate limit. Aggregate limits are restored (for purposes of future occurrences only) when the policy is renewed for a new policy period.

The CGL coverage form contains two aggregate limits:

1. The **general aggregate limit** is the most the insurer will pay for the sum of the following:

    *   Damages under Coverage A except for damages included in the "products-completed operations hazard"
    *   Damages under Coverage B
    *   Medical expenses under Coverage C

2. The **products-completed operations aggregate limit** is the most the insurer will pay under Coverage A for damages included in the "products-completed operations hazard."

The **products-completed operations hazard**, as defined in the CGL coverage form, includes all bodily injury and property damage occurring away from premises owned or rented by the named insured and arising out of the named insured's product or work. The term does not include the following:

1. Products that are still in the named insured's physical possession
2. Work that has not been completed or abandoned

Injury or damage resulting from item 1 or 2 above is part of the premises and operations liability exposure and would be subject to the general aggregate limit. To illustrate, suppose that a customer is shopping inside the insured's store. If the customer is injured by a defective product held for sale by the insured, the customer's claim would be subject to the *general aggregate* limit because the accident occurred on the insured's premises. If the injury had occurred after the customer bought the product and took it away from the insured's premises, the resulting claim would be subject to the products-completed operations aggregate limit.

Personal and Advertising Injury Limit

The **personal and advertising injury limit** is the most the insurer will pay for the sum of all personal and advertising injury to one person or organization. All sums paid under this limit reduce the general aggregate limit.

General aggregate limit
The most the insurer will pay during the policy period for the sum of (1) damages under Coverage A, except damages because of injury or damage included in the products-completed operations hazard, (2) damages under Coverage B, and (3) medical expenses under Coverage C.

Products-completed operations aggregate limit
The most the insurer will pay during the policy period for damages because of injury or damage included in the products-completed operations hazard.

Products-completed operations hazard
All bodily injury and property damage occurring away from the named insured's premises and arising out of the named insured's product or work. The hazard does not include (1) products still in the named insured's physical possession or (2) work that has not been completed or abandoned.

Personal and advertising injury limit
The most the insurer will pay for all personal and advertising injury to one person or organization.

Each Occurrence Limit

The **each occurrence limit** is the most the insurer will pay for the sum of the following arising out of a single occurrence:

1. Damages for bodily injury and property damage under Coverage A
2. Medical expenses under Coverage C

The each occurrence limit is the most the insurer will pay for a single occurrence, regardless of the number of persons insured, the number of claims or suits brought, or the number of persons or organizations making claim. All sums paid under this limit reduce the general aggregate limit or the products completed operations limit, depending on the nature of the claim.

Damage to Premises Rented to You Limit

The **damage to premises rented to you limit** is the most the insurer will pay under Coverage A for either (1) damage by a cause other than fire to any one premises rented to the named insured or (2) damage by fire to any one premises rented to the named insured or temporarily occupied by the named insured with the owner's permission. All sums paid under the damage to premises rented to you limit are subject to the each occurrence limit and also reduce the general aggregate limit.

Medical Expense Limit

The **medical expense limit** is the most the insurer will pay for Coverage C medical expenses resulting from bodily injury to one person. All sums paid under the medical expense limit are subject to the each occurrence limit and also reduce the general aggregate limit.

Application of CGL Limits

An example will clarify the application of the CGL limits. Assume that beginning January 1, the Always Best Corporation (ABC) was insured for a one-year period under an occurrence CGL coverage form with the following limits:

General aggregate	$2,000,000
Products-completed operations aggregate	2,000,000
Personal and advertising injury	1,000,000
Each occurrence	1,000,000
Damage to premises rented to you	100,000
Medical expense	5,000

Occurrence 1: On February 1, a fire in a building rented to ABC caused the following losses for which ABC was held liable (except for the medical payments, which were paid without regard to liability):

Fire damage to the rented building	$150,000
Medical payments to ten injured customers ($1,000 each)	10,000
Bodily injury to others	300,000

The medical payments claims and bodily injury claims would be paid in full, for $310,000. Only $100,000 of the fire legal liability claim would be payable because of the fire damage limit. The total of $410,000 is within the each occurrence limit. The remaining general aggregate limit is $1,590,000 ($2,000,000 – $410,000).

Occurrence 2: On July 10, an elevator fell in the building rented to ABC, injuring fifteen customers. ABC was held liable for $1,500,000 in damages for the customers' injuries.

The $1,500,000 in damages resulting from the elevator collapse exceeds the each occurrence limit of $1,000,000. Thus, the insurer will pay only $1,000,000 for that occurrence. The general aggregate limit is now reduced to $590,000 ($1,590,000 – $1,000,000).

Occurrence 3: On November 27, ABC committed an advertising injury offense when it improperly used a picture of an actor in its advertising material. The damages awarded to the actor were $800,000.

The $800,000 damages for the advertising injury offense are within the personal and advertising injury limit. However, the general aggregate has been reduced to $590,000. Consequently, the insurer is only liable for $590,000. ABC itself would bear the balance of the loss.

Occurrence 4: On December 8, one of ABC's customers was injured by a defective product sold by ABC. The customer won a judgment of $900,000 in damages against ABC.

The insurer would pay $900,000. The bodily injury was within the products-completed operations hazard and thus subject to the products-completed operations aggregate limit. The products-completed operations aggregate limit was not reduced by prior claims during the policy period, and the $900,000 damages were less than the $1,000,000 each occurrence limit.

If this claim had been one that was subject to the general aggregate limit (for example, a claim by a customer who tripped and fell on a slippery floor), the insurer would have had no duty to defend the insured or pay damages. The general aggregate limit was used up by occurrence 3, above.

CGL CONDITIONS

The CGL coverage form contains several conditions that supplement the common conditions discussed in Chapter 2. The CGL conditions, listed below, are described in the corresponding sections that follow:

1. Bankruptcy
2. Duties in the event of occurrence, offense, claim, or suit

3. Legal action against us
4. Other insurance
5. Premium audit
6. Representations
7. Separation of insureds
8. Transfer of right of recovery against others to us
9. When we do not renew

Bankruptcy

Bankruptcy or insolvency of the insured does not relieve the insurer of any of its policy obligations. The insurer remains obligated to defend the insured and pay judgments or settlements as though the insured had remained solvent.

Duties in the Event of Occurrence, Offense, Claim, or Suit

If the insured does not perform the duties required by this condition, the insurance company may be relieved of its duty to defend and pay claims. Thus, the insured must understand and fulfill these duties.

Whenever the named insured becomes aware of an occurrence or an offense that may result in a claim, notice must be given to the insurer as soon as practicable. The notice may be either oral or written, and it should state the following:

1. How, when, and where the occurrence happened
2. The names and addresses of any injured persons and any witnesses
3. The nature and location of any damage or injury resulting from the occurrence or offense

When a claim or suit is actually brought against any insured, the named insured must do the following:

1. Immediately record the details of the claim or suit and the date received
2. Notify the insurer in writing as soon as practicable

The named insured (or any other insured involved in a claim or suit) is required to do the following:

1. Immediately forward to the insurer copies of any legal papers received in connection with the suit
2. Authorize the insurer to obtain any legal records or other documents
3. Cooperate with the insurer in the investigation or settlement of the claim or in the insurer's defense against the suit
4. Assist the insurer in any action against any third party that may be liable to the insured because of the injuries or damage for which claim is made

Finally, the condition states that no insured may make voluntary payment, assume any obligation, or incur any expense without the insurer's consent.

Any voluntary payments made by an insured or expenses incurred by an insured without the insurer's consent must be paid by the insured. The only exception is that the insured may incur expenses for first aid at the time of the occurrence.

Legal Action Against Us

The legal action condition provides that no person or organization can bring the insurer into any suit seeking damages from an insured. Insurers believe that a suit that includes an insurance company as a defendant may encourage a jury to award higher damages or to award damages in cases where damages would not be awarded otherwise. (Some states permit third-party claimants to sue insurers directly, regardless of this provision.)

The condition also states that no person or organization can bring suit to enforce the CGL coverage part unless that party has fully complied with all policy conditions. For example, the insured could not sue the insurer (to get the insurer to pay a third-party claim) unless the insured had first forwarded all legal papers to the insurer, cooperated in the defense, and so on.

Other Insurance

The other insurance condition explains how the amount the insurer is obligated to pay on a claim is determined if the insured has other insurance that also covers the claim. For the purposes of the other insurance condition, all applicable coverages are classified as either excess insurance or primary insurance.

When CGL Is Excess

CGL coverage is excess insurance if the other insurance is any of the following:

1. Fire, extended coverage, builders risk, installation risk, or similar coverage on the named insured's work

2. Fire insurance on premises rented to the named insured or that the named insured temporarily occupies with the owner's permission

3. Insurance that the named insured purchases to cover its liability as a tenant for damage to premises rented to the named insured or temporarily occupied by the named insured with the owner's permission

4. Aircraft, auto, or watercraft coverage

5. Any primary insurance available to the named insured covering liability for damages arising out of premises or operations for which the named insured has been added by endorsement as an additional insured

If CGL coverage is excess, the insurer has no obligation to provide defense for any claim or suit that another insurer has a duty to defend against. However, if no other insurer provides defense, the excess (CGL) insurer will do so. In such a case, the excess insurer takes over the insured's right to recover defense costs from the other insurer.

If a claim is covered by two or more excess insurers, they share the amount of loss in excess of all primary insurance. The procedure is discussed under "Methods of Sharing" below.

When CGL Is Primary

All applicable insurance not defined as excess is considered primary and begins to pay at the first dollar of loss or when the deductible or self-insured amount, if any, is exceeded. Primary insurers are obligated to provide defense for covered claims until their limits of insurance have been exhausted by the payment of settlements or judgments. If two or more primary insurers cover the claim, they share the loss up to their combined limits of insurance.

Methods of Sharing

If two or more policies apply at the same level, either primary or excess, the policy provides for two methods of sharing: (1) contribution by equal shares and (2) contribution by limits. If all applicable policies permit contribution by equal shares, that method is used. Otherwise, contribution by limits is used.

Contribution by Equal Shares

Contribution by equal shares
Method of sharing loss when two or more policies apply; each insurer pays an equal amount until the claim is fully paid or until one insurer exhausts its limit; if so, the other insurer pays the remainder of the claim (up to its limit).

Under **contribution by equal shares**, each insurer contributes an equal amount to the payment of the claim until the claim is fully paid or until each insurer exhausts its limit of insurance, whichever occurs first. Assume, for example, that Luckless Manufacturing Company (LMC) has two liability claims arising from separate occurrences and that these claims are covered under two of LMC's primary liability policies. The applicable each occurrence limits of insurance for the two policies are as follows:

Insurer	Limit
A	$500,000
B	$1,000,000

For a claim of $300,000, each insurer would contribute $150,000. That amount would cover the claim in full and is within the limits of both policies.

A claim of $1,200,000 would be distributed in two stages. First, each insurer would contribute $500,000, equal to A's limit. Since Insurer B has not exhausted its limit, it would contribute an additional $200,000 to cover the rest of the claim.

Contribution by Limits

Contribution by limits
Method of sharing loss when two or more policies apply; each insurer pays that proportion of the claim that the insurer's limit bears to the total of all applicable insurance.

Under **contribution by limits**, each insurer pays that proportion of the claim that its limit bears to the total of all applicable insurance. However, no insurer will pay more than its applicable limit of insurance.

Using the policies of LMC as described above, Insurer A's limit ($500,000) is one-third of the total applicable limits ($1,500,000) of both policies. Consequently, Insurer A would pay one-third of each claim, but not more than its limit of $500,000. Insurer B's limit ($1,000,000) is two-thirds of the total applicable limits. Thus, Insurer B would pay two-thirds of any claim, but not more than its limit. Using contribution by limits, the two claims against LMC would be distributed as follows:

Insurer	$300,000 Claim	$1,200,000 Claim
A	$100,000	$400,000
B	$200,000	$800,000

Notice that Insurer A paid less when the claims were shared using contribution by limits. As a general rule, contribution by equal shares is more advantageous to the insurer with the higher limits, and contribution by limits is more advantageous to the insurer with the lower limits.

Premium Audit

CGL policies are often issued with estimated premiums. The final premium is determined after the policy has expired, based on the insured's payroll, sales, or attendance during the policy term, or some other rating base that could not be determined precisely at the policy inception. The premium audit condition requires the named insured to keep adequate records to permit correct calculation of the premium and to make such records available to the insurer on request. The named insured must promptly pay for any additional premiums resulting from the audit. If the audit shows the earned premium to be less than the original estimate, the insurer is obligated to return the excess to the named insured, subject to any policy minimum premium.

Representations

The representations condition states that the named insured, by accepting the policy, agrees to the following:

1. The statements in the declarations are accurate and complete.
2. The statements in the declarations are based on representations made by the named insured to the insurer.
3. The insurer has issued the policy in reliance on the named insured's representations.

This condition places a heavy burden on the named insured to read the policy declarations and to be sure that the representations made in the negotiation of the policy are accurate.

Separation of Insureds

The separation condition states that the insurance provided by the policy applies separately to each person insured. This condition can benefit an insured under certain circumstances. For example, one insured might intentionally injure a third party. The policy should not provide any coverage for the insured who caused the injury (unless inflicted with reasonable force to protect a person or property from harm). However, because of the separation condition, the policy would still provide coverage for any other insured (such as an employer or partner) who might be liable for the injury. Also, if one insured sues another insured, coverage is still provided for the insured who has been sued, subject to the other conditions and exclusions of the policy.

The condition is subject to two restrictions. First, the limits of insurance apply to all persons insured and are not increased because two or more persons are insured. Second, any rights or duties specifically assigned to the first named insured are not applicable to any other insured.

Transfer of Right of Recovery Against Others to Us

If the insured has any right to recover from any third party all or any part of a claim paid by the insurer, that right must be transferred to the insurer. In legal terminology, the insurer is subrogated to the rights of the insured to recover the amount paid. The insured must do nothing after a loss to impair this right and, upon the insurer's request, must assist the insurer in any reasonable manner to enforce the right of recovery. This policy condition was known as the *subrogation* provision in earlier policies. The insurer's right to subrogate arises because the insurer defends and pays damages on behalf of the insured.

When We Do Not Renew

If the insurer opts not to renew the policy, it must give written notice of non-renewal to the first named insured at least thirty days before the expiration date of the policy. If the notice is mailed, proof of mailing is adequate proof of notice.

Many states have adopted specific regulations that supersede this policy provision. In such cases, an endorsement is normally attached to the policy detailing the required provisions. Even if the endorsement is not attached to the policy, the regulations supersede the policy renewal provision.

CLAIMS-MADE CGL COVERAGE FORM

The occurrence version of the CGL coverage form has been the basis for discussion in this chapter and in Chapter 8. However, insurers prefer to insure some organizations on the claims-made version of the CGL coverage form.

The occurrence CGL form covers bodily injury or property damage that occurs during its policy period, *regardless of when claim is made*. A claim made today for injury that occurred twenty years ago could be covered under an occurrence policy that was in effect twenty years ago. If the injury was considered to have been "occurring" during the intervening years as well, coverage might even be triggered under any occurrence-basis policies in effect during those years. In recent years, many such "long-tail" claims have been made for latent injury caused by exposure to asbestos and other substances.

For example, in 1993, two leading insurance companies agreed to pay up to $3 billion for claims on policies they had issued almost forty years earlier for Fibreboard Corporation, a manufacturer of asbestos products. Fibreboard faced claims from over 145,000 people who maintained they were injured by its products as far back as 1950.

A problem posed for insurers by these long-tail claims is that their ultimate cost cannot be accurately predicted when the insurer develops the premium for the policy. The insurer may not realize that the insured's product can cause latent injury, and the unanticipated claims, made many years in the future, may be subject to liberalized law or inflated monetary values. As a result, the policy premiums charged by the insurer may be inadequate to pay covered claims. This poses significant challenges to insurance capacity and even insurer solvency.

The claims-made CGL coverage form was developed to address this problem. The discussion that follows describes the principal features of the claims-made form. These features include the following:

- Claims-made trigger
- Retroactive date
- Extended reporting periods

Claims-Made Trigger

In the claims-made coverage form, Coverage A and Coverage B are both subject to a **claims-made coverage trigger.** The basic requirement of the trigger is that the claim for bodily injury, property damage, or personal and advertising injury must be first made against any insured during either the policy period or an extended reporting period provided by the policy. (Extended reporting periods are described in more detail below.)

Claims-made coverage trigger
The event that triggers coverage under the claims-made CGL coverage form: the first making of a claim against the insured during the policy period.

The claims-made form states that a claim will be deemed to have been made at the earlier of the following times: (1) when notice of the claim is received and recorded by any insured or by the insurer or (2) when the insurer settles the claim. The coverage form also states that notice of an *occurrence* (such as "Today a customer slipped and fell on our floor. . . .") is not notice of a *claim or offense* (such as "Today we received suit papers from a customer who slipped and fell on our floor last month. . . .").

Retroactive Date

An additional requirement of the claims-made form is that the injury or damage for which claim is made must have occurred on or after the policy's retroactive date, if any, but not after the end of the policy period. Similarly for Coverage B claims, the personal and advertising injury offense must have been committed on or after the retroactive date but not after the end of the policy period. Thus, the **retroactive date** is the date on or after which bodily injury

Retroactive date
The date on or after which bodily injury or property damage must occur (or a personal and advertising injury offense must be committed) in order to be covered.

or property damage must occur, or a personal and advertising injury offense must be committed, in order to be covered.

A claims-made policy may contain no retroactive date, a retroactive date that is the same as the policy inception date, or a retroactive date that is before the policy inception date.

- If it has no retroactive date, the policy will cover claims first made during its policy period, regardless of when the bodily injury or property damage occurred or when the personal and advertising injury offense was committed.

- If the policy has a retroactive date (shown in the CGL declarations), the policy will not cover claims for (1) bodily injury or property damage that occurred before the retroactive date or (2) personal and advertising injury offenses committed before the retroactive date, even if claim is first made during the policy period.

Extended Reporting Periods

Extended reporting period
An additional period (also called a "tail") following the expiration of a claims-made policy. During this period the expired policy covers claims first made against the insured, provided the injury occurred after the retroactive date (if any) and before policy expiration.

Claims-made policies have a feature called an **extended reporting period,** often referred to as a "tail." An extended reporting period is a time period following the expiration date of a claims-made policy. The insurer agrees to pay any claim first made during the extended reporting period if the claim is for an injury that occurred after the retroactive date and before the policy expiration date. In other words, an extended reporting period only extends the period within which claim can be made. It does not extend the period within which the injury must have occurred.

The claims-made CGL coverage form automatically includes a basic extended reporting period for no additional premium. The basic tail runs for five years from the policy expiration date. Claims first made within that five-year tail are covered, but only if both of the following conditions are met:

1. The injury occurred (or the offense was committed) on or after the retroactive date, if any, and before the policy expiration date
2. The insured reported the occurrence to the insurer within sixty days after the policy expired

The claims-made CGL form also permits the insured to obtain, for an additional premium, a supplemental extended reporting period. The supplemental tail lasts indefinitely and does not require that the occurrence be reported within sixty days after policy expiration. In addition, the supplemental tail restores the expiring policy's aggregate limits to their original levels, but only for claims first received and recorded during the supplemental extended reporting period. If the named insured wishes to buy the supplemental extended reporting period, the named insured must request it from the insurer in writing no later than sixty days after the policy's expiration date. The supplemental extended reporting period does not go into effect until the named insured pays the additional premium for it.

Illustration of Retroactive Date

LMC purchased a one-year claims-made CGL policy with an inception date of January 1, 2001. The retroactive date was also January 1, 2001. On January 1, 2002, the policy was renewed for an additional year. The retroactive date for the renewal policy remained January 1, 2001. Before January 1, 2001, LMC was covered by occurrence form policies.

On July 1, 2002, claim was first made against LMC for injury B, which occurred on December 1, 2001. Given these facts, as depicted on the time line below, the claim was covered under the 2002 policy, since it was the policy in effect when the claim was made and the injury occurred after the policy's retroactive date.

On November 1, 2002, another person first made claim against LMC for injury A, which occurred on July 1, 2000. This claim would not be covered by the 2002 policy, since the injury occurred before the retroactive date. The claim would be covered under the occurrence policy that was in effect in 2000.

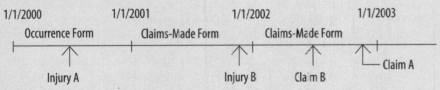

If the retroactive date of the renewal policy had been advanced to January 1, 2002, claim B would not have been covered under the 2002 policy. Even though claim would have been made during the policy period, the injury would have occurred before the retroactive date.

Non-ISO Claims-Made Forms

The ISO claims-made CGL form has not achieved widespread acceptance. Most organizations are still insured under occurrence policies for their general liability exposures. However, claims-made forms are widely used to provide professional liability and other specialty coverages (which will be described in Chapter 13). These forms are independently developed by the insurers that use them, and their claims-made features usually differ from those of the ISO form. For example, independent forms seldom include an automatic extended reporting period. Any extended reporting period must be purchased separately and is usually limited to one to three years rather than the unlimited reporting period offered by the ISO supplemental tail.

CGL ENDORSEMENTS

A wide variety of endorsements are available for modifying the CGL coverage form to meet particular needs. These endorsements can be categorized as follows:

1. State endorsements

2. Exclusion endorsements
3. Classification endorsements
4. Miscellaneous endorsements

State Endorsements

Some states have laws or regulations requiring special policy provisions. They may, for example, require earlier notice of cancellation or nonrenewal than that provided by the standard policy. Other states restrict the insurer's right to cancel coverage midterm or require the insurer to state the reason for cancellation. State endorsements are usually mandatory and must be attached to all policies providing coverage in the states to which they apply.

Exclusion Endorsements

ISO provides many exclusion endorsements, all of which restrict coverage in some way. Examples of such endorsements are listed below:

- The *Exclusion—Personal and Advertising Injury Endorsement* excludes Coverage B—Personal and Advertising Injury Liability.

- The *Exclusion—Employees and Volunteer Workers as Insureds Endorsement* modifies the Who Is an Insured section of the policy to eliminate insured status for the named insured's employees and volunteer workers.

- The *Total Pollution Exclusion Endorsement* eliminates coverage for any injury, damage, or cleanup costs resulting from the actual, alleged, or threatened discharge of pollutants.

- The *Exclusion—Designated Product Endorsement* excludes liability arising out of specified products of the insured.

Some of the classification endorsements discussed below also fit the category of exclusion endorsements.

Classification Endorsements

Many endorsements are available for adapting the CGL policy to the needs of certain classes of business organizations. These endorsements may either restrict or expand coverage under the form. Two examples of endorsements in this category are as follows:

- The *Seed Merchants—Coverage for Erroneous Delivery or Mixture and Resulting Failure of Seed to Germinate Endorsement* is added to a CGL policy covering a seed merchant. The endorsement clarifies that the policy will cover erroneous delivery of seed, errors in mechanical mixture of seeds, and failure of seed to germinate if the failure results from specified causes.

- The *Exclusion—Professional Services—Blood Banks Endorsement* excludes bodily injury or property damage arising out of the insured's rendering of or failure to render professional services as a blood bank. Blood banks ordinarily obtain professional liability coverage under a separate policy.

Miscellaneous Endorsements

Examples of the miscellaneous endorsements that can be used to add coverages, deductibles, or insureds to a CGL policy are briefly discussed below. Some miscellaneous endorsements amend certain coverages or the limits of insurance, and others modify the claims-made CGL form to provide supplemental extended reporting periods or to exclude specified locations, products, or work.

The *Boats Endorsement* can be used to extend CGL coverage to any watercraft described in the endorsement and owned or used by or rented to the insured.

The *Deductible Liability Insurance Endorsement* enables the insured to apply deductibles to the bodily injury and property damage liability coverages, either separately or combined. The deductibles may be on either a per-claim or a per-occurrence basis.

Over forty endorsements are available to include specific types of persons or organizations as insureds under a CGL policy. For example, the *Additional Insured—Vendors Endorsement* includes as an insured any person or organization (the vendor) specified in the endorsement. The vendor is covered for bodily injury or property damage liability arising from distributing or selling any of the named insured's products listed in the endorsement.

Other endorsements can be used to include such additional insureds as club members, condominium unit owners, townhouse associations, lessors of leased equipment, state or political subdivisions, users of golf carts, charitable institutions, and grantors of franchises.

RATING CGL COVERAGE

The formula used to determine the premium for a CGL policy is as follows:

$$\text{Rate} \times \text{Rate exposure} = \text{Premium.}$$

The rate depends on the nature of the insured organization and its susceptibility to liability losses. The rate exposure reflects the size of the business operations to be insured, not the type of losses to which the business is susceptible. For example, because of its production volume, the manufacturer of 1 million toys a year is more likely to be sued for products liability than a manufacturer that produces 50,000 similar toys a year. Such differences are reflected in the rate exposure. The unit in which the rate exposure is measured is called the **premium base**.

An insurer that writes CGL insurance develops a rate for each business classification that it is willing to insure. The classifications used to reference these rates are listed in the classification table of the ISO *Commercial Lines Manual*. The classification table lists more than 1,000 types of operations, each assigned an identification number called the **class code**. The class code used for a particular organization represents the description in the classification table that best fits the operations of the organization. For some businesses,

Premium base
The unit in which the rate exposure is measured, such as gross sales or payroll.

Class code
A numeric code representing the description in the rating classification table that best fits a particular organization's operations.

Certificate of insurance
A brief description of insurance coverage prepared by an insurer or its agent, commonly used by policyholders to provide evidence of insurance.

Certificates of Insurance

Many organizations demand that firms doing business with them provide evidence of insurance. Furthermore, rating rules for both workers compensation and general liability insurance require that the insured either obtain proof of insurance from contractors or subcontractors employed by the insured or pay a higher premium. The customary method of providing such evidence is a **certificate of insurance.** A certificate of insurance is a brief outline of the coverage in force when the certificate is issued. An example of a certificate is shown in Exhibit 9-2.

Two problems arising from certificates of insurance for general liability insurance are (1) the requirements for notice of cancellation and (2) the inclusion of additional insureds.

Most certificate holders want to receive written notice of cancellation from the insurer if the insurer cancels the insurance described in the certificate. The cancellation provision included in the certificate states that the insurer will attempt to mail written notice but that failure to mail such notice will not impose any liability on the insurer. Only an endorsement to the policy can obligate the insurer to give notice.

In addition to requiring certificates of insurance, some organizations want to be added as additional insureds to the policies covering the firms with whom they do business. Merely adding wording to that effect to the certificate without endorsing the policy has been held to be ineffective. Again, an endorsement to the policy is required.

Certificates are frequently prepared by insurance producers. Extreme care is necessary when preparing a certificate to be sure that the coverage described in the certificate accurately reflects the policy coverage. Furthermore, certificates should only be prepared by producers who have been authorized to do so by the insurer. Making an error or exceeding authority when preparing a certificate can expose the producer to professional liability.

more than one class code applies because the business operations involve two or more separately described classifications.

Two CGL rates apply for most classifications:

1. A premises-operations rate
2. A products-completed operations rate

For organizations having little or no risk of incurring products-completed operations liability losses (such as photo finishing labs or florists), only a premises-operations rate is used. The small cost of providing products liability coverage for such insureds is included in their premises-operations rate.

Premium Base

The premium base used in rating CGL coverage for any given business is also indicated in the classification table. In general, organizations of the same kind have the same premium bases:

- Mercantile businesses (retail stores, for example) are rated using a premium base of gross sales.

EXHIBIT 9-2

Certificate of Liability Insurance

ACORD™ **CERTIFICATE OF LIABILITY INSURANCE**	DATE (MM/DD/YYYY) 10/1/02

PRODUCER	
A.M. Able Agency 250 Main St. Workingtown, PA 19000 (215) 697-0000	THIS CERTIFICATE IS ISSUED AS A MATTER OF INFORMATION ONLY AND CONFERS NO RIGHTS UPON THE CERTIFICATE HOLDER. THIS CERTIFICATE DOES NOT AMEND, EXTEND OR ALTER THE COVERAGE AFFORDED BY THE POLICIES BELOW.

INSURED	INSURERS AFFORDING COVERAGE	NAIC #
BLS Construction 3000 Industrial Highway Workingtown, PA 19000	INSURER A: Insurance Company A	
	INSURER B: Insurance Company B	
	INSURER C: Insurance Company C	
	INSURER D:	
	INSURER E:	

COVERAGES

THE POLICIES OF INSURANCE LISTED BELOW HAVE BEEN ISSUED TO THE INSURED NAMED ABOVE FOR THE POLICY PERIOD INDICATED. NOTWITHSTANDING ANY REQUIREMENT, TERM OR CONDITION OF ANY CONTRACT OR OTHER DOCUMENT WITH RESPECT TO WHICH THIS CERTIFICATE MAY BE ISSUED OR MAY PERTAIN, THE INSURANCE AFFORDED BY THE POLICIES DESCRIBED HEREIN IS SUBJECT TO ALL THE TERMS, EXCLUSIONS AND CONDITIONS OF SUCH POLICIES. AGGREGATE LIMITS SHOWN MAY HAVE BEEN REDUCED BY PAID CLAIMS.

INSR LTR	ADD'L INSRD	TYPE OF INSURANCE	POLICY NUMBER	POLICY EFFECTIVE DATE (MM/DD/YY)	POLICY EXPIRATION DATE (MM/DD/YY)	LIMITS	
A		**GENERAL LIABILITY** [X] COMMERCIAL GENERAL LIABILITY [ ] CLAIMS MADE [X] OCCUR GEN'L AGGREGATE LIMIT APPLIES PER: [ ] POLICY [ ] PROJECT [ ] LOC	SP 0002	7/1/02	7/1/03	EACH OCCURRENCE DAMAGE TO RENTED PREMISES (Ea occurence) MED EXP (Any one person) PERSONAL & ADV INJURY GENERAL AGGREGATE PRODUCTS - COMP/OP AGG	$ 1,000,000 $ 100,000 $ 5,000 $ 1,000,000 $ 2,000,000 $ 2,000,000
A		**AUTOMOBILE LIABILITY** [X] ANY AUTO [ ] ALL OWNED AUTOS [ ] SCHEDULED AUTOS [ ] HIRED AUTOS [ ] NON-OWNED AUTOS	SP 0002	7/1/02	7/1/03	COMBINED SINGLE LIMIT (Ea accident) BODILY INJURY (Per person) BODILY INJURY (Per accident) PROPERTY DAMAGE (Per accident)	$ 1,000,000 $ –NA– $ –NA– $ –NA–
		GARAGE LIABILITY [ ] ANY AUTO				AUTO ONLY - EA ACCIDENT OTHER THAN EA ACC AUTO ONLY: AGG	$ $ $
B		**EXCESS/UMBRELLA LIABILITY** [X] OCCUR [ ] CLAIMS MADE [ ] DEDUCTIBLE [ ] RETENTION $	3XS-1522-25	7/1/02	7/1/03	EACH OCCURRENCE AGGREGATE 	$ 10,000,000 $ 10,000,000 $ $ $
C		**WORKERS COMPENSATION AND EMPLOYERS' LIABILITY** ANY PROPRIETOR/PARTNER/EXECUTIVE OFFICER/MEMBER EXCLUDED? If yes, describe under SPECIAL PROVISIONS below	29934-31	7/1/02	7/1/03	[ ] WC STATUTORY LIMITS [ ] OTHER E.L. EACH ACCIDENT E.L. DISEASE - EA EMPLOYEE E.L. DISEASE - POLICY LIMIT	 $ 100,000 $ 500,000 $ 100,000
		OTHER					

DESCRIPTION OF OPERATIONS / LOCATIONS / VEHICLES / EXCLUSIONS ADDED BY ENDORSEMENT / SPECIAL PROVISIONS

Building Contractor / Work site at Certificateholder's Premises

CERTIFICATE HOLDER	CANCELLATION
CCC Real Estate 25 2nd St. Workingtown, PA 19000	SHOULD ANY OF THE ABOVE DESCRIBED POLICIES BE CANCELLED BEFORE THE EXPIRATION DATE THEREOF, THE ISSUING INSURER WILL ENDEAVOR TO MAIL _____ DAYS WRITTEN NOTICE TO THE CERTIFICATE HOLDER NAMED TO THE LEFT, BUT FAILURE TO DO SO SHALL IMPOSE NO OBLIGATION OR LIABILITY OF ANY KIND UPON THE INSURER, ITS AGENTS OR REPRESENTATIVES. AUTHORIZED REPRESENTATIVE A.M. Able

ACORD 25 (2001/08)   © ACORD CORPORATION 1988

- Contracting businesses are rated on the basis of payroll.
- Building and premises risks (apartments and hotels) may be rated on the basis of area, gross sales, or the number of units in the building.
- Special events (concerts, sporting events, exhibitions, and so on) might be rated on the number of admissions to the event.

Once the premium base to be used in the rating of a particular policy is known, information about the organization must be gathered carefully and completely in order to measure rate exposure accurately. Specific rules govern what is and is not to be included in any of the rate exposures used to rate CGL insurance.

As explained earlier in connection with the premium audit condition, the actual premium for a CGL policy is often calculated at the end of the policy period after the rate exposure can be determined accurately. That premium is then reconciled with the estimated premium the insured paid at the beginning of the policy period.

Other Rating Considerations

Depending on the coverage choices that an insured has made, other factors are considered in determining a CGL premium. Increased limits factors are used to generate higher premiums for policies written with coverage amounts higher than the basic limits. If the insured has chosen not to buy certain coverages included automatically in the CGL form—personal and advertising injury, medical payments, or fire damage liability, for instance—premium credits are given for such reductions in coverage. Coverage can be written subject to a deductible, which reduces the premium.

When coverage is written on a claims-made basis, the usual rates are modified by claims-made factors. These factors reduce the usual rates slightly to account for the fact that claims-made policies do not (unless an additional premium is paid) cover some accidents that occur during the policy period but result in claims made after the policy has expired. An occurrence policy covers such accidents regardless of when claim is made.

MISCELLANEOUS LIABILITY COVERAGE FORMS

ISO files several miscellaneous liability coverage forms in addition to the CGL coverage forms. These forms, which are briefly described below, can be used to cover significant loss exposures that the CGL forms exclude.

Liquor Liability Coverage Form

Liquor Liability Coverage Form
Form that covers liquor liability of insureds in the business of manufacturing, distributing, selling, serving, or furnishing alcoholic beverages.

The **Liquor Liability Coverage Form** can be used to provide liquor liability insurance for insureds that are in the business of manufacturing, distributing, selling, serving, or furnishing alcoholic beverages and are therefore subject to the liquor liability exclusion in the CGL policy. In the Liquor Liability Coverage Form, the insurer agrees to pay those sums that the insured becomes legally obligated to pay as damages because of bodily injury or property damage resulting from the selling, serving, or furnishing of any alcoholic beverage. If, for example, the insured was sued by a motorist who was injured by a driver who became intoxicated at the insured's bar allegedly as a result of a bartender's negligence, the Liquor Liability Coverage Form would defend the insured and pay damages, up to its limit, for any judgment or settlement.

Products/Completed Operations Liability Coverage Form

The **Products/Completed Operations Liability Coverage Form** can be used to provide products and completed operations coverage separately from the CGL coverage form. This form might be used when the insured manufactures or sells a particularly hazardous product. In such a case, the insurer that writes the insured's commercial package policy may exclude products and completed operations liability from its CGL form. The insured may then purchase the missing products and completed operations liability coverage from another insurer that specializes in insureds with hazardous products. This insurer could write a separate policy using the Products/Completed Operations Coverage Form.

Owners and Contractors Protective Liability Coverage Form

When an independent contractor is performing operations on a property owner's premises, the property owner sometimes requires the contractor to provide a policy that protects the property owner against liability for bodily injury or property damage that arises out of either of the following:

1. The operations of the contractor at the specified location
2. Acts or omissions of the property owner in connection with the general supervision of such operations

The **Owners and Contractors Protective Liability Coverage Form** can be used to provide this insurance. This coverage form automatically terminates as soon as the contractor's work is completed or put to its intended use.

Railroad Protective Liability Coverage Form

Railroad protective liability coverage is a specialized type of owners and contractors protective liability insurance. Railroads customarily require contractors working on or adjacent to railroad property to buy this coverage to protect the railroad against claims resulting from the contractors' work. The **Railroad Protective Liability Coverage Form** can be used to provide this coverage.

Pollution Liability Coverage Forms

In addition to several pollution coverage endorsements, ISO coverage forms are available for insuring pollution liability arising out of designated sites and

Products/Completed Operations Liability Coverage Form
Form that covers products and completed operations liability separately from the CGL coverage form.

Owners and Contractors Protective Liability Coverage Form
Form purchased by a contractor to protect a property owner against liability for bodily injury or property damage arising out of (1) the contractor's operations at the specified location or (2) acts or omissions of the property owner in connection with the general supervision of such operations.

Railroad Protective Liability Coverage Form
Form that covers a railroad against claims arising out of a contractor's work on or adjacent to a railroad property and that is purchased by the contractor.

underground storage tanks. These and other types of environmental insurance will be discussed in more detail in Chapter 13.

SUMMARY

In addition to the named insured, various other persons and organizations may also be insured under the CGL coverage form. These other insureds include (but are not limited to) spouses of individual named insureds, partners and their spouses (if the named insured is a partnership), employees and volunteer workers of the named insured, the named insured's real estate manager or legal representative, operators of the named insured's mobile equipment, and organizations newly acquired by the named insured.

The CGL coverage form is subject to the following limits of insurance:

- General aggregate limit—the most the insurer will pay during the policy period for medical expenses under Coverage C, damages under Coverage B, and damages under Coverage A other than damages included in the "products-completed operations hazard"

- Products-completed operations limit—the most the insurer will pay for Coverage A damages included in the "products-completed operations hazard"

- Personal and advertising injury limit—the most the insurer will pay for damages under Coverage B

- Each occurrence limit—the most the insurer will pay for medical expenses under Coverage C and damages under Coverages A and B arising out of any one occurrence

- Damage to premises rented to you limit—the most the insurer will pay for the named insured's liability for damage to premises rented to or temporarily occupied by the named insured

- Medical expense limit—the most the insurer will pay for Coverage C medical expenses resulting from bodily injury to one person

The conditions included in the CGL coverage form relate to bankruptcy of the insured, the insured's duties in the event of loss, legal action against the insurer, other insurance, premium audits, representations, separation of insureds, subrogation, and the insurer's duties when it does not renew the policy.

Insurers use a claims-made version of the CGL coverage form for insuring some organizations that have long-tail liability exposures. The claims-made CGL coverage form covers claims first made during the policy period for injury or damage that occurred after the retroactive date, if any, shown in the policy. The claims-made coverage form contains a basic extended reporting period provision. This provision provides a five-year period for reporting claims first made after the end of the policy period because of injury or damage that occurred before the policy period ended. For an additional premium, the insured can obtain a supplemental extended reporting period, which provides a period of unlimited duration for reporting claims first made after the policy period for injury or damage that occurred before the end of the policy period.

Endorsements to the CGL policy serve several purposes, such as meeting requirements of individual states, adding or excluding coverages, making special provisions for certain classes of business, or including other persons or organizations as additional insureds.

The premium for a CGL policy is determined by multiplying applicable rates by the insured's rate exposure. The premises-operations and products-completed operations rates for a given organization depend on its class code. The rate exposure is a measure of the size of the organization stated in units of the applicable premium base: gross sales, payroll, and area are common examples.

In addition to the CGL coverage form, several miscellaneous liability coverage forms are filed by ISO to meet special needs. These coverage forms include the following:

* Liquor Liability Coverage Form
* Products/Completed Operations Coverage Form
* Owners and Contractors Protective Liability Coverage Form
* Railroad Protective Liability Coverage Form
* Various pollution liability forms

Chapter 10

Direct Your Learning

Commercial Automobile Insurance

After learning the content of this chapter, you should be able to:

- Describe the loss exposures that create the need for commercial automobile insurance.

- Given a case about a commercial automobile insurance loss, explain whether coverage applies and determine the amount, if any, the insurer will pay for the loss.

  - Explain the symbol system used to activate coverage under the Business Auto Coverage Form.

  - Explain what is covered and what is excluded by the liability and physical damage coverages of the Business Auto Coverage Form.

  - Explain the conditions of the Business Auto Coverage Form.

  - Describe the business auto coverages that may be added by endorsement to the Business Auto Coverage Form.

- Describe the coverages and exclusions in the Garage Coverage Form.

- Explain how the Motor Carrier Coverage Form differs from the Business Auto Coverage Form.

- Explain how the premium is determined for vehicles that are (a) non-zone rated and (b) zone rated.

OUTLINE

Automobile Loss Exposures

Business Auto Coverage Form

Garage Coverage Form

Motor Carrier Coverage Form

Rating Commercial Auto Insurance

Summary

Develop Your Perspective

What are the main topics covered in the chapter?

The most commonly used form for insuring commercial autos, the Business Auto Coverage Form, covers both auto liability and physical damage exposures. Endorsements can be added to provide other coverages such as auto medical payments, uninsured/underinsured motorists, and auto no-fault. This chapter explains these topics, and describes specialized forms for auto dealers and motor carriers.

Consider the loss exposures facing a local auto dealer.

- How might these exposures differ from the auto exposures of most other organizations?

Why is it important to learn about these topics?

Almost every organization has auto exposures, even if the organization does not own any automobiles. Your knowledge of loss exposures and policy provisions will help you select commercial auto coverage correctly to meet a particular insured's needs.

Review the Business Auto Coverage Form.

- What features make it versatile enough to meet the diverse auto insurance needs of most organizations?

How can you use what you will learn?

Evaluate the auto loss exposures of an organization you know well.

- Review the laws of the state in which the organization operates and recommend appropriate commercial auto coverages for this organization.

- Why did you choose these coverages?

Chapter 10

Commercial Automobile Insurance

The ownership, maintenance, or use of automobiles creates both property and liability loss exposures. As you saw in earlier chapters, commercial property and general liability forms exclude auto exposures. This chapter examines auto loss exposures and three standard coverage forms that are used to insure commercial auto loss exposures:

- The Business Auto Coverage Form meets the needs of the majority of organizations.
- The Garage Coverage Form is used to insure automobile dealers and similar businesses.
- The Motor Carrier Coverage Form is used to insure businesses that use automobiles to transport property of others or, in some cases, their own property.

AUTOMOBILE LOSS EXPOSURES

Automobile loss exposures include both property exposures and liability exposures.

Property Exposures

Any organization that has a financial interest in one or more automobiles is exposed to loss if those vehicles are damaged or destroyed. The main consequences of damage to or destruction of an auto are as follows:

1. Decrease in or loss of the auto's value
2. Loss of use of the auto until it can be repaired or replaced

Auto physical damage insurance can be used to cover damage to or destruction of an auto. Ordinarily, the insurer pays the cost of repairing the vehicle or its actual cash value, whichever is less.

To a limited extent, loss of use of an auto is insurable under a rental reimbursement endorsement to auto physical damage insurance. If a covered auto is disabled by a covered cause of loss, the insurer will reimburse the insured, up to a stated limit, for the cost to rent a substitute vehicle. In that way, the insured can continue operations and avoid loss of income.

Automobiles are subject to many of the same causes of loss that can damage property at a fixed location, such as fire, hail, windstorm, and vandalism. Because autos are mobile, they are highly susceptible to some additional perils, such as collision, overturn, and theft. However, the mobility of autos makes them less susceptible than fixed property to certain other perils. For example, a car can often be quickly driven away from rising floodwaters, an approaching forest fire, or other perils that could destroy stationary property.

Liability Exposures

Most organizations own or use autos and are thus exposed to auto liability. Liability can arise from the business use of owned, hired, or borrowed autos or even from the operation of employees' autos on behalf of the business. Furthermore, one organization can assume the auto liability of another organization by contract. These different aspects of the auto liability exposure are described in more detail below.

Owned Autos

Perhaps the most likely way a business can incur auto liability is when an employee of the business, while operating an auto owned by the business, negligently injures other persons or damages their property. As long as the employee operates the vehicle within the scope of his or her employment, the liability for resulting injuries and damage ordinarily falls on the employer as well as the employee. This rule of placing liability on the employer, known as the doctrine of *respondeat superior* ("let the employer answer"), is based on the fact that the employee was acting on behalf of the employer at the time of loss. The employer's liability in this situation is also referred to as vicarious liability.

Under the common law (the law that is made and applied by judges), the owner of an auto is not liable for negligent operation of the vehicle by someone who is not acting on behalf of the owner. To illustrate, suppose that John's Garage allows a customer to borrow one of John's business vehicles as a loaner while the customer's car is being serviced. If the customer injures another person by negligently operating John's vehicle, John should not have any liability for resulting damages.

This common-law rule does not apply in all states, however. Many states have enacted laws that make the owner of an auto liable for injuries arising out of the use of the auto by borrowers.

Commercial auto insurance covers liability of the insured arising out of the "ownership, maintenance, or use" of a covered auto. Thus, the insured's liability in any of the situations described above would be covered by commercial auto insurance, assuming the owned auto is a covered auto.

Autos Not Owned by the User

In several situations an organization can become liable for injury or damage to others resulting from the use of autos it does not own. In addition, a business that services, repairs, or otherwise attends to customers' autos can become liable for damage to cars left in its custody.

Hired and Borrowed Autos

An organization may hire autos from others for terms ranging from a few hours to a number of years. A rental period of six months or longer is usually referred to as a "lease," and shorter rental periods are typically called "rentals." In either case, the organization hiring the auto can be held legally liable for injury resulting from operating the vehicle. Similarly, the person or organization that borrows an auto from another can be held liable for injury arising from operating the borrowed vehicle.

An organization that hires or borrows autos can also become liable for damage to the hired or borrowed auto itself. This liability may be based either on negligence of the user or on a contractual duty to return the auto in the same condition as when hired, normal wear and tear excepted. These exposures are typically insured by purchasing auto *physical damage* insurance on hired autos.

Liability Assumed Under Contract

An auto rental agreement or lease may contain a hold harmless agreement whereby the renter, or lessee, agrees to indemnify the owner for the owner's liability to others arising out of use of the hired auto. As already discussed, the lessee is normally liable for damage resulting from use of the vehicle, even in the absence of the contract. However, the hold harmless agreement could have the further effect of obligating the lessee to reimburse the owner for amounts the owner is required to pay for injury to others arising out of the owner's faulty maintenance of the auto. Subject to certain restrictions, commercial auto insurance covers auto liability assumed by the insured under contracts, including auto rental agreements and leases.

Employers Nonownership Liability

Some employees use their own cars in performing their job duties. A sales representative, for example, may use his or her own car to drive to customers' offices. Because the auto is being used to further the employer's business, the employer is exposed to liability for such use. The exposure has traditionally been referred to as **employers nonownership liability**. Insurance for this exposure can be arranged under each of the commercial auto forms described in this chapter.

Employers nonownership
liability
An employer's liability for its
employees' operation of their autos
in the employer's business.

Bailee Loss Exposures

Some businesses, such as repair shops, service stations, and parking lots, take temporary possession of customers' autos. Accordingly, these "auto businesses" face the bailee loss exposures described in Chapter 7 in connection with inland marine insurance. A bailee is legally liable for damage to customers' property only if the damage occurs as a result of the bailee's negligence. However, in order to maintain good customer relations, many bailees choose to make "goodwill" payments for customers' losses even when the bailees are not legally obligated to do so. The garage coverage form, discussed later in this chapter, contains optional garagekeepers insurance provisions for covering customers' autos.

Other Auto Exposures

Other auto exposures arise from legislative actions by the various states. Most states have enacted either an auto no-fault law or an uninsured motorists law. A number of states have enacted both.

Auto No-Fault

Auto no-fault law
State statute that requires motorists to purchase (or requires insurers to make available) insurance that provides minimum first-party benefits to injured persons regardless of fault.

In an attempt to reduce litigation arising from auto accidents, several states have enacted **auto no-fault laws**. These laws require motorists to purchase (or require insurers to make available) insurance that provides minimum first-party benefits to injured persons without regard to fault or negligence. Some of these laws also limit the injured person's right to sue unless the injuries meet a certain threshold. In some states, the threshold is expressed in terms of a dollar quantity of damages resulting from the injury. (For example, motorists cannot sue for accidents resulting in less than $2,000 in damages.) In other states, the threshold is expressed as a definition of "serious injury." Unless a motorist sustains "serious injury" as defined, he or she cannot sue.

Where no-fault auto laws are in effect, motorists may be required to buy auto no-fault coverage (also known as personal injury protection). This coverage is added to the Business Auto Coverage Form by endorsement.

Uninsured Motorists

Uninsured motorists law
State statute that requires auto insurers to offer uninsured motorists coverage to all insured motorists who are their policyholders.

Uninsured motorists laws are in effect in most states. They establish that a vehicle owner can obtain insurance, under his or her auto policy, to pay for injuries caused by another motorist who is uninsured (or underinsured) and, as a result, unable to pay. Some states allow the policyholder to reject the coverage by signing a release stating that the coverage is not wanted. Uninsured (and underinsured) motorists insurance can be added to the Business Auto Coverage Form by endorsement.

BUSINESS AUTO COVERAGE FORM

Business Auto Coverage Form
Form that covers automobile loss exposures for all types of organizations other than auto dealers and motor carriers.

The **Business Auto Coverage Form** is used for insuring all types of organizations other than auto dealers and motor carriers. The Business Auto Coverage Form, along with business auto declarations and any applicable endorsements, can be included in a commercial package policy or issued as a monoline policy.

The business auto declarations form is longer and more detailed than the declarations for most other coverage forms. In addition to the usual information contained in any declarations form, the business auto declarations form includes various schedules for recording applicable coverages, covered autos, limits, deductibles, premiums, and rating and classification information.

The Business Auto Coverage Form consists of the following five sections:

Section I—Covered Autos

Section II—Liability Coverage

Section III—Physical Damage Coverage

Section IV—Business Auto Conditions

Section V—Definitions

Sections I through IV are discussed in numerical order below. The various definitions from Section V, however, are introduced as the defined terms are encountered in Sections I through IV.

Section I—Covered Autos

The Business Auto Coverage Form allows great flexibility in designating covered autos for the various coverages available under the policy. A coverage chosen by the named insured need not apply to all covered autos. For example, the insured might want to provide liability coverage for all autos and physical damage coverage for specifically described autos only.

The mechanism used to indicate the autos to which each coverage applies is a series of nine numerical **coverage symbols**, defined in Section I of the coverage form. The appropriate symbol or symbols are entered beside each coverage in the schedule of coverages and covered autos in the declarations. An illustration of how the schedule might be completed is shown in Exhibit 10-1. The coverage symbols are defined in the sections that follow.

Coverage symbol
Numeric symbol used in a commercial auto policy to indicate which autos are covered for particular coverages.

The policy definition of "auto," which applies throughout the business auto form, is a land motor vehicle, trailer, or semitrailer designed for travel on public roads, other than mobile equipment. The policy definition of "mobile equipment" is the same lengthy definition as that of the CGL coverage form, which was discussed in Chapter 8. Consequently, mobile equipment (which is generally covered under the CGL coverage form) is basically excluded under the business auto form. A semitrailer, one of the terms used in the definition of "auto," is a trailer that has wheels at the rear only. The truck tractor that tows a semitrailer also supports the forward portion of the semitrailer.

Symbol 1—Any Auto

If symbol 1 is entered for a coverage, that coverage is provided for any auto, including autos owned by the named insured, autos the named insured hires or borrows from others, and other nonowned autos used in the insured's business. Symbol 1 provides the best protection for the insured. Ordinarily this symbol is used for liability coverage only. Sometimes insurers are unwilling to use symbol 1 because of the all-encompassing coverage triggered by that symbol.

Symbol 2—Owned Autos Only

If symbol 2 is entered for a coverage, that coverage applies to all autos owned by the named insured. For liability insurance only, coverage is also provided for a nonowned trailer while it is attached to a power unit owned by the named insured. ("Power unit" is not defined in the coverage form, but the term refers to a truck tractor used to pull a semitrailer. "Trailer," defined in the coverage form, includes, but is not limited to, a semitrailer.) Symbol 2 does not cover hired or borrowed autos or other autos the named insured does not own. Symbol 2 is also used for physical damage and medical payments coverages.

Symbol 3—Owned Private Passenger Autos Only

When symbol 3 is entered beside a coverage, that coverage is provided only for private passenger autos owned by the named insured. This symbol does not include trucks or buses owned by the named insured or any kind of auto not owned by the named insured.

Symbol 4—Owned Autos Other Than Private Passenger Autos

If symbol 4 is entered for a coverage, that coverage is provided for all autos owned by the named insured except private passenger autos.

Symbol 5—Owned Autos Subject to No-Fault

Symbol 5 is normally entered only on the personal injury protection (PIP) or added PIP line of the declarations. It provides PIP coverage only for those autos that are required by law to have it.

Symbol 6—Owned Autos Subject to a Compulsory Uninsured Motorists Law

Symbol 6 is normally used only for uninsured motorists coverage. It indicates that coverage is provided only for autos that are required by law to have uninsured motorists coverage.

Symbol 7—Specifically Described Autos

If this symbol is used, coverage applies only to those autos specifically described in the policy and for which a premium is shown in the policy. It also includes, for liability coverage only, any trailer not owned by the insured while it is attached to one of the covered power units.

Symbol 8—Hired Autos Only

Symbol 8 provides coverage only for autos leased, hired, rented, or borrowed by the named insured. It does not cover autos leased, hired, rented, or borrowed from the named insured's employees or members of their families.

EXHIBIT 10-1

Schedule of Coverages and Covered Autos

ITEM TWO

SCHEDULE OF COVERAGES AND COVERED AUTOS

This policy provides only those coverages where a charge is shown in the premium column below. Each of these coverages will apply only to those "autos" shown as covered "autos"."Autos" are shown as covered "autos" for a particular coverage by the entry of one or more of the symbols from the Covered Auto Section of the Business Auto Coverage Form next to the name of the coverage.

COVERAGES	COVERED AUTOS (Entry of one or more of the symbols from the Covered Autos Section of the Business Auto Coverage Form shows which autos are covered autos)	LIMIT THE MOST WE WILL PAY FOR ANY ONE ACCIDENT OR LOSS	PREMIUM
LIABILITY	1	$	$
PERSONAL INJURY PROTECTION (or equivalent No-fault coverage)	5	SEPARATELY STATED IN EACH PIP ENDORSEMENT MINUS $_____ Ded.	$
ADDED PERSONAL INJURY PROTECTION (or equivalent added No-fault coverage)	5	SEPARATELY STATED IN EACH ADDED PIP ENDORSEMENT	$
PROPERTY PROTECTION INSURANCE (Michigan only)		SEPARATELY STATED IN THE P.P.I. ENDORSEMENT MINUS $_____ Ded. FOR EACH ACCIDENT	$
AUTO MEDICAL PAYMENTS		$	$
UNINSURED MOTORISTS	6	$	$
UNDERINSURED MOTORISTS (When not included in Uninsured Motorists Coverage)	6	$	$
PHYSICAL DAMAGE COMPREHENSIVE COVERAGE	7, 8	ACTUAL CASH VALUE OR COST OF REPAIR, WHICHEVER IS LESS MINUS $_____ Ded. FOR EACH COVERED AUTO. BUT NO DEDUCTIBLE APPLIES TO LOSS CAUSED BY FIRE OR LIGHTNING. See ITEM FOUR For Hired Or Borrowed "Autos".	$
PHYSICAL DAMAGE SPECIFIED CAUSES OF LOSS COVERAGE		ACTUAL CASH VALUE OR COST OF REPAIR, WHICHEVER IS LESS MINUS $_____ Ded. FOR EACH COVERED AUTO FOR LOSS CAUSED BY MISCHIEF OR VANDALISM. See ITEM FOUR For Hired Or Borrowed "Autos".	$
PHYSICAL DAMAGE COLLISION COVERAGE	7, 8	ACTUAL CASH VALUE OR COST OF REPAIR, WHICHEVER IS LESS MINUS $_____ Ded. FOR EACH COVERED AUTO. See ITEM FOUR For Hired Or Borrowed "Autos".	$
PHYSICAL DAMAGE TOWING AND LABOR (Not Available in California)		$_____ For Each Disablement Of A Private Passenger "Auto"	$
		PREMIUM FOR ENDORSEMENTS	$
		* ESTIMATED TOTAL PREMIUM	$

* This policy may be subject to final audit.

Symbol 9—Nonowned Autos Only

Symbol 9 provides coverage only for autos not owned, leased, hired, or borrowed by the named insured while such autos are used in connection with the named insured's business. Symbol 9 includes autos owned by the named insured's employees or members of their households but only while used in the named insured's business or personal affairs. Symbols 8 and 9 are normally used only for liability coverage. If symbol 1 is used for liability coverage, then symbols 8 and 9 do not need to be shown in order to provide coverage for hired and nonowned autos; symbol 1 includes such coverage. If another symbol is shown for liability coverage—for example, symbol 2 or 7—most insureds should add symbols 8 and 9 to obtain hired and nonowned autos coverage.

Exhibit 10-2 summarizes the symbols and their use for business auto coverage.

Coverage for Newly Acquired Autos

If any of symbols 1 through 6 is shown for a coverage, that coverage applies to vehicles of the type indicated by the symbol if such vehicles are acquired during the policy term. Coverage for newly acquired vehicles of the type indicated by the symbol is automatic, without any requirement that the insurer be notified of the acquisition. The insurer typically discovers any newly acquired autos when it audits the insured at the end of the policy period. Likewise, a premium auditor will determine the actual nonowned and hired auto exposure. The insured must then pay an additional premium for the actual exposures covered during the policy period. However, many insurers do not audit policies that generate smaller premiums.

If symbol 7 is shown for a coverage, autos acquired during the policy term are covered from the time of acquisition *only* if both of the following conditions are met:

1. The insurer insures all autos owned by the named insured, *or* the newly acquired auto replaces a covered auto.
2. The named insured asks the insurer to cover the newly acquired auto within thirty days after the acquisition.

Other Covered Items

If the coverage form provides *liability* insurance, trailers with a load capacity of 2,000 pounds or less are covered automatically for liability insurance. "Mobile equipment" is automatically covered for liability while being carried or towed by an auto that has liability coverage. Also covered, *for liability insurance only*, is an auto used as a temporary substitute for a covered auto that is out of service because of its breakdown, repair, service, loss, or destruction.

Section II—Liability Coverage

The liability coverage provisions of the business auto form include a coverage agreement, a definition of who is insured, coverage extensions, exclusions, and a limit of insurance clause.

EXHIBIT 10-2

Description of Covered Auto Designation Symbols

Symbol		Description Of Covered Auto Designation Symbols
1	Any "Auto"	
2	Owned "Autos" Only	Only those "autos" you own (and for Liability Coverage any "trailers" you don't own while attached to power units you own). This includes those "autos" you acquire ownership of after the policy begins.
3	Owned Private Passenger "Autos" Only	Only the private passenger "autos" you own. This includes those private passenger "autos" you acquire ownership of after the policy begins.
4	Owned "Autos" Other Than Private Passenger "Autos" Only	Only those "autos" you own that are not of the private passenger type (and for Liability Coverage any "trailers" you don't own while attached to power units you own). This includes those "autos" not of the private passenger type you acquire ownership of after the policy begins.
5	Owned "Autos" Subject To No-Fault	Only those "autos" you own that are required to have No-Fault benefits in the state where they are licensed or principally garaged. This includes those "autos" you acquire ownership of after the policy begins provided they are required to have No-Fault benefits in the state where they are licensed or principally garaged.
6	Owned "Autos" Subject To A Compulsory Uninsured Motorists Law	Only those "autos" you own that because of the law in the state where they are licensed or principally garaged are required to have and cannot reject Uninsured Motorists Coverage. This includes those "autos" you acquire ownership of after the policy begins provided they are subject to the same state uninsured motorists requirement.
7	Specifically Described "Autos"	Only those "autos" described in Item Three of the Declarations for which a premium charge is shown (and for Liability Coverage any "trailers" you don't own while attached to any power unit described in Item Three).
8	Hired "Autos" Only	Only those "autos" you lease, hire, rent or borrow. This does not include any "auto" you lease, hire, rent or borrow from any of your "employees", partners (if you are a partnership), members (if you are a limited liability company) or members of their households.
9	Nonowned "Autos" Only	Only those "autos" you do not own, lease, hire, rent or borrow that are used in connection with your business. This includes "autos" owned by your "employees", partners (if you are a partnership), members (if you are a limited liability company), or members of their households but only while used in your business or your personal affairs.

Coverage Agreement

In the liability coverage agreement, the insurer expresses three distinct duties:

1. A duty to pay damages
2. A duty to pay "covered pollution cost or expense"
3. A duty to defend the insured

Each of these duties is described in more detail below.

Duty To Pay Damages

The insurer agrees to pay all sums an "insured" must legally pay as damages because of "bodily injury" or "property damage" to which the insurance applies, caused by an "accident" and resulting from the ownership, maintenance, or use of a covered "auto." The terms in quotation marks are defined in Section V of the coverage form, as follows:

> "Insured" means any person or organization qualifying as an insured in the Who Is An Insured provision of the applicable coverage. . . .
>
> "Bodily injury" means bodily injury, sickness or disease sustained by a person including death resulting from any of these.
>
> "Property damage" means damage to or loss of use of tangible property.
>
> "Accident" includes continuous or repeated exposure to the same conditions resulting in "bodily injury" or "property damage".
>
> "Auto" means a land motor vehicle, trailer or semitrailer designed for travel on public roads but does not include "mobile equipment".

The insurer's obligation to "pay all sums" is governed not only by these definitions but also by the exclusions, policy limit, and other conditions to be discussed later.

Duty To Pay "Covered Pollution Cost or Expense"

The business auto form is subject to a broad pollution exclusion, discussed later in this chapter, which eliminates almost all coverage for bodily injury or property damage resulting from the escape of pollutants that are being transported by a covered auto. However, the business auto form covers certain pollution costs and expenses, such as those resulting from the escape of fuel or other fluids needed for the normal running of the covered auto.

In the event of a pollution incident, damages for bodily injury and property damage are not the only consequences for which the insured can be held liable. The insured can incur various costs and expenses as the result of demands by governmental authorities or private citizens that the insured clean up or otherwise respond to the effects of pollutants.

To address this exposure, the insurer agrees to pay all sums that the insured must legally pay as "covered pollution cost or expense." In order for pollution cost or expense to be covered, it must be caused by an accident and must result from the ownership, maintenance, or use of a covered auto. In addition, the same accident that causes the pollution cost or expense must also result in bodily injury or property damage covered by the policy. The business auto policy is subject to a broad pollution exclusion discussed later in this chapter. Cleanup costs for any incident excluded by the pollution exclusion are not covered.

Unlike defense costs, covered pollution cost or expense is not paid in addition to the stated limit of liability. All payments for covered pollution cost or expense reduce the applicable limit.

Duty To Defend

The insurer has the right and the duty to defend any insured against any claim or suit alleging damages that would be covered under the policy. The claim or suit only needs to *allege* damages that would be covered. Hence, the insurer must defend against even false or fraudulent claims or suits as long as they allege covered damages.

The coverage form defines "suit" to include not only civil proceedings but also an arbitration proceeding or any other alternative dispute resolution proceeding to which the insured must submit or does submit with the insurer's consent. The duty to defend ends when the insurer has paid its applicable policy limit in full or partial settlement of the claim. The costs of defending the claim are payable in addition to the limit of insurance.

Who Is an Insured

Many persons in addition to the named insured may be covered under the liability insuring agreement. Who is insured for liability coverage depends on the circumstances of the accident.

The named insured is an insured for *any covered auto*. If, for example, symbol 1 is shown for liability coverage, the named insured is an insured for *any* auto. If only symbol 7 is shown for liability coverage, the named insured is an insured only for specifically described autos.

Anyone other than the named insured is an insured while using with the named insured's permission a covered auto owned, hired, or borrowed *by the named insured*. However, the following restrictions apply:

- The owner or anyone else from whom the named insured hires or borrows a covered auto is not an insured, unless the covered auto is a trailer connected to a covered auto owned by the named insured. If, for example, ABC Company hires a car from A-1 Auto Rentals, A-1 will not be an insured under ABC's business auto liability coverage.

- An employee of the named insured is not an insured if the covered auto is owned by the employee or a member of the employee's household. For example, Sue is not an insured under her employer's business auto liability coverage while operating her car on an errand for her employer. (Sue's employer, however, *is* insured for this use of Sue's car if the policy includes either symbol 1 or symbol 9 for liability coverage.)

- A person using a covered auto while working in the business of selling, servicing, repairing, or parking autos is not an insured unless that business is the named insured's. For example, a mechanic of Bob's Brake Shop is not an insured under ABC's business auto liability coverage while test-driving ABC's car.

- Anyone other than the named insured's employees or partners, or a lessee or borrower of a covered auto or any of their employees, is not an insured while moving property to or from a covered auto. If, for example, employees of Jones Warehouse are unloading ABC Company's truck, the Jones employees are not covered under ABC's business auto liability coverage.

- If the named insured is a partnership, a partner of the named insured is not an insured for a covered auto owned by that partner or by someone residing in that partner's household.

- If the named insured is a limited liability company, a member of the named insured is not an insured for a covered auto owned by that member or by someone residing in that member's household.

Any person or organization (other than those excluded above) held liable for the conduct of an "insured" is also an insured. To illustrate the application of this provision, assume that an employee of XYZ Corporation operates an auto covered under ABC's business auto insurance. XYZ's employee causes an accident, and XYZ is held to be liable for its employee's conduct. Because of the provision under discussion, XYZ will be an insured under ABC's auto insurance. (XYZ's employee will also be an insured because of the earlier provision relating to "anyone else" other than the named insured.)

Coverage Extensions

The business auto liability provisions include coverage extensions for supplementary payments and for increased protection while a covered auto is out of the state where it is licensed.

Supplementary Payments

Business auto liability coverage provides six supplementary payments that are similar in most respects to those provided in the CGL coverage form. As under the CGL coverage form, these supplementary payments are payable in addition to the limit of insurance.

Out-of-State Coverage Extensions

If a covered auto is outside the state where it is licensed, the limit of insurance is, if necessary, increased on that auto to the minimum required by the outside jurisdiction in which the auto is being operated. Also, if the outside jurisdiction requires a different type of coverage, the policy provides such coverage automatically.

For example, assume that a business auto policy has a $50,000 limit for liability insurance and that a covered auto is driven out of state through two other states. If the first outside state requires a minimum limit of $100,000, the limit is increased automatically to $100,000 while the auto is in that state. If the second outside state requires no-fault coverage, the insured's policy will automatically provide no-fault coverage while the auto is in that state.

Exclusions

The exclusions that appear in the liability coverage section, listed in the box below, impose several limitations on the liability coverage agreement.

Business Auto Liability Coverage Exclusions

- Expected or Intended Injury
- Contractual Liability
- Workers Compensation
- Employee Indemnification and Employers Liability
- Fellow Employee
- Care, Custody, or Control
- Handling of Property

- Movement of Property by Mechanical Device
- Operations
- Completed Operations
- Pollution
- War
- Racing

Expected or Intended Injury

Bodily injury or property damage expected or intended from the standpoint of the insured is excluded.

Contractual Liability

Liability assumed by contract or agreement is excluded, but the exclusion does not apply to the following:

1. Liability that the insured would have in the absence of the contract
2. Damages assumed in an "insured contract," provided the injury or damage occurs after the contract is executed

The definition of "insured contract" found in Section V of the coverage form lists the types of contracts in which an assumption of liability is covered. In many ways, this definition resembles the definition of "insured contract" in the CGL coverage form. For example, both definitions include leases of premises. The business auto form covers liability assumed under a lease of premises only if the liability being assumed arises out of the ownership, maintenance, or use of an auto; the CGL form covers liability assumed under a lease of premises if the liability being assumed does *not* arise out of the ownership, maintenance, or use of an auto. The same distinction applies to the other types of insured contracts.

Under the business auto definition, the following are insured contracts:

1. A lease of premises.
2. A sidetrack agreement.
3. An easement or license agreement except in connection with construction or demolition operations on or within fifty feet of any railroad property.
4. An obligation, as required by ordinance, to indemnify a municipality, except in connection with work *for* a municipality.
5. That part of any other contract or agreement in which the named insured assumes the tort liability of another to pay damages because of bodily injury or property damage, if the agreement pertains to the named insured's business.
6. Any auto rental or lease agreement entered into by the named insured or any employee of the named insured as part of the named insured's business. However, the agreement will not be considered an "insured contract" to the extent that it obligates the named insured or the employee to pay for property damage to a rented or leased auto.

An insured contract does not include that part of any contract or agreement that:

*   Indemnifies anyone for injury or damage arising out of construction or demolition operations within fifty feet of any railroad property;
*   Pertains to the loan, lease, or rental of an auto to the named insured if the auto is loaned, leased, or rented *with a driver*; or
*   Holds a trucker harmless for the named insured's use of a covered auto over a route or territory the trucker is authorized to serve by public authority.

Workers Compensation

Like the CGL form, the business auto form excludes any liability under a workers compensation, disability benefits, or unemployment compensation law.

Employee Indemnification and Employers Liability

This exclusion is also nearly identical to one found in the CGL coverage form. The effect is to eliminate, subject to two exceptions, coverage for bodily injury to employees of the insured that should be covered under workers compensation and employers liability insurance. The two exceptions that allow coverage for employee injury are (1) injury to domestic employees not entitled to workers compensation and (2) liability assumed by the insured under an insured contract.

Fellow Employee

The business auto form excludes bodily injury to any fellow employee of any insured that arises in the course of the fellow employee's employment. If, for example, one of ABC's drivers negligently strikes another ABC employee with a truck while they are at work, ABC's business auto coverage will not protect the driver against any legal action the injured employee might be able to bring against the driver. By endorsement (for an additional premium), the fellow employee exclusion can be either deleted entirely or modified so that it does not apply to specified employees, job titles, or position.

Severability of Interests Clause

The business auto definition of "insured" contains a sentence commonly known as the severability of interests clause. It reads as follows: "Except with respect to the Limit of Insurance, the coverage afforded applies separately to each insured who is seeking coverage or against whom a claim or 'suit' is brought."

In a number of cases, the severability of interests clause has been crucial in interpreting the exclusion of bodily injury to an employee of the "insured." The effect has been to allow coverage for injury sustained by employees of the *named* insured when the insured against whom the employees made claim was some insured other than the named insured.

To illustrate, say that Sally, an employee of Ray's Hardware Store, is struck by a Ray's Hardware Store delivery truck driven by Dan. Dan is not a store employee; he is Ray's cousin. Dan borrowed the truck so that he could move his furniture to his new apartment. Sally makes claim against Dan, who qualifies as an insured under Ray's business auto policy. Although Ray's policy excludes bodily injury to an employee of the insured, this exclusion does not eliminate coverage for Sally's claim against Dan: Sally is not an employee of the insured *against whom she is making claim* (Dan).

Care, Custody, or Control

There is no coverage for property owned by the insured or in the care, custody, or control of the insured. Property owned by the insured can be insured under an appropriate form of property insurance. Property of others in the care, custody, or control of the insured is frequently insured under inland marine coverage. For example, motor truck cargo insurance, described in Chapter 7, covers property of others being transported by the insured.

Handling of Property

This exclusion helps to define the scope of coverage for accidents occurring during the loading or unloading of autos. The exclusion eliminates coverage for bodily injury or property damage resulting from the handling of property under the following conditions:

- *Before* property is moved from the place where it is accepted by the insured for movement into a covered auto

- *After* it has been moved from a covered auto to the place where it is finally delivered by the insured

Consequently, the exclusion does not apply to—and thus there is coverage for—accidents that occur while property is being moved (1) into a covered auto from the place where the insured has accepted the property or (2) from a covered auto to the place where the insured is delivering the property.

If, for example, two employees of an appliance store damage a hallway wall while moving a clothes washer from their delivery truck to a second-floor apartment, the store's business auto insurance will cover the damage to the wall, because the property damage occurred before the washer was moved to the place of final delivery.

As discussed in Chapter 8, the CGL coverage form excludes "loading and unloading" and defines that term in the same manner as set forth above, thus avoiding duplication of business auto coverage. The CGL form *covers* the exposures that exist in connection with property before loading begins or after unloading is completed.

Movement of Property by Mechanical Device

The business auto form excludes bodily injury or property damage resulting from movement of property by a mechanical device unless the device is attached to the covered auto or is a hand truck. To illustrate, movement of property by a mechanical hoist attached to a flatbed truck is covered; movement of property by a conveyor belt not attached to the truck is excluded by the business auto form (but covered by the CGL form).

Operations

This exclusion eliminates coverage for the operation of several specified types of equipment attached to covered autos. The specified types of equipment are "cherry pickers" and similar devices used to raise or lower workers; air compressors, pumps, or generators; and equipment used for spraying, welding, building cleaning, geophysical exploration, lighting, or well servicing. In the absence of this exclusion, the business auto form might otherwise be considered to cover the operation of such equipment because it is attached to a covered auto. The CGL policy covers the operation of such equipment, whether attached to an auto or not.

To illustrate, assume C&D Electric has a service truck with a cherry picker mounted on it. The driver of the truck causes an accident while driving to a work site. The resulting liability is covered under C&D's business auto insurance. After the truck reaches its work site, a passerby is injured as a result of C&D's operation of the cherry picker. The resulting liability is excluded by C&D's business auto insurance and covered by C&D's CGL insurance.

Completed Operations

This exclusion clarifies that the business auto form provides no insurance for completed operations performed with the insured's autos. For example, injury resulting from allegedly negligent snowplowing performed (and completed) by the insured would not be covered.

Pollution

With few exceptions, the business auto pollution exclusion eliminates coverage for bodily injury or property damage resulting from the discharge of any pollutants being transported or stored in, or moved to or from, a covered auto.

Pollution Caused When an Insured's Vehicle Collides With an Oil Tank Truck

Question: Betty negligently collided with an oil tank truck owned by Superior Oil Company while she was driving the delivery truck owned by her firm, Betty's Floral Service. As a result of the collision, the oil carried by the tank truck leaked onto the ground and into a nearby stream. The cost to clean up the resulting pollution exceeded $200,000. Is Betty covered by her business auto policy?

Answer: Yes. The pollution exclusion applies to pollutants that are discharged from a covered auto or being transported by or on behalf of the insured. Because the oil that spilled was not being transported by Betty or in a covered auto under Betty's policy, she would have coverage. Similarly, Betty would have coverage for pollution liability if she backed into a chemical storage tank as she was trying to park in a customer's parking lot; the oil that spilled was not being transported in (or moved to or from) a covered auto.

By a specific exception, the exclusion does not apply to the escape of fuels, lubricants, fluids, exhaust gases, or other similar pollutants needed for functioning of the covered auto. If, for example, gasoline leaks from the fuel tank of a covered auto after a collision, liability for the spill is covered.

War

Liability assumed under contract for damage caused by war, civil war, insurrection, rebellion, or revolution is excluded, even if the liability is assumed under an "insured contract."

Racing

Much as the CGL policy excludes racing of mobile equipment, the business auto form excludes covered autos while used in organized races or demolition contests. Practice or preparation for such activities is also excluded.

Limit of Insurance

Business auto liability coverage is subject to a combined single limit of insurance applicable to all bodily injury, property damage, and covered pollution cost or expense arising from a single accident. No annual aggregate limit applies. The single limit is the maximum amount the insurer will pay for all claims arising *from a single accident* regardless of the number of vehicles, the number of drivers, or the number of claimants involved.

Repeated exposure to essentially the same circumstances is considered to be a single accident. For example, if a truck is driven across the sidewalk repeatedly over several months, all of the damage it causes to the sidewalk would be considered a single accident.

An endorsement is available to provide split limits of insurance. The endorsement shows a per person limit and a per accident limit for bodily injury and a per accident limit for property damage.

Section III—Physical Damage Coverage

Section III of the business auto form provides auto physical damage insurance. The primary purpose of the coverage is to insure loss of or damage to autos owned by the insured. However, coverage can also be arranged to cover autos hired or borrowed by the insured.

Available Coverages

Three basic physical damage coverages are available for the insured to choose from:

1. Collision
2. Comprehensive
3. Specified causes of loss

Any one of these coverages can be purchased alone. More often, however, the named insured selects either (1) collision and comprehensive or (2) collision and specified causes of loss. Since comprehensive coverage encompasses all of the specified causes of loss, those two coverages are never purchased on the same autos.

In addition to the three basic physical damage coverages, the business auto form includes provisions for optional towing and labor coverage, an extension covering transportation expenses, and an extension covering loss of use of rental autos. These coverages and coverage extensions are described below.

Collision Coverage

Collision coverage
Coverage for direct and accidental loss or damage to a covered auto caused by collision with another object or by overturn.

Collision coverage insures "loss" to a covered auto caused by collision with another object or by overturn. The coverage form defines "loss" as direct and accidental loss or damage. The form does not define "collision" or "overturn." "Collision" is generally understood to mean a striking together with violent impact. "Overturn" is generally considered to include any incident in which a vehicle loses its equilibrium; the vehicle does not have to turn over completely.

Comprehensive Coverage

Comprehensive coverage
Coverage for direct and accidental loss or damage to a covered auto by any peril except collision or a peril specifically excluded.

Comprehensive coverage insures loss to a covered auto by any peril except collision or overturn or a peril specifically excluded. This is essentially the same approach to defining covered perils as is used in the Causes of Loss—

Special Form, thus covering unnamed, unanticipated perils as long as they are not specifically excluded.

Glass breakage, damage resulting from hitting a bird or an animal, and damage caused by falling objects or missiles, although they might otherwise be considered losses caused by collision, are paid under comprehensive if the auto is insured for comprehensive. This provision usually benefits the insured, since most insureds carry lower deductibles on comprehensive than on collision coverage.

If glass breakage is caused by collision, however, it can be covered by collision (and not under comprehensive) at the option of the insured. In that way, the insured can avoid the application of two deductibles when collision damage to the auto is accompanied by glass breakage.

Specified Causes of Loss Coverage

A somewhat less expensive alternative to comprehensive coverage is **specified causes of loss coverage**. This coverage insures loss to a covered auto caused by fire, lightning, explosion, theft, windstorm, hail, earthquake, flood, mischief, or vandalism. It also insures loss resulting from the sinking, burning, collision, or derailment of a conveyance transporting the insured vehicle.

Specified causes of loss coverage
Coverage for several named perils instead of all perils except those specifically excluded.

Towing and Labor Coverage

Towing and labor coverage reimburses the insured for necessary towing and labor costs resulting from the disablement of a covered *private passenger* auto. The labor must be performed at the place of disablement. The limit for this coverage, selected by the insured, is the most that the insurer will pay for each disablement.

Towing and labor coverage
Coverage for necessary towing and labor costs due to the disablement of a covered private passenger auto; coverage requires that the labor must be performed at the place of disablement.

Transportation Expenses

The coverage extension for **transportation expenses** pays for substitute transportation when a private passenger type auto has been stolen if it is insured for comprehensive or specified causes of loss. The insurer agrees to pay costs of substitute transportation actually incurred by the named insured, subject to a daily limit of $20 and a total limit of $600. Payments begin forty-eight hours after the theft, and they end when the insured auto is returned to use or when the insurer pays for the auto. Such payments may extend beyond the expiration of the policy.

Transportation expenses
Coverage extension for substitute transportation costs incurred when a private passenger type auto has been stolen; applies only if the auto is insured for comprehensive or specified causes of loss.

The coverage extension applies only if the auto is of the private passenger type and is stolen. Some insureds want broader coverage, which can be provided through the Rental Reimbursement Coverage Endorsement. The endorsement covers the cost of renting a substitute auto for a designated auto of *any* type that has suffered a loss due to *any* covered peril, subject to maximum daily and aggregate limits.

Loss of Use Expenses

When the insured rents an auto, the rental agreement may obligate the insured to pay for physical damage to the auto that occurs during the rental period, as well as resulting loss of use of the auto, regardless of whether the insured is at fault in causing the damage. Although an organization can buy physical damage insurance on hired autos (through symbol 8), such coverage applies only to the physical loss and not to the resulting loss of use. The coverage extension for **loss of use expenses** provides up to $20 a day, to a maximum of $600, to cover that exposure. These limits can be increased by endorsement.

Loss of use expenses
Coverage extension that pays loss of use of a rental auto when an insured becomes contractually obligated to make such payments.

Exclusions

Auto physical damage insurance is subject to comparatively few exclusions. Like virtually any other type of property insurance, it excludes nuclear hazards and war or military action. Notably, however, auto physical damage insurance does not exclude earthquake, flood, or other water damage.

Business auto physical damage insurance excludes certain types of losses that are likely to occur as a normal consequence of prolonged use of the vehicle or the owner's neglect. Thus, wear and tear, freezing, mechanical or electrical failure, and road damage to tires are excluded unless they result from other loss insured by the coverage form. For example, an auto with comprehensive coverage may be stolen. If the auto suffers a mechanical breakdown and tire damage resulting from abusive driving by the thief, the mechanical breakdown and tire damage would not be excluded because the proximate cause of the loss was a covered peril (theft).

The business auto form excludes many, but not all, types of electronic equipment in a covered auto. In fact, the drafters of the form have gone to great lengths to specify exactly what types of electronic equipment are excluded and which are covered. These exclusions have been redrafted several times in recent years to keep up with technological change.

The insurer will not pay for loss to the following:

1. Tapes, records, discs, or similar devices
2. Radar detectors and similar devices
3. Any equipment, whether permanently installed or not, that receives or transmits audio, visual, or data signals and that is not designed solely for the reproduction of sound
4. Any accessories used with the equipment described in item 3 above

If the insured wishes to insure such equipment, coverage can usually be added to the business auto form by using special endorsements.

The exclusion contains some detailed exceptions. In summary, these exceptions reinstate coverage for (1) sound-reproducing equipment permanently installed in the auto (or removable from a housing unit that is permanently installed in the auto) and (2) electronic equipment necessary for the normal operation of the auto.

Like business auto liability coverage, the physical damage section excludes coverage for autos while used in organized races or demolition contests, including practice or preparation for such activities.

Finally, the physical damage section excludes "diminution in value," which the form defines as "the actual or perceived loss in market value" resulting from a covered auto being repaired.

Limit of Insurance

The most the insurer will pay for a physical damage loss is the *smaller* of the following:

1. The actual cash value of the property at the time of loss
2. The cost of repairing or replacing the property with other property of like kind or quality

Deductible

The insurer's payment *for each covered auto* is reduced by any applicable deductible shown in the declarations. Thus, if two of the insured's vehicles collide with each other, two deductibles will apply.

A deductible applicable to comprehensive coverage does not apply to loss by fire or lightning. This exception can be of considerable value to an owner of a fleet of autos that are garaged at the same location and therefore susceptible to total loss by fire. In the absence of this exemption, the insured would have to bear a portion of the loss equal to the amount of the deductible times the total number of cars destroyed.

Section IV—Business Auto Conditions

Conditions that apply to all coverages under the business auto form are contained in Section IV of the form. Some of the conditions are similar to those found in the CGL form. Others are specific to auto insurance. The first five conditions are loss conditions, and the remaining eight conditions are more general in nature.

Appraisal for Physical Damage Losses

If the named insured and the insurer cannot agree on the amount of loss, either may call for an appraisal. Each will then appoint an appraiser, and the appraisers will appoint a "competent and impartial" umpire. The appraisers then determine actual cash value and the amount of loss payment. Any item on which the appraisers cannot agree is submitted to the umpire, and an award in writing, signed by any two of the three, is binding on both parties. Each party pays its own appraiser, and both parties share the cost of the umpire. This procedure applies only to disagreements about the amount of loss and not to disagreements as to coverage.

Duties in the Event of Accident, Claim, Suit, or Loss

The insured's duties after loss are essentially the same as those imposed by the CGL policy. The named insured must give prompt notice of accident or loss to the insurer or its agent and assist the insurer in obtaining the names of injured persons or witnesses. Also, both the named insured and any other person who seeks liability coverage under the policy (for example, the driver of an insured vehicle) must do the following:

1. Cooperate with the insurer in its investigation and defense of the accident or loss.
2. Immediately send to the insurer copies of any notices or legal papers received in connection with the accident or loss.
3. Submit to physical examinations by physicians selected and paid by the insurer as often as the insurer may reasonably request.
4. Authorize the insurer to obtain medical reports and other medical information.

Moreover, no insured can commit the insurer to make any payment either for damages or expenses.

If the claim is for loss or damage to a covered auto, the named insured must do the following:

1. Promptly notify the police if the insured auto or any of its equipment is stolen.
2. Do what is reasonably necessary to preserve the property from further loss.
3. Permit the insurer to inspect and appraise the damaged vehicle before it is repaired.
4. Agree to be examined under oath at the insurer's request and give a signed statement.

Legal Action Against the Insurer

No legal action can be brought against the insurer under any coverage until the named insured and the insured bringing the action, if different, have complied with all provisions of the coverage form. In addition, under the liability coverage, no action can be brought against the insurer until either a court has determined that the insured is liable for the loss or the insurer has agreed in writing that the insured is liable for the loss.

Loss Payment—Physical Damage Coverages

The insurer has three options with regard to damaged or stolen property:

1. To pay to repair or replace the property
2. To return the property at the expense of the insurer and repair any damage caused by theft

3. To keep all of the property and pay an agreed or appraised value

Transfer of Rights Against Others

The insured may have a right to recover a loss from some other party, usually because the other party caused the loss. If the insurer pays the loss, it is entitled, under this condition, to take over the insured's right of recovery from the other party. This right is referred to as "subrogation." The insured must not do anything to impair the insurer's right of recovery and must do everything reasonably necessary to secure and preserve that right.

Bankruptcy

The first of eight general conditions relates to bankruptcy. Bankruptcy or insolvency of the insured does not relieve the insurer of any of its obligations under the policy. If the insured is relieved through bankruptcy of any obligation to pay a liability claim, the insurer is still obligated to make payment just as it would have been if the insured had remained solvent.

Concealment, Misrepresentation, or Fraud

In case of fraud by the named insured relative to business auto coverage, the coverage is void. It is also void if any insured *intentionally* conceals or misrepresents a material fact about the coverage form, any autos covered, the insured's interest in any covered auto, or a claim under the coverage form. A material fact is one that would have changed the underwriting decision in some way.

Liberalization

If the insurer revises the form to provide more coverage at no increase in premium, the coverage applies to existing coverage as of the date the revision is effective in the insured's state.

No Benefit to Bailee—Physical Damage Insurance Only

Railroads and other transporters of property sometimes try to gain the benefit of the property owner's insurance by inserting a provision in their bill of lading stating that they are not liable for any loss for which the shipper is reimbursed by insurance. This provision in the bill of lading could invalidate the insurer's right of subrogation against the transporting company. Accordingly, the "no benefit to bailee" condition attempts to preserve the insurer's subrogation rights by stating that the insurer does not recognize any assignment of coverage or any other grant of coverage to any person or organization that holds, stores, or transports property for a fee.

Other Insurance

Business auto coverage may be either primary or excess, depending on the circumstances of the accident or loss. For any covered vehicle owned by the named insured, the coverage is primary. For any covered auto not owned by the named insured, the coverage is excess, and the insurance, if any, carried by the owner of the auto is primary.

For purposes of hired auto (symbol 8) physical damage coverage, any auto the named insured leases, hires, rents, or borrows is deemed to be a covered auto owned by the named insured. Such an auto is therefore covered on a primary basis. However, there is no coverage for an auto that is hired or borrowed *with a driver*.

Coverage for trailers follows the autos to which they are attached. Thus, coverage is excess for a trailer attached to an auto not owned by the named insured, and coverage is primary for a trailer attached to an auto owned by the named insured. The coverage is primary for a covered trailer owned by the named insured when it is not attached to any auto.

Regardless of the above provisions, business auto liability coverage is primary for any liability assumed under an insured contract.

If two or more policies of the same level (either excess or primary) apply to the same loss, each policy contributes to the loss in the proportion that its limit bears to the total limits of all policies of its level.

Illustration of Other Insurance Provision

To illustrate the other insurance provision, assume that two primary policies apply to the same claim. Policy A has a $100,000 limit, and Policy B has a $300,000 limit. If the claim amounted to $40,000, Policy A, which has one-fourth of the total limits, would pay $10,000, and Policy B, which has three-fourths of the total limits, would pay $30,000.

Premium Audit

The premium shown on the declarations, which the insured pays at policy inception, is an estimate. The actual premium will be determined by a premium audit and will be based on actual exposures at the end of the policy period. If the final premium is less than the estimate, the named insured gets a refund. If the final premium is greater than the estimate, the named insured must pay the difference.

Policy Period, Coverage Territory

Accidents and losses are covered if they occur (1) during the policy period shown on the declarations and (2) within the coverage territory. The coverage territory includes the United States of America, its territories and possessions, Puerto Rico, and Canada. Losses and accidents involving a covered auto while being transported between the covered territories are also covered.

A worldwide coverage territory applies to covered autos of the private passenger type that are leased, hired, rented, or borrowed without a driver for a period of thirty days or less. The insured's liability for damages must be determined in a suit in the United States, Puerto Rico, or Canada, or in a settlement to which the insurer agrees.

Two or More Coverage Forms or Policies Issued by the Insurer

A special rule applies when an accident or a loss is covered by two or more policies issued by the same insurer or affiliated insurers. In that case, the maximum amount the insurer or affiliated insurers will be required to pay is the highest limit provided under any one policy. However, this does not apply to any coverage specifically purchased as excess over business auto coverage, such as a commercial umbrella liability policy.

Coverages Added by Endorsement

Apart from the liability and physical damage coverages, all of the coverages listed in the schedule of coverages and covered autos in the business auto declarations must be added by endorsement if they are purchased. The provisions for these coverages are described below.

Medical Payments

Auto medical payments coverage pays for medical expenses incurred by occupants of a covered auto, regardless of whether the driver of the auto was at fault in the accident. Medical payments coverage, by paying a small bodily injury claim without any determination of liability, can sometimes prevent an injured passenger from making a costlier liability claim against the driver.

More specifically, the Auto Medical Payments Endorsement covers the reasonable and necessary medical and funeral expenses incurred by a person injured by an accident while entering into, riding in, or alighting from a covered auto. If the named insured is an individual proprietorship, it covers the named insured and members of his or her family while occupying *any* auto or if struck by an auto while a pedestrian. Payments for any one person may not exceed the limit stated in the declarations. Because no aggregate limit applies, the insurer may pay several times the limit if several persons are injured.

There is no coverage if the injury occurs in the course of employment and is covered under workers compensation. War, nuclear radiation, and radioactive contamination are excluded.

Auto medical payments coverage
Coverage for medical expenses incurred by occupants of a covered auto, regardless of whether the auto's driver was at fault in the accident.

Personal Injury Protection and Added Personal Injury Protection

If the insured is subject to an auto no-fault law, the required **personal injury protection (PIP) coverage** can be added to the policy by endorsement. Because benefit levels and other features of no-fault laws vary from state to state, a separate PIP endorsement exists for each no-fault state. In some no-fault

Personal injury protection (PIP) coverage
Coverage for medical expense, income loss, and other benefits stipulated in an auto no-fault plan.

states, benefit levels can be increased above the minimum required levels by using an *added personal injury protection endorsement.*

The benefits provided by a typical PIP endorsement consist of the following:

1. Medical and rehabilitation expenses
2. Income loss benefit
3. Substitute services benefit
4. Death benefits to survivors

The substitute services benefit pays the cost of purchased services that would have been performed by the injured person if the injury had not occurred. An example is the cost of a housekeeper to do the work usually performed by a person before his or her injury.

The limits of the coverage are specified in the applicable state law and are also usually included in the coverage endorsement. The exclusions applicable to the coverage vary with state law.

Uninsured Motorists Insurance

Uninsured motorists coverage
Coverage for injury of an insured person injured by an at-fault uninsured motorist; pays the amount of coverage (subject to policy limits) the uninsured motorist's liability insurance would have paid if that motorist had been insured.

Uninsured motorists coverage is a cross between no-fault insurance and liability insurance. It resembles no-fault insurance in that the benefits are paid to the injured person by his or her own insurer. It resembles liability insurance in that benefits are paid only if the injuries were caused by an uninsured motorist under circumstances that would make the uninsured motorist liable for the injuries. If these conditions are met, the uninsured motorists coverage pays the injured person the amount, subject to policy limits, that the uninsured motorist's liability insurance would have paid if he or she had been insured.

In most states, uninsured motorists coverage is applicable only to bodily injury. In some states, uninsured motorists coverage can be extended to cover property damage as well.

The uninsured motorists insurance covers any person injured by an uninsured motorist while riding in an auto insured under the policy for uninsured motorists coverage. In addition, if the named insured is an individual proprietorship, the policy covers the named insured and members of his or her family while riding in any auto or if struck by an uninsured motorist while a pedestrian. "Uninsured motorist" is defined in the policy to include the following:

1. A driver of a vehicle for which no liability insurance is provided at the time of the accident
2. A driver of a vehicle for which liability insurance is provided, but with limits less than those required by state law
3. A hit-and-run driver

A driver of a governmental vehicle or a vehicle owned by a person or an organization that has qualified as a self-insurer under state law is *not* an uninsured motorist for purposes of this coverage.

An insured can also purchase *underinsured motorists coverage*. Although the details of coverage differ from state to state, the basic purpose of under-insured motorists coverage is to cover injuries caused by motorists who have liability insurance but for an amount less than the insured's limit for underinsured motorists coverage. In some states, underinsured motorists coverage is included in uninsured motorists coverage and does not need to be purchased separately.

GARAGE COVERAGE FORM

Insurers have long recognized that the general liability and auto liability exposures of a business engaged in selling, servicing, storing, or parking autos are often closely intertwined. By 1935, insurers had developed a standardized garage liability policy, which provided, in one form, the equivalent of general liability and auto liability coverage. In 1978, ISO introduced its Garage Policy, which included three coverages under one form:

- Garage liability coverage
- Garagekeepers coverage (covering damage to customers' autos in the insured's care, custody, or control)
- Auto physical damage coverage (including a reporting form option for auto dealers' inventories).

The current **Garage Coverage Form** provides the same coverages as the Garage Policy did, but in a modular format that allows it to be written as either a monoline policy or part of a commercial package policy. Until July 2002, ISO manual rules allowed the Garage Coverage Form to be written for two categories of insureds:

1. *Auto dealers.* This category includes both franchised auto dealers (for example, an authorized Ford or Honda dealer) and nonfranchised auto dealers (for example, a used car dealer); it does not include trailer dealers.

2. *Auto service operations.* This category includes repair shops, service stations, storage garages, public parking facilities, tow truck operators, and franchised or nonfranchised *trailer* dealers.

Effective July 2002, ISO removed auto service operations from the eligibility rules for the Garage Coverage Form. Consequently, insurers that use ISO forms and rules will insure only auto dealers under the Garage Coverage Form and will use the CGL and business auto forms to insure auto service operations. Some insurers may choose to deviate from ISO rules and continue to offer the Garage Coverage Form (or a policy similar to it) to auto service risks. Accordingly, the discussion that follows still refers to nondealer insureds in some situations.

Garage Coverage Form
Form that covers the automobile and general liability loss exposures of auto dealers.

The Garage Coverage Form contains six sections:

Section I—Covered Autos

Section II—Liability Coverage

Section III—Garagekeepers Coverage

Section IV—Physical Damage Coverage

Section V—Garage Conditions

Section VI—Definitions

Section I—Covered Autos

This section parallels Section I of the business auto form. The symbols for use with the garage form range from 21 through 31.

- Symbols 21 through 29 correspond in most respects to business auto symbols 1 through 9.

- Symbol 30 is used for providing garagekeepers coverage on customers' autos left with the named insured for service, repair, storage, or safekeeping.

- Symbol 31 covers dealers' autos and autos held for sale by nondealers or trailer dealers.

Section II—Liability Coverage

This broad insuring agreement provides bodily injury and property damage liability coverage comparable to that provided by the CGL form (occurrence version) and the business auto coverage form. The insurer agrees to pay "all sums the insured legally must pay as damages because of bodily injury or property damage . . . caused by an accident and resulting from *garage operations*." The policy definition of garage operations is as follows:

> The ownership, maintenance or use of locations for garage business and that portion of the roads or other accesses that adjoin these locations. "Garage operations" includes the ownership, maintenance and use of the autos indicated in Section I of this coverage form as covered "autos". "Garage operations" also includes all operations necessary or incidental to a garage business.

Despite its similarities to CGL and business auto coverage, garage liability coverage contains some provisions that differ from those of the CGL and business auto forms.

Garage liability coverage is restricted to liability arising out of "garage operations." If the insured opens a new business that is neither a garage nor incidental to the existing garage business, it will not be covered by garage liability coverage. A CGL coverage form, in contrast, automatically covers any additional type of business that the insured may enter into during the policy period.

Garage liability coverage for products is virtually identical to that provided under the CGL coverage form, provided the product was made or sold in a garage business. By endorsement to the garage form, the named insured can purchase *broad form products coverage*, which eliminates the exclusion of property damage to the named insured's products. This additional coverage is subject to a $250 deductible.

Garage liability coverage provides completed operations insurance subject to a $100 deductible. For example, assume that during an oil change, an employee of the insured installs the oil filter improperly, allowing oil to drain from the engine and resulting in engine damage when the customer drives the car. Costs to repair the engine will be covered subject to a deductible of $100.

Regarding auto liability coverage, the garage liability section contains an exclusion that is not found in the business auto form. The exclusion eliminates liability coverage for any covered auto while leased or rented to others. However, the exclusion does not apply to—and thus there is coverage for—a covered auto the named insured rents to a customer whose auto is being serviced or repaired by the named insured. If the named insured wants liability coverage on autos it rents to other persons, coverage can be arranged by endorsement.

Customers of the named insured qualify as insureds for auto liability coverage only if the named insured's business is an auto dealership. However, a customer who has no other available insurance can only recover the limit required by the state's compulsory insurance or financial responsibility law, even if that is less than the garage liability limit. For an additional premium, customers can be covered for the full limit of insurance.

Garage liability coverage does not provide the following coverages contained in the CGL coverage form: personal and advertising injury, host liquor, fire damage, incidental medical malpractice, and nonowned watercraft. However, these coverages can be added as a package to garage liability coverage by the Broadened Coverage—Garages Endorsement.

Coverage for garage operations *other than auto* is subject to an annual aggregate limit. An "each accident" limit applies to both auto claims and other-than-auto claims.

Section III—Garagekeepers Coverage

Garagekeepers insurance covers the insured's liability for damage by a covered cause of loss to autos left in the insured's care while the insured is attending, servicing, repairing, parking, or storing the autos in the garage operation. Garagekeepers coverage is desirable because garage liability coverage excludes damage to property in the insured's care, custody, or control.

The causes of loss that can be insured against under garagekeepers coverage are collision, comprehensive, and specified causes of loss. The specified causes of loss are fire, explosion, theft, and mischief or vandalism. Like other types

Garagekeepers insurance
Insurance that covers the insured's liability for damage by a covered cause of loss to autos left in the insured's care while the insured is attending, servicing, repairing, parking, or storing the autos.

of liability insurance, garagekeepers coverage also pays the cost of defending the insured against suits alleging covered losses.

For an additional premium, garagekeepers coverage can be extended to cover loss to customers' autos regardless of whether the insured is legally liable. This coverage option, known as direct coverage, allows a garage business to preserve customer goodwill by compensating its customers for their losses even if the garage has no legal obligation to do so. The coverage is provided not by endorsement but simply by marking a box in the garage declarations form. Two options are available: direct excess and direct primary. Exhibit 10-3 shows the wording of the two options.

When the **garagekeepers direct excess option** applies, the insurer will still pay covered losses for which the insured is legally liable on a primary basis; however, when the insured is not legally liable for a covered loss, the insurer will pay in excess of what the customer can recover under his or her own auto physical damage insurance.

When the **garagekeepers direct primary option** applies, the insurer will pay all covered losses on a primary basis, regardless of whether the insured is legally liable and regardless of whether the customer can recover under his or her own insurance.

Some restaurants, hospitals, or other organizations have incidental valet parking operations that pose the same loss exposures faced by garages. Although these types of organizations are not eligible for the Garage Coverage Form, they can obtain garagekeepers coverage by endorsement to their business auto coverage.

Garagekeepers direct excess option

Option that modifies garagekeepers coverage to include coverage in situations when the insured is not legally liable for loss to a customer's auto; this additional coverage applies in excess of what customers can collect under their own insurance.

Garagekeepers direct primary option

Option that modifies garagekeepers coverage so that it will pay all covered losses on a primary basis, regardless of whether the insured is legally liable and regardless of whether customers can recover under their own insurance.

EXHIBIT 10-3

Garagekeepers Direct Coverage Options

DIRECT COVERAGE OPTIONS

Indicate below with an "X" which, if any, Direct Coverage Option is selected.

☐ EXCESS INSURANCE

If this box is checked, Garagekeepers Coverage remains applicable on a legal liability basis. However, coverage also applies without regard to your or any other "insured's" legal liability for "loss" to a "customer's auto" on an excess basis over any other collectible insurance regardless of whether the other insurance covers your or any other "insured's" interest or the interest of the "customer's auto's" owner.

☐ PRIMARY INSURANCE

If this box is checked, Garagekeepers Coverage is changed to apply without regard to your or another "insured's" legal liability for "loss" to a "customer's auto" and is primary insurance.

© ISO Properties, Inc., 2000.

Section IV—Physical Damage Coverage

Garage physical damage insurance provides the collision, comprehensive, and specified causes-of-loss coverages available under the business auto form. In most ways, garage physical damage insurance is subject to the same provisions as business auto physical damage insurance. Notable differences are described below.

Dealers' Autos

Autos held for sale by a dealer are not listed individually in the policy but are insured in the aggregate, subject to a single overall limit. The insurer makes entries on the auto dealers' supplementary schedule to indicate the types of autos (new, used, demonstrator) covered and the interests covered (owned, financed, consignment, and so forth). A reporting form, which requires the dealer to report the value of such vehicles either monthly or quarterly, is available for dealerships when the value of such vehicles on hand fluctuates widely from month to month. Under a reporting form, the annual premium is calculated on the basis of the insured's reports of values. The deductible may apply to loss caused by any covered peril or only to loss caused by theft, vandalism, or mischief.

Exclusions

Garage physical damage insurance contains several exclusions that are not found in the business auto form.

The false pretense exclusion eliminates coverage for loss to a covered auto resulting from someone's causing the named insured to *voluntarily* part with the auto by trick, scheme, or other false pretense. The exclusion also eliminates coverage for an auto the insured has acquired from a seller who did not have legal title. If, for example, the rightful owner repossesses the auto, the insured cannot recover for the loss under garage physical damage insurance. Coverage for false pretense losses can be arranged by adding the False Pretense Coverage Endorsement for an additional premium.

Another exclusion eliminates collision coverage for any covered auto while being driven or transported from the point of purchase or distribution to its destination if such points are more than fifty road miles apart. Because the "driveaway" exposure can be significant, insurers do not want to cover it without being able to assess the risk and charge an appropriate additional premium. The coverage is added by attaching the Dealers Driveaway Collision Coverage Endorsement.

Other exclusions eliminate coverage for the named insured's expected profit, for "diminution in value" (as discussed earlier), and for loss to any auto stored at a location not shown in the declarations if the loss occurs more than forty-five days after the named insured begins using the location.

Section V—Garage Conditions

The general conditions of the garage form are virtually identical to those of the business auto form.

Section VI—Definitions

The garage form contains most of the same definitions used in the business auto form. However, some additional definitions appear in the garage form to facilitate the garage form's combination of general liability and auto liability coverage. Consequently, the garage form contains definitions for terms such as "garage operations," "products," and "work you performed," and it expands the definition of "insured contract" to include the same types of contracts that are covered in the CGL. The garage form does not have a definition of "mobile equipment" because the garage form's definition of "auto" ("a land motor vehicle, trailer or semitrailer") includes mobile equipment.

MOTOR CARRIER COVERAGE FORM

ISO has developed two forms for insuring firms that use trucks to transport property of others. The Truckers Policy (now the Truckers Coverage Form) was introduced in the late 1970s for insuring the auto exposures of any person or organization in the business of transporting goods, materials, or commodities for others.

Motor Carrier Coverage Form
Form that covers businesses that use autos to transport property of others or, in some cases, their own property.

Because of the deregulation of the trucking industry since the truckers form was introduced, the truckers form is no longer as useful as it once was. Accordingly, ISO introduced the **Motor Carrier Coverage Form** in 1994 to serve as a more flexible alternative to the truckers form. The discussion that follows focuses on the Motor Carrier Coverage Form. (In most respects, the truckers form and the motor carrier form are similar.)

Eligibility

Under ISO *Commercial Lines Manual* rules, any "motor carrier" is generally eligible for the motor carrier form. The manual defines "motor carrier" to include any person or organization providing transportation by auto in the furtherance of a commercial enterprise. This definition is broad enough to encompass any of the three basic types of carriers:

1. Common carriers, who offer their transportation services indiscriminately to the general public
2. Contract carriers, who transport property only for those with whom they have chosen to enter into contracts of carriage
3. Private carriers, who transport their own property

The lines between these three types of carriers are blurred. For example, a private carrier may occasionally operate as a common carrier or contract carrier in order to keep its trucks working to capacity. Thus, the broad definition of "motor carrier" allows the motor carrier form to be used for any organization that might need it.

Contrast With Business Auto Form

The motor carrier form is similar in most respects to the business auto form but contains some provisions that address specific characteristics of the trucking business. These differences from the business auto form are described below.

Coverage for Owner-Operators

Motor carriers commonly hire independent contractors known as **owner-operators**. These owner-operators use their own trucks to haul property for the motor carriers that hire them. The terms of hire are spelled out in a lease, which may apply to a single trip, to several trips, or for a specified period. The motor carrier customarily provides liability insurance for owner-operators while they are operating under lease for the motor carrier.

Owner-operators
Individuals who lease themselves and their trucks to motor carriers to transport property for the motor carrier.

Accordingly, the Motor Carrier Coverage Form provides insured status to the lessor of a covered auto that is leased to the named insured under a written lease agreement. However, the lessor (that is, the owner-operator) is an insured only while the auto is being used in the named insured's business as a motor carrier. In addition, the written agreement must not contain an agreement requiring the lessor to hold the named insured harmless.

The owner-operator's liability coverage under the motor carrier's insurance ends as soon as the owner-operator has completed his or her obligations under the lease. For example, the lease may only apply until a trailer load of goods is delivered in a distant city. While driving home or to another job, the owner-operator will not have liability insurance unless he or she has a separate policy.

An owner-operator's own coverage is often provided under a business auto policy that has been modified with the Truckers—Insurance For Non-Trucking Use Endorsement. This endorsement excludes liability coverage for the covered auto while it is used to carry property in any business or in the business of anyone to whom the auto is rented. Thus, the policy covers the owner-operator while he or she is not insured under a motor carrier's policy. This type of coverage is often called **bobtail and deadhead coverage**, because bobtailing (operating a power unit without a trailer) and deadheading (operating with an empty trailer) are the most common situations in which an owner-operator is not covered under the motor carrier's policy.

Bobtail and deadhead coverage
Coverage for an owner-operator's use of his or her truck while not under lease to a motor carrier (and therefore not covered under the motor carrier's auto policy).

Owner-operators may also need or want physical damage insurance, uninsured motorists insurance, personal injury protection, or medical payments coverage under their own auto policies.

Trailer Interchange Coverage

Trailer interchange agreement
A contract under which two motor carriers agree to swap trailers.

In addition to the use of owner-operators, another unique feature of the trucking business is the common use of trailer interchange agreements. A **trailer interchange agreement** is a contract under which a motor carrier agrees to swap trailers with another carrier. Normally, each carrier agrees to indemnify the other for any damage that occurs to the other's trailer while in the borrowing carrier's possession. Thus, trailer interchange agreements create liability exposures for the parties to these agreements.

Trailer interchange coverage
Coverage for a motor carrier's liability for damage to trailers in its possession under a written trailer interchange agreement.

A motor carrier can cover its liability for damage to trailers in its possession under written trailer interchange agreements by purchasing **trailer interchange coverage** under the motor carrier form. The insurer also agrees to defend the insured against claims or suits alleging covered damage. The provisions for trailer interchange coverage are contained in the Motor Carrier Coverage Form. These provisions can be activated by placing the appropriate coverage symbol (69) beside whichever of the following are desired:

- Trailer interchange comprehensive coverage
- Trailer interchange specified causes-of-loss coverage
- Trailer interchange collision coverage

Physical Damage Exclusion

Another difference between the business auto and motor carrier forms is that physical damage coverage under the motor carrier form excludes loss to a covered auto while in someone else's possession under a trailer interchange agreement. If the insured wants its own physical damage coverage to apply to its trailers while in another carrier's possession under a trailer interchange agreement, this exclusion can be eliminated by showing the appropriate coverage symbol (70) for physical damage insurance.

RATING COMMERCIAL AUTO INSURANCE

Commercial autos can be rated using rules found in the automobile division of the ISO *Commercial Lines Manual*. Under these rules, the rating procedure to be used for a particular insured depends on which of five classification subsections the insured's autos fall into. Separate rating procedures apply to (1) private passenger vehicles, (2) trucks, tractors, and trailers, (3) public transportation vehicles, (4) garages, and (5) special types of vehicles. The procedures for trucks, tractors, and trailers and private passenger vehicles are described below.

Private Passenger Vehicles

Premiums for private passenger autos insured under a business auto form are obtained directly from private passenger premium tables. Liability premium tables list premiums by rating territory and policy limit. Physical damage tables list comprehensive and collision premiums by rating territory, the vehicle's "original cost new," and the deductible amount chosen. These premiums are not multiplied by rating factors.

Trucks, Tractors, and Trailers

A large part of the loss experience for any trucking operation depends directly on the area in which the insured's trucks are operated. The exposures faced by a local delivery truck are different from those encountered by a large tractor-semitrailer used for cross-country hauling. Except for light trucks (one of the truck weight classifications discussed below), any vehicle in the truck, tractor, or trailer category that is regularly operated over a route that takes it more than 200 miles from its principal garaging location must be zone rated to account for the different hazards facing local and long-distance driving.

Primary Factor

The first step in rating a vehicle (whether zone rated or not) is to determine the vehicle's *primary factor*. The primary factor depends on the vehicle's *size class*, its *business use*, and its *radius class*. The characteristics that determine the primary factor are listed in Exhibit 10-4 and described in the sections that follow.

EXHIBIT 10-4

Primary Rating Factors for Trucks, Tractors, and Trailers

1. Size Class (determined by gross vehicle weight—GVW)

   - Light

   - Medium

   - Heavy

   - Extra-heavy

2. Business Use

   - Service

   - Retail

   - Commercial

3. Radius Class

   - Local (within 50 miles)

   - Intermediate (between 51 and 200 miles)

   - Long distance (beyond 200 miles)

Size Class

There are four size classes for trucks (light, medium, heavy, and extra-heavy) determined by the vehicle's gross vehicle weight (GVW). GVW is the vehicle's maximum loaded weight specified by the manufacturer. In addition, there are two size classes for truck-tractors (heavy and extra-heavy) determined by the vehicle's gross combination weight (GCW). GCW is the maximum loaded weight for a truck-tractor and its semitrailer or trailer together.

Business Use

Business use for trucks, tractors, and trailers is categorized as service, retail, or commercial. Service use describes the use of vehicles to carry workers, equipment, supplies, and so forth to or from job sites at which the vehicle generally remains parked for most of the workday. Retail use principally involves pickup and delivery of property to or from individual households. Commercial use is the category into which vehicles are put if they do not qualify for the service or retail use categories.

Radius Class

Primary factors are also governed by the radius of the area within which the vehicle is operated—within 50 miles of the principal garaging location (local), between 51 and 200 miles (intermediate), and beyond 200 miles (long distance). **Zone rated vehicles** are medium and larger trucks in the long-distance class.

Zone rated vehicles
Trucks in the medium and larger size class that are operated beyond a 200-mile radius of the principal garaging location and that are subject to zone rating, which considers the territories in which insured vehicles operate.

Premium Computation

After the primary factor has been determined, premium computation methods differ depending on whether the vehicle is zone rated or not.

Non-Zone Rated Vehicles

A truck, tractor, or trailer is not zone rated if it is a light truck operating over any distance or a larger truck operating predominantly within 200 miles of its principal garaging location. When a commercial auto is not zone rated, the primary factor (already discussed) is added to a secondary factor associated with the nature of the insured's business operations. The sum of the primary factor and the secondary factor is called the combined factor.

Secondary factors correspond to a number of industry classifications. Depending on the degree of hazard that is characteristic of the particular industry, these factors either increase or decrease the primary factor.

The base premiums for liability and physical damage coverage are multiplied by the combined factor. Base *liability* premiums are determined on the basis of the policy limit and the territory in which the auto is principally garaged. Base *physical damage* premiums are determined on the basis of the vehicle's age and its cost new.

Zone Rated Vehicles

After the primary factor has been determined for a zone rated vehicle, its physical damage and liability premiums are calculated by applying the primary factor to base premiums. Secondary factors are not used for zone rated autos.

Base premiums for zone rated autos are affected by the various geographical zones in which the vehicles are operated, because liability and collision losses are much more likely in metropolitan areas than on the open road. Moreover, the probability of some comprehensive physical damage losses, such as theft or windstorm, varies from one region of the country to another. Base physical damage premiums also depend on the vehicle's cost new, the current age of the vehicle, the type of vehicle (with respect to collision coverage), and the chosen deductible.

SUMMARY

Auto property loss exposures exist for any organization that owns one or more autos. Physical damage to or loss of an auto from many different causes of loss can reduce the auto's value or reduce business income until the vehicle can be repaired or replaced.

The auto liability exposure is the possibility that the organization may have to defend itself against, and perhaps pay damages as a result of, suits alleging negligent ownership, maintenance, or use of autos. Liability can arise from owned autos, hired or borrowed autos, or employees' autos operated on behalf of the organization. In addition, one organization may assume by contract the auto liability of another organization. Some auto businesses, such as dealers and repair shops, have a bailee liability exposure for customers' autos.

The Business Auto Coverage Form, together with business auto declarations and any applicable endorsements, can be included in a commercial package policy or issued in a monoline policy. The business auto form contains five sections.

Section I contains nine descriptions of covered auto symbols. These symbols are entered in a schedule in the declarations to indicate which autos are covered for each coverage selected.

Section II contains the provisions for auto liability insurance including an insuring agreement, a definition of who is an insured, supplementary payments, out-of-state extensions, exclusions, and a limit of insurance clause.

Section III contains four optional insuring agreements for auto physical damage insurance: collision, comprehensive, specified causes of loss, and towing and labor. Other provisions of Section III include coverage extensions, exclusions, a limit of insurance clause, and a deductible clause.

Section IV contains conditions, and Section V contains definitions. Among the coverages that can be added by endorsement are personal injury protection, auto medical payments, and uninsured motorists.

Because the auto exposures of a garage are difficult to separate from its general liability exposures, the Garage Coverage Form combines auto liability and CGL coverage. Garage physical damage coverage can be extended to cover an auto dealer's inventory of autos on a reporting basis.

The garage form also includes optional provisions for garagekeepers insurance, which covers damage to customers' autos in the insured's care, custody, or control. Garagekeepers insurance applies on a legal liability basis unless the insured pays an extra premium for direct coverage.

The Motor Carrier Coverage Form resembles business auto coverage in most ways. However, because of frequent leasing arrangements within the trucking industry, the motor carrier form provides coverage for the owner-operators who lease their trucks to the named insured. The motor carrier form also includes provisions for trailer interchange insurance, which covers the insured's liability for damage to trailers of others while in the insured's care, custody, or control.

An owner-operator who hauls under lease with a trucker can cover its liability for "deadheading" or "bobtailing" by purchasing a business auto policy with the Truckers—Insurance for Non-Trucking Use Endorsement.

Private passenger vehicles are rated from private passenger premium tables. The methodology for rating trucks, tractors, and trailers depends on whether the vehicle must be zone rated or not. A vehicle is zone rated if it is a "medium" or "large" truck operating more than 200 miles from its principal garaging location. The premiums for zone rated vehicles reflect the various zones in which they are operated.

Direct Your Learning

OUTLINE

Businessowners Policies

Farm Insurance

Summary

Businessowners Policies and Farm Insurance

After learning the content of this chapter, you should be able to:

■ Explain what kinds of businesses are generally eligible for coverage under a businessowners policy (BOP).

■ Compare the property coverages typically contained in a BOP with the direct damage and business income/extra expense coverages available under an ISO commercial property coverage part.

■ Describe the property coverages, in addition to those of the ISO commercial property coverage part, that are commonly included in BOPs.

■ Compare the liability coverage typically provided by a BOP with the CGL coverage form.

■ Explain how BOPs are rated and why that approach to rating is a competitive advantage.

■ Describe the purpose of each of the insuring agreements (A through G) of the ISO farm policy.

■ Compare the causes of loss that can be insured under the ISO farm policy with those that can be insured under the ISO causes-of-loss forms for commercial property.

■ Describe the agricultural coverages that farmers may need in addition to those provided by farmowners policies.

Develop Your Perspective

What are the main topics covered in the chapter?

This chapter describes two types of package policies in addition to the commercial package policy (CPP): the businessowners policy (BOP) and the farm policy.

Consider the insurance needs of small businesses.

- What property and liability coverages are usually included (or available as options) in a BOP?

- What additional property and liability coverages might a typical small business need to obtain separately that the BOP does not cover?

Why is it important to learn about these topics?

Most organizations that meet insurers' eligibility requirements are insured under BOPs. Farm policies are often handled by insurers and agencies that specialize in that line. Knowing the basic concepts of the coverage under the BOP and under farm insurance will help you understand when to choose those types of coverages to meet customers' needs.

Compare the BOPs of two or more insurance companies.

- In what ways are they the same? In what ways do they differ?

How can you use what you will learn?

- Identify and evaluate the loss exposures of a small business or a farm.
- Select a BOP or a farm policy that best meets the needs of the particular customer.

Chapter 11

Businessowners Policies and Farm Insurance

This chapter primarily discusses two kinds of policies that resemble the homeowners policies written for individuals and families: businessowners policies and farm policies. Businessowners policies (BOPs) are used to insure small and medium-sized enterprises. They provide most of the coverages discussed in previous chapters that such firms might need except for workers compensation, automobile (other than hired and nonowned auto liability), and inland marine. In format, rating, and underwriting, they resemble homeowners policies. Most farm policies also resemble homeowners insurance because an owner-occupied dwelling is usually a major part of a family farm's insurable exposures with the result that the typical farm insurance policy is a blend of a homeowners policy and commercial coverage for farm operations.

BUSINESSOWNERS POLICIES

The owners of most small to medium-sized businesses have similar and relatively uncomplicated insurance needs and dislike having to purchase multiple policies. Insurers and producers find processing costs for low-premium policies too high to profitably handle these insureds' needs in separate, individually underwritten, low-premium policies. To meet these challenges, insurers offer a **businessowners policy (BOP)**, which provides a package of property and liability coverages to meet the needs of smaller insureds.

BOPs cover buildings and business personal property, and many BOPs automatically include business income and extra expense coverage. Other common coverages—such as employee dishonesty, money and securities, signs, and glass—are either included automatically or available as options.

BOPs resemble homeowners policies in the way they package basic coverages and in the simplified rating used to determine the premium. This approach offers advantages to insureds, insurers, and producers. Insureds gain the convenience of one policy that meets most of their needs at a reduced premium cost and often with coverages included that they might otherwise overlook. The reduced number of coverage options and the simplified rating procedures lower handling costs for insurers and producers, enabling them to keep or gain market share. In fact, many insurers do not individually underwrite BOP

Businessowners policy (BOP)
A package policy that combines, in a simplified manner, most of the property and liability coverages needed by small and medium-sized businesses such as stores, offices, and apartment buildings.

policies; they use highly automated systems to further reduce the cost of handling these policies. To generate additional savings, some insurers operate service centers that handle the day-to-day servicing of these policies, thus freeing producers from this work and achieving the efficiencies that can come with large-scale operations.

The first BOPs were developed in the 1970s by individual insurers rather than by advisory organizations. In response to pressure from its member companies for a competitive product, ISO introduced a BOP program in 1976. The American Association of Insurance Services (AAIS) also offers a BOP program for its member insurers. Although these standard forms are available, many insurers, including some of the largest writers of BOPs, use independently developed BOP forms and rules.

Because no one policy form dominates the BOP market, this chapter discusses the typical characteristics of BOP policies rather than the specifics of any one form. The emphasis will be on the differences between BOPs and commercial package policies. The chapter will use the generic title "BOP," even though some insurers use specialty names to identify their small business package policies.

Because of the differences in coverage provided by different insurers, policy forms should be carefully reviewed when one policy is being compared with another—even if both policies are titled "businessowners." Understanding the separate coverages discussed in Chapters 2 through 9 can facilitate the comparison.

Eligibility for BOPs

Because BOPs are class rated, insurers issue policies only to insureds that fit within the contemplated class. Furthermore, as will be discussed in more detail later, BOPs are rated based on the amount of property coverage; liability insurance is not separately rated. Therefore, a BOP is not suitable for classes of insureds that have more complex liability exposures. (The recent trend to include some construction contractors in BOP policies may seem to be an exception to this rule, but insurers offer BOP-type policies only to smaller contractors in relatively less-hazardous trades.)

Every insurer writing businessowners insurance has eligibility rules to define the types of businesses that it will accept. Insurers have underwriting guidelines that further limit the risks that they will accept. Typical eligibility rules include the classifications discussed below.

Retail, Wholesale, Service, or Processing Buildings and Personal Property

The first classification includes the so-called Main Street businesses—furniture stores, clothing stores, hardware stores, offices, and the like. Usually an eligible building must be occupied principally for retail, wholesale, service, or processing purposes and contain not more than a certain maximum total floor area, such as 15,000 or 25,000 square feet. Coverage for building and personal property owned by the same firm can be covered in one policy. In the case of leased premises, separate policies are issued for the owner and the tenants.

Apartment Buildings

Apartment buildings and residential condominium buildings are another eligible class, although insurers commonly restrict coverage to buildings of a particular size, such as not more than six stories or sixty apartments. Incidental office occupancies are permitted, and most incidental retail, service, or processing occupancies are also permitted, usually with the stipulation that they do not exceed a certain number of square feet in total. Commercial tenants of the building—the incidental occupancies described above—are also generally eligible for BOPs. Residential tenants who want personal property and personal liability coverage can be insured under homeowners policies designed for tenants (form HO-4) or unit owners (form HO-6).

Office Buildings

Office buildings, including office condominiums, are eligible subject usually to the proviso that the building not exceed a certain height (such as six stories) or a certain total floor area. A building may contain apartments and, as with apartment buildings, most incidental retail, service, or processing occupancies are permitted generally with the stipulation that they do not exceed a certain maximum number of square feet in total, such as 15,000 or 25,000 square feet. Most of the tenants in office buildings are eligible for BOPs. Even when the building itself is too large to come within an insurer's BOP eligibility rules and guidelines, tenants may be eligible. For example, no insurer would write a BOP for the Empire State Building, but many of its tenants are eligible for coverage if they meet the other eligibility requirements.

Contractors

Under rules used by some insurers, smaller construction contractors are eligible for BOP coverage. There is usually a limit on total receipts and payroll, such as not more than $3 million in annual receipts and annual payroll not exceeding $300,000. General contractors are usually not eligible, and neither are contractors that are regarded as presenting higher risks or requiring specialized underwriting, such as demolition or wrecking contractors, contractors that use cranes, and contractors that have engaged in insulation work at any time, among others.

Restaurants

In response to the growth of fast-food restaurants and restaurants with limited cooking facilities, BOPs are often available for these businesses. Insurers feel that many restaurants of this type do not pose the same underwriting problems as traditional restaurants.

Typically, eligible fast-food restaurants may include cooking processes as long as the restaurant maintains an automatic fire extinguishing system equivalent to that recommended by the National Fire Protection Association (NFPA) Standard #96.

Risk Categories Generally Eligible for BOPs

"Main Street" businesses	Retail, wholesale, service, or processing buildings and personal property—not exceeding certain total floor area.
Apartment buildings	Not exceeding certain number of floors or units.
Office buildings	Not exceeding certain number of floors or total floor area.
Contractors	Not exceeding certain amounts for total receipts and payroll. General contractors and hazardous trades usually ineligible.
Restaurants	With limited cooking facilities.

Other Eligible Occupancies

Eligibility rules vary from insurer to insurer, and it has been said facetiously that for almost any given risk, there is probably some insurer, somewhere, that will provide a BOP. This is not literally true; no insurance company would write a BOP for General Motors, and GM's risk managers would not accept the coverage even if it were offered. With very few exceptions, insurers restrict their BOPs to smaller businesses, but a wide range of small businesses can be eligible for at least one insurer's BOP.

Ineligible Operations

The following types of risks are usually not eligible in BOP programs:

- Automobile businesses
- Bars, grills, and large restaurants
- Manufacturing firms
- One- or two-family dwellings other than multiple-unit garden apartment complexes
- Places of amusement
- Financial institutions

These are only generalized examples. Most of the largest writers of BOP policies use independently filed forms and eligibility criteria.

Insurance for Home-Based Businesses

One of the trends of the last quarter of the twentieth century was the explosion in the number of home-based businesses resulting from technological advances and the shift to a service economy. The standard, unendorsed homeowners policy provides little protection for home-based businesses. Three ways (under ISO rules and forms) to obtain the needed coverage are (1) adding one or more activity-focused endorsements to the homeowners policy, (2) adding the Home Business Insurance Coverage Endorsement to the homeowners policy, and (3) obtaining a separate commercial policy.

The activity-focused endorsements include the following:

*   The Business Pursuits Endorsement extends homeowners liability coverage to cover bodily injury and property damage liability arising out of the insured's business activities. However, coverage does not apply to a business owned or controlled by the insured.

*   The Home Day Care Coverage Endorsement extends the homeowners liability, medical payments, building, and personal property coverages to cover home day care operations that would otherwise be excluded or limited.

*   The Incidental Farming Personal Liability Endorsement is available for homeowners who sell fruit, vegetables, poultry, and other agricultural products raised on their residence premises, but coverage applies only to operations that are not the insured's principal occupation. If agricultural operations *are* the insured's principal operation, farm insurance, as discussed later in this chapter, is needed.

The second alternative is the Home Business Insurance Coverage Endorsement. Designed for a business that is conducted from the insured's home, this endorsement provides a wider range of coverages than the homeowners endorsements described above. The home business endorsement includes property and liability coverages normally found in a commercial insurance policy. In general, the home-based businesses insured with this endorsement are smaller than those usually insured under a BOP.

The third alternative is a separate commercial policy such as the BOP or even a commercial package policy. A BOP or commercial package policy serves the needs of an insured who has a more complex operation or whose homeowners insurer is unwilling to provide coverage by endorsement.

BOP Forms

A BOP is a freestanding package policy. It cannot be added to a commercial package policy. A typical BOP consists of the following:

*   Policy declarations containing the same types of information found in the declarations for commercial package policies

*   One of two optional property coverage forms for insuring buildings and personal property—a named-perils form and a special ("all-risks") form

- A number of other coverages such as business income, employee dishonesty, and mechanical breakdown either included as part of the form or available as options
- Liability coverage that resembles the CGL form discussed in Chapters 8 and 9
- Common policy conditions either as a separate form or as part of the other forms
- Endorsements specifically developed for use with the BOP program

In most respects, the BOP coverages are similar to the coverage forms discussed in earlier chapters, so this chapter will not discuss most of the separate provisions. Instead, the discussion will focus on areas of major differences, first in property coverages and then in liability coverages.

Property Coverage Differences

Some of the major differences in property coverage between BOP policies and commercial property policies include the following:

- Perils covered
- Replacement cost as standard valuation provision
- No coinsurance provision
- Shorter list of property not covered
- Automatic seasonal increase in amount of insurance
- Business income and extra expense coverage included
- Other property-type coverages included or available as options
- Property coverage options generally not available in BOPs

Perils Covered

The ISO commercial property policy offers three causes-of-loss forms: basic, broad, and special. Most insurers offer only two versions of the BOP property coverage: a named-perils form, similar to the commercial property broad form; and a special form. The special form predominates; in fact, some insurers (as well as the 2002 ISO businessowners program) offer only the special form, with an endorsement available to change coverage to named perils.

Replacement Cost as Standard Valuation Provision

The standard valuation provision in BOPs is replacement cost, whereas the standard valuation provision in commercial property policies is actual cash value. Most insurers offer actual cash value as an option for BOPs, just as replacement cost is an option in commercial property policies.

No Coinsurance Provision

BOPs are characteristically written without a coinsurance or other insurance-to-value requirement in the policy. Insurers have relied on producers and underwriters to be certain that the insured carried insurance equal to full insurable values. While coinsurance requirements can be suspended in commercial property policies by the agreed value option, underwriters are careful in granting that option, with the result that most commercial property forms, other than BOPs, written for smaller insureds are subject to coinsurance.

In 1995, because many insurers felt that BOP insureds were not carrying adequate amounts of insurance, ISO introduced an insurance-to-value provision in its BOP forms similar to the insurance-to-value provision in homeowners policies. To collect full replacement cost, the insured must carry insurance equal to at least 80 percent of the insurable value of the covered property. Otherwise, recovery is limited to (1) actual cash value or (2) a proportion of the loss equal to the amount of insurance carried divided by 80 percent of the insurable value, whichever is greater. In its 2002 BOP revision, ISO has introduced an option to remove the insurance-to-value requirement by endorsement. Many insurers currently do not include an insurance-to-value provision in their BOPs; however, its use is becoming more widespread. AAIS has included an insurance-to-value requirement similar to the ISO provision in its most recent BOP revision.

Shorter List of Property Not Covered

In most BOPs, the list of property not covered is considerably shorter than the comparable list of property not covered in the Building and Personal Property Coverage Form (BPP). There are two principal reasons for this difference:

1. Some of the "property not covered" exclusions in the BPP are not needed in a BOP because they apply to types of businesses that are not eligible for a BOP in the first place. For example, wharves or docks are often not excluded in BOPs because the types of insureds eligible for BOP coverage rarely have them.

2. Insurers are willing to offer broader coverage because the insureds eligible for a BOP are generally lower-risk, more homogenous types of businesses. For example, the following, which are excluded in the commercial property forms discussed earlier, are often *not* excluded in BOPs: cost of excavations, underground pipes, foundations below the lowest floor, and retaining walls.

Automatic Seasonal Increase Provision

Some BOPs provide a novel solution to the problem of fluctuating values. They contain a **seasonal increase provision** that acts somewhat like the peak season endorsement discussed in Chapter 2 except that it applies automatically. Provided the insured carries an amount of insurance equal to 100 percent of its average monthly personal property value for the twelve months preceding the loss, the business personal property limit will automatically increase by 25 percent.

Seasonal increase provision
A provision commonly included in BOPs to address fluctuating personal property values.

The seasonal increase provision can be advantageous for an insured whose inventory has increased beyond the personal property limit at the time of a loss. For example, if Bill's Gift Shop carried a $100,000 limit for personal property and had an average monthly personal property value of $100,000 for the twelve months immediately before a loss, Bill's Gift Shop could collect up to $125,000 for the loss. If Bill's Gift Shop carried $95,000 insurance, or even $99,000, the amount would not be increased. And, of course, if the loss were $150,000, Bill would still be underinsured. Some BOP insurers offer a peak season endorsement in addition to the automatic coverage to enable the insured to meet an expected seasonal surge in values that will exceed 25 percent.

Business Income and Extra Expense Coverage Included

One of the distinguishing features of most BOPs is the automatic inclusion of business income and extra expense coverage. In commercial package policies, business income and extra expense coverage is provided by a separate form and is subject to its own underwriting requirements, such as a completed business income worksheet. Insurers seldom require any special underwriting for business income coverage in a BOP.

Moreover, business income and extra expense coverage under the BOP is usually not subject to coinsurance, monthly limitation, or even a total dollar limit. However, most BOPs apply a time limit that is not present in the commercial property business income forms: under a typical BOP, business income loss and extra expenses are payable for only twelve consecutive months following the occurrence of the direct physical damage. In some cases, ordinary payroll coverage is limited to ninety days.

Some insurers do apply a dollar limit in addition to the twelve-month limitation. For example, some BOPs limit business income and extra expense coverage to an amount equal to 20 percent of the building insurance limit plus 100 percent of the personal property insurance limit. This can be a significant difference from the twelve-month limitation. In one case, an office tenant with a $25,000 personal property insurance limit sustained a business income loss in excess of $1 million. Since the loss was incurred in less than twelve months and its BOP did not have a dollar limit, its insurer paid over $1 million. Under the alternative approach described above, payment would have been limited to $25,000. However, insurers that use this approach may offer the option to remove the dollar limitation for an increase in premium.

Many BOPs do not include business income coverage for dependent property exposures, as is available through the dependent properties endorsements to the business income coverage forms used with the commercial package policy program. Dependent property coverage can be important for a small business located in a shopping mall if the small business depends on one or more large "anchor stores" in the mall to draw customers to the insured's store.

Some insurers offer all business income coverage only as an option, not as a part of their standard BOP form.

Other Property Coverages Included or Available as Options

In keeping with the goal of minimizing the number of policies an insured requires and reducing the complexity of the policy, many coverages that require separate coverage parts or separate policies in the commercial package program are either included as part of the BOP or available as options. The trend has been for an ever-increasing number of coverages and endorsements to be included in BOP programs. Although this trend conflicts with the goal of simplification, it makes the BOP policy suitable for an increasing number of insureds. However, not all insurers offer all options, and certain insureds cannot find the exact coverage combination that they desire in any insurer's BOP. Exhibit 11-1 lists other property coverages that are often included or available as options in BOPs.

EXHIBIT 11-1

Property Coverages Available in BOPs

- Employee dishonesty (BOPs do not usually use the employee theft wording discussed in Chapter 5. Even ISO, which has filed employee theft wording in its crime forms, has stayed with employee dishonesty wording in its 2002 BOP filings.)

- Money and securities, when special-form property coverage applies; or burglary and robbery, when named-perils property coverage applies

- Forgery

- Interior and exterior glass (Some insurers have included glass coverage as part of the building and contents coverage so that no additional or optional coverage is needed.)

- Outdoor signs

- Mechanical breakdown (boiler and machinery)

- Money orders and counterfeit paper currency

- Computer coverage

- Accounts receivable

- Valuable papers and records

The limits for these coverages are often quite low, with only limited or no options for higher limits. The coverages may also not be as broad as those available in the commercial package program or in separate policies. However, they generally satisfy the needs of most small businesses.

Property Coverage Options Generally Not Available in BOPs

Some coverage options are almost never offered under BOPs because they are not needed by the small businesses that BOPs are intended for or because they require individualized underwriting attention. For example, the manufacturer's selling price endorsement is not included because manufacturers are generally not eligible for BOPs. Similarly, blanket coverage for separate locations, which is particularly useful to cover larger, multi-location risks, is not permitted because insureds that need blanket coverage do not fit well into the class-rated, simplified-underwriting structure of the BOP.

Businessowners Property Loss Example

The following loss example illustrates several of the points discussed above.

College Bookstore was insured under a BOP that provided $300,000 coverage on the building and $120,000 on business personal property. The policy included business income coverage for twelve months, had a 25 percent seasonal increase provision, and did not have any insurance-to-value requirement.

Shortly after midnight on August 20 (during the policy period), a natural-gas explosion damaged College Bookstore's building and its contents. The building loss was $260,000 on a replacement cost basis and $215,000 on an actual cash value basis. Because the explosion occurred just before the beginning of the fall semester when the store's inventory was at a seasonal peak, the business personal property loss—primarily books—was $160,000 on a replacement cost basis and $135,000 on an actual cash value basis. The average value of College Bookstore's business personal property for the twelve months preceding the loss was $110,000.

College Bookstore could not resume business until repairs were completed and inventory was restocked on January 1. The resulting loss of business income was $125,000.

The insurable values at the time of the loss were as follows:

Building:	$350,000 replacement cost
	$300,000 actual cash value
Business personal property:	$250,000 replacement cost
	$225,000 actual cash value

College Bookstore was previously insured under a commercial property policy containing the Building and Personal Property Coverage Form (BPP) and related provisions described in Chapters 2 and 3. Under that policy, College Bookstore carried $300,000 coverage on the building and $120,000 on personal property, both subject to 80 percent coinsurance. None of the coverage options in the BPP had been activated, and the policy did not include a business income form.

Questions:

Disregarding any deductibles:

1. How much can College Bookstore collect under its current BOP?
2. How much could College Bookstore collect if its previous commercial property policy were still in force?

Answer to Question 1:

College Bookstore can collect $535,000 under its current BOP, calculated as follows:

Building: Because there is no insurance-to-value requirement in its BOP and the BOP loss valuation is replacement cost, College Bookstore can collect $260,000 for the building loss.

Business Personal Property: College Bookstore was underinsured for business personal property. However, the amount of insurance it carried was more than the average business personal property value for the preceding twelve months. Thus, College Bookstore would collect $150,000 because the amount of insurance ($120,000) would be increased by 25 percent ($30,000) in accordance with the seasonal increase provision.

Business Income and Extra Expense: College Bookstore would collect $125,000 for its business income loss because the interruption did not last more than twelve months.

Answer to Question 2:

If it were still covered by its commercial property policy, College Bookstore could collect $335,000, calculated as follows:

> *Building:*
>
> Amount of insurance carried: $300,000
>
> Amount of insurance needed: $240,000
> (calculated as .80 × $300,000)

Since the amount of building insurance is more than the amount required to satisfy the coinsurance requirement, College Bookstore would collect $215,000 for the building loss—the amount of the loss on an actual cash value basis. Replacement cost applies in the commercial property policy only when that option is activated.

Business Personal Property: The business personal property loss exceeded the amount of insurance. Therefore, College Bookstore would have collected $120,000 for business personal property, the amount of its insurance. The BPP does not include a seasonal increase provision unless a higher peak season amount is added by endorsement.

Business Income and Extra Expense: College Bookstore's previous policy would not have paid any part of the business income loss. No business income and extra expense coverage is provided in a commercial property policy unless a business income form and amount of insurance are made part of the policy.

Liability Coverage Differences

BOP liability coverage is similar in most ways to that provided by the occurrence version of the Commercial General Liability (CGL) Coverage Form discussed in Chapters 8 and 9. BOP liability insurance usually provides the following coverages:

- Bodily injury and property damage liability coverage (including coverage for premises and operations, products and completed operations, and liability assumed under contract)
- Personal and advertising injury liability coverage
- Medical payments coverage

A few of the differences between typical BOP liability coverage and the ISO CGL form are discussed below. Again, individual forms vary and must be carefully reviewed.

Limits of Liability

The types of limits (such as "each occurrence," "general aggregate," and "products/completed operations aggregate") applicable to BOP liability coverage are generally similar to those of the CGL policy, which were discussed in Chapter 9. However, in their businessowners policies, insurers typically offer insureds fewer options as to the amounts that can be selected for these limits. In a typical BOP, the minimum liability limit is higher and the maximum limit lower than those available with a CGL policy. Few insurers offer per occurrence limits greater than $2 million in their BOPs. In many BOPs, the general aggregate limit is fixed at twice the each occurrence limit, and the products/completed operations aggregate is equal to the each occurrence limit. In a CGL policy, subject to the insurer's underwriting guidelines, the aggregate limits can be any amounts in excess of the occurrence limit, up to $20 million in some cases.

For BOP insureds that want higher limits of liability than those available in a BOP, an excess or umbrella liability policy (to be discussed in Chapter 13) can solve the problem. However, the minimum premiums that normally apply to excess and umbrella liability policies can make that option disproportionately expensive for some smaller insureds.

Professional Liability

BOP liability coverage is generally subject to an exclusion eliminating coverage for bodily injury or property damage due to the rendering of or failure to render any professional service. When a CGL policy is issued to a provider of professional services, such as a physician, an accountant, or an engineer, the ISO *Commercial Lines Manual* requires that a professional liability exclusion be added to the policy, so that there is effectively little difference between the BOP and CGL in this regard. However, some BOPs automatically provide professional liability coverage for retail drugstores by excepting such stores from the professional liability exclusion.

A more important difference is the optional professional liability coverage endorsements available for use with BOP liability coverage. In many cases, BOPs can be endorsed to cover the professional liability exposures of certain types of insureds such as pharmacies, barbers, beauticians, veterinarians, funeral directors, optical and hearing aid stores, and printers. There are no counterparts to these endorsements among the ISO endorsements for the CGL policy. Unless insured by a BOP, an insured desiring one of these coverages must purchase a separate professional liability policy or an independently filed package policy designed for a particular type of business.

Hired and Nonowned Autos Liability Coverage

Hired and nonowned autos liability coverage, like that provided by using symbols 8 and 9 of the Business Auto Coverage Form, discussed in Chapter 10, is usually offered by BOPs, either as part of the form or by endorsement. For an insured that owns no automobiles, the availability of hired and nonowned auto coverage under the BOP eliminates the need to obtain a separate business auto policy. This is a major advantage for smaller insureds. If they do not own any autos they often overlook the need for, or cannot obtain, a separate policy covering hired and nonowned autos liability. Yet, almost every business at some time or another uses rented, leased, borrowed, or employee-owned autos.

Other Liability Options

BOPs sometimes include other liability options. For example, the 2002 BOP program of ISO offers (1) coverage to self-storage facilities for damage to customers' goods, which is otherwise written on inland marine forms; and (2) coverage to motels for damage to guests' property, which is otherwise written as part of crime coverage. Including options like these is in keeping with the goal of providing one policy that covers most of a business's insurance needs.

Liability Coverage Options Generally Not Available in BOPs

As was the case with some property coverage options, certain liability coverage options are not part of most BOP programs because the insureds that need them generally do not qualify for BOPs. For example, claims-made BOP liability coverage is not available; claims-made coverage is usually reserved for covering liability exposures that need special underwriting and are therefore not suitable for BOP programs.

Rating BOP Coverage

Rating a BOP is much less complicated than rating comparable coverages provided by a commercial package policy as detailed in Exhibit 11-2. BOP rating resembles homeowners insurance rating. Rating procedures for a BOP are generally based on the amounts of coverage provided for building and personal property. BOPs are class rated; specific rates are not used.

The property rates include "loadings" (built-in charges) for business income, liability coverage, and any additional coverages that are automatically included. As a result, the rates do not have to be computed separately for each of those coverages. In addition, rating optional BOP coverages is much simpler than rating the comparable coverages in a commercial package policy.

EXHIBIT 11-2

Rating a BOP Versus Rating a Commercial Package Policy

Coverage	Businessowners Policy (BOP)	Commercial Package Policy (CPP)
Building	Rated based on appropriate factors	Rated based on appropriate factors
Personal Property	Rated based on appropriate factors	Rated based on appropriate factors
Business Income	Often included in the basic rate	Separately rated
General Liability	Included in the basic rate for standard limits	Separately rated
Employee Dishonesty	Sometimes included in the basic rate. If not, rating is usually simple.	Separately rated
Hired and Nonowned Autos	Simplified rating to calculate the additional premium	Separately rated

---

Some insurers use a separate rating procedure for BOP liability coverage, especially in the case of contractor insureds. Most insurers who offer BOP-type policies for contractors rate the liability coverage for eligible contractors separately from the property coverages by applying a separate liability rate to the insured's payroll, receipts, or number of full- and part-time employees.

If rating a risk manually, the rater looks up the applicable building and personal property rates in simple rate tables. More likely, the rater enters some basic data into an insurer-supplied computer program or directly online and the premium is calculated automatically. Insurers' rating takes into account the following variables:

1. Territory. Tornadoes are more frequent in the Midwest, theft losses are higher in metropolitan areas, and so on.
2. Construction of the building (such as frame, joisted masonry, or fire resistive).
3. Public fire protection.
4. Occupancy of the building.
5. Whether the building is sprinklered or nonsprinklered.
6. Deductible applicable. The standard deductible for most insurers is $250 or $500 per loss. Percentage discounts apply for higher deductibles.

The rates are increased by appropriate factors if the insured wants increased limits for liability insurance. If the insured has purchased optional coverages, the policy premium is increased, either by adding a premium charge for each optional coverage requested or by applying an increased rate factor to the insured values.

FARM INSURANCE

For most of U.S. history, farms and ranches were owned by families that lived and worked on their land. Thus, a farm or a ranch was both a residence and a family business. Today, many of the larger farms are owned by agribusiness corporations and worked by employees who may or may not live on the farm property. (In the discussion that follows, the words "farm" and "farmer" are intended to mean "farm or ranch" and "farmer or rancher.")

The insurance forms that evolved for covering farmers—called "farmowners policies"—were designed to cover both the residential loss exposures and the farming business exposures of family farmowners. In general terms, a **farmowners policy** can be described as a package policy consisting of residential insurance and commercial property and liability insurance, with some special provisions to cover loss exposures unique to farms.

To accommodate both types of farm ownership, many insurers now offer farm insurance policies that use a modular approach. When the insured is a traditional farm family that lives on its own farm, a form covering residential property exposures is included in the policy along with other forms that cover the farm business exposures. When the insured is an agribusiness corporation (see box below), the form covering residential property exposures can be omitted if there are no residential buildings to be insured.

ISO and AAIS both file forms, rules, and loss costs for farm insurance, but many of the leading writers of this line use their own independently developed forms that may differ considerably from the ISO and AAIS forms. The discussion of farm insurance that follows provides a brief overview of the ISO farm forms as examples of the various farm insurance forms in current use.

Farmowners policy
A package policy designed to cover residential property (such as a farm family's house and belongings); property used in farming (such as mobile equipment, livestock, and barns); and personal and farm liability exposures.

Insurance for Large Agribusiness Operations

Agriculture has changed dramatically in the past several decades. Many enterprises blend farming and commercial activities, a combination referred to as "agribusiness." Large agribusiness operations include huge chicken or hog processing plants, feed manufacturers, cotton gins, and grain elevator operators, to name a few. These insureds can be covered by commercial package policies combining property, liability, inland marine, and other coverages discussed in earlier chapters or, in some cases, by a farm policy. Some insurers have developed forms that offer both personal and commercial general liability coverages to meet the needs of some insureds.

Because it is often difficult to match the exposures and coverages of agribusiness enterprises using conventional forms, AAIS has developed an Agricultural Output Policy specifically for these enterprises.

ISO Farm Forms

The ISO farm program (ISO forms no longer carry the "farmowners" label) includes various forms and endorsements that can be combined in either a separate farm policy or a commercial package policy. The fundamental forms of the ISO farm program are described below.

Farm Dwellings, Appurtenant Structures and Household Personal Property Coverage Form

The Farm Dwellings, Appurtenant Structures and Household Personal Property Coverage Form contains the following four coverages, which are comparable in most respects to Coverages A through D of homeowners policies:

Coverage A—Dwellings

Coverage B—Other Private Structures Appurtenant to Dwellings

Coverage C—Household Personal Property

Coverage D—Loss of Use

Coverage B excludes structures, other than private garages, that the named insured uses principally for farming purposes. Similarly, Coverage C insures only household personal property and excludes "farm personal property" other than office fixtures, furniture, and office equipment.

Farm Personal Property Coverage Form

The ISO Farm Personal Property Coverage Form contains two coverages:

Coverage E—Scheduled Farm Personal Property

Coverage F—Unscheduled Farm Personal Property

The insured can choose either or both of these coverages, described in more detail below.

Coverage E—Scheduled Farm Personal Property

Coverage E applies to only those classes of farm personal property for which a specific limit of insurance is shown in the declarations. The types of property that can be insured under Coverage E include farm products, materials, and supplies; farm equipment; various types of livestock; and several other classes of farm personal property. In addition to insuring specified *classes* of farm personal property, Coverage E can also be used to cover individually scheduled *items* of farm personal property, such as a particular tractor or combine owned by the insured. Coverage restrictions and sublimits apply to some of the eligible classes.

Coverage F—Unscheduled Farm Personal Property

Coverage F insures unscheduled farm personal property under a single limit. To discourage underinsurance, Coverage F is subject to an 80 percent coinsurance clause. In contrast, Coverage E is not subject to a coinsurance requirement.

Coverage F excludes an extensive list of property. Some of the excluded items are household personal property; animals other than "livestock" as defined in the policy; racehorses or show horses; trees, plants, shrubs, or lawns; certain crops and poultry; and vehicles primarily designed and licensed for road use (other than farm wagons and farm trailers).

Barns, Outbuildings and Other Farm Structures Coverage Form

This coverage form contains provisions for Coverage G—Barns, Outbuildings and Other Farm Structures, which can be used to insure all types of farm buildings and structures (other than the dwelling and private garages) on either a scheduled or a blanket basis.

ISO Farm Coverages

Covering Residential Exposures:

Coverage A—Dwellings

Coverage B—Other Private Structures Appurtenant to Dwellings

Coverage C—Household Personal Property

Coverage D—Loss of Use

Covering True Farming Exposures:

Coverage E—Scheduled Farm Personal Property

Coverage F—Unscheduled Farm Personal Property

Coverage G—Barns, Outbuildings and Other Farm Structures

Extra Expense and Business Income Coverage

The Farm Personal Property Coverage Form and the Barns, Outbuildings and Other Farm Structures Coverage Form both include extra expense coverage if the policy declarations page shows a limit for that coverage. An ISO farm policy can also be endorsed to cover loss of farm income resulting from damage to farm buildings or farm personal property by a covered cause of loss. The coverage endorsement is titled Disruption of Farm Operations.

Causes of Loss Form

As in the commercial property coverage part, three levels of covered causes of loss can be purchased under the ISO farm program: basic, broad, and special. All of the policy provisions for these three levels of coverage are contained in the Causes of Loss Form—Farm Property. The insurer marks the declarations page accordingly to indicate which level of coverage applies.

Basic Causes of Loss

The basic causes of loss in the farm policy are the same as those found in the commercial property Causes of Loss—Basic Form plus four additional perils:

- Theft
- Collision
- Earthquake (covering livestock only)
- Flood (covering livestock only)

The collision peril has three aspects: (1) collision damage to covered farm machinery, (2) death of covered livestock resulting from contact with vehicles, and (3) collision damage to other farm personal property. The earthquake and flood perils apply only to loss (by death) of covered livestock.

Broad Causes of Loss

The broad causes of loss in the ISO farm program include all of the basic causes of loss plus all other named perils included in the commercial property broad form and the homeowners broad form. Death of livestock resulting from some additional perils is also covered. These additional perils are electrocution, drowning, accidental shooting, attacks by dogs or wild animals, and accidents in loading or unloading.

Special Causes of Loss

This level of coverage corresponds to that provided by the homeowners special form and the commercial property special form. Most of the exclusions of the farm coverage are identical to, or closely resemble, the exclusions and limitations found in the commercial property special form. However, some are modified either to address the particular exposures of farms or to emulate homeowners special-form coverage. Livestock, poultry, and many other types of farm products are not eligible for farm special-form coverage under ISO manual rules.

Farm Inland Marine Coverage Forms

The ISO farm program includes the following inland marine floater forms:

- Mobile Agricultural Machinery and Equipment Coverage Form
- Livestock Coverage Form

Mobile agricultural machinery and equipment and livestock can both be insured under the Farm Personal Property Coverage Form through Coverage E or Coverage F. However, when an insured wishes to insure either or both of those classes of farm personal property and no others, the insurance can be arranged using the separate inland marine forms. As under the Farm Personal Property Coverage Form, special-form coverage on livestock is not available under the Livestock Coverage Form.

Farm Liability Coverage Form

The Farm Liability Coverage Form is designed to cover both the personal and commercial liability exposures that a farmowner might have. Thus, the form combines elements of both homeowners liability coverage and commercial general liability coverage, along with special provisions that correspond to unique aspects of farm liability exposures.

Specialty Farm Coverages

Standard farmowners policies do not cover some loss exposures for which farmers frequently want coverage. Examples of the specialty coverages that can meet farmers' needs are crop hail insurance, federal crop insurance, and animal mortality insurance.

Crop Hail Insurance

A traditional form of crop insurance offered by private insurers is referred to as **crop hail insurance**. Crop hail policies cover crop loss resulting from hail and are frequently extended to cover additional perils such as fire, windstorm accompanying hail, damage caused by livestock, and vehicles. Such policies may also cover harvested crops against named perils while being transported to the first place of storage.

Crop hail insurance
Insurance offered by private insurers that covers crops against loss caused by hail and often other perils.

Federal Crop Insurance

Various crop insurance programs are also available from the Federal Crop Insurance Corporation (FCIC), a governmental insurer subject to the Risk Management Agency (RMA), a division of the U.S. Department of Agriculture.

One of FCIC's crop insurance plans is **Multiple Peril Crop Insurance (MPCI)**. MPCI policies insure farmers against unexpected production losses from natural causes, including drought, excessive moisture, hail, wind, flood, hurricanes, tornadoes, and lightning. MPCI policies do not cover losses resulting from neglect, poor farming practices, or theft.

Multiple Peril Crop Insurance (MPCI):
Insurance offered by the federal government that covers unexpected crop production losses due to natural causes such as drought, excessive moisture, hail, windstorm, and flood.

Other coverage plans are available through FCIC and RMA. To make coverage affordable, the federal government subsidizes premiums. These programs are marketed and serviced by participating private insurers but reinsured by the federal government.

Animal Mortality Insurance

The livestock coverage provided by most farm policies is not adequate for some farmers and ranchers. In addition, non-farmers often own valuable animals that they would like to insure for their full value. Farm policies normally only cover loss of livestock by specified causes such as electrocution, accidental shooting, or drowning. Owners of high-valued animals often want to insure against loss of their animals by any fortuitous cause, including illness or disease.

Animal mortality insurance
Insurance that covers loss of valuable animals by (1) death resulting from accident, injury, sickness, or disease or (2) theft, subject to exclusions.

One example of livestock coverage designed to meet special needs is animal mortality insurance. **Animal mortality insurance** is essentially term life insurance on animals. This type of insurance might be purchased to cover farm animals such as valuable horses, registered cattle, or calves being grown and exhibited under sponsorship of a club (such as 4-H). Animal mortality insurance is also bought by owners of racehorses, show dogs, circus animals, and laboratory animals. Animal mortality insurance generally covers against loss of the insured animal by (1) death resulting from accident, injury, sickness, or disease or (2) theft, subject to exclusions.

SUMMARY

Two types of commercial insurance policies that resemble homeowners insurance policies can be used to provide property and liability coverage for eligible risks: businessowners policies and the farm policies.

Businessowners policies (BOPs) are designed to cover most small and medium-sized enterprises. A BOP is class rated with the premium for property and liability coverages determined by the amount of property insurance purchased. Because BOPs are class rated and often not individually underwritten, eligibility for BOPs is limited to smaller, more homogenous types of businesses.

Most insurers' rules limit the size and types of firms that can be covered by a BOP. For example, eligibility may be restricted to retail, wholesale, or office occupancies of not more than 25,000 square feet. Certain types of business are usually ineligible in any event, such as auto businesses; bars, grills, and large restaurants; manufacturers; and financial institutions.

A BOP is a freestanding package policy. It cannot be added to a commercial package policy. Many insurers offer two versions that differ primarily in the extent of property coverage, one being a named-perils form and the other a special form.

Business income coverage is usually included in the policy. In many cases, the business income coverage is subject to no limit other than a twelve-month restoration period, but some insurers do apply a dollar limit. BOP business income coverages do not contain coinsurance provisions or monthly percentage limits.

BOP forms include liability coverage that closely resembles the occurrence-basis CGL form discussed in Chapters 8 and 9. No separate rating is required for BOP liability coverage unless the insured wishes to increase the limit of liability or add optional liability coverages. Many insurers are willing to add certain professional liability coverage endorsements to their BOPs. Employee dishonesty and mechanical breakdown coverages are either included as part of the BOP form or available as options.

When BOPs were first written, only a few optional coverages were available. The trend, however, has been to broaden an insured's choices. The latest ISO version offers almost all the endorsements that eligible businesses might need.

Farm policies are designed specifically to cover the property and liability loss exposures of farmers and ranchers, including both personal exposures and commercial farming exposures. The coverages provided by a farm policy typically insure the following:

- Dwelling buildings
- Appurtenant structures (other than farm structures)
- Household personal property
- Loss of use of the above types of property
- Farm personal property (scheduled, unscheduled, or combination of both)
- Barns and other farm buildings
- Liability coverage (residential and farm)

Farmers often want additional types of coverage that are not usually available in farm policies. These specialized coverages include crop hail insurance, federal crop insurance, and animal mortality insurance.

Chapter 12

Direct Your Learning

OUTLINE

Workers Compensation Statutes

The Workers Compensation and Employers Liability Policy

Rating Workers Compensation Insurance

Summary

Workers Compensation and Employers Liability Insurance

After learning the content of this chapter, you should be able to:

■ Given a case about employee injury or illness, explain whether the Workers Compensation and Employers Liability (WC&EL) Policy applies and the nature and extent of coverage.

- Describe the workers compensation and employers liability exposures, and explain how the WC&EL policy addresses those exposures.

- Describe the requirements for benefits to be payable under workers compensation laws.

- Describe the various workers compensation benefits.

- Describe the persons and types of employment typically covered by workers compensation laws.

- Explain how Part One of the WC&EL policy provides the benefits required by state workers compensation laws.

- Explain why employers liability insurance is needed and how Part Two of the WC&EL policy addresses this need.

- Explain the purpose of Part Three—Other States Insurance in the WC&EL policy.

- Explain the need for and the coverages provided by the voluntary compensation endorsement and the LHWCA coverage endorsement.

■ Describe the methods employers use to meet the financial requirements of workers compensation laws.

■ Explain how workers compensation policies are rated.

Develop Your Perspective

What are the main topics covered in the chapter?

This chapter examines the liability loss exposures of employers for occupational injuries and diseases of their employees. The chapter also describes the principal policy for insuring these exposures, the Workers Compensation and Employers Liability (WC&EL) Insurance Policy, and the rating process for this policy.

Consider the possible injuries you could sustain arising from your employment.

- Do you know what types of benefits your employer would be required to provide under the applicable workers compensation law?

Why is it important to learn about these topics?

Nearly every business with employees needs WC&EL insurance. A thorough understanding of workers compensation statutes, the standard WC&EL policy, coverage endorsements, and rating methods will enable you to understand how this type of insurance operates, and how to arrange appropriate coverage to suit your customers' needs.

Assume that you are the risk manager for a chain of retail stores in all fifty states.

- Would it be possible for you to buy one WC&EL policy covering your operations in all states? Explain.

How can you use what you will learn?

Imagine that you are an insurance agent. One of your customers has just implemented a loss control program designed to lessen the frequency and severity of employee injuries.

- Which would be more immediately responsive to your customer's new loss control program, experience rating or retrospective rating? Why?

Chapter 12
Workers Compensation and Employers Liability Insurance

Workers compensation and employers liability insurance responds to two basic loss exposures faced by employers:

1. The legal responsibility to pay benefits to employees as required by state workers compensation statutes

2. The cost to defend against, and possibly pay, liability claims made against the employer on account of bodily injury to an employee

This chapter examines the common characteristics of workers compensation statutes, the provisions of the standard workers compensation and employers liability insurance policy, and the rating of workers compensation and employers liability insurance.

Workers compensation and employers liability insurance
Insurance that provides (1) coverage for benefits an employer is obligated to pay under workers compensation laws and (2) coverage for employee injury claims made against the employer that are not covered by workers compensation laws.

WORKERS COMPENSATION STATUTES

Before the enactment of workers compensation statutes, workers injured in industrial accidents could, under the common law, sue their employers for damages resulting from the injury. It was up to the employee to establish that the employer was at fault for the injury. The following defenses were available to employers:

- The employee contributed to the accident.
- The employee assumed the risk of injury when he or she took the job.
- A fellow worker was responsible for the accident.

It was difficult for employees to overcome these defenses, and the majority of injured workers received nothing. Even when employees successfully pursued their claims, court delays placed a financial strain on their families. Furthermore, the system created antagonism between employers and employees.

These problems led industrialized nations to adopt workers compensation laws, beginning with Germany in 1887. The first states in the United States to enact workers compensation statutes were New York, in 1910, and Wisconsin, in 1911. Today, each of the United States, the District of Columbia, Puerto Rico, Guam, and the U.S. Virgin Islands, as well as each of the

Workers compensation statute
State statute that obligates employers, regardless of fault, to pay specified medical, disability, rehabilitation, and death benefits for their employees' job-related injuries and diseases.

Canadian provinces, have enacted **workers compensation statutes**. These laws provide "no-fault" protection by removing the right of employees to sue their employers while obligating employers to compensate injured employees even if negligence is not involved. In return for definite payment, the employer's liability is limited (but not eliminated) by statute. The system has the effect of guaranteeing injured workers prompt payment while reducing costs and court workloads arising out of litigation.

Requirements for Benefits

Workers compensation statutes provide benefits for medical expenses and wage loss resulting from either occupational injury or occupational disease.

To be covered under a workers compensation statute, an injury or disease must (in most states) arise out of *and* in the course of employment. In other words, the cause of the injury or disease must be related to the employment, and the occurrence must take place while the employee is engaged in work-related activities. For example, the statute would cover an employee who was injured when he fell off a ladder while changing a light bulb in his office: the injury arose out of and in the course of employment. In contrast, court decisions in some states have held that an employee shot by a jealous lover while at work was not covered by workers compensation: the injury did not arise out of employment.

Generally, the employee is covered for any work-related injury sustained while the employee is at the place of employment or traveling for the employer. Injuries occurring while the employee is on his or her way to or from work at a fixed location are generally not covered by the statute.

Although workers compensation laws originally had no specific provisions for occupational diseases (diseases thought to be caused by work or the work environment), the workers compensation laws of all states now include benefits for occupational diseases. Most occupational diseases become evident during employment or soon after the exposure to injurious conditions, although for some exposures the disease may be latent for a long time. Consequently, many states provide extended periods of time for the discovery of these slowly developing diseases. Although some states cover only occupational diseases that are specifically named in the law, the majority of states provide coverage for all occupational diseases.

Not all diseases contracted in the course of an occupation can be attributed to the work or occupational exposure. For example, the common cold is generally not a covered disease. In general, there must be a cause and effect relationship between the occupation and the disease.

Benefits Provided

A typical workers compensation statute imposes absolute liability on employers for the benefits provided under the statute. (Absolute liability is liability imposed without regard to fault.) The intent is that an employee be at least partially compensated for expenses and loss of earnings incurred as a result of an occupational injury or disease. The benefits prescribed by the various state workers compensation laws generally include medical benefits, disability income benefits, rehabilitation benefits, and death benefits.

Workers Compensation Benefits

- Medical benefits
- Disability income benefits
- Rehabilitation benefits
- Death benefits

Medical Benefits

In most instances, the workers compensation law provides full and unlimited medical expense benefits for a covered injury or disease. These benefits include medical, hospital, surgical, and other related medical-care costs, including physical therapy and prosthetic devices. As a rule, first-dollar benefits are provided; no deductible or coinsurance provisions are imposed on the employee as under most medical insurance plans. Depending on state law, the injured employee may have the right to select his or her own doctor or may be limited to a choice from a panel designated by the employer or its insurance company.

Disability Income Benefits

Workers compensation statutes typically classify disabilities as follows:

- **Temporary partial disability**, meaning that the injured worker is unable to perform some duties of a job for a definite period of time, such as thirty or sixty days. After that period, the worker will be able to resume all job duties.

- **Temporary total disability**, meaning that the injured worker is unable to perform any job duties for a specific period of time but will ultimately recover and be able to resume all job duties.

- **Permanent partial disability**, meaning that the injured worker suffers an irreversible injury, such as the loss of sight in one eye. However, the worker will be able to resume some job functions.

- **Permanent total disability**, meaning that the injured worker will never be able to perform any job functions.

Disability income benefits are intended to compensate an injured employee for wage loss in any of the above categories. Unlike medical benefits, income benefits are payable subject to a deductible in the form of a waiting period. Disability benefits do not begin until the waiting period has expired. The waiting period varies from three to seven days, depending on the state. If disability continues beyond a specified number of days, most laws provide for payment of benefits retroactive to the date of injury.

Temporary partial disability
A disability that prevents an injured worker from performing some job duties for a definite time period.

Temporary total disability
A disability that prevents an injured worker from performing any job duties for a specific period but that ultimately allows the worker to resume all job duties.

Permanent partial disability
A disability due to an irreversible injury that allows an injured worker to resume some job duties.

Permanent total disability
A disability that prevents an injured worker from ever being able to perform any job duties.

The benefit is payable weekly and is expressed as a percentage of the employee's average weekly wage at the time of disability. Maximum and minimum weekly benefit amounts vary widely from state to state.

State laws also require compensation for a specific number of weeks for the loss (or loss of use) of specific body parts such as fingers. These injuries are referred to as "scheduled" injuries because the injuries and corresponding benefits are listed in a document called a schedule. Scheduled injuries do not generally create permanent total disability, but the resulting permanent impairment is assumed to produce long-term loss of wages. As a result, the benefits for scheduled injuries are payable without regard to actual wage loss. In most states, the compensation for scheduled injuries is in addition to any other temporary disability benefits payable.

Rehabilitation Benefits

Rehabilitation of injured workers is a goal of the workers compensation system, and most state laws include some rehabilitation benefits. The primary rehabilitation benefit prescribed is the payment of expenses for complete medical treatment and medical rehabilitation. Vocational rehabilitation may also be required by law. Most workers compensation laws provide a maintenance allowance to injured workers during rehabilitation in addition to other compensation benefits. Many insurers provide rehabilitation services extending beyond the requirements of the law. Often, rehabilitation can cut the cost of a workers compensation claim by shortening the length of time that the injured employee is disabled. All parties benefit from rehabilitation. The employer and its insurer often save loss costs, and the injured worker is returned to productive employment. Thus, rehabilitation also benefits society as a whole.

Death Benefits

Death benefits include a flat amount for burial expense and partial replacement of the worker's former weekly wage. The burial expense allowance varies among the states. The percentage of wage loss payable also varies by state and depends primarily on the number and types of dependents. Some states provide a maximum benefit expressed as either a total amount or a time period.

Benefit Administration

Most states have a workers compensation board or industrial commission with responsibility for administering the workers compensation law. A few states employ the courts to administer claims instead of a specific administrative agency.

To initiate a claim, the injured worker notifies the employer of the injury. The employer submits an injury report to the insurer, which then transmits the report to the administrative agency. If the claim is not contested by

Employees With Pre-Existing Disabilities

Injured workers who have sustained partial yet permanent impairments that preclude returning to their prior jobs, or prospective employees with disabilities, may face great difficulty in finding suitable employment. All too often, prospective employers are reluctant to hire impaired or disabled workers, fearing the new job responsibilities will aggravate or otherwise magnify an already existing injury or occupational illness. There have been several legislative responses to this problem. One was the creation of second-injury funds in most states beginning in the years following World War II. Another was Congressional passage in 1990 of the Americans With Disabilities Act (ADA).

Second-injury funds were established to encourage employers to hire partially impaired workers and to help these workers obtain gainful employment. Should additional injury occur to an already impaired worker that results in a total or near total impairment, the applicable fund will pay a portion of the claim. Although the precise method of sharing the losses varies among the states, the basic idea is to limit the second employer's share of the loss to what would have been payable for the second injury if the first injury had not occurred.

For example, if an employee lost one eye in the first injury and the other eye in the second injury, total disability benefits would be payable after the second injury. However, the second employer would be required to pay only the benefit for the loss of one eye. The second-injury fund would pay the difference between the benefit for the loss of one eye and the benefit for permanent total disability.

This arrangement is attractive to employers, who do not want to be assessed, unfairly, for the amount of benefits payable for a total impairment. Usually, second-injury funds are established by assessing both workers compensation insurers and self-insurers in the particular state.

The Americans With Disabilities Act (ADA) was enacted to foster equal employment opportunity for the disabled. Among other provisions, ADA requires employers to make reasonable accommodation to enable disabled employees and applicants to perform their jobs. ADA and other federal and state laws prohibit discrimination against disabled workers as long as they can do their work. A number of states have decided that ADA and similar laws have reduced the need for second-injury funds. Consequently, several states and the District of Columbia have eliminated second-injury funds, preferring to rely on other laws to accomplish the goal of providing equal job access for workers with disabilities.

the employer, it is usually settled by agreement. The injured employee and the employer's insurer agree on a settlement. The agreement must be in compliance with the workers compensation law and is subject to review by the workers compensation agency. Some states use a direct payment system that does not require an agreement before benefits begin. Under this system, benefits are paid immediately, and the administrative agency reviews the amounts paid to determine compliance with the law.

If the claim is contested by the employer or by the insurance company on behalf of the employer, most states require a hearing by an officer of the administrative agency. The decision of the hearing officer may be appealed to the workers compensation board or commission and then to the appropriate court.

Persons and Employments Covered

Workers compensation statutes apply to virtually all industrial workers and most other kinds of private employment. The statutes of some states exempt employers with fewer than a stipulated number of employees, and many statutes specifically exclude certain employments such as farm labor, domestic workers, and casual employees. (A casual employee is one hired for only a short period, usually to accomplish a particular task.)

Many states provide workers compensation protection for all or certain classes of public employees. Some employees are excluded because alternate plans are provided for them. For example, federal statutes govern the rights of various classes of employees to recover benefits or damages from their employers for occupational injury or disease. Examples of such classes of employees are federal government workers, maritime workers, and interstate railroad workers.

Employee Status

Employee
A person hired to perform services for another under the direction and control of the other party, called the employer.

Entitlement to benefits under a workers compensation law depends on whether a person qualifies as an employee according to the law. An **employee** is a person hired to perform services for another under the direction and control of the other party, called the employer.

Independent Contractors

Independent contractor
A person (or organization) hired to perform services without being subject to the hirer's direction and control regarding work details.

Sometimes it is hard to determine whether an individual is an employee or an independent contractor. Unlike employees, **independent contractors** are not subject to direction and control regarding the details of the work. They agree to perform a task meeting the specifications stipulated in the contract but are free to use their own judgment and methods in performing the task. They may also employ others to perform the task, but they remain responsible under the contract for its completion.

Employment status is a question of fact, not of law. If doubt arises concerning whether an individual is an employee or an independent contractor, a court or an administrative body decides the issue on the basis of the facts. The legislative mandate generally calls for the workers compensation law to be applied liberally. Therefore, the courts have interpreted the definition of an employee broadly to provide protection to those who seek it.

An independent contractor might also employ others. An independent contractor, like all other employers, must provide workers compensation benefits for its employees. In many states, if the contractor does not provide workers compensation insurance, the responsibility and the expense fall on the principal (the firm that uses the contractor's services). Furthermore, if a firm does not have certificates of insurance from the contractors it uses, its workers compensation insurer may require it to pay workers compensation insurance premiums based on the cost of the work sub-contracted. To be certain that the contractor has workers compensation insurance in force, the principal usually requires the contractor to provide a certificate of insurance as evidence of the insurance in force when the certificate was issued. Certificates of insurance were discussed in Chapter 9.

Leased Employees and Temporary Employees

Many organizations use leased employees, temporary employees, or both. Leased employees differ from temporary employees. Temporary employees are hired for short-term assignments to cope with peak loads or to replace an employee who is out ill, on vacation, etc. The firm supplying the temporary employee provides workers compensation for temporary employees; the temporary is an employee of the providing firm, not the firm that is using his or her services.

In contrast with temporary employees, leased employees have all the outward appearance of regular employees. They work continuously for the same firm and are subject to control by the firm just as they would be if they were direct employees of the firm. Technically, however, they are co-employees of the leasing contractor, sometimes referred to as a professional employer organization (PEO), and the client-company. Sometimes a firm will transfer its employees to the PEO and then lease them back. The PEO is responsible for all payroll taxes, employee benefits, and workers compensation coverage. Generally, a separate workers compensation policy is written showing the names of the PEO and the client company although the requirements imposed by law vary from state-to-state.[1]

Out-of-State Application of Laws

When a worker travels into another state and is injured in the other state, questions arise as to how to apply the workers compensation laws of the states involved. Most state laws have extraterritorial provisions dealing with this issue. Extraterritorial provisions provide that employees can receive benefits provided by the law of the state in which they are hired even if the accident occurs in another state.

For example, Sue, an account executive for an insurance agency in State A, is injured while meeting with an insured in the insured's office in State B. Sue can collect workers compensation benefits under the State A law. Sue may also have a right instead to claim benefits under the State B law because she was injured in State B. A problem might arise if Sue claimed benefits under the State B law and the State B benefits exceeded those provided under the State A law.

The determination of which state's law applies depends on the provisions of the laws in question. Typical considerations include the following:

1. Place and nature of employment
2. The place where the employee was hired
3. The employee's place of residence
4. The state in which the employer is domiciled

The problem is complicated by different coverage and benefit provisions in the various states. For example, a truck driver might live in Massachusetts, work for a trucking firm in Pennsylvania, and drive through many states as part of the employment. According to the laws of about half of the states, if the driver is injured, a compensation claim conceivably could be filed in the state where the injury occurred, where the employment principally occurred, or where the employee was hired. Because benefit levels vary from state to state, the employee, when permitted to choose which law will apply, can select the workers compensation law with the most generous benefits.

Federal Jurisdiction

As noted earlier, occupational injuries of most maritime workers, employees of interstate railroads, and certain other workers are under the jurisdiction of federal law. Federal jurisdiction over these workers' injuries arises either as a result of specific federal statutes or because the work location comes within the jurisdiction of admiralty (maritime) law.

United States Longshore and Harbor Workers' Compensation Act (LHWCA)
A federal statute that eliminates the right of maritime workers (other than crew members of vessels) to sue their employers; requires such employers to provide injured or ill workers with benefits like those provided by state workers compensation statutes for work-related injury or illness.

The **United States Longshore and Harbor Workers' Compensation Act (LHWCA)** provides an exclusive remedy to injured maritime workers (workers engaged in longshoring or shipbuilding) subject to the act. Like state workers compensation statutes, the LHWCA eliminates the right of injured workers to sue their employers but prescribes compensation for work-related injuries without regard to fault. Congress has also extended the LHWCA to cover some government-related employment.

Jones Act
A federal statute that permits injured members of a vessel's crew (or survivors of a deceased crew member) to sue their employer for damages due to the employer's negligence.

Officers and crew members of vessels are not covered by the LHWCA. However, they have various legal remedies they can pursue for job-related injuries. One of the remedies is provided by the United States Merchant Marine Act of 1920, more commonly known as the **Jones Act**, which permits an injured crew member (or his or her survivors, in the case of death) to sue the employer for damages resulting from the employer's negligence. Admiralty law, the branch of federal law that governs most maritime matters, provides additional remedies to injured crew members, including the following:

- A lawsuit against the employer for injury resulting from unseaworthiness of the vessel
- An injured crew member's right to "maintenance" (food and shelter) and "cure" (medical attention), regardless of whether the employer was at fault

Interstate railroad workers, like the officers and crew of vessels, can sue their employers for injuries resulting from employer negligence. This remedy is provided by the Federal Employers' Liability Act.

Employees in Foreign Countries

Employees who are temporarily working outside the United States are generally covered by the extraterritorial provision of the workers compensation law of the state where they regularly work, provided they have not been out of the United States for longer than the time limit specified in the applicable law. The time limit can be as much as six months in some states but as little as thirty days in others.

In addition to time-limited coverage, another problem for firms with employees out of the country is that workers compensation laws in the United States may not provide coverage for repatriation expense or endemic disease. Repatriation expense is the added cost of transporting an ill, injured, or deceased employee back to his or her home area; such transportation can be very costly. Endemic disease refers to a disease that is prevalent in a particular country, for example, malaria in tropical countries.

Many insurers offer foreign voluntary workers compensation coverage, either as an endorsement to an insured's workers compensation policy or as part of a separate foreign insurance policy. Foreign voluntary workers compensation coverage provides "home-state" coverage without a time limit for U.S. employees who are working outside the country and also often includes coverage for repatriation expense and endemic disease.

In most countries outside the United States, the local coverage for occupational injury and disease is very different from that of the U.S. workers compensation system. Only a few countries have workers compensation laws comparable to those found in the United States and Canada. In almost all other countries, employees are treated for on-the-job injuries and occupational disease under the nation's medical insurance program. Disability benefits for employment-related conditions are provided by the social insurance that applies to all disabilities. In many countries, employees retain the right to sue their employers. Consequently, employers with employees in these countries need employers liability insurance with a coverage territory encompassing the foreign countries in which the employer operates.

Methods for Meeting the Employer's Obligation

Most workers compensation statutes require employers to demonstrate financial ability to pay any claims that may arise. Possible methods of meeting this obligation include the following:

- Private insurance
- Insurance through assigned risk plans
- Insurance through state funds or employers mutual insurance companies

- Qualified "self-insurance" plans
- Excess insurance
- Pools

Not every state allows all of these methods.

Private Insurance

An employer can meet its workers compensation obligation by purchasing insurance from a private insurer licensed to write workers compensation coverage in the state. In return for the premium, the insurance company promises to pay the benefits and assume most administrative duties required by law for work-related injuries.

Assigned Risk Plans

Some businesses cannot obtain private insurance because they do not meet insurers' underwriting criteria. Because of the compulsory nature of workers compensation, a firm without insurance could be forced out of business. Assigned risk plans exist to make insurance available. An employer rejected by private insurers can apply to the assigned risk plan in the appropriate state to obtain coverage.

State Funds and Employers' Mutuals

In approximately one-half of the states, state funds provide workers compensation insurance. Territorial funds are in effect in Puerto Rico and the U.S. Virgin Islands. Although controlled by the state government, these state and territorial funds operate in essentially the same manner as private insurance companies. The most significant difference is that they accept any good faith applicant for insurance in the state, and no assigned risk plan is necessary. In most jurisdictions, the fund competes with private insurers. In a few other jurisdictions, only the state fund may provide workers compensation coverage. The legislatures in a handful of states have created employers' mutual insurance companies that also accept virtually all applicants but, unlike state funds, are not controlled by the state.

Competitive State Funds

Competitive state fund
A facility, owned and operated by a state government, that provides workers compensation insurance and that also permits private insurers to sell workers compensation insurance (i.e., to compete with the state fund) in that state.

In all but five of the states with state funds, the state funds sell workers compensation insurance in competition with private insurance companies and are thus called **competitive state funds**. An employer in these states can purchase insurance from either a private insurer or the state fund. In some states, the competitive state fund is the largest writer of workers compensation insurance—sometimes writing more than half of the total premium volume for that line of business in the state.

Monopolistic State Funds

Five states (North Dakota, Ohio, Washington, West Virginia, and Wyoming) plus Puerto Rico and the U.S. Virgin Islands require all workers compensation insurance to be purchased from the state or territorial fund. Because no private insurer is licensed to write workers compensation coverage in these jurisdictions, the state or territorial funds have no competition and are thus known as **monopolistic state funds** or **exclusive state funds**. Workers compensation coverage, but not necessarily employers liability coverage, is available from these funds. Competitive state funds and employers mutual insurance companies usually do provide employers liability coverage.

All Canadian provinces have boards or commissions with complete jurisdiction over workers compensation. These boards are similar in concept and organization to monopolistic state funds in the United States.

Employers' Mutual Insurance Companies

Instead of establishing state funds, the legislatures in a few states have created **employers' mutual insurance companies** to operate in their states. (The legislature for each such state creates only a single employers' mutual insurance company to operate within that state.) These companies closely resemble any other mutual insurance company except that they are typically required by their charters to provide workers compensation insurance to any qualified employer in the state. Unlike state funds, these mutual companies are not instrumentalities of the state; however, like competitive state funds, they do compete with other insurers. State employers' mutual insurance companies are often the largest writers of workers compensation insurance in their states.

Self-Insurance

Almost all states allow employers to retain the risk of workers compensation losses if they demonstrate the financial capacity to do so by meeting certain requirements.

To qualify as a self-insurer, an employer must post a surety bond with the workers compensation administrative agency of the state to guarantee the security of benefit payments. In addition, most states require evidence of an ability to administer the benefit payments and services mandated by the law. Self-insurance is usually practical only for employers with a large number of employees in a given state.

Excess Insurance

An employer that qualifies for self-insurance may decide to purchase excess insurance to cover catastrophic losses. Excess workers compensation insurance includes the following types:

1. Aggregate excess
2. Specific excess

Aggregate excess insurance (also called "stop loss excess") requires the employer to retain a stated amount of loss from the first dollar during a

---

Monopolistic state fund, or exclusive state fund
A facility, owned and operated by a state government, that provides workers compensation insurance and that does not permit any other insurers to sell workers compensation insurance in that state.

Employers' mutual insurance company
A mutual insurer established by a state's legislature to write workers compensation insurance for any qualified employer in the state.

Aggregate excess insurance
Insurance that covers losses only after the insured has retained a stated amount of aggregate loss during the policy period.

specified period of time, usually one year. For example, if the insurance required a retention of $200,000, the employer would pay losses up to an aggregate amount of $200,000. The insurer would pay any losses above $200,000 up to some stated limit such as $5 million. The amounts of the retention and the insurer's maximum limit are negotiated.

Specific excess insurance
Insurance that covers loss due to a single occurrence only for the amount that exceeds the policy retention.

Specific excess insurance also requires a retention limit, but the retention is for one loss or all losses from one occurrence. If covered losses from one occurrence exceed the retained limit, the insurer would pay any additional losses from that occurrence, up to the policy limit. Examples of aggregate and specific excess insurance are shown in Exhibit 12-1.

EXHIBIT 12-1

Aggregate Excess Versus Specific Excess

Aggregate Excess Policy

$250,000 aggregate retention		$5,000,000 maximum limit
Losses from separate occurrences	#1	$ 85,000
	#2	75,000
	#3	190,000
	#4	35,000
Total losses		$385,000
Aggregate retention		250,000
Aggregate excess policy will pay		$135,000

Specific Excess Policy

$100,000 per occurrence retention		$1,000,000 maximum limit
Losses from separate occurrences	#1	$ 85,000
	#2	75,000
	#3	190,000
	#4	35,000

Since loss #3 exceeds its $100,000 retention, the specific excess policy will pay $90,000. Specific excess and aggregate excess are sometimes written in one policy. In that event the specific excess would be calculated first. The aggregate excess loss payment would be based on the total amount of losses less (1) the payment under the specific coverage and (2) the aggregate retention.

Pools

In some states, organizations may join with one another to form pools (also known as trusts) to provide members with workers compensation insurance.

Often inaccurately referred to as "self-insured pools," these pools function in a manner similar to a small insurance company. Members' contributions to the pool are usually calculated in a manner similar to the premium for a workers compensation policy.

The pool processes and pays workers compensation claims on behalf of the participating entities. Frequently, claims-processing and administration are handled by an unrelated firm called a third-party administrator (TPA). The board of directors of the pool is typically composed of executives of some of the pool's members.

Pools claim that they can provide workers compensation coverage more efficiently because pool members are involved. Furthermore, because they often deal directly with their members, pools claim to have lower costs for selling and servicing the coverage than commercial insurers do. The pools' competitors (commercial insurers) emphasize the high level of skills that many commercial insurers have developed to handle workers compensation insurance. They also point out that pool members are liable for losses of all members, not just their own losses, in the event that the pool does not have sufficient resources. In addition, in most states, pools are not covered by state guarantee funds. To increase the comfort level of its members and to avoid a catastrophically large loss, pools generally purchase excess insurance, which was described above.

THE WORKERS COMPENSATION AND EMPLOYERS LIABILITY POLICY

In the United States, workers compensation insurance is provided under a standard form known as the "workers compensation and employers liability insurance policy." This form is maintained and filed in most states by the National Council on Compensation Insurance (NCCI), an organization that will be described in more detail later in this chapter in connection with workers compensation rating.

The **Workers Compensation and Employers Liability Insurance Policy (WC&EL policy)** combines coverage for both of the following:

1. Obligations imposed by workers compensation statutes
2. Employee injury claims that are not covered by workers compensation statutes

The policy contains uniform provisions even though workers compensation benefits vary by state. It is possible to use the same policy in various states because the applicable workers compensation laws are incorporated by reference in the policy. Thus, the covered workers compensation benefits are not itemized in the policy. The benefits specified in the applicable statute govern the types and amounts of benefits payable by the insurer.

Workers Compensation and Employers Liability Insurance Policy (WC&EL policy)
Policy used in most states to provide workers compensation and employers liability insurance.

A complete WC&EL policy consists of the following documents:

1. Information page
2. Policy form
3. Endorsements (if any apply)

These documents are not designed to be included in the ISO commercial package policy format. WC&EL coverage is provided by a separate policy that stands on its own.

Information Page

The information page is equivalent to the declarations page of other policies. The WC&EL information page is divided into four major parts or "items," as shown in Exhibit 12-2.

Item 1 gives essential information about the insured, including the insured's name and mailing address, the type of legal entity, and workplaces other than the insured's mailing address.

Item 2 shows the coverage period. Coverage begins and ends at 12:01 A.M. at the address of the insured given in Item 1.

Item 3 summarizes the coverage provided by the policy. Benefits required by the workers compensation law of the state or states listed in Item 3.A. will be paid in the event of an injury to an employee. This space should normally list all states in which the insured has operations and the insurer is licensed to provide coverage. Item 3.B. shows the limits of liability under the employers liability coverage for bodily injury by accident and by disease. An entry in Item 3.C. indicates that workers compensation coverage will be extended automatically to additional states if the insured expands operations. In addition, all endorsements and schedules attached to the policy at inception are listed on the information page or in a schedule attached to the policy.

The information necessary to calculate the estimated policy premium appears in Item 4. It includes a description of the classification(s) (explained later) assigned to the insured's business. This description and the corresponding code number are taken from the appropriate workers compensation manual. Another column contains the insured's estimate of what the remuneration (payroll) will be for the period covered by the policy. The estimated payroll is shown beside each classification.

The next column shows the rate applicable to each classification. Usually the rate is expressed in dollars of premium per $100 of payroll. The last column shows the estimated premium determined by multiplying the estimated payroll by the rate for each classification.

EXHIBIT 12-2

WC&EL Information Page

WORKERS COMPENSATION AND EMPLOYERS LIABILITY INSURANCE POLICY
INFORMATION PAGE

Insurer:

POLICY NO.
0 1 2 3 4 5 6 7 - 9

1. The Insured: ABC Corporation   _____ Individual   _____ Partnership
   Mailing address: 2000 Industrial Highway   __X__ Corporation or _____
                     Workingtown, PA 19000

   Other workplaces not shown above:

2. The policy period is from ___10/1/02___ to ___10/1/03___ at the insured's mailing address.

3. A. Workers Compensation Insurance: Part One of the policy applies to the Workers Compensation Law of the states listed here:

   B. Employers Liability Insurance: Part Two of the policy applies to work in each state listed in Item 3.A. The limits of our liability under Part Two are:

Bodily Injury by Accident	$ 100,000	each accident
Bodily Injury by Disease	$ 500,000	policy limit
Bodily injury by Disease	$ 100,000	each employee

   C. Other States Insurance: Part Three of the policy applies to the states, if any, listed here:

   All states except those listed in Item 3.A. and ND, OH, WA, WV, and WY

   D. This policy includes these endorsements and schedules:

   See Schedule

4. The premium for this policy will be determined by our Manuals of Rules, Classifications, Rates and Rating Plans. All information required below is subject to verification and change by audit.

Classifications	Code No.	Premium Basis Total Estimated Annual Remuneration	Rate Per $100 of Remuneration	Estimated Annual Premium
Sheet Metal Shop	0454	300,000	11.53	34,590
Clerical Office	0953	275,000	0.49	1,348
		Experience Modification of 1.382 Applied		13,728
		Estimated Premium Discount		(4,869)
		Total Estimated Annual Premium	$	44,797
Minimum Premium $ 1,273		Expense Constant	$	140

Countersigned by _____

WC 00 00 01 A

Policy Form

The standard WC&EL policy form includes a general section and the six parts listed below:

- Part One—Workers Compensation Insurance
- Part Two—Employers Liability Insurance
- Part Three—Other States Insurance
- Part Four—Your Duties If Injury Occurs
- Part Five—Premium
- Part Six—Conditions

General Section

The general section explains the nature of the policy and defines important terms. The first paragraph explains that the policy is a contract and that the parties are "you" (the insured) and "we" (the insurer). The insured is the employer named in Item 1 of the information page. The policy states that if that employer is a partnership, coverage applies to the partners only in their capacity as employer of that partnership's employees.

The general section defines "workers compensation law" to mean "the workers or workmen's compensation law and occupational disease law of each state or territory named in Item 3.A. of the Information Page." Any amendments during the policy period are included, but provisions of a statute that relate to nonoccupational disability benefits are not included within this definition. Moreover, the definition is limited to *state* laws. The United States Longshore and Harbor Workers' Compensation Act and other federal laws are not included.

The term "state" means any of the fifty states or the District of Columbia. Coverage for the workers compensation law of a United States territory applies only when Item 3.A. of the information page explicitly names that territory.

Covered locations are defined to include all workplaces listed on the information page and all of the insured's workplaces in states listed in Item 3.A. unless other insurance or self-insurance applies.

Part One—Workers Compensation Insurance

The coverage provided by Part One obligates the insurer to pay all compensation and other benefits required of the insured by the workers compensation law or occupational disease law of any state listed in Item 3.A. of the information page. The employer automatically receives coverage for all benefits required by that state's workers compensation law for all locations, operations, and employees as designated by the law. The policy applies to all operations of the employer except those otherwise insured or specifically excluded by endorsement.

The coverage applies to bodily injury by accident and by disease. The accident must occur during the policy period, and the last exposure to disease in the employment of the insured must occur during the policy period.

According to the policy, the insurer will pay the benefits required by the workers compensation law. The policy shows no dollar limit for these benefits. Any applicable limits would be those found within the law itself. Part One of the policy contains no exclusions.

The insurer has the right and duty to defend claims covered by the policy. The insurer also agrees to pay additional costs, such as the expense of investigating a claim and litigation costs.

The policy provides that the insured will reimburse the insurer for any penalties required under a workers compensation law because of (1) willful misconduct, (2) illegal employment, (3) failure to comply with health and safety laws and regulations, and (4) discrimination against employees who claim workers compensation benefits.

When the insurer pays compensation or employers liability benefits on behalf of an insured, any right of recovery the insured or the injured employee may have against a third party becomes the right of the insurer.

The policy also recognizes the legal requirements that directly obligate the insurance company to pay workers compensation benefits to any injured employee or, in the event of death, to the employee's dependents. Because the contract is made primarily for the benefit of employees and their dependents, they have a direct right of action against the insurance company.

For the protection of the employee, the policy provides that the obligations of the insurance company will not be affected by the failure of the employer to comply with the policy requirements.

All workers compensation laws covered by the policy become a part of the insurance contract just as if they were written into the policy, and employees have the rights to compensation defined by those laws. If the policy and the applicable workers compensation law conflict, the policy will automatically conform with the law.

Part Two—Employers Liability Insurance

Part Two of the policy, which provides employers liability coverage, is structured like a traditional liability policy, containing an insuring agreement and exclusions.

Employers Liability Insuring Agreement

The insurer agrees to pay damages that the insured becomes legally obligated to pay because of bodily injury to an employee. The bodily injury must be caused by accident or disease and arise out of and in the course of the employee's employment. The insurer also agrees to defend the insured against claims or suits seeking covered damages.

There are ways in which an employer can be held liable under the common law as the result of employee injuries. The following are examples:

- An employee of the insured sues a third party (such as a machine manufacturer) for an occupational injury, and the third party then sues the employer. The third party's suit might allege, for example, that the employer was negligent in maintaining the defective machine and that the employer must therefore indemnify the manufacturer for all damages the manufacturer had to pay to the employee.

- The spouse or a family member of an injured employee sues the employer for loss of companionship or services (such as housekeeping or yard work that the employee would otherwise have performed) resulting from the injury. (Many states do not permit such suits.)

Another requirement of Part B is that the employment out of which the injury arises must be necessary or incidental to the insured's work in a state or territory listed in Item 3.A. of the information page. This provision is not a requirement that the injury must *occur* in one of the states or territories listed. For example, an employee might be injured after driving into an unlisted state to buy supplies for work being performed in a listed state. Even though the injury occurred outside the listed state, the injury still arose out of employment that was necessary or incidental to the insured's work in a listed state.

The same coverage triggers apply to employers liability coverage that apply to workers compensation coverage.

- For bodily injury *by accident*, the policy that is in effect when the *injury occurs* is the policy that applies.

- For bodily injury *by disease*, the policy that is in effect on the employee's *last day of last exposure* to the conditions causing or aggravating the injury is the policy that applies.

Employers Liability Exclusions

Like most other liability policies, employers liability coverage is subject to exclusions that prevent overlapping coverage with other forms of insurance and eliminate coverage not intended by the insurer.

Statutory Obligations   In keeping with the basic purpose of employers liability coverage, several exclusions are aimed at eliminating coverage for claims that would be covered under various statutes, including the following:

- Any workers compensation, occupational disease, unemployment compensation, or disability benefits law
- The Longshore and Harbor Workers' Compensation Act (LHWCA)
- The Federal Employers' Liability Act (which gives workers on interstate railroads the right to sue their employers for injuries resulting to any degree from the employer's negligence)
- Any other federal workers compensation or occupational disease law

Also excluded is bodily injury to a master or member of the crew of any vessel. Masters and crew members of vessels are not eligible for LHWCA benefits but can pursue remedies described earlier in this chapter.

Various endorsements are available for deleting or modifying most of the exclusions listed above in order to extend the policy to cover those liabilities. The endorsement for covering LHWCA obligations is discussed later in this chapter. A shipowner's liability for crew injuries, although insurable by endorsement to the WC&EL policy, is usually covered under the shipowner's protection and indemnity policy (see Chapter 7).

Injury Outside the United States or Canada   Employers liability coverage does not apply to bodily injury that occurs outside the United States, its territories or possessions, and Canada. However, this exclusion does not apply to injury to a resident or citizen of the United States or Canada who is *temporarily* outside the places listed above.

Liability Assumed Under Contract   Employers liability coverage does not apply to liability assumed under contract—even if the insured has assumed another party's liability for injury to the insured's own employee. (As noted in Chapter 8, the CGL policy, by way of an exception to the "employers liability" exclusion in that policy, covers the insured against liability assumed under contract for injury to an employee of the insured. In almost every other instance, the CGL policy excludes liability for injury to an employee of the insured.)

Other Exclusions   Employers liability insurance also does not apply to any of the following:

1. Punitive damages for injury or death of any illegally employed person
2. Bodily injury to employees employed in violation of the law with the knowledge of the insured or any executive officers of the insured
3. Bodily injury intentionally caused by the insured
4. Damages arising out of employment practices, including (but not limited to) demotion, evaluation, harassment, discrimination, and termination
5. Fines or penalties imposed for violation of federal or state law
6. Damages payable under the Migrant and Seasonal Agricultural Worker Protection Act

Limits of Liability

Unlike workers compensation coverage, employers liability coverage is subject to limits of liability stated in the policy. The three limits that apply to employers liability coverage are as follows:

1. The "bodily injury by accident" limit is the most that the insurer will pay for bodily injury resulting from any one accident, regardless of the number of employees injured.

2. The "bodily injury by disease—policy limit" is the most that the insurer will pay for bodily injury by disease, regardless of the number of employees who sustain disease.

3. The "bodily injury by disease—each employee" limit is the most that the insurer will pay for bodily injury by disease to any one employee.

Defense costs, as well as supplementary payments similar to those covered under the CGL coverage form, are covered in addition to the limits of liability. As in the CGL policy, the insurer has no duty to pay defense costs or supplementary payments after it has paid the applicable limit of insurance.

Part Three—Other States Insurance

Other states insurance
Insurance that automatically extends coverage to the insured's operations in any state listed in Item 3.C. of the WC&EL information page.

Employers need workers compensation coverage if they expand their operations into states not listed in Item 3.A. of the information page when the policy is issued or last renewed. This coverage, called **other states insurance**, is incorporated within the policy form as Part Three. It extends workers compensation and employers liability coverage to operations in any state listed in Item 3.C. of the information page. If coverage applies to a state designated in Item 3.C., and the insured begins operations in that state, the policy provides the same coverage as if that state were listed in Item 3.A. The policy requires the insured to "Tell us at once if you begin work in any state listed in Item 3.C. of the Information Page."

If the insured has operations in a particular state on the effective date of the policy but that state is not listed in Item 3.A., the insured must notify the insurer within thirty days or else no coverage will apply for that state. Thus, when operations are *known* to exist in a particular state, that state should be listed in Item 3.A. When operations do not currently take place in additional states but *could* be extended into those states, those states should be listed in Item 3.C. Naturally, states in which the insurer is not licensed to write workers compensation insurance (including those that have monopolistic state funds) should not be included for either item.

If an insurance company is licensed in all states, the wording used in Item 3.C. often reads: "All states except those listed in Item 3.A. and ND, OH, WA, WV, and WY." This protects the insured if it commences operations in any state other than those listed in Item 3.A. (which are already covered) or in any state other than the five monopolistic fund states (where it would be illegal for the insurer to provide workers compensation insurance). Insurers will also exclude states in which they are not licensed or in which they do not wish to provide coverage for underwriting reasons.

Stopgap coverage
Coverage for employers liability that private insurers provide to employers operating in a monopolistic fund state that does not include such insurance in its workers compensation policies.

If the insured anticipates operating in a state with a monopolistic workers compensation fund, the insured should obtain workers compensation insurance from the appropriate state agency. Because the workers compensation policies issued by monopolistic state funds do not include employers liability insurance, many employers buy a type of employers liability insurance called **stopgap coverage**. This coverage is often provided by the same insurer that provides the insured's general liability insurance.

Part Four—Your Duties If Injury Occurs

Part Four explains the duties of the insured when a loss occurs. The insured must promptly notify the insurer of any injury, claim, or suit. The insured must also cooperate with the insurer, attend hearings and trials at the request of the insurer, and help secure witnesses. The insured cannot, except at his or her own expense, voluntarily make any payment, assume any obligation, or incur any expenses except for immediate medical and other services at the time of injury as required by the workers compensation law.

Part Five—Premium

Workers compensation premiums are based on the insured's payroll, which cannot be precisely determined until after the policy expires. Part Five explains premium determination procedures, establishing the role of insurance company manuals in determining premium and stipulating that the manuals and the premium may change during the policy period. The policy tells the insured that the classifications and rates shown on the information page may change if they do not accurately describe the work covered by the policy.

Part Five also defines payroll as the premium base and stresses that it includes the remuneration of executive officers and the payroll of employees of uninsured contractors and subcontractors. The audit provision explains the insurer's right to examine and audit the insured's books and records at any time during the policy period and within three years after expiration insofar as such books and records relate to the policy. It explains why the final premium may be different from the estimated premium and shows how the premium will be determined on cancellation of the policy. The insured must keep records of information needed to compute the policy premium and provide such records to the insurer when requested.

The premium shown on the information page is an estimated premium. The final premium is determined by a process known as an audit. In general terms, an audit is defined as an examination of records or financial accounts to check their accuracy. In insurance usage, it refers to an examination of an insured's financial records to determine the premium for a prior period. Most audits are conducted annually a few months after the policy expiration. However, for insureds that generate substantial premiums, the insurer may require quarterly, or even monthly, audits. The audit may be performed by an insurance company representative, known as a premium auditor, or an independent auditor hired by the insurer, or the insured may be asked to perform a self-audit and report the payroll amounts to the insurance company.

Part Six—Conditions

The policy conditions limit or define the rights and obligations of the parties to the insurance contract. The conditions address insurer inspections, policy years, assignment, cancellation, and who represents the insured.

Inspection

The inspection condition gives the insurer permission to inspect a policy-holder's workplaces and operations. These inspections allow the insurer to assess whether safe practices are employed and proper precautions taken for the safety of employees. These inspections are valuable to all involved parties. The insurer's safety recommendations help the insurance company avoid losses, they reduce the cost of workers compensation insurance for the employer, and they protect employees from injury.

Although this condition states that the insurer is permitted to inspect work-places, the policy does not require the insurer to perform inspections. When such services are performed, the policy indicates that this does not constitute an undertaking to warrant that any workplaces, operations, machinery, or equipment inspected are safe or healthful.

Occasionally an injured employee will sue the insurer asserting that the insurer was negligent in failing to detect a hazardous condition in the work-place and that the insurer's negligence contributed to the employee's injury. Most courts have held that the inspection provision protects the insurance company from such claims, but there have been court decisions in favor of injured employees.

Long-Term Policy

If the policy period is longer than one year, each year is considered separate as far as policy provisions are concerned, and premium is computed in accordance with the manual rules and rates in effect for that year. An exception is a three-year fixed-rate policy that would carry an endorsement modifying this provision. Such three-year policies are rarely issued.

Assignment

As with almost every other form of insurance, the workers compensation policy cannot be assigned without the insurer's consent. Because of the complexity of auditing a policy that has been assigned to a new insured, insurers almost never consent to the transfer of a workers compensation policy. Insurers generally prefer to cancel the existing policy and issue a new policy.

Cancellation

The cancellation condition states the rights of the insurer and the insured to cancel the policy. However, this condition is subject in all cases to any requirements of the workers compensation law, and some laws restrict the insurer's right of cancellation. According to the cancellation condition, the insurer must provide at least ten days' notice before cancellation becomes effective. The insured may cancel the policy at any time.

Sole Representative

The first named insured acts on behalf of all insureds for premium payment, refund, cancellation, and other rights and duties under the policy.

Endorsements

Despite the flexibility built into the standard WC&EL policy, a number of situations require modification of standard policy provisions by adding an appropriate endorsement to the policy. Two of the more important endorsements are examined below.

Voluntary Compensation Endorsement

The workers compensation laws of most states exempt some types of employment from statutory workers compensation benefits. The most commonly exempted occupations are farm labor, domestic employment, and casual labor. In some cases, the law does not apply to employers with fewer than a certain minimum number of employees. The workers compensation laws of some states do not apply to partners, sole proprietors, or executive officers. Even when exempt persons are not entitled to workers compensation benefits by law, benefits may be extended to them by voluntary action.

In cases where WC&EL coverage is not required by law, an employer may want to purchase the coverage. CGL policies, as discussed in Chapter 8, exclude coverage for claims for bodily injury to an employee of the insured arising out of and in the course of employment by the insured. Employers liability coverage would cover such claims by employees not subject to the workers compensation law.

The **Voluntary Compensation and Employers Liability Endorsement** amends the standard WC&EL policy to include an additional coverage called "voluntary compensation." The additional coverage does not make employees subject to the workers compensation law, but it obligates the insurance company to pay, on behalf of the insured, an amount equal to the compensation benefits that would be payable to such employees if they were subject to the workers compensation law designated in the endorsement.

The voluntary compensation endorsement states that if an employee entitled to payment under the endorsement brings a suit under the common law, the coverage provided by the endorsement reverts to employers liability insurance. The insurer will defend the insured against the employee's suit and pay any settlement awarded, subject to the stipulated limits of liability.

Voluntary Compensation and Employers Liability Endorsement
Endorsement that amends the WC&EL policy to cover employees who are not subject to a workers compensation statute.

LHWCA Coverage Endorsement

The United States Longshore and Harbor Workers' Compensation Act follows the same principles as the state workers compensation laws. In some circumstances, an employer may be subject to both the LHWCA and the state workers compensation law at the same time. Although both of these exposures may be insured, they must be covered and rated separately.

Coverage can be provided by adding the **United States Longshore and Harbor Workers' Compensation Act Endorsement** to the WC&EL policy. The endorsement amends the definition of "workers compensation law" to include the LHWCA with respect to operations in any state designated in

United States Longshore and Harbor Workers' Compensation Act Endorsement
Endorsement that amends the WC&EL policy to cover the insured's obligations under the LHWCA.

the endorsement's schedule. (In practice, many WC&EL insurers are unwilling to add LHWCA coverage because of the unfavorable loss experience associated with the LHWCA.)

RATING WORKERS COMPENSATION INSURANCE

Most states require insurers to belong to an approved advisory organization in order to write workers compensation and employers liability insurance. This organization gathers statistics for workers compensation in those states. Different organizations may exist for different states. The designated organization files with the supervisory authority the manuals for classifications, rules, rates (or loss costs, depending on the state), rating plans, and policy forms on behalf of its members.

The National Council on Compensation Insurance (NCCI) serves as the filing agency for insurers in most states and prepares standard forms and endorsements. Several states have independent rating bureaus for workers compensation insurance. Some of these use the services of NCCI. Other states make their own rates and issue their own rules and manuals. However, the procedures generally resemble those of NCCI.

Workers compensation insurance protects employers from losses resulting from the work-related injuries or diseases of employees as determined by statute. The premium for that protection should reflect the exposure to such losses. The exposure varies considerably according to the size of the employer's work force and the degree of hazard in the work performed. Workers compensation premiums reflect these two factors because the premium depends on the amount of the employer's payroll (the basis of premium) and the type of business (classification) involved.

Basis of Premium

With only a few exceptions, the premium base for workers compensation insurance is remuneration (that is, payroll). Payroll serves as an effective premium base because it varies directly with the exposure covered by the insurance, it is relatively easy to determine and verify from available records, and it is not readily subject to manipulation by the insured.

A business obtaining workers compensation insurance may not know how many employees it will have during the coming year. The policy, however, bases the premium on the manual rate for the applicable classification per $100 of payroll for the year. At the inception of the policy, the insured pays an estimated premium based on an estimate of the annual payroll, and a premium auditor may examine the insured's records at the end of the policy period (or at shorter intervals during the policy period) to determine the actual payroll. The insurer then calculates the actual earned premium. If it is greater than the deposit premium, the insured receives a bill for the additional premium due. If it is less, the insured receives a refund. However, the premium cannot fall below the minimum premium shown in the manual for the governing classification. The minimum premium is the lowest premium that can be charged for a policy, and it varies according to classification and state.

Classifications

Rates for workers compensation insurance vary considerably according to the classification of workers. The class rating system serves to identify groups of similar employments whose experience is then combined for the purpose of establishing rates. To achieve this result, however, both premiums and losses must be accurately and consistently assigned to the proper classes. Any business may involve many different operations in widely varying combinations. Some of these operations may be extremely hazardous, while others are not. The classification rules attempt to delineate classification procedures that are both equitable and simple to apply.

The classification section of the workers compensation manual alphabetically lists several hundred classifications. Other than the so-called standard exception classifications (such as clerical employees), each one describes a particular business. For each employer, it is necessary to determine the basic classification that best describes the business of the employer within the state so that the employer's exposure base and loss experience can be pooled with all similar businesses. Generally, an employer is not permitted to divide payroll between two or more governing classifications. These points are explained below.

Governing Classification

A governing classification is one that best describes an insured's activities. With only a few exceptions, all its employees at any one location are assigned to that classification. For example, a furniture manufacturer and an auto repair shop may each employ painters as part of their operations. To compute the workers compensation premium, the payroll for furniture painters will be assigned to the furniture manufacturing classification, whereas the payroll for auto body painters will be assigned to the auto body repair shop classification.

Standard Exception Classifications

The payroll for certain employees is separately rated. These classifications, called standard exception classifications, apply to the following:

- Clerical office employees and drafting employees, provided they work in an area physically separated from other operations
- Telecommuting clerical and drafting employees
- Salespersons, collectors, or messengers
- Drivers, chauffeurs, and their helpers

The payrolls for employees in these classifications are shown separately on the policy and take the rates applying to the standard exception classification, not the rate for the governing classification. For some classifications, however, the manual indicates that certain standard-exception payroll is to be included in the governing classification. For example, Code 5183 reads: "Plumbing NOC and drivers." ("NOC" means "not otherwise classified.") Therefore, the payroll for drivers employed by a firm classified as code 5183 would be assigned to the plumbing classification and not rated separately on the policy.

Premium Adjustments

The premium determined by applying the rates to the exposures can be modified by any one of several adjustments.

WC&EL Premium Adjustments

- Experience rating
- Retrospective rating
- Premium discount
- Merit or schedule rating factors

- Rate deviations
- Expense constant
- Deductible credit
- Dividend plans

Experience Modification

Experience rating plan
Rating plan that increases or reduces the premium for a future period based on the insured's own loss experience for a period in the recent past.

Under an **experience rating plan,** the premium applicable to a particular insured is increased or decreased for a future period based on that insured's loss experience for a period in the recent past. The past period is usually the three years beginning four years before policy inception. For example, an insured's premium for 2001 might be adjusted based on that insured's loss experience for the years 1997, 1998, and 1999. The premium for 2001 would be reduced if the insured's losses were lower than expected for the class, and increased if the insured's losses were higher.

Rating rules provide that insureds whose workers compensation premiums have reached certain amounts are subject to experience rating modification. The experience rating computation produces an **experience modification,** or mod, which serves as a rate multiplier. If the mod is less than 1.00, the premium is reduced, and vice versa. See Exhibit 12-2 for an example.

Experience modification
A rate multiplier derived from the experience rating computation.

The required average premium varies from state to state, but generally ranges from $2,500 to $5,000 a year. Experience rating provides an incentive to insureds to implement loss control measures that reduce workplace accidents.

Retrospective Rating

Retrospective rating plan
A rating plan that increases or reduces an insured's premium for a policy period based on the insured's own losses during the same period.

Under a **retrospective rating plan**, an insured's premium for a given period is reduced or increased based on that insured's losses during the same period.

The insured pays an estimated premium at the beginning of the period and receives either a refund or a bill for an additional premium after the end of the period, depending on the losses during the period. A formula for calculating the retrospective premium adjustment, subject to minimum and maximum premiums, is written into the policy at its inception. Underwriters sometimes require retrospective rating plans as a condition of providing insurance for marginal accounts that may generate high losses. Conversely, insureds that expect lower than average losses may find retrospective rating attractive, particularly when combined with an effective loss control program that reduces claim frequency and severity.

Premium Discount

Many of the expenses of providing workers compensation do not increase proportionately with increases in premium. For example, the costs of policy issuance and premium collection generally do not increase with the size of the premium. Underwriting expense does increase with the size of the premium, but it generally does not cost 100 times as much to underwrite a policy with a $100,000 premium as it does one with a $1,000 premium. Furthermore, the percentage paid to producers as a commission is usually reduced as the premium increases. In recognition of these lowered expenses, the *premium discount plan* provides an increasing credit for premiums in excess of a certain minimum.

Merit or Schedule Rating Factors

In many states, the premium can also be modified by a *merit or schedule rating* factor to give the insured credit for conditions that exceed those normally expected, such as superior housekeeping, excellent employee training, and on-site medical facilities.

Rate Deviations

In some states, insurers are permitted to apply a rate deviation factor (for example, 10 percent) to the premium as calculated by the rating manual. Insurers generally reserve these credits for better risks, although competitive pressures sometime result in average risks receiving a deviated premium.

Expense Constant

An **expense constant** is a flat charge designed to cover administrative expenses, such as policy issuance and record keeping, that are common to all policies. An expense constant is applied regardless of the size of the policy premium. Not every state calls for an expense constant charge. Where they are applied, they generally amount to less than $200 per policy.

Expense constant
A flat charge to cover administrative expenses, such as policy issuance and record keeping, that are common to WC&EL

Deductibles

In almost all non-monopolistic states, an insured can reduce its premium by electing a deductible plan. The deductible applies to both medical and lost-time claims on a per claim basis. The credit for smaller deductibles is not substantial (for example, about 1 percent of premium for a $100 deductible, and 3 to 6 percent for a $500 deductible), but the added incentive to reduce workplace accidents is beneficial for all parties.

Large deductible plan
A plan that allows insureds to self-insure most of their workers compensation claims without establishing a qualifying self-insurance plan; WC&EL policy with deductibles in the $50,000 to $250,000 range.

Large deductible plans, those with deductibles in the $50,000 to $250,000 per claim range, greatly reduce the premium and are available in most states. Insureds electing such plans are, in effect, self-insuring most of their workers compensation exposure since most claims are less than the deductible. Large deductible plans avoid the complications of setting up a true self-insurance plan. The insurance company does all the administrative work connected with workers compensation claims, and the insured reimburses the insurer for claim payments up to the deductible limit per occurrence. Above the deductible, the insurance coverage functions as a per-claim stop loss. In some cases aggregate stop-loss protection is also included.

Dividend Plans

For policies written on a dividend plan, the cost of the insurance can be reduced by dividends declared by the insurance company. Two general types of dividend plans are available: a flat dividend plan and a sliding-scale dividend plan. Under a *flat-dividend plan*, all eligible policies receive the same percentage of premium as a dividend regardless of their individual loss experience. Under a *sliding-scale dividend plan*, the size of the dividend varies with the insured's own experience; the lower the insured's loss ratio, the higher the dividend percentage. In sliding-scale dividend plans, no dividend is paid when the loss ratio for the expiring year exceeds a certain percentage, usually 45 to 60 percent.

Insurers offer dividend plans to insureds with good safety records and at least a certain minimum premium size. In discussing dividend plans with insureds, it is important to point out that dividends cannot be guaranteed. Dividends are paid after expiration of the policy and then only at the rate declared by the insurer's board of directors. On occasion, the directors may reduce the dividend rate or not declare any dividend at all.

SUMMARY

Workers compensation laws were adopted to assure workers and their families of prompt payment for occupational injuries and diseases and resulting disabilities or deaths. For an injury or disease to be covered under a typical workers compensation law, the injury or disease must arise out of and in the course of employment.

The benefits provided by workers compensation laws include medical benefits, disability income benefits, death benefits, and rehabilitation benefits. The amounts collectible for these benefits are defined in the applicable law.

Workers compensation laws apply to most employees. Some of the workers that are not covered by state workers compensation laws include federal government employees, maritime workers, and employees of interstate railroads.

The extraterritorial provisions in most state laws provide benefits for employees injured outside their home state. Extraterritorial coverage for employees temporarily located in foreign countries is usually limited to six months or less. Voluntary foreign workers compensation coverage can provide coverage without time limit and may include repatriation expense and endemic disease coverage.

Employers can meet their workers compensation obligations by buying workers compensation insurance from private insurers, assigned risk plans, or state workers compensation insurance funds, or by joining pools. Alternatively, larger employers can self-insure (retain) their workers compensation exposure if they meet certain tests specified in the applicable workers compensation law. A combined approach is to self-insure up to a certain point and purchase excess insurance above that point.

Workers compensation insurance is mainly provided under a standard form called the Workers Compensation and Employers Liability Insurance Policy (WC&EL policy). The policy not only covers the insured's obligations under workers compensation laws but also provides employers liability coverage. Employers liability coverage protects the insured against claims for employee injuries that are not subject to workers compensation.

The workers compensation part of the policy obligates the insurer to pay all compensation and other benefits required of the insured by the workers compensation law of any state listed in Item 3.A. of the policy's information page (declarations). Coverage for federal compensation laws, such as the Longshore and Harbor Workers' Compensation Act, is excluded unless coverage is extended by endorsement.

The employers liability part of the policy obligates the insurer to pay damages that the insured becomes legally obligated to pay under the common law because of bodily injury by accident or disease to an employee. The bodily injury must arise out of and in the course of the employee's employment and not be covered under a workers compensation law. The insurer also agrees to defend the insured. Several exclusions apply to employers liability coverage.

A policy feature called "other states insurance" extends the policy to cover obligations under workers compensation laws of states in addition to those listed in Item 3.A. of the information page. Such additional states, however, must be listed in Item 3.C. of the information page.

Common endorsements to the WC&EL policy include voluntary compensation coverage (providing workers compensation benefits for employees not subject to a workers compensation law) and Longshore and Harbor Workers'

Compensation Act coverage (covering an employer's obligations under the LHWCA).

The premium base for WC&EL insurance is ordinarily the insured's payroll. The premium base is multiplied by a rate that depends on the insured's classification.

Certain types of employees, such as clerical workers and drivers, are assigned to separate classifications called standard exception classifications. In all but a few cases, an employee's payroll cannot be divided among two or more classifications.

An estimated premium is usually charged at the beginning of the policy period. At the end of the policy period, the insured's actual payroll figures are used to determine the final premium.

The premium determined by applying the rates to the exposures can be modified by experience rating factors, retrospective rating plans, premium discount percentages, merit or schedule rating factors, rate deviations, expense constants, deductible credits, and dividend plans.

CHAPTER NOTE

1. For more information on PEOs, see Kirk A. Goeldner, "Professional Employee Organizations—Opportunities and Considerations," *CPCU Journal*, Spring 1999, pp. 17–20; and Joseph J. Occhiogrosso, "Professional Employers for Small Companies," *Management Accounting*, December 1998, pp. 38–42.

Direct Your Learning

OUTLINE

Excess and Umbrella Liability Insurance

Professional Liability Insurance

Aircraft Insurance

Environmental Insurance

Coverage for Foreign Operations

Surety Bonds

Summary

Miscellaneous Coverages

After learning the content of this chapter, you should be able to:

■ Given a case, determine the amount that will be paid for a claim under primary insurance and excess or umbrella liability insurance.
  • Compare excess and umbrella liability policies.
  • Describe the applicability of the self-insured retention (SIR) in an umbrella liability policy.
  • Describe the effect of the "maintenance of underlying insurance" condition in umbrella liability policies.

■ Describe the differences between professional liability policies and CGL policies.

■ Describe professional liability loss exposures and the corresponding professional liability coverages using physicians and insurance producers as examples.

■ Describe the loss exposures insured by the following:
  • Directors and officers liability insurance
  • Employment practices liability insurance
  • Employee benefits liability insurance
  • Fiduciary liability insurance

■ Describe the coverages that can be included in an aircraft insurance policy.

■ Describe the various types of environmental insurance policies that are currently available.

■ Identify the foreign loss exposures a United States domiciled organization could have that would not be covered under standard property and liability insurance policies, and explain how those exposures can be insured.

■ Describe the characteristics of surety bonds.

■ Describe the guarantee provided by each of the bonds discussed in this assignment.

Develop Your Perspective

What are the main topics covered in the chapter?

This chapter surveys several additional types of loss exposures and insurance, including excess and umbrella liability insurance, professional liability insurance, aircraft insurance, environmental insurance, coverage for foreign operations, and surety bonds.

Review the limits of insurance provided under a CGL policy.

- Are these limits sufficient to cover the loss exposures facing the organization?
- What type of policy could extend the limits of this coverage?

Why is it important to learn about these topics?

Most organizations face at least one of the specialized or unusual exposures covered under the policies in this chapter. Knowing that these policies exist for these exposures, and how the policies apply coverage, will enable you to help customers cover losses that are not otherwise covered under many standard policies.

Consider the loss exposures facing professionals such as lawyers or accountants who provide professional services to others.

- What type of policy covers liability arising out of their rendering of professional services?

How can you use what you will learn?

Analyze the loss exposures of an organization.

- Does this organization face unusual or specialized loss exposures?
- What coverages from this chapter would you recommend to properly insure against these loss exposures?

Chapter 13
Miscellaneous Coverages

The types of insurance described in preceding chapters of this text cover the common property and liability exposures of most organizations. Many other forms of commercial insurance are available to cover specialized or unusual exposures. This chapter surveys several commercial insurance coverages that fill gaps left by the more basic policies.

The chapter will first examine excess and umbrella liability policies that provide additional amounts of insurance above one or more "primary" liability policies and, in some cases, provide broader coverage than the primary policies. The chapter will then describe professional liability policies designed to treat specific exposures that are not covered by CGL or auto policies. The chapter concludes with discussions of aircraft insurance, environmental insurance, coverage for foreign exposures, and surety bonds.

EXCESS AND UMBRELLA LIABILITY INSURANCE

Excess liability insurance and umbrella liability insurance are two similar types of coverage that organizations buy mainly to extend the limits of their CGL, commercial auto, and other "primary" liability policies.

Need for Excess or Umbrella Liability Coverage

To understand why excess or umbrella insurance is needed, it is helpful to review three basic characteristics of liability insurance that are not shared by property insurance.

1. Difficulty in estimating maximum possible loss for liability exposures
2. Layering of liability coverages
3. Effect of aggregate limits

Maximum Possible Loss

Most *property* loss exposures have a reasonably clear **maximum possible loss (MPL)**. For example, the maximum possible building loss for a building that would cost $2 million to rebuild is, simply, $2 million. There is no comparable way to estimate MPL for most liability exposures. Awards to injured persons can, in severe cases, reach staggering totals. A Coca-Cola distributor paid more

Maximum possible loss (MPL)
The largest loss that could be sustained in a particular occurrence or by a particular property.

than $145 million to settle claims growing out of the collision of one of its delivery trucks with a school bus. Even property damage claims can involve enormous settlements; the cleanup costs alone for the *Exxon Valdez* oil spill in Prince William Sound on the Alaskan coast exceeded $2.5 billion.

Moreover, million-dollar verdicts have become increasingly frequent. There were no million-dollar verdicts in the U.S. before 1962, but in 2000 there were hundreds of million-dollar verdicts and twenty-seven verdicts that exceeded $100 million.[1]

Although most organizations are not likely to experience million-dollar liability losses, the possibility of a large liability loss exists for virtually any business, regardless of the size of the business and the type of service or product the business offers.

Layering of Coverage

Another difference between property and liability coverage is the way in which insurers provide high limits of coverage. Most property exposures are covered entirely by one insurer. If several insurers participate on the risk, they generally do so on a pro rata basis: each insurer shares proportionately in all losses.

In contrast, high-limit liability insurance is generally arranged in two or more "layers." That is, the coverage provided by the first (or "primary" insurer) must be totally exhausted before the next layer of insurance makes any payment. (Property insurance for highly valued properties is also sometimes arranged in layers, but that is the exception.) The primary layer of liability insurance seldom exceeds $1 million per occurrence. Each successive layer often provides $5 million, $10 million, $25 million, or more dollars of coverage. It is estimated that the total limit of liability insurance available in the world insurance market for any one insured exceeds $1.6 billion.[2]

Effect of Aggregate Limits

Unlike property insurance, liability insurance is usually subject to an aggregate limit for the policy period. Thus, even if a business is never faced with a verdict that exceeds the *each occurrence* limit of one of its primary liability policies, the business could have several liability losses during one policy year that could reduce its *aggregate* limit, leaving a subsequent loss underinsured or uninsured.

For example, assume that an insured has CGL coverage with a $1,000,000 each occurrence limit, a $2,000,000 general aggregate limit, and a $2,000,000 aggregate limit for products and completed operations. If the insured has four products liability losses for $500,000 each during the policy period, the policy will pay nothing for later products liability losses that occur during the same policy period, even if no claim exceeds the each occurrence limit. ($500,000 × 4 = $2,000,000—the aggregate limit.)

Insurance Treatment

The large liability loss exposures described above can be insured with additional policies known as excess liability policies and umbrella liability policies. These policies provide limits of insurance in excess of the limits of an "underlying" primary policy or policies.

Excess or umbrella liability coverage comes into play when the amount of damages exceeds the each occurrence limit of an underlying policy or when the aggregate limit of an underlying policy has become depleted by prior claims during the policy period. Umbrella liability policies may also cover some claims that are not covered at all by the underlying policy or policies.

Excess Liability Insurance

An **excess liability policy** may take any of three basic forms:

1. A "following form" subject to the same terms as the underlying policy
2. A self-contained policy subject to its own terms only
3. A combination of the two types above

A following-form excess policy covers a liability loss that exceeds the underlying limits *only if the loss is covered by the underlying insurance.* To illustrate, assume that an insured has an underlying liability policy with an each occurrence limit of $1,000,000 and a following-form excess policy with an each occurrence limit of $1,000,000. If a claimant obtains a judgment of $1,250,000 against the insured for bodily injury covered by the underlying policy, the underlying policy will pay the each occurrence limit of $1,000,000, and the excess policy will pay the remaining $250,000. The application of the primary and excess policies to the claim is illustrated in Exhibit 13-1.

A self-contained excess policy applies to a loss that exceeds the underlying limits *only if the loss is also covered under the terms of the excess policy.* For example, the excess policy may not cover injury within the products-completed operations hazard, even though the underlying policy does. In that case, the excess policy will not pay for a products liability claim, even though the claim was covered by the underlying policy and exceeded the each occurrence limit of the underlying policy.

Alternatively, an excess policy may combine both of the above approaches by incorporating the provisions of the underlying policy and then modifying those provisions with additional conditions or exclusions in the excess policy.

Umbrella Liability Insurance

The term "umbrella liability" is generally used to describe a type of excess insurance that is broader than ordinary excess liability policies. Although ordinary excess policies may apply in excess of one or more underlying policies,

Excess liability policy
Policy that covers liability claims in excess of the limits of an underlying policy or a stated retention amount.

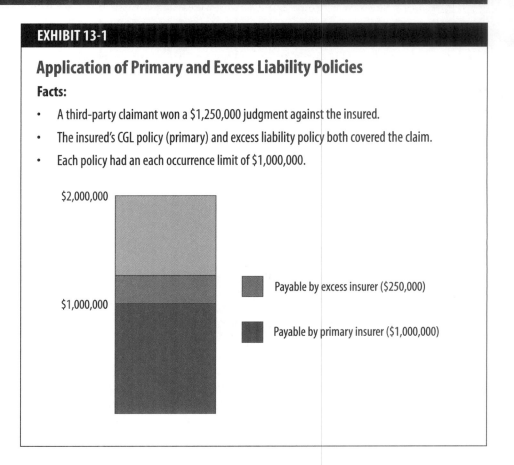

EXHIBIT 13-1

Application of Primary and Excess Liability Policies
Facts:

*   A third-party claimant won a $1,250,000 judgment against the insured.
*   The insured's CGL policy (primary) and excess liability policy both covered the claim.
*   Each policy had an each occurrence limit of $1,000,000.

Payable by excess insurer ($250,000)

Payable by primary insurer ($1,000,000)

Umbrella liability policy
Policy that provides excess coverage over several primary policies (typically CGL, auto, and employers liability) and that may also provide drop-down coverage.

an **umbrella liability policy** almost always provides excess coverage over several primary policies, such as CGL, auto liability, and employers liability. The distinguishing feature of umbrella liability policies is coverage that is broader in some respects than that of the underlying policies, thus providing primary coverage for certain occurrences that would not be covered by any of the underlying policies. In contrast, ordinary excess liability policies tend to be on the same terms as the underlying coverage or even on narrower terms than the underlying.

An umbrella liability policy thus performs three functions. Like an ordinary excess liability policy, it (1) provides additional limits above the each occurrence limits of the insured's primary policies and (2) takes the place of the primary insurance when primary aggregate limits are reduced or exhausted. In addition, it (3) covers some claims that are not covered by the insured's primary policies, subject to a retention (an amount of loss retained by the insured).

Drop-down coverage
Coverage provided by many umbrella liability policies for (1) claims not covered at all by the underlying policies and (2) claims that are not covered by an underlying policy only because the underlying policy's aggregate limits have been depleted.

Drop-Down Coverage

The latter two functions—providing primary coverage when either the underlying aggregate limits are exhausted or the underlying policy simply does not cover the type of loss that has occurred—are often referred to as **drop-down coverage**.

To illustrate the first function of drop-down coverage (which may also be performed by an ordinary excess policy), assume that a manufacturer has the following occurrence-basis policies:

1. A CGL policy with an each occurrence limit of $1,000,000 and a products-completed operations aggregate limit of $2,000,000
2. An umbrella policy with an each occurrence limit of $5,000,000 and an aggregate limit of $5,000,000

During one policy period, the primary CGL insurer pays products liability claims totaling $2,000,000, exhausting the aggregate limit. If the insured is sued by a consumer who alleges he was injured by the insured's product during the same policy period, the umbrella policy will "drop down" to defend the insured and/or pay damages (subject to the umbrella policy's limits) as if the umbrella policy were primary insurance. If subsequent products liability claims are made against the insured for injury that allegedly occurred during the policy period, the umbrella policy will defend or pay those claims also. The umbrella insurer's obligation to defend and pay ceases when its limits are exhausted.

As an example of the second aspect of drop-down coverage, assume that a manufacturer has a CGL policy and an umbrella liability policy. A products liability suit is brought against the manufacturer in a country not included in the CGL coverage territory. The CGL policy covers products liability worldwide but only if the suit is first made in the United States or Canada. Thus, in this case, the CGL policy does not apply. However, if the umbrella policy does not contain the same territorial restriction on products suits, it will "drop down" and handle the claim as though it were the primary policy.

When a claim covered by the umbrella policy is not covered at all by any primary policy, the drop-down coverage is subject to a retention (also known as a **self-insured retention** or **SIR**). If the retention shown in the umbrella is $25,000, for example, the umbrella will pay that part of the claim that exceeds $25,000, subject to the applicable limits of insurance under the umbrella policy. (See Exhibit 13-2.) Retentions vary in amount, from as low as $500 for a very small business to $1,000,000 or more for the largest businesses. In many policies, particularly those issued to small businesses, the retention does not apply to defense costs. Coverage for these costs is provided in full, often referred to as "first-dollar defense coverage."

Self-insured retention (SIR)
An amount that is deducted from claims that are payable under an umbrella liability policy and that are not covered at all by any primary policy.

The retention does *not* apply when the umbrella is (1) paying in excess of a claim covered by the primary policy or (2) dropping down to pay a claim because the primary policy's aggregate limit has been exhausted.

Required Underlying Limits

Each insurer writing umbrella liability policies has its own requirements for the types and amounts of underlying insurance that the insured must have.

EXHIBIT 13-2

Application of Umbrella Policy to Claim Not Covered by Primary Policy

Facts

- A $200,000 claim was covered by the umbrella policy but not by any of the primary policies.
- The umbrella policy had an each occurrence limit of $1,000,000 and a $25,000 SIR.

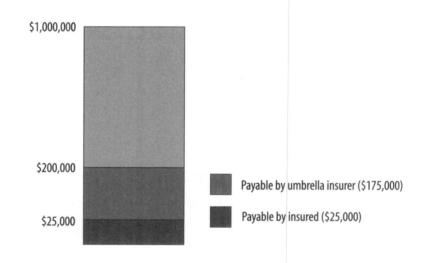

Payable by umbrella insurer ($175,000)

Payable by insured ($25,000)

(For purposes of readability, this exhibit is not drawn to scale.)

For example, an umbrella insurer might require the insured to have the following primary coverages and limits:

Commercial General Liability

- $1,000,000 each occurrence
- $2,000,000 general aggregate
- $2,000,000 products and completed operations aggregate

Business Auto Liability

- $1,000,000 combined single limit

Employers Liability

- $100,000 bodily injury each accident
- $100,000 bodily injury by disease each employee
- $500,000 disease aggregate

The umbrella limits apply in full in excess of each of the underlying coverages. Thus, if an insured with the underlying limits shown above also carried a

$10,000,000 umbrella policy, the total coverage available for one occurrence covered by the CGL policy and the umbrella would be $11,000,000 ($1,000,000 primary plus $10,000,000 umbrella), but the total coverage for one employers liability claim would be only $10,100,000 ($100,000 primary plus $10,000,000 umbrella). If the umbrella policy included a $25,000 retention for coverages it provided on exposures not covered in the primary policies, the $10,000,000 coverage would apply above the $25,000 retention. Exhibit 13-3 illustrates the interaction of the primary and umbrella limits discussed above.

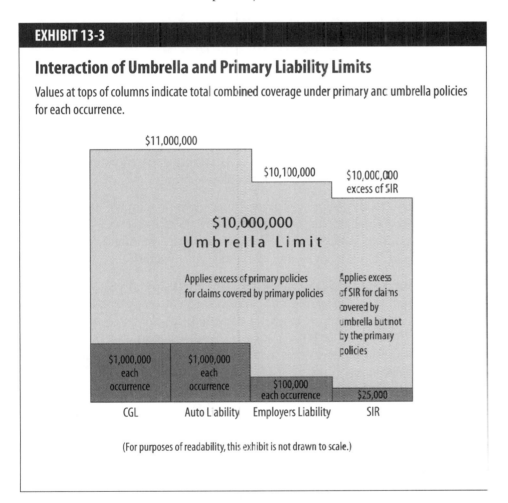

EXHIBIT 13-3

Interaction of Umbrella and Primary Liability Limits

Values at tops of columns indicate total combined coverage under primary and umbrella policies for each occurrence.

$11,000,000

$10,100,000

$10,000,000 excess of SIR

$10,000,000 Umbrella Limit

Applies excess of primary policies for claims covered by primary policies

Applies excess of SIR for claims covered by umbrella but not by the primary policies

$1,000,000 each occurrence

$1,000,000 each occurrence

$100,000 each occurrence

$25,000

CGL   Auto Liability   Employers Liability   SIR

(For purposes of readability, this exhibit is not drawn to scale.)

Aggregate Umbrella Limits

The previous example ignores any aggregate limit in the umbrella policy. Almost all umbrella policies now contain aggregate limits that operate like the aggregate limits in the primary insurance. In some cases, the aggregate limit applies to all claims under the umbrella; in other cases, the aggregate limit applies only to coverages that are subject to an aggregate in the underlying policies.

If the umbrella policy in the previous example included an aggregate limit, then the total available insurance would be reduced by payments on other claims payable by the umbrella policy. For example, assume that the umbrella policy described in the example had a $10,000,000 each occurrence limit *and a $10,000,000 aggregate limit.* Assuming also that no other claims had been paid by either policy, if a $3,000,000 premises liability claim was paid ($1,000,000 by the primary policy and $2,000,000 by the umbrella), only $9,000,000 would be available for the next covered claim—$1,000,000 (the balance of the underlying aggregate) from the primary policy and $8,000,000 (the balance of the umbrella aggregate) from the umbrella.

Broad Insuring Agreement

Many umbrella liability policies contain one comprehensive insuring agreement instead of several specific ones. A common approach is for the insurer to promise to pay the amount in excess of the underlying limit that the insured becomes legally obligated to pay as damages for bodily injury, property damage, personal injury, or advertising injury arising out of an occurrence to which the policy applies, subject, of course, to the umbrella policy's limit.

The definitions of bodily injury, property damage, personal injury, and advertising injury in an umbrella policy may differ from those in the underlying policies. For example, personal injury could be defined to include an offense, such as discrimination, that is not covered by the underlying insurance.

Some umbrella policies use two insuring agreements, often referred to as "A" and "B." In effect, these policies combine an excess policy and an umbrella policy in one policy. Insuring agreement A is an excess coverage applying over the underlying policies. Insuring agreement B applies to occurrences for which coverage is available under the umbrella but not in the underlying policies.

Occurrence and Claims-Made Coverage Triggers

Umbrella policies are usually occurrence forms. However, the underlying primary policies sometimes include both occurrence and claims-made coverages (such as a claims-made CGL policy and an occurrence-basis auto liability policy).

Gaps in coverage can occur when the umbrella or excess policy has a different coverage trigger than the underlying coverage. To avoid this problem, some insurers provide both occurrence and claims-made triggers in their umbrella policies. These policies provide that the trigger for the umbrella coverage will be the same as that used for the underlying coverage.

Exclusions

Like a CGL or an auto liability policy, an umbrella liability policy contains exclusions that restrict the broad coverage granted by the insuring agreement. Although the exclusions of umbrella policies resemble those found in underlying policies, there is usually some variation. In fact, much of the broadened coverage provided by umbrella liability policies is achieved by using exclusions in the umbrella policy that have narrower application than the exclusions of the underlying policies.

To illustrate, an umbrella policy might contain a watercraft exclusion that is stated not to apply to any watercraft, owned or nonowned, less than *fifty* feet long. In contrast, the watercraft exclusion of the underlying CGL coverage form is stated not to apply to nonowned watercraft less than *twenty-six* feet long. Consequently, the umbrella policy will provide drop-down coverage for owned boats less than fifty feet long and for nonowned boats between twenty-six and fifty feet long.

Another possibility is that the umbrella policy will contain an exclusion that does not exist in any of the underlying policies. For example, the umbrella policy may exclude claims for bodily injury arising from exposure to lead even though no such exclusion appears in the primary policy. In such a case, the umbrella policy provides narrower coverage than the underlying insurance for the particular exposure.

Conditions

The principal differences between the general conditions of primary liability policies and umbrella policies concern maintenance of underlying insurance and the coverage territory.

Maintenance of Underlying Insurance

The **maintenance of underlying insurance condition** obligates the insured to maintain all required underlying coverages in full force and effect during the policy period, except to the extent that their aggregate limits become reduced by payment of claims. The insured further agrees to notify the insurer promptly if any underlying policy is changed or replaced by a policy issued by another insurer.

Failure To Maintain Underlying Limits   If the underlying insurance is not maintained, the umbrella policy will apply as though the underlying insurance *had* been maintained. That is, a claim that would have been covered by an underlying policy, had it been kept in force, will only be covered for the amount that exceeds the limit of the underlying policy. The umbrella policy will not drop down to pay claims that would have been covered by the required underlying policy.

Concurrent Inception and Expiration   Umbrella and excess policies should have the same inception and expiration dates as the underlying policies. Policies that have the same inception and expiration dates are said to be "concurrent." This is important because the maintenance of underlying insurance provision often requires that the underlying insurance remain in full force except for reduction in the aggregate limit due to payments of claims arising out of occurrences *during the policy period.* The last four words

Maintenance of underlying insurance condition
A condition that obligates the insured of an umbrella liability policy to maintain all required underlying coverages in full force and effect during the policy period.

are italicized to emphasize a possible problem for insureds. If the policies are not concurrent, the aggregate limit in an underlying policy might be reduced by a claim occurring before the umbrella policy's inception date. In that event, the insured would not be in compliance with the maintenance of underlying insurance provision and would have a gap in coverage for subsequent claims.

To illustrate this point, assume that the insured has a CGL policy running from January 1, 2002, to January 1, 2003, with a $1,000,000 each occurrence limit and $2,000,000 aggregate limits. On March 1, 2001, the insured purchased a $5,000,000 umbrella policy that requires underlying CGL limits of $1,000,000 each occurrence and $2,000,000 aggregate. The CGL insurer made a payment of $600,000 to settle a claim occurring on February 1, 2002. On July 15, 2002, the collapse of an exterior wall of the insured's building seriously injured four pedestrians. Each of the resulting claims was settled for $750,000, for a total of $3,000,000. The primary CGL insurer would pay $1,400,000, which would exhaust its general aggregate limit because the insurer had already paid $600,000 to settle the earlier claim. The umbrella insurer would only pay $1,000,000 of the remaining $1,600,000 in damages because the insurer would calculate its payment as if the full $2,000,000 aggregate were available for losses in the year beginning March 1, 2001. The insured would be faced with an uninsured loss of $600,000.

If the policy periods of the primary and umbrella policies cannot be made concurrent, the insured's agent or broker should ask the umbrella insurer to endorse its policy to permit impairment of the aggregate limit in the underlying policy.

Coverage Territory

Most umbrella policies provide worldwide coverage, in contrast with the more limited coverage territories ordinarily found in primary policies. However, some umbrella policies require that suit be brought in the United States or Canada.

PROFESSIONAL LIABILITY INSURANCE

The word "profession" has historically been associated with occupations referred to as the learned professions—law, medicine, education, and the clergy—expanded in more recent times to include engineers and architects. It would therefore seem logical that "professional liability insurance" should refer to liability insurance for those professions, and in fact that was its original meaning and it is still used, in certain circumstances, to convey that meaning. However, as new liability exposures have evolved because of increased litigiousness, expansion of legal theories of liability accepted by the courts, and the proliferation of knowledge-based occupations, "professional liability insurance" is now available for more occupations than just those traditionally classified as professions. These additional occupations range from analytical chemists to veterinarians, the common thread being liability for the failure to use the degree of skill expected of a person in the particular field.[3]

Furthermore, **professional liability insurance** is now also used to describe coverages such as directors and officers liability, employment practices liability, and other coverages not included in CGL or commercial auto policies. Despite the seeming differences between these coverages and traditional professional liability policies, the similarities of policy terms and the techniques used in underwriting and marketing these new coverages have led to this grouping. In this text, unless the context specifically indicates otherwise, "professional liability" should be understood to refer to this broad range of coverages. Accordingly, the professional liability section of this chapter discusses not only the traditional types of professional liability policies covering doctors, lawyers, and other providers of professional services, but also the following types of policies:

- Directors and officers liability
- Employment practices liability
- Employee benefits liability
- Fiduciary liability

In part because of the broadening of the term "professional liability," these exposures are also known as "malpractice" or "errors and omissions." "Malpractice liability" is commonly used to describe liability in connection with occupations that involve contact with the human body, ranging from physicians to beauticians. "Errors and omissions liability" is more likely to be used to describe professional liability for occupations such as accounting, insurance production, law, and engineering. However, there is no consistent use of the terms, and in some cases they are used interchangeably. Professional liability, however, is generally understood to include all of these occupations.

Professional Liability Insurance for Specific Occupations

This section discusses the traditional type of professional liability insurance that is written for individuals or organizations engaged in particular professions or occupations. Because the liability exposures of one profession (such as medicine) may differ considerably from the liability exposures of another profession (such as engineering), insurers use different policies to insure each. In most cases, only a few insurers that specialize in a particular type of professional liability insurance write that type of insurance. Specialization is necessary to develop the skills required to successfully underwrite the risks and handle claims that differ from the more usual types.

Most professional liability insurance is written on forms independently developed by individual insurers as opposed to standard forms. The sections

Professional liability insurance
Insurance that covers persons engaged in various occupations against liability due to their rendering or failing to render professional services, exclusive of the exposures covered under their CGL policies; describes various other types of insurance such as directors and officers liability, employment practices liability, and fiduciary liability.

that follow first describe professional liability policies generally, in terms of their usual differences from CGL policies, and then describe the loss exposures and corresponding policy provisions for two specific occupations: physicians and insurance producers (agents and brokers).

Differences Between Professional Liability and CGL Policies

Many of the provisions in professional liability policies written to cover providers of professional services resemble those found in CGL policies; however, there are important differences. Four common differences concern the following issues: (1) use of a claims-made trigger, (2) consent-to-settle requirements, (3) selection of defense counsel, and (4) the use of deductibles.

Claims-Made Trigger

Many professional liability coverages develop "long-tail" claims—that is, claims that are presented long after the policy has expired. A classic case involves professional liability of obstetricians. In most states, a statute of limitations provides that claims are barred unless a lawsuit is filed within a specified period. For negligence claims, this period is often two years. In such states, most negligence claims are unenforceable unless suit is begun within two years after the date of the injury. However, the time limit does not begin to run until the injured person has reached majority (eighteen years in most states). Thus, it is not unusual for an obstetrician who is alleged to have negligently inflicted an injury on a newborn infant to be faced with a claim as many as twenty years later. The same pattern exists for other professions. For example, a building may collapse years after the architect prepared the allegedly deficient plans. Consequently, insurers prefer to use claims-made professional liability policies in order to avoid liability for such claims under policies that expire years before the claim is eventually submitted.

The claims-made approach was discussed in Chapter 9 in connection with the CGL policy. The primary difference between independently developed claims-made forms and the ISO claims-made CGL form is in the extended reporting period provisions. The ISO form automatically includes a basic extended reporting period that allows up to five years for the first making of a claim for injuries that occurred during the policy period. For an additional premium, the insured can purchase a supplemental extended reporting period that provides an unlimited time period to receive the claim for injuries that occurred during the policy period.

In contrast, the claims-made provisions found in independently developed professional liability policies sometimes do not contain any automatic extended reporting period. Any extended reporting period must usually be specifically requested and paid for, and few (if any) professional liability policies offer an *unlimited* extended reporting period; one to three years is more usual.

Consent to Settle

The CGL policy provides that the insurer may, at its discretion, settle any claim or suit; the insured is seldom involved in that decision and has no policy-given right to prevent a settlement that the insurer wants to make. In contrast, because professional or business reputations may be at stake in claims under professional liability policies, the insured frequently is given the right to participate in the decision to settle a claim in such policies.

The policy may provide that the insurer cannot settle a claim without the insured's consent. If the insured does not consent to settlement, the insurance company, at its expense, must then (unless the policy provides otherwise) continue to defend the insured and pay any judgment that the court may award.

More typically, professional liability policies provide that if the insured does not agree to a proposed settlement, the insured must take over the defense and pay any further defense expenses as well as the amount of any judgment or settlement that exceeds the amount for which the insurer could have settled the claim. This provision is sometimes informally referred to as a "hammer clause," because it usually compels the insured to agree to the settlement proposed by the insurer. To lessen the harshness of this provision, some policies provide that the insured and the insurer will share the additional defense and settlement costs that ensue when an insured refuses to consent to a settlement.

Selection of Defense Counsel

Under a CGL policy, the insurer selects and pays the attorneys that defend the insured against claims that would be covered by the policy. In contrast, some professional liability policies give the insured the right to select counsel, usually subject to the insurer's approval of the qualifications of the attorney selected by the insured. Some professional liability policies give the insured the option to assume the defense even though the policy otherwise provides that the insurer shall have the duty to defend.

Deductibles

Although CGL insurance is often written with a deductible or retention for larger insureds, most small to mid-size accounts have CGL coverage with no deductible. In contrast, professional liability insurance is usually subject to a deductible. Most professional liability insurers have mandatory minimum deductibles for their various classes of professional liability business, with higher deductibles as an option. The minimum deductible on a professional liability policy for a provider of professional services might range from $1,000 to $10,000 per claim. The minimum deductibles for directors and officers liability policies, employment practices liability policies, and fiduciary liability policies can range widely, depending on the insured's size and the insurer's marketing and underwriting strategies.

Classifications Requiring Professional Liability Exclusions on Their CGL Policies

Insurers routinely endorse their CGL policies to exclude professional liability when insuring persons or organizations that render certain professional services. The ISO *Commercial Lines Manual* requires the use of a professional liability exclusion for numerous occupations, some of which are listed below. Each of these occupations may have a need for professional liability insurance.

Ambulance services	Health or exercise clubs
Analytical chemists	Hearing aid stores*
Barber shops	Inspection or appraisal companies
Beauty parlors	Insurance agents
Blood banks	Insurance companies
Cemeteries	Laboratories—research, development, or testing
Computer manufacturers	
Cosmetic, hair, or skin preparation stores	Marine appraisers or surveyors
	Medical offices
Crematories	Medical or X-ray laboratories
Drugstores*	Optical goods stores*
Electronic data processing operations	Penal institutions
Engineers or architects	Saunas and baths
Fire departments	Tanning salons
Funeral homes or chapels	Tattoo parlors
Health-care facilities	Veterinarians or veterinary hospitals

* Professional services exclusion is not required for drugstores, hearing aid stores, and optical goods stores if products liability coverage is included.

Physicians Professional Liability

A physician's professional liability usually arises from improper performance in the practice of the profession that results in injury. A few of the medical errors that cause injury and can result in liability are as follows:

- Failure to properly diagnose a disease, resulting in more serious illness, disability, or even death
- Improper performance of a surgical procedure, causing injury to a patient
- Failure to warn a patient of the hazards involved in a course of treatment
- Leaving a surgical instrument or other foreign object in a patient following surgery

Physicians can also be held liable for administrative errors or omissions connected with their medical practice. For example, a physician who serves on a hospital's accreditation committee may be held liable for injury resulting from improperly refusing hospital staff privileges to another physician.

The insuring agreement in a typical physicians professional liability policy covers damages resulting from "providing or withholding professional services" by the insured or anyone else for whose acts the insured is legally responsible (such as a nurse working under the insured doctor's supervision). The insuring agreement also covers liability arising out of the insured's service on a formal accreditation board. The damages that the insurer will pay on behalf of the insured are not restricted to those for bodily injury or property damage. Damages for libel, slander, defamation, invasion of privacy, and similar offenses are generally covered by professional liability policies unless specifically excluded.

Insurance Agents and Brokers Errors and Omissions Liability

A few of the errors or omissions for which insurance agents or brokers have been held liable to their clients include the following:

- Failure to properly advise the client regarding his or her insurance needs
- Failure to obtain insurance for a client in a timely manner after agreeing to do so
- Failure to renew a policy at expiration without giving prior notice to the client
- Failure to properly advise the client regarding appropriate limits

Insurance producers can also become liable to the insurance companies they represent. For example, an agency that binds coverage that the insurance company has not authorized the agency to bind can be held liable to the insurer if any claims are made under the coverage.

Although there is no standard insurance agents and brokers errors and omissions liability policy, the policies issued by various insurers are similar. A typical policy agrees "to pay on behalf of the insured all sums that the insured becomes legally obligated to pay as damages . . . arising out of any negligent act, error or omission . . . in the conduct of the insured's business [as an insurance agent or broker]."

A policy exclusion makes it clear that the policy does not cover damages for bodily injury or damage to tangible property. For example, the policy would not cover a claim made by a pedestrian who tripped and fell on a poorly maintained sidewalk in front of the insured agent's office and sued the agent for damages. The policy may, however, pay damages indirectly related to either bodily injury or property damage. For example, an insurance agent's client might be sued for bodily injury resulting from an auto accident. If, because of the agent's negligence, the client does not have insurance to cover the damages and the client sues the agent for negligence, the agent's errors and omissions policy would pay the client's damages. The damages that the insurance agent would become legally obligated to pay would have resulted from the agent's negligent failure to procure insurance rather than from bodily injury.

Other Exclusions

Certain exclusions are common to most professional liability policies. For example, most policies exclude contractual liability, punitive damages, and the insured's dishonest, criminal, or malicious acts.

Professional liability policies for some professions contain specialized exclusions. For example, professional liability policies for lawyers and accountants may exclude liability arising from practice before the Securities and Exchange Commission. Insurance agents and brokers errors and omissions policies may exclude liability for failure to remit premium refunds or policy dividend payments to insureds.

Conflicts and Overlaps With the CGL Policy

As noted in the text box on page 13.16, ISO manual rules require that CGL policies issued to certain professionals contain a professional liability exclusion endorsement. Moreover, some professional liability policies exclude bodily injury and property damage. Nevertheless, coverage conflicts sometimes arise between CGL and professional liability insurers.

For example, if a patient falls off the examining table in a physician's office, is the cause of the accident defective maintenance of the examining table (probably covered by the physician's CGL policy)? Or is the cause of the accident the failure of the physician to monitor a patient suffering from vertigo (probably covered by the physician's professional liability policy)? In one such case, the court ordered both insurers to share the loss.[4]

The standard recommendation for avoiding such disputes is to obtain professional liability insurance and CGL coverage from the same insurer. However, that is often not possible, given the limited number of insurers writing professional liability insurance. When coverage has been placed with separate insurers, any claim with a possible overlap in coverage should be reported to both insurers. Investigation of the claim by the insurers may clarify whether it is a general liability or a professional liability claim.

Directors and Officers Liability Insurance

The directors of a computer manufacturing company were sued by a shareholder who alleged mismanagement when a new disk drive failed to achieve any substantial sales volume, resulting in a drop in the stock price. The claim was settled for $16 million. A major oil company and two of its senior executives were hit with a $69 million jury verdict in a wrongful termination lawsuit brought by two former officers.[5]

As these and hundreds of other cases show, the individuals who serve as the directors and officers of a corporation can be sued, as individuals, for breach of their corporate duties. Frequently, the plaintiffs are stockholders of the corporation, who may feel that they have been harmed financially by negligent management of the corporation. In other cases, the suit may be brought by employees of the corporation or by outsiders, such as customers or clients.

In recognition of the potentially devastating liability exposure faced by individual directors and officers, corporations usually agree to indemnify their directors and officers for the costs resulting from suits against them. The laws of several states permit or even require corporations to provide such indemnification to their directors and officers.

Thus, the directors and officers liability exposure affects both the individual directors and officers and the corporation itself. Many corporations protect themselves and their directors and officers against this exposure by purchasing **directors and officers (D&O) liability insurance**. There is no standard form for D&O liability insurance. Each insurer offering the coverage develops its own policy.

Because stockholders are the largest class of claimants, it is sometimes assumed that directors and officers liability insurance is not needed by corporations with no public stockholders (known as "closely held" corporations) or by nonprofit corporations. However, the Tillinghast-Towers Perrin *D&O Liability Survey* has shown, year after year, that more than half of all D&O claimants are not stockholders. Claimants can include employees, competitors, customers, and regulators.

Directors and officers (D&O) liability insurance
Insurance that covers a corporation's directors and officers against liability for their "wrongful acts" that would not be covered under a CGL or auto policy; also covers the sums that the insured corporation is required or permitted by law to pay to the directors and officers as indemnification.

Insuring Agreements

A D&O policy ordinarily contains two insuring agreements:

1. The first agreement covers the directors and officers of the insured corporation for their personal liability as directors or officers that results from a "wrongful act." "Wrongful act" is usually defined to include any breach of duty, neglect, error, misstatement, misleading statement, omission, or other act done or wrongfully attempted by the directors or officers.

2. The second insuring agreement, often referred to as company reimbursement coverage, covers the sums that the insured corporation is required or permitted by law to pay to the directors and officers as indemnification for suits alleging wrongful acts by directors or officers.

D&O insurance is written on a claims-made basis. The availability and terms of extended reporting periods vary among policies but generally are not as liberal as those of the ISO claims-made CGL policy. For example, some D&O policies allow the insured to purchase an extended reporting period (or "discovery period") only if the policy is canceled or not renewed by the insurer. Moreover, the discovery period is generally not more than three years.

Exclusions

Virtually all D&O policies exclude bodily injury and damage to tangible property. (As explained in Chapter 9, CGL insurance covers the directors and officers of the insured corporation against liability resulting from bodily injury or damage to tangible property.) D&O policies ordinarily exclude liability for pollution and nuclear hazards as well.

Other exclusions found in D&O policies eliminate coverage for claims made against directors or officers because of the following:

1. Libel or slander
2. Gaining any personal profit to which they were not legally entitled
3. Failure to effect or maintain adequate insurance for the corporation
4. Certain violations of the Securities Exchange Act
5. Acts of deliberate dishonesty
6. Liability under the Employee Retirement Income Security Act (ERISA)

Some of these exclusions can be eliminated or modified by negotiation with the insurer.

Other Provisions

The costs of defending against D&O suits are notoriously high. Although D&O policies usually cover the costs of defending against claims alleging loss covered by the policy, these costs are typically subject to policy limits instead of being payable in addition to policy limits as in standard CGL policies.

Deductibles

D&O policies are usually subject to both a flat deductible amount and a specified percentage of participation by the insured in all losses exceeding the retention. To illustrate, assume that KRE Corporation has a D&O liability policy with a $1 million limit, a $25,000 deductible, and a 5 percent participation. If KRE's insurer settles a covered D&O claim for $100,000, KRE and its insurer will pay the amounts shown below:

KRE will pay the deductible	=	$25,000
KRE will pay 5% of the remaining $75,000	=	$3,750
The insurer will pay 95% of $75,000	=	$71,250

A higher deductible often applies to the company reimbursement coverage than to the insuring agreement that covers the directors and officers directly.

Entity Coverage

When first developed, D&O policies were written in the name of the corporation, but the corporation was usually not an insured. The reimbursement coverage of a D&O policy written in that way will pay the corporation for payments it makes to indemnify its directors and officers.

However, if the corporation itself is named as a defendant in a covered suit, as occurred in the oil company case mentioned above, the insurer under such a policy will not defend the corporation or make any payment to settle claims against the corporation.

Many insurers now offer the option to include the corporation as an insured. This option is referred to as **entity coverage**. Because the corporation is often named as a defendant in a lawsuit alleging wrongful acts by the directors and officers, entity coverage can be a worthwhile extension of the D&O policy. However, there are disadvantages for the directors and officers. They will have to share the limits of liability with the corporation and, because of potential conflicts of interest, separate legal counsel may be required for the corporation, which would increase defense costs and reduce the limits available to pay claims when defense costs are payable within the limits. An even more difficult problem may be the danger that the entire policy—that is, 100 percent of the policy limits—may be attached by the bankruptcy trustee in the event of a corporate bankruptcy, leaving the directors and officers with no protection at all.

Entity coverage
Coverage extension of D&O liability policies for claims made directly against a corporation (the "entity") for wrongful acts.

D&O Coverage for Smaller Corporations and Nonprofits

D&O coverage was originally developed to meet the needs of the largest corporations. However, the growth of claims against all corporations has created a need for this coverage by entities of all sizes, including even small nonprofit organizations. Smaller corporations and nonprofit organizations often find that outside directors will not serve on their boards unless such coverage is provided. Policies written for smaller entities are similar to D&O policies written for large corporations except that policies for smaller entities are more frequently written to include the organization as an insured.

Employment Practices Liability Insurance

The growth of federal and state legislation dealing with employment discrimination and sexual harassment, the changing legal views on wrongful termination, and the increasing tendency of aggrieved parties to turn to the courts for settlement of such disputes have caused insurers to specifically exclude coverage for such employment-related claims from CGL policies. To fill this gap in coverage, insurers offer **employment practices liability (EPL) insurance**—sometimes called "employment-related practices liability insurance." [6]

Employment practices liability (EPL) insurance
Insurance that covers an organization, its directors and officers, and its employees against claims alleging damages because of wrongful employment practices such as sexual harassment, wrongful termination, and unlawful discrimination.

Although both ISO and AAIS have developed forms, most EPL policies are written by insurers using their own independently developed forms. Coverage typically applies to the insured's liability for wrongful employment practices. Definitions of wrongful employment practices vary from policy to policy, but generally include work-related acts such as the following:

- Sexual harassment
- Wrongful termination and wrongful failure to hire, promote, or grant tenure
- Wrongful demotion, reassignment, or discipline

- Unlawful discrimination against someone in a legally protected class
- Invasion of privacy
- Defamation
- Intentional infliction of emotional distress

Typical exclusions eliminate coverage for claims arising from labor disputes and collective bargaining; reorganization, downsizing, or closure of operations; violations of federal laws that establish fiduciary responsibilities for employers to their employees; and claims arising from the bankruptcy, insolvency, receivership, or liquidation of the employer.

EPL policies are usually written on a claims-made basis. Extended reporting periods of from one to three years are usually provided with an additional premium required to activate them.

In addition to damages paid for judgments or settlements, the cost of defense is covered, but it is often paid *within* (not in addition to) the limit of insurance.

The definition of "insured" in an EPL policy usually includes the corporation, its directors and officers, its employees, and, in most policies, its former employees. In some policies, coverage for employees applies only to managerial or supervisory employees.

Almost all policies require a minimum deductible, which generally ranges from $1,000 to $25,000, depending on various factors such as the number of employees, the type of business, and its geographic location.

Because smaller organizations seldom have the sophisticated human resources departments characteristic of larger enterprises, many insurers that write EPL coverage for smaller firms provide risk management assistance, often by third-party providers, without additional cost to their policyholders. These services can include an EPL risk management audit, toll-free telephone consultation and employee reporting line, specimen employee handbooks, and regional seminars on employment practices.

A coverage variation for smaller enterprises, particularly nonprofit and governmental organizations, is the combination of EPL coverage and D&O coverage in a single policy. This can result in a lower combined premium, but the EPL coverage in such combination policies is sometimes not as broad as that found in stand-alone policies, and separate limits are seldom provided. To provide protection for the employer in this type of policy, the policy must include entity coverage.

Employee Benefits Liability and Fiduciary Liability Insurance

Virtually all employers provide some noncash benefits as a part of the total compensation of their full-time employees. These employee benefits include health, life, and nonoccupational disability insurance; privately sponsored retirement plans; 401(k) plans; educational assistance plans; and others.

Two types of insurance—employee benefits liability insurance and fiduciary liability insurance—are the principal means of covering the liability exposures arising out of employee benefit plans.

Employee Benefits Liability Insurance

Employee benefits liability insurance covers an employer (and, in some policies, its employees who act on its behalf) against liability claims alleging improper advice or other errors or omissions in the administration of the employer's employee benefit plans. The coverage is usually provided in an endorsement to the employer's CGL policy. Examples of administrative errors include the following:

- Providing negligent advice on the selection of employee benefit programs
- Failing to enroll an employee in the employer's group health insurance program, with the result that the employee has no health insurance for a condition that would have been covered by the health insurance
- Improperly calculating a retiree's pension benefits, resulting in wrongful reduction of the retiree's retirement income

Employee benefits liability insurance is often written on an occurrence basis. This can cause a problem if the previous coverage was written on a claims-made form. An error that occurred in the prior period but was not reported until the new policy was in effect would not be covered under the new policy because the occurrence took place before policy inception. The error would not be covered under the previous policy unless an extended reporting period had been purchased when that policy terminated.

Fiduciary Liability Insurance

Providing employee benefits exposes the employer to liability under the common law and state and federal statutes. Under the common law, the employer (or professional adviser) has a duty to provide competent advice to employees regarding their choices among employee benefits. A person or an organization that breaches that duty can become liable for resulting damages.

The most comprehensive statute regarding employee benefits is the Employee Retirement Income Security Act (ERISA) of 1974. Among other things, ERISA imposes specific duties on all employee benefit plan "fiduciaries." ERISA defines as a fiduciary practically anyone whose role in employee benefits involves discretionary control or judgment in the design, administration, funding, or management of a benefit plan. (In a general sense, "fiduciary" is defined as someone who is bound by an agreement to act primarily for someone else's benefit.) A fiduciary who causes a loss to the plan by breaching the statutory duties can be held personally liable for the full amount of the loss. Moreover, the employer of the fiduciary can become vicariously liable for the loss.

In addition to facing claims for errors or omissions in carrying out their administrative duties, fiduciaries can be sued if they breach fiduciary duties involving discretionary judgment. An example of a duty involving discretionary

Employee benefits liability insurance
Insurance that covers an employer against liability claims alleging improper advice or other errors or omissions committed while administering the employer's employee benefit plans.

judgment is using due care in investing funds accumulated for an employee retirement income plan. If the plan's fiduciaries make negligent investment decisions and thus cause financial harm to the plan's participants, the participants can sue the fiduciaries. Employee benefits liability insurance does not cover liability for such discretionary judgment. **Fiduciary liability insurance** covers the exposure.

Fiduciary liability insurance
Insurance that covers the fiduciaries of an employee benefit plan against liability claims alleging breach of their fiduciary duties involving discretionary judgment.

Fiduciary liability policies also usually include coverage for administrative errors in the same manner as employee benefits liability coverage. However, many fiduciary liability policies do not include the corporation as an insured; coverage is restricted to the individual fiduciaries themselves. The corporation can sometimes be added as an insured to the fiduciary liability policy, in which case the employee benefits liability insurance coverage is duplicate insurance. Since the cost of employee benefits liability coverage is usually quite reasonable, some insureds maintain the duplicate coverage in order to obtain higher limits.

> ### Employee Benefits Versus Fiduciary Liability
>
> Employee benefits liability insurance and fiduciary liability insurance are often confused. The basic difference between them can be expressed as follows: employee benefits liability insurance covers administrative errors and omissions (such as failing to enroll an employee in a group health plan), whereas fiduciary liability insurance covers breach of fiduciary duties involving *discretionary* judgments (such as exercising poor judgment in investing funds).

AIRCRAFT INSURANCE

Aircraft insurance
Insurance that covers liability due to the insured's ownership, maintenance, or use of aircraft; physical damage to aircraft owned or used by the insured; and other aircraft loss exposures.

Aircraft insurance is purchased by a broad spectrum of insureds, ranging from the individuals who own and operate small planes for pleasure to the major airline companies that own and operate large fleets of aircraft. The purpose-of-use categories that insurers use to classify aircraft risks, shown in Exhibit 13-4, demonstrate the diverse risks covered by aircraft insurance.

Aircraft insurance in many ways resembles auto insurance. Like auto insurance, aircraft insurance policies are divided into physical damage and liability sections. Aircraft physical damage insurance is also referred to as "hull insurance," reflecting the marine insurance origins of aircraft insurance.

A fundamental difference between auto insurance and aircraft insurance is that pilots of insured aircraft must meet strict qualifications. In addition to holding both the appropriate license and current medical certification from the Federal Aviation Administration (FAA), the pilot is often required to have at least a specified number of hours of experience flying the type of aircraft insured.

EXHIBIT 13-4

Purpose-of-Use Categories

Category	Description
Airline	International, national, and regional air carriers.
Business and Pleasure	Individually owned aircraft used for owner's personal purposes with no charge made or direct profit derived from the aircraft's use.
Industrial Aid	Corporate-owned aircraft that are (1) used for transporting employees, associates, and executives and (2) flown by full-time professional pilots.
Commercial Use	Charter operators, air taxi operators, and other profit-seeking operators.
Special Use	Crop dusting, banner towing, law enforcement, pipeline patrol, hunting, etc.

In addition, except for policies covering airlines, aircraft policies cover only the plane or planes specifically described in the policy. Aircraft insurance policies written for general aviation risks (all classes of aircraft shown in Exhibit 13-4 other than airliners and military aircraft) usually have no counterpart to the "any auto" coverage provided by symbol 1 of the business auto policy.

Aircraft Hull Coverage

The two most common aircraft hull coverages are (1) "all risks—ground and flight" and (2) "all risks—not in motion."

All risks—ground and flight, the broader of the two, covers most causes of loss whether the plane is in flight or on the ground at the time of the loss.

All risks—not in motion covers the plane only when it is on the ground and not moving under its own power. Thus, coverage applies while the plane is being towed, because it is not moving under its own power. Coverage does not apply, however, while the plane is taxiing, since the plane is moving under its own power.

The principal exclusions that apply to "all-risks" aircraft hull coverage are as follows:

- Wear and tear
- Tire damage unless caused by theft, vandalism, or other physical damage covered by the policy
- Embezzlement or conversion by someone legally in possession of the aircraft (a lessee, for example)
- War

Some aircraft policies exclude losses on any aircraft whose FAA Airworthiness Certificate has become void or has been restricted.

Hull insurance on smaller aircraft is usually subject to a dollar deductible, either for a flat amount (such as $1,000) or for a stated percentage (such as 10 percent) of the plane's value. Some policies are written with a specified dollar deductible for ground coverage and a percentage deductible when the aircraft is in flight. Larger multi-engine aircraft are sometimes insured with no deductible since a deductible would not eliminate many claims; the cost to repair even minor damage to such planes can be thousands of dollars.

Aircraft Liability Coverage

Aircraft liability coverage protects the insured against third-party claims for bodily injury and property damage resulting from the ownership, maintenance, or use of insured aircraft. Separate limits of insurance usually apply to (1) bodily injury excluding passengers, (2) passenger bodily injury, and (3) property damage. Exhibit 13-5 shows how the limits might be expressed in a policy.

EXHIBIT 13-5

Aircraft Limits Illustration

• Bodily injury excluding passengers	$250,000 each person $500,000 each occurrence
• Passenger bodily injury	$250,000 each person $750,000 each occurrence
• Property damage	$500,000 each occurrence

Most insureds purchase all three coverages, but some insureds, such as cargo carriers, may not need passenger bodily injury coverage. Aircraft liability insurance can also be written with a single limit applying to all coverages.

Aircraft liability coverage typically excludes the following:

- Intentional injury, except to prevent interference with safe operations.
- Liability assumed under contract. However, some policies cover liability assumed under incidental contracts, such as a contract for use of an airport.
- Bodily injury to an employee of the insured.
- Obligations under workers compensation or similar laws.
- Damage to property owned, leased, occupied, controlled, or under the care of the insured. However, some policies provide basic limits of coverage for passengers' baggage or for damage to hangars leased by the insured.

Various provisions are included in, or can be added to, aircraft policies to cover the insured's potential liability arising out of aircraft not specifically described in the policy. Such provisions can cover newly acquired aircraft, temporary substitute aircraft, and other aircraft not owned, leased, or regularly used by the insured. For example, a sales representative might use his or her own plane to make calls on customers. The employer would need nonowned aircraft liability insurance just as it would need nonowned auto liability coverage if the salesperson used his or her own auto.

Other Aircraft Coverages

Aircraft liability insurance is often supplemented by medical payments coverage and passenger voluntary settlement coverage. These coverages provide a way to make prompt payments to injured persons and perhaps avoid liability claims that could be more costly.

Aircraft medical payments coverage is similar to the medical payments coverage available in auto policies. The coverage pays, regardless of the insured's legal liability, for reasonable medical or funeral expenses incurred by occupants of the insured aircraft.

Passenger voluntary settlement coverage, also commonly known as *admitted liability coverage*, is unique to aircraft insurance. It is normally available for industrial aid aircraft (see Exhibit 13-4). The coverage provides scheduled benefits if a passenger suffers death, dismemberment, or loss of sight. In order for benefits to become payable, both of the following actions must be taken:

1. The insured must ask the insurer to pay.
2. The claimant must release the insured from liability for all bodily injury caused by the accident.

ENVIRONMENTAL INSURANCE

The Resource Conservation and Recovery Act (RCRA) of 1976 included, among other provisions, a requirement that owners and operators of hazardous waste treatment, storage, and disposal facilities, municipal landfills, and petroleum storage tanks demonstrate financial responsibility to clean up environmental damage and compensate victims for bodily injury and property damage resulting from the release of contaminants. RCRA suggests insurance as a means of complying with this requirement. The Comprehensive Environmental Response, Compensation, and Liability Act of 1980, commonly called Superfund, imposed strict, unlimited liability on anyone involved as an owner, operator, or user of a toxic waste site. Other federal laws and legislation similar to RCRA and Superfund enacted in many states have expanded the need for environmental insurance.

Potential Loss Exposures Under Superfund Legislation

Ace Manufacturing Company disposed of its off-specification chemical materials in Joe's Dump between 1960 and 1970. Joe's Dump was licensed for this entire period by the state in which it is located under a law applicable to municipal solid waste disposal facilities. Ace had hired Sam's Sanitary Service to transport the hazardous waste material from Ace to Joe's Dump. In 1972, Joe sold his land to Wonder Products Incorporated. Wonder still owns the land but discontinued use of the landfill in 1980.

In 1984, the drinking water supply of a nearby municipality was found to be contaminated. Groundwater investigations determined that Joe's Dump was the source of the contamination. The cost to clean up, remediate, and reconstruct Joe's Dump is expected to be $30,000,000. Under CERCLA, the following parties are Potentially Responsible Parties (PRPs), subject to strict liability for the cleanup expenses:

- Joe's Dump as an owner/operator
- Ace Manufacturing Company as a waste generator
- Sam's Sanitary Service as a transporter to the site
- Wonder Products Incorporated as the current owner and a past operator of the site

All responsible parties face liability for the cleanup expenses. In this case, if Joe's Dump, Ace Manufacturing, Sam's Sanitary Service, and other PRPs were out of business at the time of the Superfund cleanup action, Wonder Products could be assessed the entire cleanup expense.

Because the comprehensive general liability policy in use in the 1970s and early 1980s excluded damage caused by sudden and accidental release of pollutants, insurers offered a new policy, titled Environmental Impairment Liability, to meet some of the needs of insureds. (The current CGL policy has an even more encompassing pollution exclusion, as discussed in Chapter 8.) From that beginning, **environmental insurance** has grown into a complex field including both first-party and third-party coverages. There is no standard environmental policy. In addition, many policies are individually negotiated so that even policies issued by the same insurer can differ from one another. Some common types of environmental insurance are briefly described below.

Environmental insurance
Insurance that covers the consequences of pollutants being released into the environment; includes a variety of first-party or third-party coverages.

- *First-party onsite cleanup coverage* covers the expense to clean up pollution on the insured's own premises. Generally, coverage is limited to previously unknown pollution, but some insurers offer coverage for (1) known pollution that was not thought to require remediation or (2) pollution that was remediated but is subsequently found to need further treatment.

- *Third-party environmental liability coverage* can cover claims for bodily injury and property damage occurring both onsite or offsite caused by pollution originating from the insured's premises, the release of contaminants during transportation, or pollution emanating from nonowned disposal sites.

- *Cleanup cost cap coverage* (also called *remediation stop-loss*) protects the insured against cost overruns in performing remediation of a contaminated site. The insurer agrees to pay the excess costs over a self-insured retention or deductible.

- *Contractors pollution liability coverage* insures contractors against liability for bodily injury and property damage arising out of remediation operations, environmental cleanup, and transportation of hazardous materials.

- *Environmental professional liability coverage* provides professional liability insurance for engineers, lawyers, consultants, laboratories, and others providing advice or services involving pollution. There is a demand for this type of coverage because almost all of the professional liability policies discussed in the previous section contain a pollution exclusion.

COVERAGE FOR FOREIGN OPERATIONS

Unlike homeowners policies, which usually provide worldwide coverage, commercial insurance policies, with only a few exceptions, restrict coverage to the United States, its territories and possessions, and Canada. Some of the exceptions are: ocean marine policies, which ordinarily provide worldwide coverage; CGL policies, which cover certain occurrences outside the covered territory if suit is instituted within the covered territory; and some other forms that offer minor coverage extensions for foreign operations. Despite these exceptions, standard policies leave insureds with foreign operations exposed to potentially serious coverage gaps.

Many countries require that certain forms of insurance be placed with local insurers. Large companies with extensive operations in foreign countries usually cover their exposures by obtaining the required local coverages and, in addition, carrying a master policy that provides primary coverage in countries that permit it and wraps around the required coverages in other countries, making coverage essentially uniform throughout the world.

At one time, small to mid-sized businesses in the United States did not have to concern themselves with foreign exposures, because they seldom had any foreign operations. Now, even relatively small firms do business around the world. See the text box for some examples of foreign loss exposures not covered by standard commercial policies.

To meet the needs of firms with foreign loss exposures, a number of insurers offer a variety of specialized coverages, including the following:

- Foreign property and business income
- Foreign liability
- Foreign supplemental and excess auto
- Foreign voluntary workers compensation and employers liability
- Foreign crime, including kidnap and ransom

Examples of Foreign Loss Exposures

- Fred, a sales representative for Computer Facilitators, Inc. (CFI), was at the end of a six-month assignment in Europe, when he injured a client by dropping his laptop computer on the client's foot. If the client sues for his injuries, CFI's CGL policy will not provide coverage, because Fred has been away from his home base within the covered territory for more than a "short time."

- Pierre, scalded while using a Hot Tubs, Ltd. (HTL), product in his home in Paris, obtained a judgment against HTL in France and then commenced a court action in the United States to collect the judgment. HTL's CGL insurer would not provide coverage because the original suit was not brought in the covered territory.

- Sue, an employee of Superior Engineering, Inc. (SPI), rented a car in a country where auto liability insurance does not apply to claims by passengers. Sue had an auto accident resulting in injuries to her passengers, and the car rental company's insurance did not cover either Sue's legal expenses to defend against the passengers' suit or pay the damages they were awarded. SPI's business auto policy would not cover the claims, because the accident occurred outside the covered territory.

- Elaine, an employee of Management Consultants (MC), contracted malaria while on temporary assignment in Southeast Asia for MC. The workers compensation law of Elaine's home state did not cover the expense of treating malaria, and consequently, MC's workers compensation policy did not cover the expense either.

- Ed, the CEO of an American corporation, was kidnapped and held for ransom while attending a conference in Europe. Although Ed's company had a crime insurance policy that included extortion, the extortion coverage did not apply because the kidnapping occurred outside the policy territory, which was limited to the United States, Puerto Rico, and Canada.

These coverages are similar to their domestic counterparts, although some are unique to foreign situations. For example, foreign voluntary workers compensation policies often include coverage for transportation expense to return disabled or deceased employees to the United States (referred to as "repatriation expense"). There are no standard forms for these coverages. Each insurer in this specialized market develops its own wordings.

SURETY BONDS

Surety bond
A written contract that expresses one party's promise to answer for another party's failure to do something as promised.

In its most fundamental form, suretyship represents the promise of one person (called the surety) to answer for the failure of another person (called the principal) to do something as promised. Suretyship, in this sense, has been used since the beginnings of civilization. Suretyship today is usually conducted by insurance companies and is evidenced by a written contract called a **surety bond**. Surety bonds are used to provide a wide range of guarantees.

Surety Bonds Contrasted With Insurance

Although there are many different types of surety bonds, they share four qualities that distinguish them from most property and liability insurance policies:

1. There are three parties to the contract.
2. The principal is liable to the surety for losses paid by the surety.
3. In theory, the surety should not sustain any losses on any surety contracts.
4. The coverage period is indefinite.

Three Parties

A surety bond is a contract that involves three parties—the surety, the obligee, and the principal. The **surety** (usually an insurance company) guarantees to the **obligee** that the **principal** will fulfill an obligation or perform as promised. For example, a surety could guarantee that a construction contractor (principal) will complete a building for a property owner (obligee) in accordance with the construction contract.

Principal Liable to Surety

If the principal fails to fulfill the obligation, the surety must either fulfill the obligation or indemnify the obligee. However, the principal becomes liable to the surety to the extent of the surety's expenditures. The surety bond, in other words, pays the obligee's loss, not the principal's, even though the principal pays the premium.

Surety Expects No Losses

Before issuing a surety bond, a surety examines the prospective principal's qualifications. A principal's qualifications are sometimes summed up as the "three Cs"—capital, capacity, and character:

1. *Capital.* Does the principal have sufficient funds and credit to finance the project and all other ongoing work?
2. *Capacity.* Does the principal have the skill, experience, staff, and equipment to execute the work successfully?
3. *Character.* Does the principal have a reputation for honoring agreements even when there are adverse developments?

At least in theory, no surety bond is issued unless the surety is satisfied that the principal is capable of performing the obligation that is the subject of the surety bond. In issuing a surety bond, the surety is attesting to the principal's ability to perform. In practice, sureties do sustain losses when a principal fails to perform and the principal does not have the funds to repay the surety. In some cases, the surety will require that the principal post collateral to make sure that the principal will be able to repay the surety if the surety has to perform on behalf of the principal.

Surety
The party (usually an insurer) to a surety bond that guarantees to the obligee that the principal will fulfill an obligation or perform as promised.

Obligee
The party to a surety bond that receives the surety's guarantee that the principal will fulfill an obligation or perform as promised.

Principal
The party to a surety bond whose obligation or performance the surety guarantees.

Indefinite Coverage Period

Surety bonds ordinarily do not terminate until the principal has fulfilled its obligations, which may take only a few days or as long as many years. Consequently, surety bonds are not issued as year-to-year contracts, and they normally do not allow either the surety or the principal to cancel them.

However, some types of surety bonds may be cancelable. Typically, bonds allowing cancellation require the surety to give notice of cancellation to the obligee. Cancellation becomes effective a certain number of days thereafter as stipulated in the bond itself or provided by law or regulation.

Other Characteristics of Surety Bonds

Other characteristics of surety bonds (which do not necessarily represent a contrast with property and liability insurance contracts) include the statutory nature of some surety bonds and the use of a limit.

Statutory Nature of Bonds

Many bonds are required by municipal ordinance or federal or state regulations or statutes. The provisions of these statutory bonds, and therefore the obligations of the three parties to the bond, are spelled out in the law. Other bonds are not required by statute. The need for a nonstatutory bond is usually established in the contract between the obligee and the principal. For example, a construction contract between a private owner and a contractor may require the contractor to obtain certain types of contract bonds.

Bond Limit

A bond is written for a set limit, sometimes called the "penalty." If the principal's obligation exceeds the limit, the surety will be liable only for the amount of the limit. However, like liability insurance policies, some bonds pay court costs and interest on judgments in addition to the stated limit. If the obligee's actual loss is less than the limit, most surety bonds provide only for the payment of the actual loss. Some surety bonds are issued on a forfeiture basis, meaning that the entire amount of the bond is paid if the principal defaults.

Types of Surety Bonds

There is no single form of bond suitable for the many circumstances that may require bonding. Surety bonds can be grouped into the following two broad categories: contract bonds and commercial surety bonds.

Contract Bonds

Contract bond
A surety bond guaranteeing the fulfillment of obligations under construction contracts or other types of contracts.

Contract bonds guarantee the fulfillment of contract obligations. In many cases, contract bonds relate to construction contracts. However, some contract bonds cover other types of contracts, such as a supplier's obligation to furnish supplies and materials for a certain period at an agreed price. The most common types of contract bonds are bid bonds, performance bonds, payment bonds, and maintenance bonds, which are described below and summarized in Exhibit 13-6.

Bid Bonds

Before awarding a supply or construction contract, the obligee may require a bid bond from each bidder. A **bid bond** guarantees that the bidder will actually enter into the contract at the price bid. If the principal fails to fulfill this obligation, the surety will pay the obligee the difference between the amount of the principal's bid and the bid finally accepted, plus any additional expenses incurred because of the contractor's default.

Bid bond
A contract bond guaranteeing that a contractor bidding on a construction or supply contract will actually enter into the contract at the price bid.

Performance Bonds

If awarded the contract, the principal must usually provide a performance bond. The **performance bond** guarantees the obligee that work will be completed in accordance with the contract. If the contractor defaults, the surety will be responsible for completing the work or paying damages to the obligee.

In some cases, a surety will find that its principal is in danger of defaulting before work actually comes to a standstill. Depending on the circumstances, the surety may take steps to help the contractor complete the work, such as lending money to the contractor, guaranteeing bank credit, or providing consultation services.

Performance bond
A contract bond guaranteeing that a contractor's work will be completed according to the contract.

Payment Bonds

Also called a labor and material bond, a **payment bond** guarantees that the contractor/principal will pay when due all of the labor and material bills arising out of the work that the contractor is obligated to perform. This guarantee is important to the owner because if subcontractors and suppliers are not paid, they may file liens against the owner's property, impairing the owner's title to the property. The payment guarantee is usually included in the contractor's performance bond but may be issued in a separate bond.

Payment bond
A contract bond guaranteeing that a contractor will pay when due all of the labor and material bills arising out of the work that the contractor is obligated to perform.

Maintenance Bonds

A **maintenance bond** guarantees the principal's work against defects in workmanship or materials for a specified period after the project is completed. Some performance bonds automatically include this coverage for one year without an additional charge.

Maintenance bond
A contract bond guaranteeing a contractor will correct defects in workmanship or replace defective materials for a specified period after project completion.

Commercial Surety Bonds

Commercial surety bonds can cover a broad spectrum of situations. The principal types of commercial surety bonds are (1) license and permit bonds, (2) public official bonds, (3) judicial bonds, and (4) federal surety bonds.

EXHIBIT 13-6

Contract Bond Comparison

	Obligee	Principal	Guarantee
Bid Bond	The owner or the party calling for the bid	The bidder	The bidder will enter into the contract and provide a performance bond if the bid is accepted.
Performance Bond	The property owner or the party having the work done	The contractor	The contract will be performed by the contractor according to plans and specifications.
Payment Bond	Same as performance bond	The contractor	The project will be free of liens—that is, certain bills for labor and materials will be paid.
Maintenance Bond	Same as performance bond	The contractor	The work will be free from defects in materials and workmanship for a specified period.

Adapted from *FC&S Bulletins,* Casualty & Surety volume, Surety B-1 (September 1990). Used with permission of the publisher, The National Underwriter Co., Erlanger, Ky.

License and Permit Bonds

License bond
A commercial surety bond guaranteeing that a licensee (such as a licensed plumber) will pay damages resulting from the licensee's violations of the duties and obligations imposed on the licensee.

Cities, states, and other political subdivisions often require persons or organizations wishing to engage in a particular business or trade to obtain a *license.* Similarly, a person or an organization wishing to exercise a particular privilege in connection with its business may be required to obtain a *permit.*

Before a license or permit is granted, the applicant is commonly required to obtain a license bond or a permit bond. A **license bond** provides payment to the obligee (the state, city, or other public entity) for loss or damage resulting from violations by the licensee of the duties and obligations imposed on the licensee. A **permit bond** serves the same purpose with respect to the duties and obligations imposed on a permit holder. For example, an operator of a liquor store may have to post a bond guaranteeing that it will not sell liquor in violation of alcoholic beverage control laws.

Permit bond
A commercial surety bond guaranteeing that a permit holder (such as a liquor store) will pay damages resulting from the permit holder's violations of the duties and obligations imposed on the license holder.

Public Official Bonds

Certain types of public officials are required by law to obtain bonds that protect the public against the official's failure to perform his or her duties faithfully and honestly. Officials generally required to obtain a **public official bond** are those whose duties involve the handling of public funds, the seizure and disposition of property, the arrest or detention of persons, or any other duties that could result in violation of the rights of others. Among the public officials required to be bonded are treasurers, tax collectors, sheriffs and deputies, police officers, judges and court clerks, notaries public, insurance commissioners, and bank examiners. In some cases, this bonding requirement can be met by the government crime form described in Chapter 5.

Public official bond
A commercial surety bond guaranteeing that a public official will perform his or her duties faithfully and honestly.

Judicial Bonds

A **judicial bond** is a statutory bond guaranteeing that a person or an organization will fulfill all obligations that the court or the law imposes on the person or organization. Judicial bonds are either fiduciary bonds or court bonds.

Judicial bond
A commercial surety bond guaranteeing that a person or an organization will fulfill all obligations that a court or the law has imposed on the person or organization.

Fiduciary Bonds
Fiduciary bonds are commonly required of persons selected or approved by courts to perform certain duties that involve holding property in trust for the benefit of others. For example, probate courts frequently appoint administrators to settle estates of deceased persons who died without wills, to appoint guardians of minors, and to appoint conservators of estates of incompetent persons. A person who is appointed to any of these positions by a court is required to post a fiduciary bond with the court. The bond guarantees that the principal will faithfully perform all duties as prescribed by law or as specified by the court.

Fiduciary bond
A judicial bond guaranteeing that persons selected or approved by courts will perform certain duties involving holding property in trust for the benefit of others.

Court Bonds
Court bonds are often required by courts in connection with lawsuits. For example, if a defendant wishes to appeal an adverse court decision, he or she must provide an appeal bond guaranteeing that the judgment will be paid if the appeal is unsuccessful. (Paying for such a bond in connection with a covered claim is part of the supplemental coverages in a CGL policy and many other liability policies.)

Court bond
A judicial bond guaranteeing that defendants or plaintiffs will perform as required by courts in connection with lawsuits.

Court bonds are also required in connection with disputes over the ownership of personal property. As an illustration, A might ask the court to compel B to return property that A claims belongs to A. The court will likely require both A and B to post court bonds until the case is decided. A's bond will guarantee that A will pay B any damages resulting from this action if it is decided in B's favor. B's bond will guarantee that B will turn the property over to A if the case is decided in A's favor.

Federal Surety Bonds

Federal surety bonds include bonds required by federal agencies that regulate activities such as immigration, the manufacture or distribution of alcohol and tobacco products, and importing and exporting. Because these bonds pose special risks, sureties often require the principal to post cash collateral in connection with the bond.

Federal surety bond
A bond guaranteeing that regulated parties will perform according to federal laws or regulations.

SUMMARY

Most organizations need higher limits of liability insurance than those normally provided by their CGL, commercial auto, and other primary liability policies. An excess liability policy or an umbrella liability policy can provide the higher limits. Both types of policies pay damages that exceed the per occurrence or aggregate limits of underlying policies. An umbrella policy may also cover, subject to a self-insured retention, claims that are not covered under any of the insured's primary policies.

Various policies are available for covering special exposures not insured under the more common forms of commercial insurance. By industry usage, many of these policies are referred to as professional liability insurance even though only a few apply to the traditional professions, and some, such as directors and officers liability and employment practices liability, seem only remotely related to professional liability.

Professional liability policies cover liability for the failure to use the degree of skill expected of a person in a particular field. Physicians, lawyers, architects, engineers, insurance agents and brokers, and persons and organizations engaged in many other occupations need these policies.

Directors and officers liability policies cover corporate directors and officers against their personal liability for wrongful acts in the scope of their corporate duties. D&O liability insurance also covers the corporation for all sums it is required or permitted by law to pay as indemnification of its directors and officers. Entity coverage, which includes the corporation as an insured, is also available under D&O policies.

Employment practices liability insurance covers an employer and its employees against claims alleging various employment-related offenses such as wrongful termination, sexual harassment, and discrimination.

Employee benefits liability insurance covers the employer (and in some cases the employees acting on its behalf) against liability for *administrative* errors and omissions (such as failing to enroll an employee in a plan). It is typically provided by an endorsement to a CGL policy.

Fiduciary liability insurance covers plan fiduciaries against liability for doing harm to employee benefit plans through *discretionary* errors and omissions in handling plan funds (such as investing plan assets unwisely).

An aircraft insurance policy can include the following coverages:

- Hull (physical damage) insurance, covering the insured aircraft on an "all-risks" basis for either "ground and flight" or "not in motion."
- Liability insurance, covering liability for bodily injury and property damage resulting from the ownership, maintenance, or use of the insured aircraft.
- Aircraft medical payments insurance, covering medical or funeral expenses incurred by occupants of the insured aircraft.

- Passenger voluntary settlement coverage, providing scheduled benefits if a passenger suffers death, dismemberment, or loss of sight.

Environmental insurance can cover (1) the cost to clean up the insured's own property and (2) liability arising from the discharge or dispersal of pollutants. It can also protect the insured against cost overruns in a cleanup of known pollutants, cover pollution liability of contractors, and provide environmental professional liability coverage for those who provide advice or services in connection with pollution.

Firms that operate outside the coverage territory, as defined in standard commercial policies, need insurance for their foreign exposures. The coverages are similar to those provided by standard policies, although there are some that are unique to foreign exposures.

In a surety bond, the surety (which is usually an insurance company) guarantees to the obligee that the principal will fulfill an obligation or perform as promised. If the principal does not perform as promised, the surety must fulfill the obligation or indemnify the obligee.

The major categories of surety bonds are contract bonds and commercial surety bonds. Contract bonds include bid, performance, and payment bonds. Major classes of commercial surety bonds are (1) license and permit bonds, (2) public official bonds, (3) judicial bonds, and (4) federal surety bonds.

CHAPTER NOTES

1. Margaret Cronin Fisk, "Big Gets Bigger: Despite 2000 Slump, Juries Remain Bullish," *National Law Journal*, February 19, 2001.

2. Howard Platzman, ed., *Limits of Liability 2001* (New York: Marsh, Inc.), p. 5.

3. "Professional Liability and Claims Made Coverage" (St. Paul, Minn.: St. Paul Fire and Marine Ins. Co., Rev. 6-94), p. 1.

4. American Casualty Company v. Hartford Insurance Company, 479 So.2d 577 (1985), cited by Westchester Chapter CPCU Research Committee, Jerome Trupin, chairman, in "Problems with Personal Injury Liability Insurance for Professionals" (Malvern, Pa.: CPCU Society, 1990), p. 11.

5. "CNA: The D&O Market," *Viewpoint* (Chicago: CNA Insurance Companies, Fourth Quarter, 1992), p. 10.

6. Much of this section is derived from information in the annual survey of Employment Practices Liability Insurance by Richard Betterley published in *The Betterley Report* (Sterling, Mass.: Betterley Risk Consultants, Inc.).

Index

Page references in boldface refer to definitions of key words or phrases.

Page references in italics refer to exhibits.

Abbreviations

ACV	Actual cash value
BIC	Business income coverage form
BPP	Building and Personal Property Coverage Form
CGL	Commercial General Liability
CLM	*Commercial Lines Manual*
CPP	Commercial package policy
D&O	Directors and officers
policy	liability policy
DIC	Difference in conditions
EBI	Extended business income
EDP	Electronic data processing
EPL	Employment practices liability
FCIC	Federal Crop Insurance Corporation
F.O.B.	Free on board
HPR	Highly protected risk
HSB	Hartford Steam Boiler Group
ISO	Insurance Services Office
MPCI	Multiple Peril Crop Insurance
MPL	Maximum possible loss
NCCI	National Council on Compensation Insurance
P&I	Protection and indemnity
PEO	Professional employer organization
PIP	Personal injury protection
PML	Probable maximum loss
RCRA	Resource Conservation and Recovery Act of 1976
SAA	Surety Association of America
SIR	Self–insured retention
WC&EL policy	Workers Compensation and Employers Liability Policy

A

ACV, building and, 2.27

Abandonment condition, BPP, **2.20**

Accident, duties in event of, Business Auto Section IV condition, 10.24

Accounting or arithmetical errors or omissions, inside and outside the premises commercial crime exclusion, 5.20

Accounts Receivable Coverage Form, **7.17**

Acts committed by you, your partners or your members, commercial crime exclusion, 5.18

Acts of employees, managers, directors, trustees or representatives, commercial crime exclusion, 5.18

Actual cash value (ACV), **2.23**

Additional conditions, BPP, 2.24–2.25

Additional coverage—collapse
  broad form, 3.10
  special form, 3.14

Additional coverages
  BIC, 4.9–4.12
  BPP, 2.12–2.15

Admitted liability coverage, aircraft, 13.27

Aggregate excess insurance, **12.13**

Aggregate limits
  CGL, 9.7
  property versus liability insurance and, 13.4
  umbrella liability policy and, 13.9–13.10

Agreed value coverage option, **4.20**

Agreed value option
  BPP deductible and, 2.20
  combining blanket insurance with, 2.32

Agreed value optional coverage, BPP, **2.26**

Agribusiness, insurance for, 11.17

Aircraft
  basic form coverage of, 3.5–3.6
  CGL Coverage A exclusion of, 8.18–8.19

Aircraft hull coverage, 13.25–13.26

Aircraft insurance, 1.9, **13.24**

Aircraft liability coverage, 13.26–13.27

All other like perils, hull insurance and, 7.22

"All-risks"
  inland marine insurance as, 7.8
  ocean cargo policies as, 7.21

Alteration, **5.10**. *See also* Forgery or alteration.

Alterations and new buildings, BIC and, 4.10–4.11

Ammonia contamination, equipment breakdown limit of insurance, 6.13

Animal mortality insurance, **11.21–11.22**

Annual transit policy, **7.11**

Antennas, BIC exclusion, 4.13

Any auto, Symbol 1, Business Auto Section I, 10.7

Apartment buildings, BOP and, 11.5

Appraisal, BIC loss condition, 4.14

Appraisal condition, BPP, **2.20**

Appraisal for physical damage losses, Business Auto Section IV condition, 10.23–10.24

Assigned risk plans, workers compensation and, 12.12

Assignment, WC&EL policy Part Six condition, 12.24

Auto, **8.18**
  CGL Coverage A exclusion of, 8.18–8.19
  mobile equipment versus, 8.19–8.20

Auto dealers, Garage Coverage Form and, 10.29

Auto insurance, commercial, 1.7

Auto medical payments coverage, **10.27**

Auto no-fault laws, **10.6**

Auto service operations, Garage Coverage Form and, 10.29

Automobile loss exposures, 10.3–10.6

"Average," marine term of, 7.21

Avoidance, **1.4**

B

BIC, 4.7–4.20
    rating, 4.24
BOP, 11.3–11.17
    commercial property insurance and, 2.3–2.4
    eligibility for, 11.4–11.7
    forms, 11.7–11.15
    rating, 11.15–11.17
BPP
    BIC finished stock exclusion and, 4.13
    equipment breakdown and, 6.3
    maximum limits for additional coverages and coverage extensions, 2.19
    valuation provision, 2.23
Bailee, **7.6**
    business auto loss exposures of, 10.5–10.6
    insurance for, 7.14
    no benefit to
        Business Auto Section IV condition, 10.25
        commercial property clause, 3.27
Bailees' customers policy, **7.14**
Bailment, **7.6**
    financial effect of loss and, 7.8
Bailor, **7.6**
Bankers blanket bond, 5.28
Bankruptcy
    Business Auto Section IV condition, 10.25
    CGL condition, 9.10
Barns, Outbuildings and Other Farm Structures Coverage Form, 11.19
Barratry, hull insurance and, 7.22
Basic causes of loss, ISO farm program, 11.20
Basic form. See Causes of Loss—Basic Form.
Benefit administration, workers compensation, 12.6–12.8
Benefits, workers compensation statutes, 12.4–12.8
Bid bond, **13.33**
Bill of lading, **7.5**
Blanket insurance, **2.30**
    advantages of, 2.31–2.32
    combining agreed value option with, 2.32
Bobtail and deadhead coverage, **10.35**

Bodily injury, CGL definition of, **8.11**
Boiler explosion, illustration of, 6.6
Boiler and machinery insurance. See Equipment breakdown insurance.
Bonds, types of, 13.32–13.35
Brands and labels, equipment breakdown insuring agreement, 6.11
Brands and Labels Endorsement, **3.23**
Breach of contract, **8.6**
Breakdown, **6.5**
Broad causes of loss, ISO farm program, 11.20
Broad form. See Causes of Loss—Broad Form.
Brokers, errors and omissions liability of, 13.17–13.18
Builders Risk Coverage Form, **3.15**
Builders risk policy, **7.10**
Building
    BIC and, 4.10–4.11
    BPP definition of, **2.8**
    vacancy of, 2.22–2.23
Building coverage, Condominium Association Coverage Form, 3.19
Building and Personal Property Coverage Form (BPP), **2.8**
Burglary, **5.27**
Business auto conditions (Section IV), 10.23–10.27
Business auto coverage, garage liability versus, 10.30
Business Auto Coverage Form, **10.6**
    Motor Carrier Coverage Form versus, 10.35–10.36
Business classes, CGL endorsements for, 9.18
Business income, **4.8**
Business income coverage forms, 4.7–4.20
    ISO farm program, 11.19
    period of restoration and, 4.8
Business income and extra expense BOP, 11.10
    equipment breakdown, 6.8–6.9
Business Income (and Extra Expense) Coverage Form, **4.7**
Business Income (Without Extra Expense) Coverage Form, **4.7**
Business Income Changes—Educational Institutions Endorsement, BIC, 4.23
Business income from dependent properties, BIC and, 4.21–4.22
Business Income From Dependent Properties—Broad Form, BIC and, 4.22

Business Income From Dependent Properties—Limited Form, BIC and, 4.22
Business income insurance, 1.6, **4.3**
Business income losses
    measurement of, 4.4–4.5
    property and perils and, 4.6–4.7
Business Income Premium Adjustment Endorsement, BIC, 4.23
Business interruption, changes in expenses during, 4.5–4.6
Business personal property, Condominium Association Coverage Form, 3.19
Business use, commercial auto rating factor, 10.38
Businessowners insurance, 1.7–1.8
Businessowners policy (BOP), **11.3**
Businessowners property loss, example of, 11.12–11.13

C

CGL
    BOP versus, 11.13–11.15
    garage liability versus, 10.30
    professional liability conflicts and overlaps with, 13.18
    professional liability policies versus, 13.14–13.16
CGL coverage, rating, 9.19–9.22
CGL coverage form, claims-made, 9.14–9.17
CGL insurance, 1.7
CGL limits of insurance
    application of, 9.8–9.9
    illustration of, 9.6
CGL policy, overview of, 8.9–8.10
CLM, **3.30**
    classification table in, 9.19
CPP, **1.10**
    BOP rating versus, *11.16*
    components of, *1.11*
Camera and Musical Instrument Dealers Coverage Form, **7.15**
Cancellation
    CPP conditions, 1.12–1.13
    WC&EL policy Part Six condition, 12.24
Cancellation as to any employee, commercial crime condition, 5.9
Care, custody, or control, Business Auto Section II exclusion of, 10.17

Cargo, freight and, 7.18
Cargo insurance, 7.19–7.21
Carriers of goods, 7.5–7.6
Catastrophic loss, commercial property insurance and, 3.24–3.25
Causes of loss
    Builders Risk Coverage Form, 3.16
    commercial property rating and, 3.31
    hull insurance, 7.22
    inland marine insurance, 7.8
    ocean cargo policies, 7.21
Causes of Loss—Basic Form, **3.4**
Causes of Loss—Broad Form, **3.9**
Causes of Loss—Special Form, **3.11**
Causes-of-loss form, **2.7**, 3.3–3.15
    BIC exclusions in, 4.12
    ISO farm program, 11.19–11.20
Certificate of insurance, **9.20**
Certificate of liability insurance, ACORD example of, *9.21*
Civil authority additional coverage, **4.10**
Civil commotion, basic form coverage of, 3.6
Civil law, **8.4**
Claims
    CGL insured's duties in event of, 9.10–9.11
    duties in event of, Business Auto Section IV condition, 10.24
    workers compensation, 12.6–12.8
Claims provisions, crime policy, 5.24–5.25
Claims-made CGL coverage form, 9.14–9.17
Claims-made coverage forms, non-ISO, 9.17
Claims-made coverage trigger, **9.15**
    CGL versus professional liability and, 13.14
    umbrella liability policy, 13.10
Class code, **9.19**
Class rating, **3.34**
Classification endorsements, CGL, 9.18
Classifications, rating workers compensation insurance and, 12.27–12.28
Coinsurance
    agreed value optional coverage and, 2.26
    BIC, 4.16–4.18
    BOP provision for no, 11.8–11.9
    BPP deductible and, 2.20
    blanket insurance requirement of, 2.31

commercial property rating and, 3.31
    example of, *2.24*
    payroll and, 4.22
Coinsurance clause, BPP, **2.24**
Coinsurance provision, equipment breakdown, 6.9
Collapse
    broad form coverage of, 3.10
    special form coverage of, 3.14
Collapse during construction, Builders Risk Coverage Form, 3.16
Collision coverage, Business Auto Section III, **10.20**
Collision liability clause, hull policy, **7.23**
Commercial Articles Coverage Form, **7.15**
Commercial auto insurance, 1.7
    rating, 10.36–10.39
Commercial bailments, 7.6
Commercial Crime Coverage Form, 5.4
Commercial crime form endorsements, 5.27
Commercial crime insurance, **5.3**
Commercial crime program, ISO, 5.4–5.27
Commercial general liability (CGL) insurance, 1.7, **8.3**
Commercial general liability (CGL) policy, overview of, 8.9–8.10
Commercial inland marine coverage forms, 7.15–7.17
Commercial insurance, **1.3**
    lines of business in, 1.5–1.9
Commercial insurance policies, 1.9–1.15
Commercial Lines Manual (CLM), **3.30**
    rating filed classes and, 7.17
Commercial package policy (CPP), **1.10**
Commercial Property Conditions, **2.7**, 3.25–3.29
Commercial property coverage, rating, 3.29–3.34
Commercial property coverage form, **2.7**
Commercial property coverage part, CPP, **2.5**
Commercial property declarations page, **2.5**
    example of, *2.6*
Commercial property forms, 3.15–3.21
    equipment breakdown and, 6.12
Commercial property insurance, 1.6, **2.3**

Commercial surety bonds, 13.33–13.35
Common carriers, **7.5**
    Motor Carrier Form and, 10.34
Common "dec" page. *See* Common policy declarations.
Common law, bailment and, 7.9
Common Policy Conditions, CPP, **1.12**
Common policy declarations, CPP, **1.10**
Communication, instrumentalities of, 7.7, 7.14
Competitive state fund, **12.12**
Completed operations, Business Auto Section II exclusion of, 10.18
Completed operations liability exposure, **8.8**
Comprehensive coverage, Business Auto Section III, **10.20**
Comprehensive Environmental Response, Compensation, and Liability Act of 1980 (Superfund), 13.27
Computer fraud coverage, **5.15**
Computer media, equipment breakdown definition exclusion of, 6.14
Concealment, **3.26**
Concealment, misrepresentation, or fraud, Business Auto Section IV condition, 10.25
Conditions
    additional, BPP, 2.24–2.25
    CGL, 9.9–9.14
    commercial crime form, 5.8–5.9
    commercial property, 3.25–3.29
    crime policy, 5.21–5.25
    equipment breakdown insurance, 6.14–6.18
    Garage Form Section V, 10.34
    umbrella liability policy, 13.11–13.12
    WC&EL policy Part Six, 12.23–12.24
Condominium Association Coverage Form, **3.19**
Condominium Commercial Unit-Owners Coverage Form, **3.20**
Condominium coverage forms, 3.18–3.21
Consent to settle, CGL versus professional liability and, 13.15
Consequential loss, equipment breakdown limit of insurance, 6.13–6.14
Consolidation—merger, crime policy condition, 5.22

Construction
 collapse during, Builders Risk Coverage Form, 3.16
 commercial property premiums and, 3.32–3.33
 increased cost of, 2.15
Contingent business income and extra expense, equipment breakdown insuring agreement, 6.11
Contingent business income and extra expense coverage, **6.11**
Continuing expenses, **4.5**
 BIC loss determination and, 4.16
Contraband, insurability of, 7.11
Contract, **8.6**
 bailment and, 7.9
 insured, 8.15
 liability assumed under, business auto, 10.5
Contract bond, **13.32**
 comparison of types of, *13.34*
Contract carriers, **7.5**
 Motor Carrier Form and, 10.34
Contractors
 BOP and, 11.5
 independent, 12.8–12.9
Contractors equipment floater, **7.10**
Contractual liability, **8.7**
 Business Auto Section II exclusion of, 10.15–10.16
 CGL Coverage A exclusion of, 8.14–8.16
Contribution by equal shares, **9.12**
Contribution by limits, **9.12**
COPE factors, commercial property premiums and, 3.32
Counterfeit paper currency. *See* Money orders and counterfeit paper currency.
Court bond, **13.35**
Coverage A—Bodily Injury and Property Damage Liability, CGL, 8.10–8.24
Coverage B—Personal and Advertising Injury Liability, CGL, 8.25–8.28
Coverage C—Medical Payments, CGL, 8.29–8.30
Coverage E—Scheduled Farm Personal Property, 11.18
Coverage F—Unscheduled Farm Personal Property, 11.18–11.19
Coverage extensions
 BPP, 2.15–2.18
 Builders Risk Coverage Form, 3.16
 Business Auto Section II, 10.14–10.15

Inside the Premises—Robbery or Safe Burglary of Other Property, 5.14
 special form, 3.14–3.15
Coverage forms, business income, 4.7–4.20
Coverage part, CPP, **1.14**
Coverage period, crime policy condition, 5.22–5.24
Coverage symbols, Business Auto, **10.7**
Coverage territory
 Business Auto Section IV condition, 10.26–10.27
 CGL Coverage A, 8.12–8.13
 commercial property condition, 3.29
 crime policy condition, 5.22
 umbrella liability policy, 13.12
Coverage triggers, umbrella liability policy, 13.10
Coverages
 Business Auto Section III, 10.20–10.22
 duplicate, Business Auto Section IV condition, 10.27
Covered autos
 Business auto schedule of, *10.9*
 Business Auto Section I, 10.7–10.10
 description of coverage symbols of, *10.11*
 Garage Form Section I, 10.30
Covered equipment
 covered property versus, 6.7
 equipment breakdown, **6.5**
Covered property, covered equipment versus, 6.7
Crime, definition of, 5.3
Crime coverages, typical, 5.17
Crime forms, government, 5.26
Crime insurance, 1.6
Crime policy conditions, 5.21–5.25
Criminal law, **8.4**
Crop hail insurance, **11.21**
Custodian, **5.13**

D

D&O liability insurance, 13.19–13.21
DIC policy, 7.13
Damage to premises rented to you limit, CGL, **9.8**
Damage to your product, CGL Coverage A exclusion of, 8.22

Damage to your work, CGL Coverage A exclusion of, 8.22
Damages, insurer's duty to pay, CGL Coverage A, 8.10–8.13
Data, equipment breakdown definition of, 6.14
Data and media, equipment breakdown limit of insurance, 6.14
Dealers, inland marine insurance and, 7.7
Dealers' autos, Garage Form Section IV, 10.33
Death benefits, 12.6
Debris removal
 BPP additional coverage of, 2.13
 equipment breakdown policies and, 6.14
Debris removal losses, examples of, 2.14
"Dec" page. *See* Common policy declarations.
Declarations, Commercial Crime Coverage Part, 5.5
Declarations page, commercial property coverage part, example of, 2.6
Deductibles
 BPP, 2.18–2.20
 Business Auto Section III, 10.23
 CGL versus professional liability and, 13.15
 commercial property rating and, 3.31
 D&O policy, 13.20
 equipment breakdown insurance, 6.16–6.17
 WC&EL policy and, 12.29–12.30
Defense costs, hold harmless agreement and, 8.15
Defense counsel, CGL versus professional liability and, 13.15
Definitions, Garage Form Section V, 10.34
Delay, BIC exclusion, 4.13
Dependent property exposures, **4.22**
Difference in conditions (DIC) policy, **7.13**
Directors and officers (D&O) liability insurance, **13.19**
Disability income benefits, workers compensation, 12.5–12.6
Discovery form, **5.4**
 ISO crime policy, 5.23
Dividend plans, WC&EL policy and, 12.30
Drop-down coverage, **13.6**

Duties after loss, crime policy condition, 5.24

Duties in the event of accident, claim, suit, or loss, Business Auto Section IV condition, 10.24

Duties in the event of loss, BIC loss condition, 4.14

Duties in the event of loss or damage, BPP loss condition, 2.21

Duty to defend, Business Auto Section II, 10.13

Duty to pay "covered pollution cost or expense," Business Auto Section II, 10.12–10.13

Duty to pay damages, Business Auto Section II, 10.12

E

E&O
equipment breakdown insuring agreement, 6.11
professional liability as, 13.13

E&O coverage, **6.11**

E&O liability, insurance agents and brokers, 13.17–13.18

EBI, 4.11

EBI additional coverage, extended period of indemnity coverage and, 4.20

EBI coverage, BIC delay exclusion and, 4.13

EDP floater, 7.13–7.14

EPL insurance, 13.21–13.22

Each occurrence limit, CGL, **9.8**

Earth movement, basic form exclusion of, 3.7

Earthquake and volcanic eruption coverage, 3.24–3.25

Electronic data processing (EDP) equipment floater, 7.13

Electronic media and records, BIC loss condition, 4.14–4.15

Employee, **12.8**
commercial crime definition of, 5.6–5.7
leased and temporary, 12.9

Employee benefit plans, commercial crime condition, 5.9

Employee benefits liability insurance, **13.23**

Employee canceled under prior insurance, employee theft exclusion, 5.19

Employee dishonesty, employee theft versus, 5.7

Employee dishonesty insurance, 5.28

Employee indemnification, Business Auto Section II exclusion of, 10.16

Employee theft
employee dishonesty versus, 5.7
employers' losses from, 5.3
exclusions, 5.19–5.20
underinsured losses and, 5.9–5.10

Employee theft coverage, **5.6**

Employees
CGL coverage of, 9.4
workers compensation in foreign countries and, 12.11
workers compensation and pre-existing disabilities of, 12.7

Employers liability
Business Auto Section II exclusion of, 10.16
CGL Coverage A exclusion of, 8.16

Employers liability insurance. See also Workers compensation and employers liability insurance.
WC&EL policy Part Two, 12.19–12.22
workers compensation and, 1.8

Employers mutual insurance company, **12.13**

Employers' mutuals, workers compensation and, 12.12

Employers nonownership liability, **10.5**

Employment practices liability (EPL) insurance, 13.**21**

Endorsements
BIC, 4.21–4.23
BPP, Peak Season Limit of Insurance Endorsement, 2.29–2.30
Business Auto Coverage Form, 10.27–10.29
CGL, 9.17–9.19
commercial property coverage and, 2.7, 3.21–3.25
ISO crime policy, 5.25–5.27
WC&EL policy, 12.25–12.26

Entity coverage, D&O policy, **13.21**

Environmental insurance, 1.9, 13.**28**

Equipment
contractors, 7.10
examples of movable, 7.7

Equipment and accessories, inside and outside the premises commercial crime exclusion, 5.20–5.21

Equipment breakdown, commercial property forms and, 6.12

Equipment breakdown insurance, 1.6–1.7, **6.3**

Equipment Breakdown Protection Coverage Form, 6.4

Equipment Dealers Coverage Form, **7.15**

Errors and omissions
equipment breakdown insuring agreement, 6.11
professional liability as, 13.13

Errors and omissions (E&O) coverage, **6.11**

Errors and omissions liability, insurance agents and brokers, 13.17–13.18

Examination of books and records, CPP conditions, 1.13

Excess insurance
CGL as, 9.11–9.12
workers compensation and, 12.13–12.14

Excess liability insurance, 13.3–13.12

Excess liability policy, **13.5**

Excess and umbrella liability insurance, 1.8

Exchanges or purchases, inside and outside the premises commercial crime exclusion, 5.20

Exclusion endorsements, CGL, 9.18

Exclusions
BIC, 4.12–4.14
basic form, 3.7–3.9
Business Auto
Section II, 10.15–10.19
Section III, 10.22–10.23
CGL
Coverage A, 8.14–8.24
Coverage B, 8.26–8.28
Coverage C, 8.30
commercial crime, 5.18–5.21
D&O policy, 13.20
employee theft, 5.19–5.20
equipment breakdown insurance, 6.11–6.12
Garage Form Section IV, 10.33
inside the premises and outside the premises, 5.20–5.21
physical damage, Motor Carrier Form, 10.36
professional liability policies, 13.18
special form, 3.11–3.14
umbrella liability policy, 13.10–13.11
WC&EL policy Part Two, 12.20–12.21

Exclusive (monopolistic) state fund, **12.13**

Expected or intended injury
  Business Auto Section II exclusion
    of, 10.15
  CGL Coverage A exclusion of, 8.14
Expediting expenses coverage, equipment breakdown insuring agreement, 6.8
Expense constant, **12.29**
Expenses, business interruption and 4.5–4.6
Expenses to reduce loss, **4.10**
Experience modification, **12.28**
Experience rating plan, **12.28**
Explosion
  basic form coverage of, 3.5
  pressure vessel, 6.7–6.8
Exposure
  commercial property premiums and, 3.33
  loss, **1.4**
Exposures
  inland marine, 7.4–7.9
  ocean marine, 7.18–7.19
  sources of liability, 8.7–8.9
Extended business income (EBI) additional coverage, **4.11**
Extended period to discover loss, **5.23**
Extended period of indemnity coverage option, **4.20**
Extended reporting period, **9.16**
Extra expense coverage, **4.9**
  BOP, 11.10
  ISO farm program, 11.19
  period of restoration and, 4.8
Extra Expense Coverage Form, **4.21**
Extra expenses, **4.5**

F

FCIC, 11.21
F.O.B. (free on board), 7.6
Faithful performance of duty, government crime forms, 5.26
Falling objects, broad form coverage of, 3.9
Farm Dwellings, Appurtenant Structures and Household Personal Property Coverage Form, 11.18
Farm inland marine coverage, 11.20
Farm insurance, 1.8, 11.17–11.22
Farm Liability Coverage Form, 11.21

Farm Personal Property Coverage Form, 11.18–11.19
Farm program (ISO), 11.18–11.21
Farmowners policy, **11.17**
Fast-food restaurants, BOP and, 11.5–11.6
Federal Crop Insurance Corporation (FCIC), 11.21
Federal Employers' Liability Act, 12.11
Federal surety bond, **13.35**
Fellow employee, Business Auto Section II exclusion of, 10.16–10.17
Fidelity bond, 5.28
Fiduciary bond, **13.35**
Fiduciary liability insurance, **13.24**
Filed classes, inland marine business, 7.9
Filed inland marine coverage, 7.15–7.17
  rating, 7.17–7.18
Film Coverage Form, **7.16**
Financial institution bond, **5.28**
Finished stock, BIC exclusion, 4.12–4.13
Fire
  basic form coverage of, 3.4
  inside and outside the premises commercial crime exclusion, 5.20
  lightning, earthquake, hull insurance and, 7.22
Fire department service charge, BPP additional coverage of, 2.13
Fire legal liability coverage, **8.24**
Fire protection, commercial property premiums and, 3.33
Floater, 7.10
Flood, basic form exclusion of, 3.8
Flood coverage, 3.24
Floor Plan Coverage Form, **7.16**
Foreign operations, insurance for, 13.29–13.30
Forgery, **5.10**
Forgery or alteration, commercial crime insuring agreement, 5.10–5.11
4-H Club, animal mortality insurance and, 11.22
Fraud, 3.25–3.26
  Business Auto Section IV condition, 10.25
Freight, **7.18**
Functional building, BPP endorsement for, 2.27–2.28
Functional replacement cost, **2.28**
Fund Transfer Fraud Endorsement, commercial crime, 5.17

G

Garage Coverage Form, **10.29**
Garagekeepers coverage (Section III), 10.31–10.32
Garagekeepers direct access option, **10.32**
Garagekeepers direct primary option, **10.32**
Garagekeepers insurance, **10.31**
General aggregate limit, CGL, **9.7**
General average, **7.21**
General damages, CGL coverage of, 8.11
General section, WC&EL policy, 12.18
Glass, broad form coverage of, 3.10
Governing classification, rating workers compensation insurance and, 12.27
Government crime forms, 5.26
Governmental action
  basic form exclusion of, 3.7
  commercial crime exclusion, 5.18

H

HPR insurance, **3.21**
  commercial property insurance and, 2.3–2.4
Hail
  basic form coverage of, 3.5
  crop hail insurance, 11.21
Hartford Steam Boiler Group (HSB), 6.3–6.4
Hazardous substance, equipment breakdown limit of insurance, 6.13
Hired autos, business auto liability and, 10.5
Hired autos only, Symbol 8, Business Auto Section I, 10.8
Hired and nonowned liability coverage, BOP and, 11.15
Hold harmless agreement, **8.7**
  defense costs and, 8.15
Home-based businesses, BOP and, 11.7
Homeowners policies, BOP and, 11.3
Hull coverage, aircraft, 13.25–13.26
Hull insurance, **7.21**
Hull policies, 7.22–7.23

I

Improvements and betterments, **2.9**
Increased cost of construction, BPP additional coverage of, 2.15
Indemnification condition, government crime forms, 5.26
Independent contractor, **12.8**
Indirect loss, commercial crime exclusion, 5.18
Inflation guard optional coverage, BPP, **2.26**
Information page, WC&EL policy, 12.16–12.17
Injury outside the United States or Canada, WC&EL policy Part Two exclusion, 12.21
Inland marine coverage, ISO farm program, 11.20
Inland marine insurance, 1.7, **7.5**
    commercial property insurance and, 2.3–2.4
    development of, 7.3–7.4
    policies of, 7.9–7.18
Inland marine loss exposures, 7.4–7.9
Inside the premises, exclusions, 5.20–5.21
Inside the Premises—Robbery or Safe Burglary of Other Property, commercial crime insuring agreement, 5.12–5.14
Inside the Premises—Theft of Money and Securities, commercial crime insuring agreement, 5.11–5.12
Inspection, WC&EL policy Part Six condition, 12.24
Inspections, equipment breakdown insurance, 6.18
Inspections and surveys, CPP conditions, 1.13–1.14
Installation floater, **7.11**
Instrumentalities of communication, inland marine insurance and, 7.7, 7.14
Instrumentalities of transportation, inland marine insurance and, 7.7, 7.14
Insurance
    risk management technique of, 1.3–1.5
    surety bond versus, 13.31
Insurance agents, errors and omissions liability of, 13.17–13.18

Insurance for highly protected risks (HPR), **3.21**
Insured
    Business Auto Section II, 10.13–10.14
    CGL, 9.3–9.6
    workers compensation, 12.8–12.11
Insured contract
    Business Auto and, 10.15
    CGL definition of, **8.15**
Insureds, Builders Risk Coverage Form, 3.15
Insuring agreements
    BIC, 4.7–4.8
    CGL
        Coverage A, 8.10–8.14
        Coverage B, 8.25–8.26
        Coverage C, 8.29–8.30
    commercial crime form, 5.4–5.17
    D&O policy, 13.19
    equipment breakdown insurance, 6.4–6.11
    umbrella liability policy, 13.10
    WC&EL policy Part Two, 12.19–12.20
Intangible property, insurance classification of, 2.4
Intentional tort, **3.6**
Interests insured, crime policy conditions, 5.22
Inventory shortages, employee theft exclusion, 5.19
ISO
    Business Auto Coverage Form, **10.6**
    CGL policy, overview of, 8.9–8.10
    CLM
        classification table in, 9.19
        rating filed classes and, 7.17
    commercial crime program, 5.4–5.27
    commercial inland marine coverage forms, 7.15–7.17
    commercial package policy program, 1.10–1.15
    program, components of, *1.11*
    commercial property coverage part and, 2.4
    Equipment Breakdown Protection Coverage Form, 6.4
    farm program, 11.18–11.21
    Garage Coverage Form, **10.29**
ISO/Surety Association of America (SAA) commercial crime program, 5.25

J

Janitor, custodian versus, 5.13
Jewelers Block Coverage Form, **7.16**
Jewelers block policy, 7.7
Joint insured, crime policy condition, 5.22
Joint or disputed loss agreement, equipment breakdown condition, **6.18**
Jones Act, **12.10**
Judgment rating, **7.18**
Judicial bond, **13.35**
Jurisdictional inspection provision, equipment breakdown insurance, 6.18

L

LHWCA, 12.10
Large deductible plan, 12.30
Law, civil and criminal, 8.4–8.5
Laws, workers compensation, 12.3–12.15
Layering, property versus liability insurance and, 13.4
Leased employees, 12.9
Legal action against insurer
    Business Auto Section IV condition, 10.24
    commercial property condition, 3.26–3.27
Legal action against us, CGL condition, 9.11
Legal expenses, commercial crime exclusion, 5.18
Legal liability, **8.4**
Legal representatives, CGL coverage of, 9.5
Liability
    carriers of goods and, 7.5–7.6
    legal, 8.4–8.7
Liability assumed under contract, WC&EL policy Part Two exclusion, 12.21
Liability coverage
    aircraft, 13.26–13.27
    BOP versus CGL, 11.13–11.15
    Business Auto Section II, 10.10–10.20
    Garage Form Section II, 10.30–10.31
    ISO farm program, 11.21

Liability coverage agreement, Business Auto Section II, 10.12–10.13

Liability coverage forms, miscellaneous, 9.22–9.24

Liability coverage options, BOP, 11.15

Liability insurance
excess and umbrella, 13.3–13.12
professional, 13.12–13.24

Liability loss, **8.3**

Liability loss exposure, **1.4**, 8.3–8.9
business auto, 10.4–10.6

Liability policies, primary and excess, illustration of, *13.6*

Liberalization
Business Auto Section IV condition, 10.25
commercial property clause, 3.27

License bond, **13.34**

Lightning, basic form coverage of, 3.4

Limit of insurance
Business Auto
Section II, 10.19–10.20
Section III, 10.23
commercial property rating and, 3.31
employee theft insuring agreement, 5.8
Inside the Premises—Robbery or Safe Burglary of Other Property, 5.14

Limits
aircraft liability insurance, 13.26
umbrella liability policy and, 13.7–13.9

Limits of insurance
BIC, 4.14
BPP, 2.18
CGL, 9.6–9.9
equipment breakdown, 6.13–6.14

Limits of liability
BOP versus CGL, 11.14
WC&EL policy Part Two, 12.21–12.22

Line of business, **1.5**

Liquor liability, CGL Coverage A exclusion of, 8.16

Liquor Liability Coverage Form, **9.22**

Livestock Coverage Form, 11.20

Loading or unloading, **8.18**

Location, commercial property premiums and, 3.33

Longshore and Harbor Workers' Compensation Act, United States (LHWCA), **12.10**

Long-term policy, WC&EL policy Part Six condition, 12.24

Loss
duties in event of, Business Auto Section IV condition, 10.24
examples of equipment breakdown, 6.4
financial effects of, 7.8–7.9
hull policy coverage of, 7.23
indirect, commercial crime exclusion, 5.18
marine term of "average" and, 7.21

Loss assessment coverage, **3.21**

Loss conditions
BIC, 4.14–4.16
BPP, 2.20–2.23

Loss control, **1.4**

Loss costs, **3.30**

Loss Covered Under This Insurance and Prior Insurance Issued by Us or Any Affiliate, crime policy condition, 5.24

Loss determination, BIC loss condition, 4.15–4.16

Loss exposure, **1.4**

Loss exposures
automobile, 10.3–10.6
business income, 4.4–4.7
examples of foreign, 13.30
inland marine, 7.4–7.9
liability, 8.3–8.9
ocean marine, 7.18–7.19
sources of liability, 8.7–8.9
Superfund, 13.28

Loss of privilege, BIC exclusion, 4.13–4.14

Loss payment, BPP loss condition, 2.21–2.22

Loss payment—physical damage coverage, Business Auto Section IV condition, 10.24–10.25

Loss Sustained During Prior Insurance, crime policy condition, 5.23

Loss sustained form, **5.4**
crime policy, 5.23

Loss of use expenses, Business Auto Section III, **10.21**

M

MPCI, **11.21**

MPL, 13.3–13.4

Mail Coverage Form, **7.16**

"Main Street" businesses, BOP and, 11.4–11.5

"Maintenance and cure," LHWCA and, 12.10

Maintenance bond, **13.33**

Maintenance of underlying insurance condition, **13.11**

Malpractice, professional liability as, 13.13

Manual rating, judgment rating versus, 7.18

Manufacturer's Selling Price (Finished Stock Only) Endorsement, BIC finished stock exclusion and, 4.13

Manufacturers' Consequential Loss Assumption Endorsement, **3.23**

Marine insurance, **7.3**
inland, 1.7
ocean, 1.7, 7.19–7.24

Maximum period of indemnity coverage option, **4.19**

Maximum possible loss (MPL), **13.3**

Medical benefits, workers compensation, 12.5

Medical expense limit, CGL, **9.8**

Medical payments coverage, aircraft, 13.27

Merchant Marine Act of 1920, United States (Jones Act), 12.10

Merger, crime policy condition, 5.22

Merit rating factor, WC&EL policy and, 12.29

Messenger, **5.14**

Miscellaneous real property coverage, **3.21**

Misrepresentation, **3.25**
Business Auto Section IV condition, 10.25

Mobile Agricultural Machinery and Equipment Coverage Form, 11.20

Mobile equipment, **8.19**
CGL Coverage A exclusion of, 8.19–8.20

Mobile equipment operators, CGL coverage of, 9.5

Money operated devices, inside and outside the premises commercial crime exclusion, 5.20

Money orders and counterfeit paper currency, commercial crime insuring agreement, 5.16–5.17

"Money," "securities," and "other property," employee theft insuring agreement, 5.7–5.8

Monoline policy, **1.10**

Monopolistic state fund, **12.13**

Monthly limit of indemnity coverage option, **4.19**

Moral hazard, market value of buildings and, 2.27–2.28

Morale hazard, market value of buildings and, 2.27–2.28

Mortgageholder, BPP condition, 2.25

Motor carrier, CLM eligibility of, 10.34–10.35

Motor Carrier Coverage Form, **10.34**

Motor truck cargo liability policy, **7.12**

Motor vehicles, inside and outside the premises commercial crime exclusion, 5.20

Movable equipment, inland marine insurance and, 7.7

Multiple Peril Crop Insurance (MPCI), **11.21**

Mutual insurer, employers', 12.13

N

NCCI
    rating workers compensation insurance and, 12.26
    WC&EL policy and, 12.15

Named insured
    Business Auto Section II, 10.13–10.14
    CGL, 9.3–9.4

Nationwide Marine Definition, **7.4**

Need for Adequate Insurance condition, Builders Risk Coverage Form, 3.17

Negligence, **8.5**

Net income, **4.4**

Net loss, **4.4**

Newly acquired autos, Business Auto coverage of, 10.10

Newly acquired or constructed property extension, BPP, 2.16

Newly acquired locations, 4.11–4.12

Newly acquired organizations, CGL coverage of, 9.5–9.6

Newly acquired premises, equipment breakdown insuring agreement, 6.10

No benefit to bailee, commercial property clause, 3.27

No benefit to bailee—physical damage insurance only, Business Auto Section IV condition, 10.25

No coinsurance, BOP provision, 11.8–11.9

No-fault, workers compensation insurance as, 12.4

No-fault laws, auto, 10.6

Noncontinuing expenses, **4.5**

Nonfiled classes, inland marine business, **7.9**

Nonfiled inland marine coverages, 7.9–7.14

Noninsurance transfer, **1.5**

Nonowned autos only, Symbol 9, Business Auto Section I, 10.9

Non-owned detached trailers extension, BPP, 2.17–2.18

Nonprofit corporations, D&O coverage for, 13.21

Nonprofit organizations, business income insurance for, 4.7

Non-zone rated vehicles, 10.38

Nuclear, commercial crime exclusion, 5.19

Nuclear hazard, basic form exclusion of, 3.7

O

Obligee, **13.31**

Occupancies, eligible, BOP, 11.6

Occupancy, commercial property premiums and, 3.33

Occurrence, **8.12**
    CGL insured's duties in event of, 9.10–9.11

Occurrence CGL coverage form, claims-made form versus, 9.14

Occurrence coverage trigger
    CGL, 8.13
    umbrella liability policy, 13.10

Ocean marine exposures, 7.18–7.19

Ocean marine insurance, 1.7, **7.19**
    inland marine versus, 7.3
    policies of, 7.19–7.24
    rating, 7.24

Off-premises services interruption, BIC exclusion, 4.12

Offense, CGL insured's duties in event of, 9.10–9.11

Office buildings, BOP and, 11.5

Open cargo policy, **7.19**

Operations
    BIC definition of, 4.8
    BIC loss determination and, 4.15
    Business Auto Section II exclusion of, 10.18
    ineligible, BOP, 11.6

Operations liability exposure, **8.8**

Optional coverages
    BIC, 4.18–4.20
    BPP, 2.25–2.27

Ordinance or law
    basic form exclusion of, 3.7
    equipment breakdown insuring agreement, 6.10

Ordinance or Law Coverage Endorsement, **3.22**

Ordinance or Law—Increased Period of Restoration Endorsement, **4.23**

Ordinary Payroll Limitation or Exclusion Endorsement, **4.22**

Organizations, CGL coverage of, 9.5–9.6

Other consequential losses, BIC exclusion, 4.14

Other insurance
    Business Auto Section IV condition, 10.25–10.26
    CGL condition, 9.11
    commercial property clause, 3.27–3.28
    crime policy condition, 5.25

Other states insurance (WC&EL policy Part Three), **12.22**

Outdoor property extension, BPP, 2.17–2.18

Out-of-state coverage extensions, Business Auto Section II, 10.14–10.15

Outside the premises
    commercial crime insuring agreement, 5.14–5.15
    exclusions, 5.20–5.21

Owned autos, business auto liability and, 10.4

Owned autos only, Symbol 2, Business Auto Section I, 10.8

Owned autos other than private passenger autos, Symbol 4, Business Auto Section I, 10.8

Owned autos subject to a compulsory uninsured motorists law, Symbol 6, Business Auto Section I, 10.8

Owned autos subject to no-fault, Symbol 5, Business Auto Section I, 10.8

Owned private passenger autos only, Symbol 3, Business Auto Section I, 10.8

Owner-operators, Motor Carrier Form and, **10.35**

Owners and Contractors Protective Liability Coverage Form, **9.23**

Ownership of property, crime policy condition, 5.22

P

P&I insurance, 7.24
PEO, 12.9
PML, BIC coinsurance and, 4.18
Package modification factors, CPP, 1.15
Package policy, **1.10**
Particular average, **7.21**
Passenger voluntary settlement coverage, aircraft, 13.27
Payment bond, **13.33**
Payroll
  rating workers compensation insurance and, 12.27–12.28
  WC&EL policy Part Five and, 12.23
Peak Season Limit of Insurance Endorsement, BPP, **2.29**
Performance bond, **13.33**
Perils, business income losses and, 4.6–4.7
Perils covered, BOP, 11.8
Perils of the seas, **7.22**
Period of restoration, **4.8**
  BIC coinsurance and, 4.19
  buildings and, 4.11
  equipment breakdown and, 6.8
  ordinances or laws and, 4.23
Permanent partial disability, **12.5**
Permanent total disability, **12.5**
Permit bond, **13.34**
Personal and advertising injury, **8.25**
  CGL Coverage A exclusion of, 8.24
Personal and advertising injury limit, CGL, **9.7**
Personal effects and property of others extension, BPP, 2.16–2.17
Personal injury protection (PIP) coverage, **10.27**
Personal property
  BOP and, 11.4–11.5
  BPP endorsement for, 2.27–2.28
  insurance classification of, 2.4
  insuring fluctuating value of, 2.28
Personal property of others
  BPP definition of, **2.10**
  BPP extension of replacement cost, 2.27
Physical damage, loss payment, Business Auto Section IV condition, 10.24–10.25

Physical damage coverage
  Business Auto Section III, 10.20–10.23
  Garage Form Section IV, 10.33
Physical damage exclusion, Motor Carrier Form, 10.36
Physical damage losses, appraisal for, Business Auto Section IV condition, 10.23–10.24
Physicians professional liability, 13.16–13.17
Physicians and Surgeons Equipment Coverage Form, **7.15**
Policies
  commercial insurance, 1.9–1.15
  commercial property coverage, 2.3–2.5
Policy changes, CPP conditions, 1.13
Policy period
  Business Auto Section IV condition, 10.26–10.27
  commercial property condition, 3.29
  umbrella liability policy, 13.11–13.12
Pollutant cleanup and removal, BPP additional coverage of, 2.15
Pollution
  Business Auto Section II exclusion of, 10.19
  CGL Coverage A exclusion of, 8.16–8.17
Pollution liability coverage forms, 9.23–9.24
Pools, workers compensation and, 12.14–12.15
Power, Heat, and Refrigeration Deduction Endorsement, **4.23**
Pre-existing disabilities, workers compensation and, 12.7
Premises liability exposure, **8.8**
Premium adjustments, WC&EL rating and, 12.28–12.30
Premium audit
  Business Auto Section IV condition, 10.26
  CGL condition, 9.13
Premium base, **9.19**
  CGL, 9.20–9.22
Premium discount, WC&EL rating and, 12.29
Premiums
  CPP conditions, 1.14
  commercial auto rating, 10.38
  commercial property factors affecting, 3.32

rating workers compensation insurance and, 12.26–12.27
Value Reporting Form and, 2.29
WC&EL policy Part Five, 12.23
Preservation of property, BPP additional coverage of, 2.13
Pressure vessel, explosion of, 6.7–6.8
Primary insurance, CGL as, 9.12
Primary rating factors, commercial auto insurance, 10.37–10.38
Principal, **13.31**
Private carriers, **7.5**
  Motor Carrier Form and, 10.34
Private insurance, workers compensation and, 12.12
Private passenger vehicles, rating, 10.36–10.37
Probable maximum loss (PML), **4.18**
Products liability exposure, **8.8**
Products-completed operations aggregate limit, CGL, **9.7**
Products-completed operations hazard, CGL, **9.7**
Products/Completed Operations Liability Coverage Form, **9.23**
Professional liability, BOP versus CGL, 11.14
Professional liability insurance, 1.9, 13.12–13.24
  definition of, **13.13**
Profit, **4.4**
Proof of loss, **2.21**
Property
  BPP coverage of, 2.8
  bailment and, 7.6
  Builders Risk Coverage Form, 3.15–3.16
  business income losses and, 4.6–4.7
  control of, commercial property condition, 3.26
  damage to, CGL Coverage A exclusion of, 8.20–8.22
  financial effects of loss of, 7.8
  handling of, Business Auto Section II exclusion of, 10.17–10.18
  hull insurance valuation of, 7.23
  impaired, CGL Coverage A exclusion of, 8.22–8.23
  inland marine insurance and, 7.5–7.6
  movement of by mechanical device, Business Auto Section II exclusion of, 10.18
  open cargo valuation of, 7.20
  ownership of, crime policy condition, 5.22

preservation of, 2.13
rating filed inland marine coverage
    for, 7.17
recovered, BPP loss condition, 2.22
transfer or surrender of, inside and
    outside the premises commer-
    cial crime exclusion, 5.21
types of, 2.4–2.5
types of dealers of, 7.7
unusual, inland marine insurance
    and, 7.7
voluntary parting with title to or
    possession of, inside and out-
    side the premises commercial
    crime exclusion, 5.21
Property coverages, BOP, 11.8–11.12
Property covered, Condominium Com-
    mercial Unit–Owners Coverage
    Form, 3.20
Property damage
    CGL definition of, **8.11**
    equipment breakdown insuring
        agreement, 6.6–6.8
Property exposures, dependent, 4.22
Property insurance, liability insurance
    versus, 13.3–13.4
Property loss (businessowners), ex-
    ample of, 11.12–11.13
Property loss exposure, **1.4**
Property loss exposures
    business auto, 10.3–10.4
    MPL and, 13.3–13.4
Property losses, criminal acts and, 5.3
Property not covered
    BOP, 11.9
    BPP, 2.10–2.12
Property off-premises extension, BPP,
    2.17
Property in transit, special form cover-
    age of, 3.14–3.15
Protection and indemnity (P&I) insur-
    ance, **7.24**
Public official bond, **13.35**
Public policy, contraband and, 7.11
Punitive damages, CGL coverage of,
    8.11
Purpose-of-use categories, aircraft
    insurance, 13.25

R

RCRA, 13.27
Racing, Business Auto Section II
    exclusion of, 10.19

Radius class, commercial auto rating
    factor, 10.38
Railroad protective Liability Coverage
    Form, **9.23**
Railroad workers, Federal Employers'
    Liability Act and, 12.11
Rate, **3.29**
Rate deviations, WC&EL policy and,
    12.29
Rating, **3.29**
    BIC, 4.24
    BOP, 11.15–11.17
    CGL coverage, 9.19–9.22
    commercial auto insurance,
        10.36–10.39
    commercial property coverage,
        3.29–3.34
    factors in CGL premium, 9.22
    filed inland marine coverage,
        7.17–7.18
    ocean marine insurance, 7.24
    workers compensation insurance,
        12.26–12.30
Real estate managers, CGL coverage
    of, 9.5
Real property, insurance classification
    of, 2.4
Recall, CGL Coverage A exclusion of,
    8.23–8.24
Records, crime policy condition, 5.24
Recovered property, BPP loss condi-
    tion, 2.22
Recoveries, crime policy condition, 5.25
Rehabilitation benefits, workers com-
    pensation, 12.6
Renewal, CGL condition, 9.14
Replacement cost, BOP valuation
    provision, 11.8
Replacement cost optional coverage,
    BPP, **2.26**
Reporting requirements, Value Report-
    ing Form and, 2.29
Representations, CGL condition, 9.13
Resource Conservation and Recovery
    Act (RCRA) of 1976, 13.27
Restaurants, BOP and, 11.5–11.6
Retention, **1.5**
    drop-down coverage and, 13.7
Retroactive date
    claims-made CGL coverage form,
        9.15
    illustration of, 9.17
Retroactive date endorsement, crime
    discovery form, **5.23**
Retrospective rating plan, **12.28**
Riot, basic form coverage of, 3.6

Risk categories, BOP, 11.6
Risk management, **1.3**
    insurance as, 1.3–1.5
Risk management process, steps in, 1.4
Robbery, **5.12**

S

SIR, 13.7
Safe burglary, **5.13**
Schedule rating factor, WC&EL policy
    and, 12.29
Seasonal increase provision, BOP, **11.9**
Self-insurance, workers compensation
    and, 12.13
"Self-insured pools," workers compen-
    sation and misnomer of, 12.15
Self-insured retention (SIR), **13.7**
Separation (of insureds), CGL condi-
    tion, 9.13–9.14
Severability of interests clause, business
    auto, 10.17
Signs Coverage Form, **7.16**
Sinkholes, basic form coverage of, 3.6
Size class, commercial auto rating fac-
    tor, 10.38
Smoke, basic form coverage of, 3.5
Snow, sleet, or ice, weight of, broad
    form coverage of, 3.9
Soft costs coverage, **7.11**
Sole representative, WC&EL policy
    Part Six condition, 12.24
Special causes of loss, ISO farm pro-
    gram, 11.20
Special damages, CGL coverage of, 8.11
Special form. *See* Causes of Loss—Spe-
    cial Form.
Specific excess insurance, **12.14**
Specific insurance, **2.30**
Specific rating, **3.33**
Specifically described autos, Symbol 7,
    Business Auto Section I, 10.8
Specified causes of loss coverage, Busi-
    ness Auto Section III, **10.21**
Spoilage Coverage Endorsement, **3.22**
Spoilage damage, equipment break-
    down insuring agreement, 6.9
Sprinkler leakage, basic form coverage
    of, 3.6
Stacking, commercial property cover-
    age and, 3.26
Standard exception classifications,
    rating workers compensation
    insurance and, 12.27–12.28

Standard Form No. 24, 5.28
Standard valuation provision, replacement cost, BOP, 11.8
State endorsements, CGL, 9.18
State funds
    competitive and monopolistic, 12.12–12.13
    workers compensation and, 12.12
Statute, **8.7**
Statutes
    WC&EL policy Part Two exclusions and, 12.20–12.21
    workers compensation, 12.3–12.15
Steam boiler explosion, illustration of, 6.6
Stop loss excess insurance, 12.13
Stopgap coverage, **12.22**
Strict liability, **8.6**
Subrogation, **3.29**. *See also* Transfer of recovery rights.
Sue and labor clause, **7.21**
Suit
    CGL insured's duties in event of, 9.10–9.11
    duties in event of, Business Auto Section IV condition, 10.24
    insurer's duty to defend against, 8.14
    Jones Act and, 12.10
Superfund, 13.27
Supplementary payments
    Business Auto Section II, 10.14
    CGL Coverages A and B, 8.28–8.29
Surety, **13.31**
Surety bond, 1.9, **13.30**
    characteristics and types of, 13.32–13.35
Suspension, BIC definition of, 4.8
Suspension condition, equipment breakdown insurance, **6.15**
Symbols, coverage, Business Auto, 10.7–10.10

T

Tail (extended reporting period), 9.16
Tangible property, insurance classification of, 2.4
Temporary employees, 12.9
    as employees in commercial crime definition, 5.7
Temporary partial disability, **12.5**
Temporary total disability, **12.5**
Theatrical Property Coverage Form, **7.16**

Theft, **5.6**
    special form exclusions of, 3.13–3.14
Theft of building materials, Builders Risk Coverage Form, 3.17
Theft, disappearance, and destruction, **5.11**
"Three Cs" (capital, capacity, character), surety bonds and, 13.31
Tort, **8.5**
Towing and labor coverage, Business Auto Section III, **10.21**
Tractors, rating, 10.37
Trading, employee theft exclusion, 5.19
Trailer interchange agreement, **10.36**
Trailer interchange coverage, **10.36**
Trailers, rating, 10.37
Transfer of recovery rights
    Business Auto Section IV condition, 10.25
    CGL, 9.14
    CPP, 1.14
    commercial property, 3.29
    crime policy, 5.25
Transfer or surrender of property, inside and outside the premises commercial crime exclusion, 5.21
Transit insurance, 7.11–7.12
Transportation, instrumentalities of, 7.7, 7.14
Transportation expenses, Business Auto Section III, **10.21**
Transportation (transit) insurance, 7.11
Trip transit policy, **7.11**
Truckers Coverage Form, Motor Carrier Form versus, 10.34
Trucks, rating, 10.37

U

Umbrella liability insurance, 13.3–13.12
    excess and, 1.8
Umbrella liability policy, **13.6**
Underlying insurance, umbrella liability policy and, 13.11
Uninsured motorists coverage, **10.28**
Uninsured motorists laws, 10.6
United States Longshore and Harbor Workers' Compensation Act (LHWCA), 12.10
United States Longshore and Harbor Workers' Compensation Act Endorsement, **12.25**

United States Merchant Marine Act of 1920 (Jones Act), 12.10
Unlawful act, 5.6
Unowned autos, business auto liability and, 10.4–10.5
Utility interruption, equipment breakdown insuring agreement, 6.9–6.10
Utility services, basic form exclusion of, 3.7–3.8
Utility Services—Time Element Endorsement, BIC, 4.23

V

Vacancy, BPP loss condition, 2.22–2.23
Valuable papers and records—cost of research extension, BPP, 2.17
Valuable Papers and Records Coverage Form, **7.17**
Valuation
    BPP loss condition, 2.23
    filed inland marine coverages and, 7.15
    open cargo policy calculation of, 7.20
    vessel, 7.23
Valuation provision
    equipment breakdown insurance, 6.15–6.16
    replacement cost, BOP, 11.8
Valuation—settlement, crime policy condition, 5.24–5.25
Value Reporting Form, BPP, **2.28**
Vandalism
    basic form coverage of, 3.6
    inside and outside the premises commercial crime exclusion, 5.21
Vehicles, basic form coverage of, 3.5–3.6
Volcanic action, basic form coverage of, 3.6
Volcanic eruption. *See* Earthquake and volcanic eruption coverage.
Voluntary Compensation and Employers Liability Endorsement (WC&EL policy), **12.25**
Voluntary parting with title to or possession of property, inside and outside the premises commercial crime exclusion, 5.21
Volunteer workers, CGL coverage of, 9.4
Voyage policy (cargo), **7.19**

W

WC&EL policy, 12.15–12.26
War
    Business Auto Section II exclusion
        of, 10.19
    CGL Coverage A exclusion of, 8.20
War and military action, basic form
    exclusion of, 3.8
War and similar actions, commercial
    crime exclusion, 5.19
Warehouse operators legal liability
    policy, **7.14**
Warehouse receipts, employee theft
    exclusion, 5.19–5.20
Warehouse to warehouse clause, **7.20**
Watchperson, custodian versus, 5.13
Water, basic form exclusion of, 3.8
Water damage
    broad form coverage of, 3.9
    equipment breakdown limit of
        insurance, 6.14

Watercraft, CGL Coverage A
    exclusion of, 8.18–8.19
Weight of snow, sleet, or ice, broad
    form coverage of, 3.9
Who is an insured
    Business Auto Section II,
        10.13–10.14
    CGL, 9.3–9.6
Windstorm, basic form coverage of, 3.5
Workers compensation
    Business Auto Section II exclusion
        of, 10.16
    CGL Coverage A exclusion of, 8.16
    employers' obligation and,
        12.11–12.15
Workers compensation and employers
    liability insurance, 1.8, **12.3**
Workers Compensation and Employers
    Liability Policy (WC&EL policy),
    12.15
Workers compensation insurance
    rating, 12.26–12.30
    WC&EL policy Part One,
        12.18–12.19

Workers compensation laws, out-of-
    state application of, 12.9–12.10
Workers compensation statutes, **12.4**

Y

Your business personal property, BPP
    definition of, **2.9**
Your duties if injury occurs, WC&EL
    policy Part Four, 12.23

Z

Zone rated vehicles, 10.39